THE OTHER HALF

Wives of Alcoholics and Their
Social-Psychological Situation

COMMUNICATION AND SOCIAL ORDER

An Aldine de Gruyter Series of Texts and Monographs

Series Editor

David R. Maines, *Pennsylvania State University*

Advisory Editors

Bruce Gronbeck • Peter K. Manning • William K. Rawlins

David L. Altheide, **An Ecology of Communication: Cultural Formats of Control**

David L. Altheide and Robert Snow, **Media Worlds in the Era of Postjournalism**

Joseph Bensman and Robert Lilienfeld, **Craft and Consciousness: Occupational Technique and the Development of World Images** (*Second Edition*)

Valerie Malhotra Bentz, **Becoming Mature: Childhood Ghosts and Spirits in Adult Life**

Herbert Blumer, **Industrialization as an Agent of Social Change: A Critical Analysis** (*Edited with an Introduction by* David R. Maines and Thomas J. Morrione)

Dennis Brissett and Charles Edgley (*editors*), **Life as Theater: A Dramaturgical Sourcebook** (*Second Edition*)

Richard Harvey Brown (*editor*), **Writing the Social Text: Poetics and Politics in Social Science Discourse**

Joo-Hyun Cho, **Family Violence in Korea**

Norman K. Denzin, **The Alcoholic Family**

Norman K. Denzin, **Hollywood Shot by Shot: Alcoholism in American Cinema**

Irwin Deutscher, Fred P. Pestello, and Frances G. Pestello, **Sentiments and Acts**

Bruce E. Gronbeck, **Sociocultural Dimensions of Rhetoric and Communication**

J. T. Hansen, Michael Patrick Madden, and A. Susan Owen, (*editors*), **Parallels: The Soldiers' Knowledge and the Oral History of Contemporary Warfare**

Emmanuel Lazega, **Communication and Interaction in Work Groups**

David R. Maines (*editor*), **Social Organization and Social Process: Essays in Honor of Anselm Strauss**

David R. Maines, **Time and Social Process: Gender, Life Course, and Social Organization**

Peter K. Manning, **Organizational Communication**

Stjepan G. Městrović, **Durkheim and Postmodernist Culture**

R. S. Perinbanayagam, **Discursive Acts**

William Keith Rawlins, **Friendship Matters: Communication, Dialectics, and the Life Course**

Vladimir Shlapentokh and Dmitry Shlapentokh, **Ideological Trends in Soviet Movies**

Jim Thomas, **Communicating Prison Culture: The Deconstruction of Social Existence**

Jacqueline P. Wiseman, **The Other Half: Wives of Alcoholics and Their Social-Psychological Situation**

THE OTHER HALF
Wives of Alcoholics and Their
Social-Psychological Situation

Jacqueline P. Wiseman

with a Foreword by Robin Room

ALDINE DE GRUYTER
New York

About the Author

Jacqueline P. Wiseman is Professor of Sociology at the University of California, San Diego. She is the author of numerous journal articles, and has written and edited half a dozen books, including *Stations of the Lost: The Treatment of Skid Row Alcoholics*, for which she received the C. Wright Mills Award.

Dr. Wiseman has been an invited participant on many research panels; in 1985 she was delegated by the Eisenhower Foundation to participate in a study of the treatment of alcoholism in the People's Republic of China.

ALDINE DE GRUYTER
A division of Walter de Gruyter, Inc.
200 Saw Mill River Road
Hawthorne, New York 10532

The paper used in this publication meets the minimum requirements of American National Standard for Information Sciences—Permanence of Paper for Printed Library Materials, ANSI Z39.48-1984.

⊚

Library of Congress Cataloging-in-Publication Data
Wiseman, Jacqueline P.
    The other half : wives of alcoholics and their social-
psychological situation / Jacqueline P. Wiseman.
        p.   cm. — (Communication and social order)
    Includes bibliographical references and index.
    ISBN 0-202-30382-9 (cloth). — ISBN 0-202-30383-7 (paper)
    1. Alcoholics—Family relationships.   2. Wives—Psychology.
3. Co-dependence (Psychology) I. Title. II. Series.
HV132.W57   1991
362.29′23—dc20   91-11740
                                                        CIP

Manufactured in the United States of America

10 9 8 7 6 5 4 3 2 1

FOR KETTIL BRUUN (1924–1985)

Director of the Finnish Foundation for Alcohol Studies
and an inspiration to researchers in that field
all over the world

CONTENTS

3. THE HOME TREATMENT

4. SEEKING TREATMENT FOR ALCOHOLISM:
    THE POLEMIC BETWEEN THE POTENTIAL
    PATIENT, THE CONCERNED WIFE, AND
    THE THERAPIST

5. THE MALEVOLENT PENDULUM: DRUNKEN
    AND SOBER BEHAVIOR OF AN ALCOHOLIC
    AS PERCEIVED BY HIS WIFE

6. THE PRIVATE TRAGEDY OF ALCOHOLISM:
    THE FAILED MARRIAGE RELATIONSHIP

FOREWORD

In these pages, a distinguished scholar in the symbolic interactionist tradition brings to us and interprets for us the stories of those who find themselves caught in a problematic and seemingly endless interaction: they are women who have come to define themselves as married to an alcoholic. Drawing on extensive interviews, Dr. Wiseman elucidates the drawn-out and agonizing process by which her informants come to their definition of the situation and of their relationship, and categorizes for us the diverse and resourceful ways they try to do something about it. Through the lens of her fieldwork and analysis, we can discern a great deal about how the wife of an alcoholic perceives and thinks about the events, predicaments, and possibilities of her marriage and her life. The analysis is strengthened by a cross-cultural dimension—the study material comes from Finland as well as the U.S.—and through interviews with comparison groups of wives of nonalcoholics and of wives of former alcoholics, whose husbands are now recovered.

Dr. Wiseman's prize-winning earlier study, *Stations of the Lost,* focused on problematic drinkers who were mostly detached from family life. The present study can be seen as complementary, in examining the impact of problematic drinking on family life. Most people who drink heavily and become defined as alcoholics in fact have families, and are married or at some time have been married.

It has long been recognized that the family bears much of the brunt of responding to problematic drinking, and that the drinking is often highly disruptive to the process and sometimes to the existence of the family. Some systems of therapy—transactional therapy, family systems therapy, and Al-Anon and other 12-step oriented therapies—insist that the alcoholism is enmeshed in family processes, and that other family members as well as the alcoholic need treatment. Some, indeed, would define alcoholism as "a family disease," and would label other family members as "coalcoholics" or "codependent." Around the concept of "codependency," a whole new mutual-help movement of Adult Children of Alcoholics (ACA) has emerged in the U.S., bringing among other effects considerable changes in the composition and process of Al-Anon.

As Dr. Wiseman's analysis underlines, among family members the spouse of the alcoholic bears a special burden. Partly this reflects the impact of problematic drinking on joint responsibilities in the nuclear family—responsibilities for such matters as housing, finances and child-raising. Beyond this, as Dr. Wiseman's respondents eloquently remind us, is the impact of the drinking on what lawyers call "consortium"—on the expectations built into marriage of the "company, affection and service" of the other spouse.

Dr. Wiseman's respondents are not only spouses, but also women. In both of the societies of her study, as she points out, this means their earnings will on average be less than a man's, and that they will be defined as having primary responsibility for any children of the marriage. Economically, they will have a greater incentive somehow to continue the marriage. Their gendered upbringing will probably also make it more difficult emotionally for them to cut the marital tie. Whatever the reason, a husband is considerably more likely than a wife to divorce a problematic drinker. Studies that try to interview husbands still married to alcoholics (e.g., Ames 1982) usually have to make do with fewer subjects than Dr. Wiseman was able to find.

As women, Dr. Wiseman's respondents are assigned special responsibilities regarding drinking. Both in Finland (Holmila 1988) and the U.S. (Room 1989), men are more likely than women to be heavy drinkers, and attempts at social control of drinking within the family are predominantly women's attempts to control men. In Holmila's study of young couples in the general population of Helsinki, two-thirds of husbands viewed their wives' efforts to control their drinking rather positively, as a part of a wife's caring and love for her husband (1988, p. 53). Wives who were very dissatisfied with the marriage were in fact somewhat less likely than wives with a lower level of dissatisfaction to attempt to control their husbands' drinking (p. 86). A study of Finnish welfare actions in the 1940s and 1950s documents the state's routine enlistment of wives as control agents over their husbands' drinking (Järvinen, 1991). In his analysis of life stories told by Finnish working-class male alcoholics, Alasuutari (1986) reports the husband's version of events: an alternation over the life course between heavy-drinking break-outs to freedom and independence and periods of settling down with a controlling wife. In both societies, then, women bear a double burden of control with respect to drinking: they are supposed not only to control their own drinking, but also to try to control the drinking of their men.

As wives of actively drinking alcoholics, Dr. Wiseman's primary subjects thus find themselves in multiple binds. The husband's continued drinking is visible evidence of their failure in the wifely duty of controlling his drinking; meanwhile the husband is expressing the utmost resentment about their efforts to carry out this duty. Often the wife still has residual positive feelings for him, no matter how he has behaved. She is tied economically to his actions, no matter how irresponsible. She is supposed to look to him and to no other for intimacy and sexual satisfaction, no matter how brutal, disgusting, or impotent he may be. In these circumstances, it is not surprising that a minority of wives of alcoholics sink into the emotional exhaustion and inertia described by Dr. Wiseman in Chapter 8. It is a testament to their spirit and resilience that the majority do not.

Robin Room
Alcohol Research Group
Medical Research Institute of San Francisco

References

Alasuutari, Pertti. 1986. "Alcoholism in Its Cultural Context: The Case of Blue-Collar Men." *Contemporary Drug Problems* 13:641–86.

Ames, Genevieve. 1982. *Maternal Alcoholism and Family Life: A Cultural Model for Research and Intervention.* Unpublished Ph.D. dissertation, medical anthropology, University of California, San Francisco.

Holmila, Marja. 1988. *Wives, Husbands and Alcohol: A Study of Informal Drinking Control within the Family.* Helsinki: Finnish Foundation for Alcohol Studies, vol. 36.

Järvinen, Margaretha. 1991. "The Controlled Controllers: Women, Men and Alcohol." *Contemporary Drug Problems* 18 (forthcoming).

Room, Robin. 1989. "The U.S. General Population's Experience of Response to Alcohol Problems." *British Journal of Addiction* 84:1291–1304.

PREFACE

Research goals are not created instantly and in a vacuum. Nor are these goals, once clearly delineated, necessarily achieved overnight. My experience is that research of value results from the convergence of background knowledge with the emergent insight or question prompted by some actual occurrence. This has proved to be particularly true in my ethnographic cross-cultural investigation of wives of alcoholics.

The catalyst in this research study was the invitation of Kettil Bruun, late director of the Finnish Foundation for Alcohol Studies, to research the social aspects of alcoholism in his country. Dr. Bruun was impressed with my work on skid row alcoholics, *Stations of the Lost* (Prentice-Hall 1970, since reprinted by University of Chicago Press, 1979). With characteristic generosity, he offered to support me in the research topic of my choice. Although I hadn't at that point in time finalized a definite research goal, I nevertheless accepted his kind invitation.

While preparing our home for rental during our absence, we hired a neighbor to re-do our kitchen. He had recently lost his job—as a result (we found out in due time) of a serious drinking problem. At one point, he confided in us that his wife's family had offered to buy him a pickup truck if he were to stop drinking, but he told them he would rather drink.

Here, indeed, is where scholarly background in a subject area and a real-life incident caused a researcher to formulate a problem. At that moment, I began to wonder what strategies wives of alcoholics use to get their husbands to quit or modify their drinking? An auxiliary inquiry was—what works and what doesn't?

This, indeed, was the topic presented to Kettil on my arrival in Finland. He placed the facilities of the Finnish Foundation for Alcohol Studies at my disposal, and I began work. A simultaneous translator, Pia Rosenqvist (a sociology graduate student and linguist), was assigned to my study, and I started running advertisements to get volunteer subjects. A short time into the study, however, I realized that none of the strategies used by wives to get their husbands to stop or modify drinking behaviors really worked. My study, as framed, was a study of failure.

At the same time, as a result of the data collected, I also began to see that other dynamics of the situation of the wife of an alcoholic were worth pursuing. Women talked about the difficulty they had in deciding whether their husbands were indeed alcoholics (or just social heavy drinkers). Not only had they developed an impressive array of strategies to get their husband to stop drinking, but they also had to make their way through a maze of professional treatments. Brutality alternated with super-kindness. They described the effect his drinking had on them and their marriage; they told me about managing their lives while remaining in the marriage. It was a vastly broader scope for my study than originally conceived. And even these insights did not constrict the goals of the study. Eventually, I began to see that what happened during the periods of drinking could affect whether the man was later able to maintain sobriety.

Obviously, such questions meant finding out *in detail* about the interaction between spouses and its myriad effects *over time.* Further, what did these behaviors mean to the power relationship between the spouses. This meant seeing complex situations and even more complex reactions to them from the point of view of the wife, and then fitting the pieces together into a comprehensible and cohesive whole, the tapestry of their lives, as it were.

Portions of my research in Finland were published in a Finnish journal and a French journal. Additionally, papers drawing on the research data from Finland were presented at various scholarly meetings following my return. In addition, my colleagues in Finland kept me up to date on developments there in my research subject area. While I was writing the monograph intended on Finnish Wives of Alcoholics, Herbert Blumer suggested to me that a parallel study of American wives would strengthen the Finnish findings through comparison. Data for this second study (funded by the National Institute of Alcohol Abuse and Alcoholism) was completed in 1980, with supplemental data obtained in 1985 and beyond.

An interesting variable in this ongoing research was the advent of the women's rights movement some years earlier, which was well underway in the United States when I began this work. Further, I found the movement had made a start in Finland (primarily among the professional class). Finland had a mixture of greater openness to female professionals than did the United States, combined with less equality between spouses than many Americans professed. Yet for all the publicity on the new position of women, the wives in either country who volunteered for this study seemed traditional in their inability to leave bad marriages. Of course, a great many of these women were housewives who had reached middle age without having obtained any special skills training or any career experience. They had established their future in marriage and family. Even for those with skills and experience, opportunities for well-paying jobs on career ladders were limited, although not as greatly as in the United States. Thus, these women continued to cling with determination to married status, despite the fact that their husband had let them down. Subsequent re-interviewing and reviewing of the research of others over the years (up through the middle and late 1980s) revealed no major differences in the reactions of these wives.

The picture in Finland had begun to change, and some changes have been noted by American researchers as well., These data are primarily statistical. Thus, while they do not offer any substantive description of the *dynamics of interaction* among future couples in the area of alcoholism control, *clues* are available concerning how a new generation of Finns and Americans may cope with an alcohol problem in their marriage.

In Finland, with the growing women's rights ideology, women are beginning to act more like their male counterparts. The prevalence of abstinence, which had been high among women in Finland, has declined and women are drinking (Sulkunen 1987). Additionally, more women are drinking to get drunk, although this is still a rare phenomenon (Ahlström 1987). More drinking by both sexes is taking place in the home, which means that women in Finland who at one time did not know how much their husband drank (and therefore had a difficult time deciding if he was an alcoholic), are seeing his intake, just as wives do in America (Simpura 1987). This new visibility of male drinking probably means that currently Finnish women are alerted somewhat earlier as to how much more their husbands are drinking than in the past. This new awareness, however, may be offset by another development: Women are now drinking in bars with their husbands, so their concern may be modified by their own behavior (Holmila 1988).

The changes taking place currently have not been uniform in their development. The increase of female drinkers and the advent of wife-husband drinking relationships has not yet changed the expectation of women as the "moral guardian" in Finland. It is still the woman who tries to limit the man's intake and her efforts and advice continue to fail. (In the United States, Room reports a "dramatic rise in a five-and-a-half year period in Americans' reported efforts to control each other's drinking," with wive's efforts exceeding that of husbands over the long term [1989a, 1989b, 1989c, 1990]).

Järvinen (1991) points out that Finnish women's expected controlling role still leaves them in a subordinate position. Perhaps this is because, for all the increase of women's drinking and their invasion of male strongholds to do it, men still drink more with other men than with women or at family gatherings (Simpura 1987). Pubs remain a male bastion (Sulkunen 1987). Men continue to exceed female intake (Alström

1987). Men on the average drink more in one week than women in one month. The general consumption in Finland had edged up a bit closer to that of the United States; it is now eight liters per person, and not seven as reported in Chapter 1.

Treatment for alcoholism has both expanded and, at the same time, become less coercive in Finland. The Social Hospital and A-Clinics still treat alcoholics, but an array of specialized clinics, such as Youth Clinics, homes for short term (7–12 days) in-patient treatment, half-way houses, overnight homes, and hostels for permanent residence of alcohol (and drug) abusers now exist. The Social Bureau moves more slowly and through several intermediate steps before forcing a husband into treatment, unless his health is in danger or he is very violent. It also monitors and supervises persons for a year after discharge from treatment. Employers also must go through several "warnings" before forcing an employee to spend vacation time at a Social Hospital, or eventually discharging him for being drunk on the job. The result of these changes is that acceptance of treatment is increasingly a voluntary matter.

In the future, alcoholism problems in Finland may be more evenly divided between men and women, and women may eventually give up the controlling role. Inasmuch as the pressure to stop drinking has not been all that successful, this may be a change for the better for both spouses. The ultimate result of the woman's movement is unknown as well. Ahlstöm (1991) and Mäkelä (1991) have suggested a new momentum of the woman's rights movement. As a result, fewer and fewer women may be willing to remain married to an alcoholic at all costs, especially since social welfare aid is more available, and by implication more acceptable than before (Ahlström 1987). Additionally, there are now temporary shelters available for battered women. On the other hand, in the daily press, many U.S. feminists report a regression, or at least a disappointing absence of progress in attaining equality.

Järvinen (1991) reports on some changes over time (from 1940 to the present) in the Finnish expectations of the female role as controller of male drinking. She closes her paper by saying, "The main male-female dualisms embraced . . . by the entire alcohol discourse of the 1940s and 1950s, is of course, intact still today." Two other important aspects of a women's condition in Finland remain unchanged; There is still a rental apartment shortage and no alimony is paid to wives.

This analysis of the lives of wives of alcoholics is written in the ethnographic present. Only another ethnographic close-up of marital interaction will tell us whether any appreciable changes have occurred in the interactive dynamics of living with an alcoholic as revealed by this study.

I am grateful to many generous colleagues in Finland for their help and their gracious hospitality. I treasure the time I spent with them. So many gave a hand, that not all names come back, but Salme Ahlstrom, Kettil Bruun, Leila Iivonen, Klause Mäkelä, Elina Haavio-Mannila, Sirkka-Liisa Säilä, Juha Partanen, Esa Österberg and the ever-present Pia Rosenqvist (who has continued in this field of research) are certainly prominent among them. In the United States, I am grateful to Patrick Biernacki, Rae Blumberg, Don Cahalen, Kaye Fillmore, Setsu Gee, Joseph Gusfield, Dorothy Miller, Ron Roisen, and Robin Room, Harry Specht, Connie Weisner, and Al Wright for their suggestions. Additionally, both Robin Room and Don Cahalen opened the extensive libraries of the alcohol research institute to me as well as offered me opportunity to present data in colloquia and get feedback from experts there.

David Maines, editor of the Aldine series in which this book appears, offered many helpful suggestions and I am especially grateful as well to Arlene Perazzini, managing editor, for her patience and creativity in the production of the book.

I also wish to thank the many wives of alcoholics in both countries who took me in their confidence and shared their lives with me. Later, after I had written the analysis, other wives of alcoholics, social workers, counselors and scholars in the field listened to various aspects of this stud presented in papers and aided me in testing the validity of the findings.

Stan Wiseman edited a great many of my chapters and papers on this subject through the years and bore, without complaint, the persons who surmised (erroneously) that he must be the husband who "inspired" the topic.

Finally, I wish to acknowledge the continuing impact of Herbert Blumer, John Clausen, Erving Goffman, and David Matza on my research. They were my mentors at University of California, Berkeley, and although none of them ever read this study and so could not have offered any suggestions about it, I imagined what they might say or do at various junctures in the data-gathering and the analysis. I have tried to meet what I felt would be their expectations.

References

Ahlström, Salme. 1987. "Women's Use of Alcohol." Pp. 109–134 in *Finnish Drinking Habits: Results from Interview Surveys Held in 1968, 1976 and 1984*, edited by Jussi Simpura (translated by Andrew McCafferty). Helsinki: The Finnish Foundation for Alcohol Studies, V. 35.

———. 1991. In private conversation with me.

Holmila, Marja. 1988. *Wives, Husbands, and Alcohol: A Study of Informal Drinking Control within the Family.* Helsinki: The Finnish Foundation for Alcohol Studies, V. 36.

Järvinen, Margaretha. 1991. The Controlled Controllers. "Women, Men, and Alcohol." *Contemporary Drug Problems* 18 (forthcoming).

Mäkelä, Klaus. 1991. In private conversation with me.

Room, Robin. 1989a. "Spouse Reports Versus Self-Reports of Drinking in General Population Surveys." Paper presented at 15th Annual Alcohol Epidemiology Symposium, Kettil Bruun Society for Social and Epidemiological Research on Alcohol, Mastricht, the Netherlands.

———. 1980b. "Worries, Concerns, and Suggestions: Informal Processes in the Social Control of Drinking." Paper presented at the annual meeting of the Society for the Study of Social Problems.

———. 1989c. "The U.S. General Population's Experience of Responding to Alcohol Problems. *British Journal of Addiction* 84:1291–1304.

———. 1991. "Comments and Suggestions: Responses to Drinking within U.S. Families, 1990." Paper presented at Symposium on Alcohol, Family and Significant Others, Kettil Bruun Society for Social and Epidemiological Research on Alcohol, Vuoranta, Finland.

Simpura, Jussi. 1987. "A Typical Autumn Week's Drinking." Pp. 79–103 in *Finnish Drinking Habits: Results from Interview Surveys Held in 1968, 1976, and 1984*, edited by Jussi Simpura (translated by Andrew McCafferty). Helsinki: Finnish Foundation for Alcohol Studies. V. 35.

Sulkunen, Pekka. 1987. "Abstinence." Pp. 38–54 in *Finnish Drinking Habits: Results from Interview Surveys Held in 1968, 1976, and 1984*, edited by Jussi Simpura (translated by Andrew McCafferty). Helsinki: Finnish Foundation for Alcohol Studies. V. 35.

Wiseman, Jacqueline P. *Stations of the Lost: The Treatment of Skid Row Alcoholics.* Englewood Cliffs, N.J.: Prentice-Hall. (Reissued by University of Chicago Press, 1979.)

CHAPTER 1

Introduction

In recent history, industrialized societies have come to recognize that heavy and apparently compulsive drinking, known as alcoholism or problem drinking, is highly detrimental to both the drinker and those close to him or her, as well as costly to communities as a whole.

At the societal level there is the expense of underwriting treatment and possibly social welfare for the alcoholic and affected dependents, plus the problem of drunk driving and its often tragic effects on both the drinker and the innocent victim. At the organizational level, there is the substantial cost to industry in terms of loss of work time and industrial accidents. At the individual level there is the health hazard created by excessive drinking, as well as the loss of self-respect and the emotional costs to next of kin. In fact, it seems indisputable that alcoholism causes human misery, wasted lives, and diverted resources that might be put to better use.

Awareness of the magnitude of the problems caused by alcoholism has resulted in various efforts at amelioration. There have been educational, legislative, religious, political, and moral attempts to limit or prevent its development. The healing and helping professions (medical, psychological, and counseling) have been requested or have volunteered to create and offer various treatment approaches. Incarceration or fines for drunk driving or public drunkenness have been instituted, as has involuntary commitment to treatment. Governments continue to tax package alcohol keeping the price high, thereby limiting its purchase and consumption. Legal hours of service and age limitations have also been instituted to restrict intake. In addition, many research institutions, both private and government-sponsored, have received grants or

Editor's Note:
   Citations for the theoretical aspects of this introduction are dispersed throughout the book, where they are discussed at greater length.

1

been created expressly to investigate the causes and treatment of alcoholism.

This emphasis on etiology and treatment of alcoholism ignores what might be termed the first line of defense in the battle with compulsive drinking behavior—the home front and the spouse. It is spouses, after all, who are usually first to become aware that their partners appear to be developing into problem drinkers. Thus, it is they who must first confront the making of a diagnosis. Once they do so, they must attempt to deal with this family crisis, and the way that they do this can affect both themselves and their drinking spouses. Yet, the parameters of this family drama are not well delineated.

To begin with, little has been known about the avenues by which spouses arrive at the decision that drinking, once seen as normal (though perhaps heavy and annoying), has progressed into alcoholism and is a serious problem. Even less is known about the various ways spouses try to deal with the problem, once they have defined it. We do know that even today their success at helping the drinker quit or cut down is limited.

The actual daily details of living with an alcoholic have not been systematically examined either. While we have a good deal of information about the physical and psychological condition of heavy drinkers resulting from many years of overindulgence, less is chronicled concerning the toll alcoholism takes on the mental and economic well-being of concerned significant others. We do not know the alternative modes people use to manage their lives when the specter of a heavily drinking marital partner is an integral part of them. And, equally important, we do not know much about the interplay between the adjustments the spouse of a problem drinker finds necessary and the alcoholic's continuing or ceasing to drink.

Goals and Focus of the Research

Wives of alcoholics in two Western industrial countries—the United States and Finland—are studied in an attempt to answer these questions. This cross-cultural approach was selected to surface broader aspects of the phenomenon of alcoholism, and the circular effects between heavy drinking and marital interaction. Finland was selected because it differs from the United States in terms of attitudes toward heavy drinking, approaches to treatment, and laws for control. Additionally, the relationship between men and women and the position of women have significant differences and similarities in both societies that encourage comparative investigation.

The overarching theoretical framework that guided data collection and analysis has been that of the symbolic interactionism of George Herbert Mead and Herbert Blumer. Within this theoretical perspective, the emphasis is on the experience and attitudes of the wife as she perceives her husband's drinking and its attendant problems. It is her story, from her point of view, and includes her feelings about where other family members fit into the problem. Additionally because of this focus on the wife's perspective, attention given here to the causes of alcoholism is limited to her belief or knowledge about it. This study does offer some clues, however, concerning effectiveness of treatment and possible factors in the continuation of problem drinking.

The Advantages of a Symbolic-Interactionist Framework

Symbolic interaction theory focuses on the mechanics and ingredients of decision-making. A central tenet is that people act rationally—if not always wisely—rather than being the unwitting victims of inner personality forces or external social pressures. Symbolic interactionist theory posits that people confront and define the situations within which they find themselves and then, in keeping with these definitions, select, construct, and execute, as best they can, what they believe to be the most appropriate action. This theory is especially effective for understanding motivation in problematic situations.

Such a perspective, applied to the wives of problem drinkers, also challenges the usefulness of various theoretical frameworks that have been applied in the past to explain the behavior of wives of alcoholic men, and the part these women might be playing in their husband's drinking behavior.

For instance, psychologists have used various versions of psychoanalytic theory in an attempt to understand a wife's response to her husband's drinking, his treatment for it, and the sobriety (or recidivism) that may follow. Within this framework her reactions to her husband's drinking have been seen as indicating certain specific "pathological" personality traits: either an unconscious need to dominate, or masochistic tendencies with a need to suffer. One of the wife's actions used to buttress this theory included her attempts to take over most aspects of running the household. Another alleged indicator of her pathology is that she continues to live with her husband and provide wifely services even though these seem unappreciated, and/or she endures being beaten during his drinking bouts and yet remains in the marriage. Psychologists also take as a major keystone to their theories the fact that when an alcoholic husband sobers up, his wife apparently experiences great stress rather than unmitigated happiness and relief. They assume that this indicates she actually wants him to remain an alcoholic (so she can continue her domination or her suffering), and for this reason will try to drive him back to drinking, although she is unconscious of these motivations.

An alternative explanation is provided by persons of functionalist persuasion, also utilizing nonrational motivation theory to analyze the same data. Within this framework, the wife of an alcoholic is seen as unconsciously creating and/or functioning as a part of a family "system" whose members have obtained an "equilibrium" that has resulted from internal and external adjustments to the drinking husband. As a result, their continued functioning actually depends on his persistent overimbibing and concomitant troublesome activities. Such a framework also can be seen as accounting for the wife's behavior while the husband drinks heavily, her apparent inability to leave her husband, her reaction to the termination of her husband's drinking, as well as ways in which she may contribute to his recidivism when he sobers up.

Symbolic interactionists do not see the wife as a captive of either the structure of her personality or of the stability of adjustment of family members to an alcoholic in their midst. In attempting to cope with and/or adjust to their husbands' problem drinking as well as the periods of treatment and sobriety, it is assumed that wives consciously construct their behavior in keeping with their definition of the situation. Furthermore, these definitions can, at any given time, change as the result of some new information and/or occurrences. Thus, all behaviors are emergent—that is, are in constant process. While perhaps surprising to the average person, many of the definitions and resulting behaviors of these women are not without logic if the situation is seen through their eyes. Thus, while some of the data in this study describe behaviors like those mentioned above in connection with other theories, they are amenable to a different analysis—when seen from the wives' perspective and coupled with other information not heretofore gathered. Such factors as a wife's initial lack of knowledge about alcoholism, naive expectations of what a wife can do to help her husband with his drinking problem (considering her presumed close relationship with him), and assumptions about professional treatment become important in her definition of the situation and how best to handle it. Concerns about maintaining the household in the face of his actions emerge as well. Also a factor in her decisions and behavior is her socialization as a woman, wife, and mother. Not surprisingly, these judgments change over time and with experience. Thus, the analysis is dynamic rather than static, as is the case with the psychoanalytic and functionalist approaches briefly touched on above.

Important Conceptual Areas in the Study

Within the general parameters of the major theoretical framework, and the substantive goals of the study, several definitional changes over time, or *definitional careers,* become apparent. These careers are pervasive throughout the study as well as being related to each other: (1) the career of the diagnosis of alcoholism; (2) the definition of alcoholism causation as a factor in coping strategies; (3) the changing marriage relationship and self-image of the wife.

Just as symbolic interaction offers a challenge to other theoretical approaches to understanding the wife of an alcoholic, so does the charting of these definitional careers furnish a challenge to other more extant views of person perception, alcoholism as a disease, and how wives in unhappy marriages manage their lives.

Thus, these definitions (and redefinitions) of several significant and interrelated situations by wives of alcoholics bring a new perspective to this important, behind-the-scenes family drama. The wife's recasting of the meaning of her husband as marriage partner, his excessive drinking, therapists and treatment, and attitudes of family and friends evolves like a many-faceted mosaic. With each new definition, the wife must arrive at a decision concerning how to act. By looking at these situations in the lives of wives of alcoholics and the meanings they have for these women, the study illustrates how change in one area of life can revise definitions and behavior in several other areas as well. Further, these changes rebound from the alcoholic and his family back to the wife and the husband in circular but idiosyncratic fashion.

The Career of the Diagnosis of Alcoholism

Initially, the focus of this research is on the wife's attempts to diagnose the meaning of her husband's heavy drinking. As she does this, it is in full knowledge that a judgment of alcoholism will change his symbolic meaning as a marriage partner, as well as set in motion new definitions of their marriage.

Person perception is usually studied by psychologists as a fairly instantaneous judgment, the kind made upon viewing a photograph or from limited contact with another person. That is, of course, one important way in which people judge others. This study, however, is concerned with the long-term diagnostic struggles of a person (in this case a wife) who is in fairly continuous contact with the person to be judged. By considering this longitudinal aspect of person perception, labeling theory also is considerably broadened. A husband who is being judged and possibly labeled can be both loved and dominant in the dyad as well. Thus, the diagnosis is complicated by a person who has the power to fight a negative decision and its resulting label.

One aspect of this long-term decision-making is that wives pay a high psychological price for their period of indecision. Having to cope as they do with both their anxiety and their husband's denials of a drinking problem, many of these women actually begin to fear for their own sanity. This unexpected construction of reality is mentioned by wives in both cultures.

Eventually the diagnosis of alcoholism crystallizes from an accumulation of clues, often because of a last straw or clincher in the form of some social deviance the wife finds explainable in no other way (although it is often a deviant behavior not directly associated with heavy drinking). The defining-encounter career then ends with wives retroactively recasting prior events by reviewing formerly ignored behavior clues, which now take on new meaning with the diagnosis of alcoholism. This certainly is a much more complex form of person perception and judgment.

Definition of Alcoholism Causation
as a Factor in Coping Strategies

Closely connected to the problem of diagnosing alcoholism is the fact that it is a phenomenon shrouded in ambiguity, mystification, and disagreement. It has been variously designated a bad habit, a disease, or a moral failing. Its etiology is not known nor has a consistently successful treatment been developed. The ideologies of alcohol causation that wives adopt, discard, and readopt and their approaches to get their husbands to stop drinking so heavily can, quite naturally, be seen to be related. By looking at the strategies the wife uses in an attempt to get her husband to quit drinking or at least decrease the amount of his intake, we can see the career of opinion transformation on the cause of alcoholism as it parallels their changing relationship. Additionally, on a theoretical level, the broader problem of engineering behavior change is highlighted by the approaches she tries.

Inasmuch as wives perceive heavy drinking as a voluntaristic act, they do not initially accept the disease model of alcoholism. Rather, their extended diagnostic decision initially launches them on another fairly long-term career—"trying to help him stop drinking." Wives' attempts at behavior change during this period include logical discussion, emotional scenes, and threats, and offer an excellent typology of approaches to social control used by laypersons in their daily life.

In addition to the *direct approach* (asking or telling someone to change or using threats as negotiation), a wife may try several indirect strategies (manipulating a person into changing unawares). Most are quite inventive attempts at changing aspects of her husband's day-to-day living patterns in such a way as to encourage or induce reduced alcohol intake.

Theoretically, what makes the case of the wife's attempt at home treatment interesting is that she is a subordinate in a power relationship trying to bring about behavior change. This is not the usual status relationship between a therapist and a client. In these efforts, wives are seen to be in dual and contradictory roles: both therapist and spouse. Furthermore, they must live with their therapeutic failures.

When wives fail at logical persuasion and indirect manipulation, they start searching for professional treatment for their husbands. This action also signals a change in their view of alcohol causation from a habit or willful behavior to a sickness or disease—a definition that has had many adherents, both lay and professional, over the years.

Defining alcoholism as a disease, plunges the wife into a treatment world that has many aspects that are both surprising and dismaying. Certainly, she is ill-equipped to sort out the many therapeutic approaches, and she is ill-prepared to accept the high rate of failure of most. Neither does she anticipate that she will become a reluctant member of a sort of therapeutic triangle.

Another facet of alcoholism as part of an interactive phenomenon is the emergence of the significance of behavior during sober periods (or, more broadly, periods of remission). The Parsonian sick role does not cover this phenomenon and researchers in the field of alcoholism have shown little interest in it. While the drunken comportment of alcoholics has been studied, it has been assumed that their behavior during periods of sobriety is no different than that of someone who overindulged briefly (that is, an unpleasant hangover, then a return to "normalcy"). However, data in this study indicate that the sober comportment of alcoholics has a different meaning for the problem drinker than for the person who occasionally overindulges, sobers up, undergoes a hangover, and experiences regret. In the marital interactive dynamics that follow, it becomes clear that, for an alcoholic, a period of sobriety is an important *precursor* to another period of drinking. As a result of analysis of these data, an expanded model of these dynamics can be shown to be involved in the ability of men to abstain for a year or more.

The Changing Marriage Relationship

Attempts by the wife to help her husband stop drinking reveal another career of evolving definitions—that of their relationship and the power she has as a result of his feelings for her. Until she fails to persuade him to cut down on his drinking for her sake, she believes she is very important in his life. After she has tried many different approaches (almost all connected in some way with what she believes to be their relationship), she reassesses his apparent lack of feeling toward her and the marital relationship, and mentally reconstructs it accordingly. This reassessment is only the first step in the gradual disintegration of the marriage relationship. As time goes by, four important areas of interaction—companionship, meals, recreation, and sex—are adversely affected by the husband's drinking.

Two other aspects common to male alcoholics that affect their behavior are revealed in this study to have qualities not usually noticed: brutality while drunk, and sexual impotence.

It is well known that some alcoholic husbands, when drunk, beat their wives. When wife beating first came to the attention of researchers, it was initially thought that drinking was a causal factor in brutality, but several studies have indicated that alcohol is not so much the cause as an excuse after the fact. This research bears out these findings, but adds an important element: the "specialization" in types of brutality toward family members by alcoholic men, as reported by their wives, has not been revealed in detail before this study. (This self-limitation in behavior in terms of selection of victim, type of brutality, and timing indicates more elements of control are present during intoxication than some theories of compulsive behavior have assumed to be the case.) Equally significant is the evidence presented that interaction between husbands and wives during sexual intercourse has an impact on the impotence reported among heavily drinking males equal to or even greater than the long-term physiological effect of alcohol consumption.

When major husband-wife roles are lost due to the husband's behavior, the wife often carries on her role without the reassurance of a counter role. Alienation and estrangement also have careers. Wives gradually cool toward their husbands and instead develop a type of quasi-primary relationship with them, maintaining mere vestiges of former roles. Furthermore, there is the loss of viable family rules and valuable family themes when the husband-wife dyad begins to break down. This makes the road back to sobriety difficult, inasmuch as it is haunted by the alcoholic's bad behavior of the past.

Where can a wife turn for help in such a situation? The stigma of alcoholism affects her as well as her drinking husband. This study contrasts the stereotypical view of family and friend help networks with the reality of reactions to the wife's needs when the problem is an alcoholic husband. Relatives (and society as a whole), who offer the wife little help in the innumerable crises she faces, pressure her to hold the marriage together. A *courtesy stigma* is experienced by wives as they lose friends and some relatives. Social invitations cease to be extended. Eventually, wives of alcoholics come to depend on and support each other—either informally or by joining Al-Anon.

When an alcoholic husband fails in important areas of marriage—becomes irresponsible and thoughtless of his wife's feelings, forces her to engage in rough sex, or, alternatively becomes impotent or even brutally beats her—does she continue to live with him because of masochistic tendencies? Alternative explanations must start with her economic situation and gender role socialization.

Perhaps the most poignant construction of reality on the part of wives of alcoholics is a sense of dependence on the marital role—even when their husbands fail to fulfill basic aspects of their part of it. This feeling of dependence is quite complex and is actually confounded with a sense of responsibility and subordinate status. A woman who feels inadequate to head a household alone is paradoxically socialized to be nurturant toward a "sick" husband, a task she combines with a sense of pride in the homemaking role. Additional factors that account for her acceptance of cruelty and even brutality on the part of her husband include economic considerations, the inhibiting factor of children, if there are any, and the resistance of the husband to divorce.

However, staying in the marriage does not necessarily mean a totally gloomy future. These wives ultimately divide into two groups: those who make a life of their own within the marriage and those who sink further and further into despair. Significantly, such factors as her age, income and occupation, usually affect a woman's chances to do something positive for herself are less potent than motivation and attitude. Furthermore, there is a circularity to how their ultimate condition evolves over time. Success breeds attempts at more success; absence of aspiration and failure increases the sense of helplessness and failure.

For those wives who can move beyond their original limiting definition of how much independence they can handle, a new construction of their self-image gradually develops. As a result, they are eventually able to build an independent life for themselves within the marriage. This metamorphosis appears to rise out of a feedback and buildup of bold (for them) actions, successes, and redefinitions of what is possible.

Finland as a Comparative Case

Finland, a country with a much smaller land area than the United States and a much more homogeneous population, offers an interesting site for comparison of alcohol problems. While Americans drink more per capita than do Finns (approximately 10 liters [*Statistical Abstract of the United States* 1990] to almost 7 liters [*Yearbook of Nordic Statistics* 1989–90]) Finns are, as a nation more concerned about their drinking problem. At one time, Finland had a much larger proportion of population reporting to be teetotalers than did the United States (Makela 1971), but that difference no longer exists today as women are joining the ranks of drinkers, as mentioned in the Preface. Finnish culture is more indulgent about intoxication and more public drunkenness is tolerated than in the United States. On the policy level, however, the Finnish government exercises more control than the United States, managing both the manufacture and distribution of alcoholic beverages. Sanctions for drunken driving are much stricter in Finland, as well (Osterberg 1977).

The brief discussion of Finland that follows will attempt to place the drinking behavior of Finns within a cultural context as it affects male drinkers (who predominate in Finland, as they do in the United States), and their wives.

Finland is often seen as part of a Scandinavian triad that includes Sweden and Norway. At times, Denmark is also viewed as part of this Nordic country group. Finland is internationally known, (along with other Scandinavian countries) as a nation of people who drink heavily. Finns see drinking as lowering tension and increasing sociability. No occasion is seen as truly festive without the serving of alcohol. When it is not offered openly, guests will bring their own supply and consume it clandestinely. As in the United States, certain annual church holidays are occasions for drinking—Christmas, Easter, Whitsunday—as are family celebrations such as announcement of engagement banns or birthdays. Work festivals (e.g., barn-raisings), which often last several days, leaving a job, after university examinations, as well as national celebrations such as Midsummer and May Day also are times for heavy drinking in Finland (Suuronen 1973). Like the United States, Finland had prohibition (1919–1932). Home distillation has not been officially permitted since 1866 (Sariola [no date]).

Drinking patterns of the two countries vary markedly. Binge drinking and heavy, concentrated intake for the purpose of becoming intoxicated is the norm in Finland. (Makela 1971; no author 1978). Men are expected to be blatant in their drunkenness. In the United States, by comparison, heavy and even problem drinkers tend to pace themselves, and try to avoid florid displays of intoxication, preferring to prove that they can "hold their liquor." In other words, in Finland occasional unrestrained drinking is seen as more attractive than regular but restrained drinking (Ahlstrom-Laakso 1973). Saturday night is a heavy drinking night. Finns also seem to feel that any time of the day is a good time to imbibe. When one passes a bar early in the morning in Finnish cities, large crowds of men can be seen having a beer or two *before* going to work. Thus, Finnish men are more likely than Americans to show up at work already partially intoxicated. American men, unless confirmed alcoholics, hold back until at least noontime, and often until late afternoon or early evening.

Because of these differences in intake patterns, Finnish citizens often see drunken men staggering about their city streets during the day, lying along side buildings or the banks of rivers, lurching in front of city buses, and making nuisances of themselves at bus stops. Americans usually see such sights only in skid row areas of cities.

The heavy drinking condoned in Finland makes it difficult for a wife to decide that her husband is drinking "too much." There are also axioms concerning drinking that are a part of a culture of tolerance of heavy drinking (Suuronen 1973):

- Don't ask if a man drinks; ask rather how he acts when he is drunk.
- No matter how much he drinks, a man is not an alcoholic if he can still work and support a wife and children.
- Liquor at weddings pays off.

The fact that drinking in Finland is much more visible than in the United States, especially in areas where it is likely to cause problems with the rest of the population, may account for the greater involvement of the Finnish government in the consumption of alcohol and the treatment of alcoholism as compared to the United States.

For instance, the government handles, through the ALKO monopoly, the wholesale buying, pricing, and reselling of all alcohol in Finland, except for "medium" beer. This control extends to the percentage of alcohol content allowed in such beverages as beer and wine. Additionally, known alcohol abusers can lose their privileges to buy. Package stores do not display alcohol in the same way that it is done by commercial stores in the United States. Rather, the stores are more like small "box stores," with a counter.

Finland has much more stringent laws concerned with driving under the influence of alcohol (DWI). The driver need not be drunk; 1.5 per ml. of alcohol is the limit. Additionally, because drunks are so visible, there is more probability of arrest for public drunkenness in Finland than in the United States (Osterberg 1977; Ahlstrom-Laakso 1971). Finns often use designated drivers who do not drink at all at social events. This became a custom many years before it became popular with Americans. In the United States the definition of drunk driving is usually restricted to persons with a fairly high blood-alcohol content established by a breatholizer or other tests (such as walking a straight line). A conviction often results in forfeiture of license to drive for a time, but no jail term is imposed on a first offender.

The Finnish government also sponsors a network of treatment facilities that include complete inpatient hospital treatment in "social hospitals," halfway houses, and outpatient care in A-Clinics. The social hospitals offer both medical and psychological therapy. The A-Clinics offer short inpatient treatment (approximately five days). These clinics are founded on the so-called "Yale Plan," which was based on voluntary commitment and five to seven-day hangover help. They also offer overnight treatment. Social hospitals, used for longer stays, were set up to accommodate a drinker's spouse and children for visits on weekends and at other times. Whole families eat together in the dining rooms. Specialized A-Clinics are available for youthful drinkers, and hostels and overnight homes are available for skid row alcoholics. (These latter two facilities offer shelter from the freezing Finnish nights, no treatment, but possible referral.) Additionally, there is a League of A-Guilds, which is a client association of Finnish A-Clinics. A-Guild members hold therapy meetings at A-Clinics. All these facilities receive financial aid from both national and city sources (Osterberg 1977; Kiviranta 1969).

Alcoholics Anonymous (AA) was established in Finland in 1948, 13 years after its founding in the United States. For its first three years, the Finnish AA was financed by the government, an unusual situation for AA, which has always maintained its independence by avoiding formal underwriting by any organization. By 1951, AA declined further governmental aid and operated its Finnish organization on the more usual plan of member maintenance (Kiviranta 1969). Currently, most AA meetings are to be found in Finnish cities. Some are held in prisons, hospitals, and other institutions for alcoholics. Finland also has an Al-Anon, which, like most American Al-Anons, is primarily used by wives of alcoholics.

Unlike the United States, where commitment for treatment is usually handled through the courts with some civil rights protection, Finland casts a much broader net to get presumed alcoholics into treatment. First of all, if a wife complains to a Social Bureau about her husband's drinking, he receives a postcard notifying him of mandatory counseling. Such counseling may include referral to an A-Clinic. If he ignores this invitation for guidance, he may be institutionalized in a social hospital against his will. Additionally, Finnish law has made employers a partner in the treatment of alcoholism. If a worker is discovered to have an alcohol problem, the employer cannot fire him, but must, instead, give him his vacation at once—to be spent in a social hospital. By law, the employee must have several opportunities at social hospital treatment before he can be fired.

The Finnish government underwrites research into alcohol use and treatment through the Finnish Foundation for Alcohol Studies. A consumer education program tries to teach citizens either to drink moderately or stay away from hard liquor entirely. No alcohol advertising has been allowed since 1969 (Osterberg 1977).

Like all Nordic societies, Finland has been solidly patriarchal until recently. In its early days, women helped men on the farm and also shouldered the responsibility for child rearing and housekeeping. Legally, the wife was subject to her husband; in fact, she was his partner in the farming enterprise. With the advent of industrialization, the more recent pattern of the man as breadwinner and the woman as housewife emerged (Skard and Haavio-Mannila 1984; Haavio-Mannila 1983).

This pattern changed when the marriage rate dropped between 1950 and 1960, resulting in an excess of single women at the same time that technology outdistanced the old guilds. Women provided a needed source of cheap labor. They were first recruited as telegraph operators, shop assistants, and secretaries, as well as primary school teachers. Still women were barred from high schools and universities and did not have the vote. (Skard and Haavio-Mannila 1984).

Along with the opportunity to work outside the home at low wages, Finnish women also began to see themselves as part of an oppressed group, and a feminist movement (primarily middle class) pushed for universal suffrage and equal educational opportunities. Working class women unionized.

The end of formal discrimination did not insure equality between the sexes, however. Although women composed almost half (45%) of the labor force in 1984, with 77% of mothers with preschool children gainfully employed, they are clustered in the lower (service) portion of a gender-segregated occupational force with little opportunity for advancement (Skard and Haavio-Mannila 1984; Kauppinen-Toropainen, Haavio-Mannila, and Kandolin 1984; no author 1982). A large proportion of the women who are employed work full-time and dominate the public sector, while men have more of the jobs in the private sector (Haavio-Mannila and Kari 1980). On the average, women are paid less than men. The best educated women in Finland do not receive a salary equal to the average monthly earnings of men (Niitamo and Hyppola 1985). It has been said by Finnish feminists that whole industries are dependent on the exploitation of cheap female labor (Skard and Haavio-Mannila 1984).

Because they are expected to do most of the housework in addition to their job, women have less free time than do men (Haavio-Mannila, Jallinoja, and Strandell 1983; Niemi, Kiiski, and Liikkanen 1981). Additionally, they have little or no discretionary money because they are expected to pay for food and the cost of running the household. This takes most of what they usually earn, given that they are on the lower rungs of the salary scales. Nevertheless, the husband has responsibility for the rent and the rest of the money (with some exceptions) is his. This can be spent on alcohol, if he wishes. This inequity is reinforced by the method of paying employees in Finland—directly to the bank. Thus, each spouse has his/her own account. However, the woman's account is more often depleted by financial responsibility for the household.

Certain other remnants of patriarchy are significant for this study. Men's drinking is segregated activity for the most part; with males meeting in pubs to talk and play darts while doing some serious drinking. Finnish women, by and large are teetotalers. Approximately 10% of the men drink almost three-fourths of the alcohol consumed by women (Makela 1971). Thus, it is most likely that Finnish men do not have their wives as drinking companions. It follows that the more a man drinks, the more often he is apart from his wife. There is an axiom in Finland that the more a wife tries to take a controlling role, the more a man will tend to drink apart from her (Holmila 1985).

Culturally, women are seen as the moral guardian of the family. A woman is expected to help the man she loves control his drinking. One saying in Finland is that it is up to a wife to make her home more attractive than the pub. Men are aware that their wives use various strategies to get them to limit their alcoholic intake. In fact, when boys first learn to drink they are told that some female member of their household will help them establish control and offer guidance as to amount. After they are married, they are told that such guidance is a "wifely duty." Some say they pay attention to their wife's attempts. Others are proud that they ignore their wife (Alasuutari [no date]; Sulkunen, Alasuutari, Kinnunen, and Natkin 1984; Homila 1985; Natkin 1984).

Finland is also known as a country with a great deal of physical violence. There is an assumption among Finns that family violence is caused by alcohol consumption (Peltoniemi 1984a,b). Certainly in the United States, alcohol consumption is highly correlated with male violence against wives. There is a lesser involvement of alcohol and child abuse. In both cases, however, the drinking may be an excuse rather than a direct cause.

Divorce is allowed for the "emotional factor" (mental cruelty, irreconcilable differences) as well as physical abuse (Haavio-Mannila and Jallinoja 1980). However, alimony is seldom awarded in Finland, and child care is difficult to collect (a phenomenon not unlike that in the United States).

Finns consider themselves to be fiercely independent. This philosophy of life has kept them, to a great extent, from turning for aid either to family, friends, or social welfare agencies (seen as the last resort) in times of stress, illness, or other emergencies (Haavio-Mannila, and Jallinoja 1980). This pride operates to discourage the wives of alcoholics from leaving their drinking and abusive husbands and accepting welfare assistance, as American women sometimes do.

This study compares and contrasts wives of alcoholics in the United States and Finland on the problems they face in defining their husbands as problem drinkers, the numerous approaches they use to get them to curb their excessive drinking, the search for successful treatment, and the effects of alcoholic husbands on them and their marriage. It also is concerned with the help—or lack of it—that wives receive from various sources, and the ways in which some wives manage to build a satisfactory life of their own and still remain married, while others sink into despair. Finally, this study looks at the circularity of husband-wife interactional effects during the husband's drunken and sober periods and the way this process of mutual influence can be seen to help explain successful abstinence from alcohol or recidivism.

One of the initially most disappointing aspects of the cross-cultural data actually turned out to be the most compelling. Although the two countries were selected to highlight differences in interactional patterns in the above areas due to cultural divergences, the most significant finding is how the phenomenon of the alcoholic husband eradicates the variations between the two countries, and is overwhelming in its consequences for wives and marriages.

CHAPTER 2

Diagnosing Alcoholism:
The Hidden Drama
on the Home Front

Introduction

A concerned wife watches her husband drink his fourth martini and shortly fall asleep in front of the television—his nightly routine. Another wife is notified by the police that her husband is in jail—arrested again for drunken driving. A third woman has observed that her husband's drinking is increasing, and that he has also become unusually touchy and quarrelsome. Each of these women wonders if her spouse's drinking is getting out of control. None of them is able to decide the issue immediately. Some continue a watchful waiting for clues; others let the matter slip from their consciousness only to have their concern rekindled by a new episode of excessive drinking or public drunkenness, which always raises unpleasant issues: What kind of a person is her husband that he could act like this? What should she do about it? What does it all mean to their marriage?

The data that will be presented indicate that her decision concerning the meaning of his drinking will be the end product of a long history of concern, clue seeking and validation, and—most importantly—soul-wrenching doubts and anxieties. For some persons other than the drinking man's wife, the answer may seem all too obvious. The only question for them is why it takes her so long. Yet, the judgment that "he is an alcoholic" is seldom easy when love and marriage are involved. How are we to understand this process by which a wife sifts through a welter of events ultimately to arrive at a diagnosis of her husband's drinking and worrisome behavior?

17

Significance of the Wife's Decision

The dynamics of this decision are of both substantive and theoretical interest. Inasmuch as wives are usually the first to notice that their husbands' drinking patterns have changed, and therefore the first to try to deal with the excessive drinking, it becomes extremely important to know how they arrive at a diagnosis of alcoholism and *why* (as the data reveal) this decision takes so much time.

Theoretically, this type of judgment, taking place as it does over quite a period of time and often concerned with interpreting changes in the person, has not been given a great deal of attention by sociologists,[1] despite its relevance to labeling theory. The career of interpretations the judge and the judged make of each other's appearance and actions as they interact before and during the time a label is considered, selected, and applied, would benefit from closer scrutiny. Judgments that have a career over an extended period of time, in which incremental changes occur between persons who are in an intimate relationship with each other, are a different type of "defining encounter" than I have described in the case of skid row alcoholics and agents of social control (Wiseman 1979:iv; 1987:323). These persons spend a very limited time together and label each other either for bureaucratic or survival purposes. Little or no personal emotion or future investment in these decisions exists. On the other hand, the wife of an alcoholic has a tremendous emotional and future investment in her husband, and the decision she makes about his drinking. In both types of encounters, the conscious efforts of the person being judged to deflect or influence the decision is an integral part of the dynamic processes and is further influenced by the status or power differential between the two.

The decisional career of wives in two cultures—the United States and Finland—will be followed from their initial considerations and ruminations that their husband is consuming a large amount of alcohol, through continuing concern about his behavior and intake, to the time when the weight of evidence tips the scale unequivocally toward a diagnosis of alcoholism.

It should be mentioned that this investigation is limited to the decisional career of wives of alcoholic men. Thus, it is these women's perceptions of their husband's drinking problem that are being studied. That their husband might see his own drinking behavior quite differently is obvious. However, the perception, cognition, and interpretation of the wives is extremely useful for reasons mentioned previously— these women are often first to "diagnose" their husband as alcoholic and then take some action that they hope will help him. This is important, because while others may suspect a drinking problem, they are much less likely to take ameliorative steps concerning it, as will be seen.

A Model for the Dynamics of Alcoholism Diagnosis

The process of deciding that a loved one is an alcoholic presents special and complex problems of perception, knowledge, and judgment for the average layperson. (Even professionals have difficulty developing foolproof criteria, as will be seen.) The amount of an alcoholic beverage consumed can occur on a continuum from "normal," with no particular social or physiological consequences, to "pathological," which causes behavioral and physical problems. No definitive boundary between labels exists. As a phenomenon (or affliction), alcoholism is equivocal. Many persons overindulge from time to time, but are not, on this basis alone, considered alcoholics. Additionally, the troublesome types of behavior that often occur in conjunction with alcohol consumption frequently take place in its absence as well, so that as indicators of alcoholism per se they are not conclusive evidence of a drinking problem. Finally, alcoholism has a long-term development in which sober periods are interspersed with drinking ones, making certainty about diagnosis particularly difficult. These decisional problems are compounded for the wife of an alcoholic due to the significance such a diagnosis has for her life, and account for the more difficult and protracted deliberations she experiences.

In order to understand this decisional career better, it is instructive at this point to look at a parallel situation—that of lay diagnosis by wives of men who are ultimately seen as mentally ill. The protracted diagnostic problem of these women can serve as a guiding framework to aid the understanding of the steps by which wives of alcoholics make their determinations. Developed by Yarrow et al. (1978:38), this model outlines how the wife defines and redefines problematic behaviors of her husband as she struggles to determine their meaning. She vacillates back and forth from deep concern to self-reassurance that she is worrying unnecessarily. Continuing occurrences of incidents rekindle doubt about the meaning of his sometimes bizarre behavior, until eventually she reluctantly decides he is mentally ill.

What are the important steps in such a decisional career? Beginning with troublesome initial events, cues accumulate and accelerate in seriousness to a point where they break through a wife's ongoing threshold of nonconcern and force her to notice. She now must address the question of what her husband's behavior means. When this first occurs, the wife usually attempts to explain away her spouse's seemingly strange activities as actually quite normal or understandable.

As the disturbing incidents continue, however, the wife finds herself in an "overlapping definitional state." Her husband's behavior fluctuates between appearing to be a "problem-not-problem" or "normal-not-normal." As her interpretations shift back and forth, she continues to collect clues; and she continues to be, by turns, concerned or tries to explain away his acts by "normalizing them" in her own mind. Eventually, another decisional threshold is reached. The weight of troublesome events begins to tip the scale. As even more upsetting behaviors follow, the case is clinched, so to speak; the decision that his behavior is not normal becomes the overriding one. The wife is forced to the conclusion that her husband is mentally ill.

With only slight modification, this model can serve as a diagnostic paradigm for decisional processes of wives of alcoholics. The major difference between the mental-illness decision as summarized from the Yarrow et al. data and the alcoholism decision to be presented lies in the types of behaviors with which the wife becomes concerned.

In order to utilize the Yarrow et al. model, wives were asked to recall the first event and/or behavior of their husband that caused them to suspect alcoholism. They were then asked what other events or behavior caused concern about problem drinking and were probed several times with "Anything else?" Then they were asked what finally convinced them that their husbands were alcoholics.[2]

Despite cultural differences, data indicate that many aspects of the diagnostic career of wives of alcoholics remain constant in both the United States and Finland, even though wives in those two countries perceive the problem of excessive drinking in different social situations. Cultural differences in perspectives on drinking behavior do, however, cause some divergence in timing and behavioral areas of concern.

In the United States, fairly heavy drinking is accepted, although drunkenness and loss of control are not. Pride in being able to "hold" one's liquor without showing its effects is a general norm. American wives are usually aware of the amount of their husband's alcohol intake because they see him drinking, inasmuch as they often accompany him on recreational outings that include alcohol. American men imbibe fairly openly at home, as well. In Finland, heavy drinking is culturally encouraged and visible drunkenness is tolerated—even subtly applauded.[3] However, wives often do not see their husband drink because this activity takes place primarily in taverns in the company of other men. Thus, Finnish wives rarely use "amount of alcohol consumed" as an early indicator of the possibility of problem drinking. They notice it later, of course, as their husband begins to need more alcohol than he can afford at tavern prices and starts drinking more frequently at home. A detailed explication of this process follows.

Early Concern about Drinking: Ambiguities and Normalizing Processes

Consumption as an Indicator in Two Cultures

Perhaps the greatest barrier to a diagnosis of alcoholism is the fact that addiction takes hold very gradually. Thus, wives in both the United States and Finland can become accustomed to their husband's imbibing and only notice incremental changes upon conscious reflection or when some untoward event, associated with alcoholism, forces their attention. These wives say, typically:

> I think there is a fine line between social drinking and alcoholic drinking . . . I think he just kind of gradually slipped over the line. (American)
>
> I have to say it was more than 10 years—almost 20—before I thought of him as an alcoholic. He was able to control it in the beginning very well. (Finn)

American wives say they were first alerted to the possibility that their husband might have a drinking problem when they noticed the increased amount of alcohol he was consuming and disturbing new aspects of his style of drinking. However, a woman's developing awareness of her husband's drinking is not so much the result of absolute amounts consumed as of the manner in which he departs from culturally desired norms of alcohol consumption. When American women tell of their initial concern about their husband's drinking, they say:

> After he puts in his day's work, when he comes home, he just wants to keep on drinking all night long. (American)
>
> [I suspected he had a drinking problem] when I went out into the kitchen at night and found him drinking straight from the bottle. (American)

These wives also say that their concern escalates as they note that their husband either actively seeks out alcohol or appears to be building his life around drinking:

> With John, he just, uh, everything he did was evolved around drinking, you know; if it was a funeral, he had to get drunk, and if it was a happy time, he had to get drunk . . . he got drunk at any and every little thing he couldn't handle. (American)

His main interest in life when he came home was his drinking, and if there was not beer in the house, he would go get some, and if we were going anywhere and if there was no chance to drink, he would not go. When we went to Disneyland, he took the monorail out to the bar. (American)

In Finland, on the other hand, where heavy drinking and drunkenness are acceptable behavior (or tolerated, at least), drinking is usually done away from home. As a result Finnish wives do not make the connection between heavy drinking and alcoholism:

Here in Finland people might drink a couple of days, all day, so even that is not an indicator [of alcoholism]. (Finn)

Well, I worried about how much he drank, I was afraid it might be a problem, but I didn't know if it was alcoholism. (Finn)

Once alcoholism is suspected, the continuing issue for most wives in either culture is to find some way to distinguish between normal or social drinking (even when heavy) and drinking that can be labeled alcoholism. This definitional problem is compounded by the fact that the wife usually knows little about alcoholism, except for some stereotypes that do not seem applicable to her husband. Further, she has very little idea of where to learn more about it. In such an informational vacuum, wives are at an almost total loss to assign meaning to their husband's drinking behavior:

I didn't know what an alcoholic was. I had no conception of it whatsoever; I had never known one—my parents drink socially but I had never been exposed to it. (American)

I knew he drank a lot, but I really didn't connect it with alcoholism. I always thought that only skid row bums were alcoholics. (Finn)

Although there are available, from such organizations as AA or alcoholism treatment clinics, both definitions of alcoholism and indicators of the development of problem drinking, no wife mentioned consulting any informational source at this stage in the diagnostic process. Indeed, had any woman looked for definitions at that early stage, there is a good chance she would have decided the material was inapplicable or seemed not very helpful in the specific case of her husband. As Robinson notes, "'alcoholism' is a messily defined notion." He goes on to explain that this is because of its complex connection with many aspects of life and many fields of scholarly endeavor:

This (the difficulty in defining alcoholism) is not surprising since any definition which purported to incorporate the physiological, biochemical, psychological, sociological, legal, moral, (and) religious nature of the phe-

nomenon, the progress of its development and likely prognosis, the indications for treatment, together with its effects upon the individual and
society could be nothing other than either totally incomprehensible or of
such generality as to bear no meaningful relationship to the empirical
world. (1973:91)

Ten years later, Chafitz echoed this sentiment:

> It is difficult to establish the fine line on the drinking continuum that
> separates social drinkers from problem drinkers. . . . It is important to
> keep in mind that with alcohol problems, as with other diseases, there is
> no point on the health-illness continuum that can serve as a universal
> guide to indicate when an individual is in trouble and requires examina-
> tion, diagnosis, and treatment. (1983:60–61)[4]

At this stage of suspecting their husband has become an alcoholic,
wives unanimously hesitate to ask the opinion of family or friends. They
feel, probably erroneously, that they alone notice the increased alcohol
consumption, and they do not want to plant seeds of suspicion among
others unnecessarily. Thus, they try to mull over the matter alone. Additionally, like the wives of mentally ill men, they go through a stage of
trying to lull their own concern, to deny what they fear to believe—an
enterprise to which drinking husbands are only too happy to contribute.

The Wife's Urge to Normalize:
The Husband's Normalizing Strategies

Festinger (1954, 1964) observes that when people receive information
which is contrary to already-accepted beliefs, the new input initiates
psychological tensions that he refers to as "cognitive dissonance."[5] He
further suggests that humans are unable to tolerate such tensions for
any lengthy period, but must resolve the matter—preferably in the direction that brings the least pain, blame, regret, or chagrin. Bennett
Berger (1981), in a reincarnated and extended version of cognitive-disso-
nance theory, uses the term "ideological work" to conceptualize how
people devise mental compromises to relieve the tension created by
situations in which their philosophy of life and reality come into conflict. Either phrase captures the human propensity to reduce apparent
contradiction and seek consistency. For instance, the wives that Yarrow
et al. studied, reinterpreted and normalized increasingly bizarre acts of
their husbands to make them seem consistent with their earlier-estab-
lished definitions of these men as rational.

This pull toward definitional consistency by interpretive normalization also occurs while wives of excessive drinkers are trying to decide
what, if anything, is wrong with their husband. Continuously confronted with behavior that is in conflict with how they think a man

should conduct himself both in private and in public, they are faced with the necessity of making sense out of actions that upset and frighten them, one aspect of which is heavy drinking. Such behavior is not constant, however. At other times their husband does not drink or act drunk. This is reassuring to wives who are aware that decisions they make about their husband can shake the foundations of their marriages. Thus, confronted with ambiguous signals and their own ambivalence, these women move back and forth during this early stage of the decisional career between reinterpreting all the undesirable evidence as really behavior that is "normal" or "understandable under the circumstances" (and thus "saving their marriage" by this definition), or seriously considering the possibility of alcoholism as the result of another troubling episode.

American women describe how they try to relieve the cognitive dissonance they experience by neutralizing their husband's drinking behavior as the normal result of unusual circumstances:

> Yes, I noticed it [the heavy drinking]. Of course, I made up all kinds of excuses for it at first. He had recently come out of a divorce and I rationalized to myself that he was just confused now; the poor guy had been misused by his first wife and had really been given a rough deal, and I swallowed it all; and you know I said I'm going to make a difference. I made up all these beautiful excuses that worked for about ten months. (American)

Wives in the United States also indicate their early resistance to seeing themselves married to an alcoholic:

> I blamed his friends, Las Vegas, and I suppose [even] after six years of his drinking everyday, I didn't blame him. But it was four years ago that it did hit me; that I was married to an alcoholic. I didn't want to be. I fought it. (American)

Finnish women also do a form of ideological work as they wrestle with the concerns caused by their husband's heavy drinking. Their initial normalizing strategies, however, are quite different from those of American wives. Some Finnish wives focus on possible personal problems they might have with their husband or the possibility that his drinking is normal practice for men when they are relaxing together:

> For two years after we were married, everything was fine, but then he started staying away from home a night or two. He would come home smelling of alcohol, but I didn't connect it with alcohol at once. I thought he wanted [sexual] pleasures. (Finn)

I didn't know what to expect in marriage. I didn't know whether or not his behavior was typical of men's behavior or not [i.e., staying away all night and drinking heavily]. (Finn)

Wives are also aided in their resistance to labeling their spouses as alcoholics by the husbands themselves, who vehemently deny having any drinking problem. Husbands appear to take one of two approaches to accomplish this: they either defend their drinking as normal or attack their wife's concern as excessive or abnormal. A wife who is attempting to explain away the worrisome aspects of a husband's behavior anyway is vulnerable to either strategy.

American and Finnish husbands defend the quantity of their alcohol intake somewhat differently, an interesting reflection of cultural differences in the two countries in this area. As American men drink openly at home, they will calmly deny to their worried wives that their imbibing has become significantly heavy:

He said he wasn't an alcoholic. That he just liked to drink. (American)

[He says] "I'm normal. What I'm doing, there is nothing wrong with it." (American)

Inasmuch as Finnish men do their drinking in bars, most arguments center on their condition when arriving home. Such challenges are interpreted by them as interfering with their male prerogative:

When I talked to him about it, he was very hard about it. He said that he could do with his money what he wished and it was not my business to interfere. He told me he would accept no interference from me with his drinking. (Finn)

As time goes on, however, the doubts and mental anguish of this early period, which have been put to rest by a wife eager to believe that there is nothing amiss and a husband equally concerned to allay her suspicions, reassert themselves. A state of perilous balance between a diagnosis of "alcoholic-non-alcoholic" emerges and every new disturbing incident tips the scales toward a verdict of problem drinking.

The Perilous Balance; the Scale-Tipping Incidents

Some of the first incidents that rekindle concern after a successful normalization result, paradoxically, from the increased attempts by the husband to quiet his wife's fears about his drinking. These acts ultimately have the opposite effect and become a signal to the wife that her husband may indeed have a drinking problem after all.

A primary classic giveaway sign is the hiding of bottles, a ruse by which the husband hopes to keep his wife from knowing the true extent of his supply and the rapidity with which it is exhausted. Wives in both cultures are jolted out of their acceptance of their husband's drinking as normal when they discover caches of alcohol.[6]

American and Finnish wives who find hidden bottles sound very similar in their descriptions of hiding places: under clothes in dresser drawers, in a bag of clothespins, hidden in the water chamber of the toilet, under the bed, and in workrooms.

Another subterfuge used by husbands to keep wives from knowing how much they are drinking is to lie about the amount of money being spent on alcohol. This ploy eventually backfires also. The drain on the budget is discovered, one way or another. Checks do not clear, or bills that were supposed to be paid are not. The duplicity involved in these lapses is seen as another piece of evidence that makes alcoholism more probable. American women describe the impact of catching their husband in lies about money matters as follows:

> He lied mostly about money. He would run tabs at bars when he promised he wouldn't and then I would inadvertently find out about it. He would lie about how much money he earned so that he would always have enough money to drink. And he would lie about what he was going to go out and do in order to get away to drink, and uh, just things I began to realize a normal person would not do. I knew there was something wrong. (American)

The clues to alcoholism offered by financial difficulties are somewhat differently structured in Finland, but they have the same effect. As mentioned in Chapter 1, frequently in that country, wives do not know how much their husband makes because men's paychecks are deposited directly to their bank accounts by employers. Accounts are not joint. As a result, the wife's first inkling that money is going for liquor instead of bills is when creditors begin to complain—an event that takes longer to develop to crisis proportions in Finland than the United States because of the greater proportion of Finnish than American wives who work outside the home. In Finland, these women often are expected to pay the basic bills—rent and clothing—from their salaries. When the food money runs short, expected car payments are not made, and other bills begin to appear, the wife realizes money that should have gone to these payments has gone to alcohol.

An even more serious scale-tipper is the drunk-driving citation. For American wives, this is seen as a major indicator of alcoholism and they often report such tickets as having a strong bearing on their final diagnosis:

> [He] was just drinking a lot at the time. He was falling down and he was arrested for drunk driving. So I just began to read articles on alcoholism. (American)

Although almost one-fourth of the American wives mention drunk driving as important in pushing them toward a diagnosis of alcoholism, only a few Finnish women gave this type of behavior as influential. This is undoubtedly because driving after any imbibing is harshly punished in Finland. A first offender may get a jail sentence of six months. Because of this, even when people drink moderately, they take a bus or taxi to their destination. Thus, driving after drinking in Finland is seen as a sign of almost total surrender to liquor, since ordinarily even persons with a long-established drinking problem are prudent enough to avoid driving a car.

The Escalation of Upsetting Incidents

Berger and Kellner (1970) have pointed out that the negotiated aspects of the marital dyad eventually culminate in understandings that become so stable that a major departure from expected behavior by one spouse can cause the other to sense something serious has gone wrong with the relationship. In tandem with the worrisome heavy drinking, the wives in both cultures are eventually confronted from time to time with husbands who "do not seem themselves," or whose behavior is "strange" or "unpredictable" or "not like them."

Reduction in Dependability

For instance, American wives began to note that their husband has become undependable in areas where he formerly was responsible:

> All of a sudden, over the past few years, everything was being put to me, and he could not or didn't want to do [anything]. . . . More and more I was taking over the responsibilities of everything. (American)

> It seemed like the activities with the children became secondary. . . . The outings started being cancelled or he was too drunk to go with us to the zoo and places like that. (American)

> He started neglecting everything else, like [getting] the car cleaned, the yard work, this type of thing. (American)

Finnish wives, on the other hand, mention lack of dependability in chores and engagements much less frequently, probably because their husbands are responsible for fewer chores and social activities with the family.

Temporary Personality Changes

Both American and Finnish wives report the occurrence of what seem to them to be disturbing temporary personality or behavior changes in their husbands that cause them to reexamine their previous suspicions about alcoholism once again:

> Well, all I can say is at times he was like a schizophrenic. I could see a progress in his personality change. (American)
>
> Well, he was just a lot different when he was drinking than when he was sober. When he was sober, he was a sweet, nice, person; and when he was drinking, he would beat me up sometimes and stuff like that. (American)
>
> There were some antisocial features to his behavior. I think that when one is staying away a lot of hours . . . and hurting someone, it must be alcoholism. (Finn)
>
> He was so changeable—like a Jekyll and Hyde. (Finn)

Upsetting Scenes and Violence

In addition to the personality changes, American wives report frightening scenes in which their husband shows uncharacteristic indifference to their safety or feelings, or those of others. These incidents also cause the women to reconsider the possibility of alcoholism:

> Coming back from a picnic with the family . . . he would get drunk at outings . . . loading up a barbecue which hadn't had the sparks out, and we'd be driving on the highway and sparks would be coming out of the truck every which way. And then he covered it with an army blanket that could have started on fire and flown on somebody else's car. I was so frightened for myself and the children. (American)
>
> He got a gun and came into the kitchen and said he was going to kill me. . . . He had me by my slacks and was dragging me around the house. . . . The next day I checked the gun and [it] was loaded, and that really scared me. (American)
>
> He tried to kill me; he threw the kitchen table through the glass sliding windows, and tore the phone off the wall. (American)

Finnish wives, left out of a great deal of their husbands' social lives, are not privy to such antics, which probably occur when their husbands are drinking away from home. They do, however, complain that their husbands are violent and beat them. They do not necessarily see this as an indicator of alcoholism, however, inasmuch as Finland has a high rate of marital and other violence. It does disturb them greatly, nevertheless.

The Psychological Price of Ambivalence

The Yarrow et al. model of lay diagnosis of mental illness has little to say about the effect on the wife of prolonged ambivalence on important matters; (the state of "he is normal-not-normal") like her husband's sanity. For wives of alcoholics, struggling with these overlapping definitions in which the scales are tipping toward "alcoholic" (at the same time their husbands are accelerating their campaign to drink undisturbed), it is a period of extreme self-doubt, stress, and fear for their own sanity in some cases.

Wives in both cultures report that when they complain about their husbands' apparent development of irresponsibility, personality fluctuations, and violence, these men often deny the charges, calling their wives nervous, neurotic, paranoid, or mad to be upset:

> He said it was all in my head [that he drank too much]. (American)
>
> He said I was physically and mentally ill. I was nervous, he said. (Finn)
>
> My husband said, "I am doing all right. You had best get some help for yourself." (Finn)

For some women, torn between their own desire to explain away problems, yet still concerned about the amount of alcohol their husbands are drinking, a type of "gaslight" phenomenon is created, making them fear they are losing their minds.[7] This occurs in both cultures:

> An alcoholic is so good at playing with your mind that I was convinced for so long that even though I knew he had a problem, I was convinced that it was my fault and I really thought I was crazy. (American)
>
> I think I was almost to the point of losing my mind. I couldn't sleep. I couldn't think; I couldn't do anything. (American)
>
> I was getting flippy. . . . I woke up in a hospital one night. I had tried to commit suicide. (American)
>
> Ten years ago I first started to feel uneasy and restless because I thought we have too much alcohol in the family. First I thought I, myself, was ill. I even went and got pictures of my brain, but then I decided it was not me—it was something else. (Finn)
>
> I was feeling so badly I went to a psychiatrist to see if I was mentally ill. He reassured me there was nothing wrong with me, and said my husband's drinking was the problem. (Finn)

Last Straws or Clinchers

As wives in both cultures go through their own periods of mental instability and, with or without professional help, finally decide that it is their husbands' drinking (and not their own nervousness) that is causing real (and not imagined) problems in their family, they are aided in this decision by incidents that for them tip the scales irrevocably toward problem drinking. Interestingly, these factors have little direct relationship to heavy drinking. Rather, they are linked by the wife to it as the causal factor.

These last straws are behaviors that indicate the marriage is in such trouble that a diagnosis of alcoholism actually can make a wife feel better—where it formerly made her feel worse. These persuasive factors include personality changes in the husband that seem more permanent than those noticed earlier, behavior on the job that gets him fired, and unmistakable signs that he is being sexually unfaithful. Alcoholism can now be seen as the cause of such actions, rather than the husband's purposeful upsetting behavior.

Seemingly Permanent Personality Changes

Wives in both cultures report the development of apparently long-term personality changes that replace the Jekyll-Hyde personality noted in the earlier sober-drunk days. Many at this juncture decide such changes are definite indicators of excessive drinking:

> I began to be more certain [he was an alcoholic] when I saw personality change. Nothing seemed to matter very much [to him]. . . . I noticed that he just didn't seem the same, I don't know how to put it. (American)

> Well, I knew he drank, but he was always very pleasant. I guess I knew he was an alcoholic when he ceased to be pleasant. (American)

> [I was certain he was an alcoholic when] he became mean and raw and brutal, and he had not been before that. Also, his memory because worse. (Finn)

Instability on the Job

When a husband's drinking begins to seriously affect his ability as a breadwinner, depleting the household budget and ruining the family's credit standing, wives become very concerned and link this with alcoholism:

> [I finally decided he was an alcoholic when] he wasn't really keeping up his job the way he should. When he came to paying bills, he was irresponsible about things like that. (American)

There is a Finnish saying that a man who drinks is not an alcoholic if he can hold a job and go to work everyday. Thus, for the Finnish wife, learning that her husband has been drunk on the job is definitive. To her, as to some American women as well, this must indicate alcoholism because it endangers the family livelihood:

> He started to neglect his work. He started to drink in the morning and if he had something else important to do, he neglected it and just drank. I thought these were typical characteristics of an alcoholic, according to what I had read. (Finn)

Unfaithfulness

Another final scale-tipper for some American wives is suspicion that her husband is having an affair. For them (perhaps to salve their pride), this is seen as incontrovertible evidence of a drinking problem, for otherwise, their reasoning goes, this sexual straying would not have happened. As these women explain it:

> He kept getting worse (about drinking), and I knew he was running around because I was getting calls from this woman. He had a young girl. (American)
>
> But then he started, at the age of 43, running around with an 18-year-old; and I don't know that means he is an alcoholic; but I didn't think he would have done it otherwise because when he was sober he didn't; he knew he was married; but when he was drunk . . . (American)

As mentioned earlier, Finnish wives used unfaithfulness to explain away heavy drinking rather than to link the two. For them, the last straw is financial insolvency and joblessness.

For wives in both cultures, however, the long period of alternating definitions is just about over. Confirming evidence is sought to make their diagnosis a certainty.

The Search for Confirmation of the Diagnosis of Alcoholism

In keeping with theories of cognitive dissonance and ideological work, Hart (1965) has pointed out the human preference for consistency of evidence for decisions. That is, once a person has decided something, he/she tends to search for confirming evidence of one kind or another. Thus, only after they are fairly certain of their diagnosis do wives of alcoholics start looking for and studying professional literature on the subject. Additionally, they mentally review past events that they had normalized as "he is not an alcoholic," and recast these situations as containing significant alternative clues that they had failed to notice or had misinterpreted.

American women say that once they are fairly certain of their diagnosis of alcoholism, they start watching educational television shows on the subject and reading pertinent articles in the newspapers. Some contact AA and ask for literature. Some visit (and eventually join) Al-Anon (the organization for wives of alcoholics). Wives from both countries say:

> I began to read articles. I saw more and more articles in magazines and newspapers. I simply began to compare his behavior with the articles I read. (American)

> I started reading how they are and all that, and I thought, "My God, he's one!" . . . I called AA and they sent a man here. (American)

> When I discovered he was ill and suffering from alcoholism, I noticed that in this town where we lived, there was no official help. So I went to the library and read up on alcoholism and read many books on it. (Finn)

One effect of these wives' new knowledge of problem drinking is to give them a more professional vocabulary by which to describe their husband's drinking behavior. Where they once talked about a man who "looked for excuses to drink," or who "drank excessively at drinking occasions," they now start describing his intake as a compulsion or say that he has lost control of drinking.[8] Where they had spoken of his drinking as an activity, they now referred to it as an illness. Heretofore unexplainable mood swings are seen as indicators of a hangover and withdrawal.

Concerned wives also resurrect and review past occurrences they had previously persuaded themselves were not significant indicators of problem drinking and redefine these as containing overlooked clues that further reinforce their current judgment:

> Looking back . . . I could see now that he was [an alcoholic], but during that time, I didn't feel that alcohol was a problem. I thought we were social drinkers. (American)

> About ten years ago . . . he rear-ended a woman driver and left the scene of the accident, but even at that time, I did not suspect he had a drinking problem. (American)

> Now I see that all of these times he came home and was rough and mean and silent and smelled of alcohol, and I wondered why he acted that way, that he was an alcoholic. At the time, I thought he was just tired from his job. (Finn)

Eventually, all pertinent past events are reinterpreted to support the diagnosis of alcoholism. Furthermore, current behavior, as it occurs, falls into these newly constructed categories. Thus, the diagnosis of alcoholism picks up momentum with the increased confirmation of added events.

The Dynamics of Perceiving and Judging: Theoretical and Substantive Significance of Short-Term versus Long-Term Definitional Processes

The dynamics of the decisions of wives of alcoholics as they haltingly diagnose their husband's drinking as pathological, indicates that there are certain circumstances where judgments about persons are arrived at only after a long period beset by contradictory evidence that causes alternative doubts, reassurances, and renewed questions. Such a decision involves collection, evaluation, and interpretation of evidence gathered over time and is in sharp contrast to the immediate judgments of persons, an area that has been extensively explored by psychologists. This study of wives weighing of problematic evidence about their husband offers an opportunity to gain insight into the complex demands of long-term judgment.

First of all, there is the longitudinal aspect. A woman in this situation must not only have a clear recall of what her husband was like before his drinking became excessive, but she must decide what is significant about changes in his physical appearance and behavior that deserve her concern. Then, the wife must see these changes as linked to heavy drinking and not other phenomena. As Robinson further points out on the same topic, such alcoholism diagnoses are situation- and setting-specific:

> The characterization "he is an alcoholic" occurs in a social order. The thoughts, concerns, activities, projects, prospects of others are more or less linked to the person who drinks. . . . The character of this linkage is partially given by the location of the drinker in a variety of social structures and institutions such as the family, the work place, the hospital, the leisure place, etc. In any of these settings "alcoholism" comes to be noticed at certain points and not at others. (1973:94)

To complicate matters further, a shift in what is worth "noticing" or "what counts" as evidence of alcoholism can be discerned over time. The balance between concern and normalization can be crucially tipped. In the end, the most persuasive clues for the wife (that the husband has become a problem drinker) are his aberrant or hurtful social behavior, which threaten either the well-being of the family or her marital relationship. (Many of these "threshold-passing" behavior patterns would be ranked as "minor criteria" by the Criteria Committee of the National Council on Alcoholism.)[9]

Perhaps more important than the immediate dynamics of the situation in establishing the linkage to alcoholism is the background context within which such attributions are made, because the decision is such a long-term process (Rose 1958; Harnett and Elder 1973; Kuehn 1974).

In case of the possibility of alcoholism of a husband, the most pertinent background aspects, according to the data, appear to be (1) the wife's unwillingness to admit to herself (for reasons of love, pride, and/or loyalty, as well as the implications such a diagnosis inevitably have for her marriage) that her husband has a serious drinking problem; (2) the wife's lack of knowledge about alcoholism; (3) the husband's persistent denial that he has a drinking problem; and, (4) the power differential between the spouses that favors the drinking husband. Little attention has been given to the generic aspects of such background factors on a judgmental decision.[10]

Equally significant is the finding of a serious psychological toll taken on the wives of alcoholics as they suspect their own sanity while being bombarded with conflicting evidence during the difficult judgment period. Their mental problems are further exacerbated by the emotionally close relationship between themselves and the person they are attempting to diagnose. At the same time, he is using power and argument to deflect the judgment. Obviously, this puts wives in a catch-22[11] situation: the fear that they are losing their minds can be overcome by deciding that the husband is an alcoholic, despite his denials. But to retain their sense of mental normality is to redefine what might be seen as a good marriage to a problematic one.

The decisional career model of wives who ultimately diagnose their husbands as mentally ill, offered by Yarrow et al., is used to aid the understanding of the parallel problems wives of alcoholics face, inasmuch as there are similarities between both the phenomena of mental illness and alcoholism and their lay diagnoses. Both maladies have an intermittent quality, so that with the coming and going of "symptoms," there is a waxing and waning of concern sufficient to force a decision as to the pathological nature of the behavior. In both cases, the judge is in an intimate relationship with the person being judged, who strongly denies have any problems.

The theory of cognitive dissonance (or, more recently, ideological work) allows us to see how past actions, formerly explained away as not indicating problems with alcohol, can be resurrected and recast to confirm the final diagnosis. Self-education in the area of alcoholism is used by the wife to reinforce her decision, not to make it initially. When wives reach this point, even impression management by their husbands is seen as an indicator of a problem, and not possible counterevidence.

Thus, the career of such a decision is long and encompasses many stages and eventual scale-tippers, as well as many aspects of person judgment that have received little systematic attention.

On a substantive level, this study of the various aspects involved in the career of wives' diagnosis of their husbands as alcoholics makes more understandable why wives seem to take so long to decide a matter that may seem obvious to others. Additionally, evidence indicates that most alcoholic males enter treatment for the first time primarily to please a spouse or other close relative. Thus, the long period of indecision is of additional substantive interest, beyond what it does to the wives' mental health. It is also a crucial turning point in the husbands' eventual acceptance of treatment (even temporarily), for once a wife is certain of her diagnosis, she can begin to try to assess various approaches for handling their mutual problem.

Notes

1. Psychologists have studied many of the types of the decisions people make about each other on the basis of various "traits" and their awareness of and/or feeling about them. Some of these decisions are arrived at in a very short period of time. Schneider et al. (1979) review some of this literature in *Person Perception*. One good example of such demands on judgmental ability is the employment interview in which one short meeting (and a curriculum vitae) may be all the data available with which to select one applicant out of a field of many (for instance Hariton 1970; Dian et al. 1972; Keenan 1976, 1977; London and Poplawski 1976; Gross and Crofton 1977; Tuller et al. 1979; Heilman and Saruwatari 1979; Imada and Hakel 1977; Sigelman et al. 1980). In addition to studies of attributions made on the basis of the stimuli being present, cognitive psychologists also investigate those resulting from the way in which persons use their memory [and its organization] to retrieve pertinent material (Ostrom et al. 1980; Ebbeson 1980). Psychologists who study the attribution process also have developed complex theories concerning the way persons decide on causality and responsibility (Shaver 1975). Their purpose is somewhat different than sociologists, however, in that they are attempting to understand how the cognitive processes work in general moreso that how they work in a specific situation.
2. Naturally, while this approach was made to approximate a step-by-step reconstruction of this decision, the time order cannot be known for certain because of the complicated and long-term nature of the development of alcoholism and decisions concerning it. Yet, there is virtually no other way to get this data. However, because of this limitation on the collection of actual longitudinal data, (as well as the sampling problems discussed in the chapter of methodology), generalizations should be made cautiously. Nevertheless, the findings deserve consideration because they offer clues to an important process of decision-making, a first step that eventually brings the alcoholic man to the attention of professionals.

3. It is not unusual to see drunken men weaving down Finland's major commercial streets during the day, or lying in gutters or parks in the city of Helsinki. Parties in Finland conventionally last until early morning—5 or 6 A.M. is not unusual. At 7 to 8 in the morning, bars can be seen crowded with men having a drink (usually beer) before going to work.

4. In 1974, *The Task Force of the Second Special Report to the U.S. Congress on Alcohol and Health* said the following about a definition of alcoholism: "There is an absence of clear definitions of problem drinking and alcoholism, but universal agreement that they represent a source of grave concern for our society" (U.S. DHEW, 1974:1). In 1984, Schuckit's clinical guide to diagnosis and treatment of alcoholism pointed out that the *Diagnostic and Statistical Manual of the American Psychiatric Association* (DSM-III) is not a great deal of help with the diagnosis of alcoholism, although it was worse in the past when it ignored life problems as well as psychological and/or physical dependence. Schuckit goes on to say that "there is no one best definition of alcoholism, and the different criteria overlap a great deal" (pp. 45–46). Chafetz (1983:68, 74) divides indicators of alcoholism into "warning signs," which are primarily physical and psychological (e.g., irritability the morning after drinking, frequent headaches, nausea, periodic confusion, mild memory loss, psychoticlike behavior, or a seizure the day after drinking), and individual *social* indicators (e.g., going to work intoxicated, drinking in order to function on the job, receiving a DWI charge, sustaining serious injuries or getting into trouble with the law while intoxicated, or doing things while intoxicated that the person claims they would not ordinarily do). Schuckit (1984:47) suggests that a definition that looks at the occurrence of serious social (work, accidents, marital problems, arrests, job layoffs) or health (cirrhosis) problems related to alcohol can be useful in defining alcoholism.

5. This press toward consistency has been noted as a phenomenon by many other psychologists, primarily of a gestaltist persuasion, and sociologists, although its actual mechanics are not well understood. Asch (1946), Heider (1967:264), and Wilde (1968) have noted that people have a marked tendency to cluster the traits of someone being judged and form an understandable unity of them. Gollin (1958) and Pewers and Secord (1973), however, have noted differing patterns of handling inconsistent data that seem associated with both the attributes of the judge as well as the person judged.

6. Trice, in his discussion of the development of alcoholism said this about the hiding of bottles: "With the hiding of his supply, the alcoholic deviates completely. This action signals a point where he has become so determined to avoid notice that he tries to deceive everyone in his life as well as himself" (1966:34). In the classic motion picture *The Lost Weekend*, the alcoholic desperately caches various bottles in his apartment, all the time trying to convince his bride-to-be that he has given up drinking. One bottle was even suspended on a string out his window.

7. *Gaslight* was a play and then a motion picture in which the villain-husband tried to convince his rich wife she was going mad by denying the reality of her perceptions until she herself began to doubt them.

8. Loss of control is a major tenet of AA. They claim that alcoholics are unable to control the amount that they drink, and that if they take one drink, they have a compulsion to continue imbibing until the supply is depleted (Chafetz, 1983; Keller, 1972:156). The slogan, "one drink away from a drunk," is intended to stop the heavy drinker from taking "that first drink." Belief in this phenomenon of loss of control apparently does aid laypersons trying to under-

stand the drinking of a loved one. As noted, it is used in the reverse by those who are trying to deny their own drinking problem when they claim that they are still "in control" of their intake and that even though they are drinking a great deal, they are doing so through preference.

9. Criteria for alcoholism diagnosis developed by the Criteria Committee, National Council on Alcoholism (1972:43–45) have been operationalized. These criteria are further categorized as to whether they are physiological, or behavioral, psychological, and attitudinal. These two major groupings are then subdivided in terms of major and minor criteria. Unfortunately, even if a wife were to see this material, the physiological indicators would be of little help to her, primarily because they focus on a stage more advanced than the period at which she first develops concern about her husband's drinking. For instance, tremors, hallucinations, withdrawal seizures, and delirium tremens, while undeniable indicators of alcoholism, usually come in the latter portion of an alcoholic's career. Thus, she uses what the council terms "minor" behavior anomalies.

While admitting that alcoholism is very difficult to diagnose, Forrest suggests gross diagnostic categories:

> Behaviorally, the diagnosis of alcoholism frequently includes marital discord and possible divorce, chronic work adjustment difficulties, extended legal complications, interpersonal and general social difficulties, identity and role conflict, and parental inadequacy; in short, this amounts to an almost total life-style constructed around drinking behavior. (1978:60)

The problem drinker "entails a life style in which major accidents, difficulties and traumas have been alcohol facilitated." (This includes automobile accidents, sexual affairs, job absenteeism, aggressive outbursts, and similar unacceptable behaviors.) Possibly of some help to wives are what have been termed the "warning signs" of alcoholism—indicators that drinking is getting out of hand. Some of these are proposed by the National Institute on Alcohol Abuse and Alcoholism (1971:no pagination):

1. the need to drink before facing certain situations
2. frequent drinking sprees
3. a steady increase in intake
4. solitary drinking
5. early morning drinking
6. blackouts (loss of memory of certain periods of time).

Other indicators of alcoholism are available. For instance, the following have been suggested by the National Institute on Alcohol Abuse and Alcoholism:

> Anyone who goes to work intoxicated has a drinking problem. Anyone who is intoxicated and drives a car has a drinking problem. Anyone who sustains bodily injury requiring medical attention as a consequence of an intoxicated state has a drinking problem. Anyone who, under the influence of alcohol, does something he contends he would never do without alcohol has a drinking problem. (1972:8)

These warning signs of alcoholism are less ambiguous than the definitions, but few wives seem aware of them at the outset of their husband's heavy drinking. It is probable that many husbands do not evidence these symptoms in the earlier stages of problem drinking. Equally important, these indicators are necessarily stated situation free, whereas actual drinking behavior is imbedded in varying real occurrences and individual martial expectations that moderate and mediate its meaning, allowing alternative explanations to surface. There are, of course, self-tests for alcoholics to take, but heavily drinking men are not likely to be exposed to them until committed to a hospital as a result of other rather flagrant evidence of alcoholism. (see, for instance, Powers and Spickard 1984; Swenson and Morse 1975; Moore 1972; Pokorny et al. 1972).

10.   For instance, strong attempts on the part of the person being judged to influence in some way the decision of the judge are usually not a variable in cognitive studies where the major interest is most often in a subject who is making a naive or "natural" presentation. Goffman (1959), however, calls our attention to times when persons are involved in "impression management" and certainly the avoidance of a deviant label would fall under that rubric.

11.   *Catch-22* was the title of a novel by Joseph Heller (1962). It referred to the construction of armed forces rules in such a way that it was impossible to avoid combat through claims of mental stress inasmuch as such a claim during war time indicated how sane the claimant really is.

CHAPTER 3

The Home Treatment

Introduction

When the long period of doubt, anxiety, and evidence-gathering culminates in the conclusion that her husband is an alcoholic, what follows might be described as a compassionate crusade by the wife, a time when she seeks to help him or "save" him. This is the beginning of a new period in the lives of the drinker and the spouse: the home treatment—a period with a career of its own during which a range of strategies are tried by the wife in the hope of accomplishing the desired reform. Once again, the reactions of American and Finnish wives parallel each other in many cases, while showing the effects of cultural differences in others.

In most cultures, almost without exception, the wife first tries to handle the problem herself rather than turning either to relatives or to professionals in the field of alcoholism treatment. It is, of course, possible (even probable) that family members already suspect or "know" that a son, son-in-law, or brother has become a problem drinker. However, not one wife in either sample was approached at this juncture by a concerned relative to discuss the matter, and most wives assumed that they had the prerogative of telling relatives and asking for help, or keeping the husband's excessive drinking a secret.

The reluctance of people to ask kin for help (because it means betraying their need for it when they are trying to maintain a trouble-free facade) is seldom discussed in the literature on family help networks. Yet it is a real issue, and some wives show a shrewd lay awareness of the lasting quality of a stigma, once revealed, even if later overcome. As they put it:

> Right now, his family thinks he is a wonderful person. If they were to discover this problem, it might affect his inheritance. (American)

I thought that if he should stop drinking, then it would not be good for her [the wife's mother] to know that he had. (Finn)

They are also loathe to let kin know that their marriage may be a failure:

Both our parents think we are a perfect couple. If I tell them about his drinking, what will they think? (American)

I haven't told my mother. She is ill and I haven't wanted to disappoint her. She thinks my marriage is quite all right. (Finn)

Additionally, most Finnish and some American wives repeatedly say that their husbands would not approve of their sharing family problems with relatives outside the immediate family. This, alone, is effective in sealing some wives' lips, for a time at least. Wives also avoid consulting professionals in the field of alcohol treatment, because that very act could also allow knowledge about a husband's drinking to get outside the family.

Although she has been told by many that alcoholism is a disease or illness, the wife, in her heart of hearts, still believes that her husband's excessive drinking is voluntary. Certainly this is the impression the husband wants her to have. Thus, she proceeds on the theory that the drinking can be halted or modified by an act of will if the husband can just be persuaded of the necessity to do so.[1] With this firm belief in the basic rationality of her spouse then, the wife sets forth with determination to convince her husband that it is imperative he change his drinking habits.

In their ameliorative efforts, wives in America and Finland face problems that are special to their cultures. Important differences between male-female relationships in each country affect the wife's direct attempts to stop her husband's heavy drinking. For some time now in modern American marriages, more than lip service is often paid to the equalitarian ideal (Clayton 1975:346–65; Reiss 1976:257–62), especially where it is assumed that a dynamic power balance is achieved in two-job marital dyads. However, more recently, marriage and family researchers have noted that merely because the wife is working does not make her a full and equal partner (Schumm et al. 1985; Scanzoni 1980; Aldous 1981; Li and Caldwell 1987). Neither can she pursue a career with the same single-minded intensity as her husband (Poloma et al. 1981), nor is she always interested in doing so. In Finland, however [and other Scandinavian countries as well (Haas 1986)], the cultural norm that a man must be dominant in his home and his marriage is sufficiently strong that even in two-job families the wife has that additional barrier to any direct, frank discussion of the issue of excessive drinking. (The Position of

Women in Finnish Society 1984).[2] The significance of these differences will become apparent as the home treatment is described in detail.

The Parameters of Persuasion to Change

There are two possible ways one person can attempt to change the behavior of another:

1. The direct approach: ask, tell, or force the person to change. (Negative and/or positive sanctions my be inferred, threatened, or applied as part of this approach.)
2. The indirect approach: manipulate the person into changing without his/her realizing such efforts are being made. That is, make the person think he/she is changing behavior of his/her own free will.

The assumptions implicit in the use of either approach are quite different.[3] The direct approach assumes people can change their behavior if they wish; those who ask assume the individual is (1) sympathetic to the person making the request, (2) cannot resist the logic of the argument offered, or (3) cannot resist because of their subordinate position in a power relationship—which means they must deal with an implied or open threat of sanction or its enactment. On the other hand, implicit in the indirect approach is the belief that either the target person is determined not to change voluntarily, regardless of the unpleasant consequences and must be manipulated to do so, or cannot change of his/her own free will.

At the outset, the wife sees her task as providing reasons for quitting so persuasive that they outweigh any motives her husband may have for drinking. She is prepared to argue and, if need be, even to nag.

In detailing this career of coping approaches, it should be noted that many of these activities on the part of wives of alcoholics have been chronicled by previous researchers. However, when Joan Jackson (1954) described some of these behaviors, she referred to them as the way family members "adjust" to alcoholism. In 1975, Orford et al. noted some 46 "coping behaviors" of wives, while James and Goldman (1971) and Steinglass (1979, 1981a,b) also reported several styles, many of them overlapping with those described here given in response to the question, When you decided your husband was an alcoholic, what did you do about it? In this analysis of a wife's strategies to get her husband to stop drinking, her varied approaches can be seen to be linked to a changing belief about the nature of alcoholism, as well as the meaning of the tie between herself and her husband.

The Direct Approach

Logical Persuasion and Its Fate

The problem of what constitutes the best means for helping a deviant back onto the normative path has long puzzled both the behavioral scientist and the social reformer. Those who attempt reforms of deviant behavior must tread a narrow line: too weak an approach will be ineffectual; too strong a push risks setting up a cycle of alienation that may ultimately drive the individual from the group entirely, and into the company of more understanding peers (Parsons 1951). The wife thus cannot expect her husband's drinking to be drastically reduced if she is only mildly critical of his failure to control excessive consumption. On the other hand, heavy-handed demands or raging denunciations may drive the drinking husband out of the home to the nearest bar, where a peer group awaits with understanding, acceptance, and support.

Compounding this double bind for the wife are the problems arising from her unique position as an amateur reformer/therapist: her emotional tie with her husband, her subordinate status vis-à-vis him, and the lack of reinforcement for her efforts—she is not a professional counselor.

Initially, when American wives try to "talk things over" with their husband, they start in a rather low-key mode, attempting a casual style while still making their concern clear. For the most part, as can be seen, the early requests center on suggestions for more moderate drinking rather than stopping altogether.

> I'd tell him, "I don't mind if you drink, I really don't, a six-pack or two is fine. But why is it like a compulsory thing? . . . That you've got to drink it . . . It can't stay in the refrigerator till the next day? Why isn't there a stopping point at all? (American)
>
> Usually when we are alone, I tell him, "You gonna start to drink again, you better be careful." But I would not nag him. I'd say, "You're drinking again. You better be careful or you'll end up in trouble." (American)

The responses these American women receive are, not surprisingly, similar to the husband's defensive answers reported when the wife is in the throes of trying to diagnose the cause of her husband's problems or their deteriorating marital relationship:

> I'm not drinking too much. It's your imagination.

Once convinced that a gentle nudge toward cutting down on alcohol intake is not going to work, American wives move on to what might be termed logical persuasion, with three major foci:

1. He had better start realizing that he has a real drinking problem, that his drinking has gotten out of hand.
2. His drinking is adversely affecting other areas of his social life and relationships with others.
3. His drinking, if continued, will ruin is health.

The escalating urgency in these appeals can be noted in these exemplary quotations from American wives:

> I told him that if he kept drinking he'd be out of a job. (American)
>
> I tried to show him what was bothering me—the fact that we didn't have any money; the car; he has ulcers also . . . the fact that he was always complaining about a headache, his stomach, and everything . . . the fact that the only time he complained about it was when he was drinking . . . the fact that he was showing up late for work. He argued about it, though. (American)

The reaction of some American husbands to these stronger arguments remains mild, and even becomes conciliatory as they agree and promise to cut down on their drinking. However, these promises are seldom kept for long:

> Well sometimes he would say he would try, and maybe I could see him maybe for a few days try to limit the amount that he took by bringing home less . . . but gradually he got back into the same old patterns again. (American)
>
> He agreed with me, but nothing ever changed. He would never argue . . . just agreed . . . said he would do something about it, but never did. (American)

At this point, some American husbands became either philosophical or somewhat defensive about their drinking:

> He just says, "You start to die the day you are born. Did you know that?" (American)
>
> [He said,] "Oh, go away and leave me alone. It's my body; it's my life. What concerns me is not any of your business." (American)

These interchanges are rather gentle compared to the majority of those occurring between drinking husbands and their wives in Finland, where there is no attempt to pretend the relationship is an equalitarian one. Finnish men often respond with anger to suggestions they drink too much. They immediately make clear that any attempt by the wife to discuss the topic with them is taboo. Those who do allow the subject to be brought up disagree in the same way that they did during the diagnostic stage. Other men change the focus of the talks to the woman's faults and complaints they have about her. Defensive criticisms by the husband can cover almost anything:

> He doesn't think of his drinking as a problem. He says I have food and shelter. Do I want more? (Finn)
>
> Either he would not answer [my discussion of his drinking], or he would get angry and tell me what I looked like. He criticized me for how I looked or how fat I was . . . especially how fat I was. (Finn)

Finnish wives often "learn" in this way that the subject of their husband's drinking is not a safe one to bring up. With such unpleasantness to face, it is not surprising that some of the Finnish wives tone down their direct approach to their husband's drinking to the point of saying almost nothing at all. Or they say nothing that can be interpreted as a challenge to his position and right to decide for himself how much he should drink. As one wife put it:

> A couple of times I remarked that everything would be better if he didn't drink. But I said it casually. (Finn)

Other Finnish wives try to avoid stirring up an angry husband by developing a schedule of his moods, in order to know when it is best and safest to talk to him about his drinking and when he is most likely to be objective about the amount:

> Just after drinking periods, he was very soft and I could talk to him about his drinking. (Finn)
>
> It's really no use trying to talk to him when he's sober, because he's so nervous then. (Finn)
>
> When he's in the middle of a hangover is a good time to talk to him. He feels so awful that he is ready to listen. (Finn)

Since loss of control suggests alcoholism (see note 8, Chapter 2), a heavy drinker often claims not to have lost control because every drink was taken consciously and purposely. This is exactly how Finnish men deny their wives' allegations of alcoholism. Rather than basing a diagnosis on amount of intake or social behavior as the wives do, the drinkers themselves consider their ability to control their drinking to suit themselves the most pertinent criterion. (American men, as was noted, speak of their "preference" for alcohol as "normal.") Finnish wives say about their husbands:

> He said that he is not an alcoholic. He said he could control it. (Finn)
>
> He said, "I can stop whenever I want, but I don't feel like stopping today." (Finn)

It might be mentioned that some American wives also take great pains not to offend their husband when voicing concern about his drinking, indicating that this minority fear their husband's rage as do Finnish women:

> I can remember trying to have talks with him, trying to convince him that this alcohol was ruining our marriage, but I was never forceful. (American)
>
> [I] just wrote notes. I tried to talk to him to see if he would open up and tell me what is bothering him. (American)

Nagging: The American Wives Escalate Their Campaign

Most American wives, unlike the Finns, do not hesitate to show anger when logical discussion fails. Many admit they openly argue with their husband concerning drinking or that they nag and complain about it. (Some claim that long periods of silence preceded their nagging in which their anger built up until they could contain it no longer.)

> I'd be a screaming, nagging bitch. That's what I became. (American)
>
> I would do the nagging and get upset at this and that. Especially when he'd stay out all night long. Then there'd be accusations. It just built up in me for all those 13 years of marriage when I never said too much to him [about his drinking]. (American)

One outcome of escalating sanctions in order to hasten reform is that such action may actually increase deviance. American men do not react with the same equanimity to a wife's nagging and quarreling that they show when she attempts logical persuasion. A husband's frequent reaction is to claim that his wife is actually driving him to drink by her continual complaining.[4]

> Well, he said I was nasty when he drank, so this is why [he said] he drank. Who wants to come home to a nasty woman? I admit, I did start to get nasty. (American)
>
> He said, "I figure I'm going to catch hell for one beer, so I might as well stay for five or six or whatever." (American)

Parenthetically, Finnish wives do not admit to nagging and their husbands seldom claim their wives drive them to drink. This is probably because heavy drinking, and even drunkenness, is not only expected behavior of men in Finland, but almost a matter of pride. Since the man assumes he is boss in his home, it would diminish his pride if he admitted he drank because of a failure of dominance rather than fulfilling his role as a traditional two-fisted drinker. The Finnish husband does, as mentioned, use complaints about his wife at an earlier juncture: to silence her when she cautiously brings up the topic of his drinking for

logical discussion. American husbands use criticism defensively to end
the nagging and also to explain their drinking:

> [He says he drinks because] I scream too much, the kids are always fight-
> ing, I'm too fat, I'm too skinny . . . His wife is a bitch . . . You know.
> (American)
>
> Once he said, "You're too fat. Stop eating and I'll stop drinking."
> (American)
>
> "It's your fault I drink," he would say. "You won't accept my job and you
> won't accept me as I am." (American)

It seems obvious that logical discussion, sweet reasonableness, or the
angry repetition of an argument that soon becomes nagging when used
by American wives, does not have much persuasive power over a heavily drinking man. Seeming acceptance of a wife's point of view by the
husband when she mildly admonishes him for his drinking does not
really carry with it any long-term reform. When the wife becomes more
forceful, the alcoholic husband begins to blame her for his problems,
leaving her in a no-win quandary. Finnish husbands are not receptive to
logical discussion regardless of how it is presented, and attempt to abort
every type of wifely persuasion before it even gets started.

The effect of this stalemate on wives is the same in both cultures—
even when reached by different polemical routes—despair and desperation. These feelings, in turn, set the stage for the switch from the logical
approach to one of the strategies of persuasion often used by women:
emotional pleading.[5]

Emotional Pleading by American and Finnish Wives

When a powerful person makes a request of a subordinate, there is
little difference between the request and a command (Heider 1967:278–
79). On the other hand, if the request is by the less powerful of the two,
it becomes a petition for a favor. When the wife of an alcoholic turns to
pleading, it is in recognition that she has failed to convince her husband
to stop drinking either by the logic of her argument or to assuage her
anger. Now, she must ask that he take this action as a favor. She is,
however, still counting on the relationship between herself and her
husband—the margin of emotional goodwill created by love and affection—to be an important factor in his granting it. Pleas at this stage in
the home treatment are often accompanied by tears and the general
discomfort of all concerned.

Wives' descriptions of how they acted when they became too emotional to continue to discuss their husband's drinking dispassionately
show great similarity in both cultures:

> I begged him, I pleaded, I cried. I was very emotional, and I cried, and I said that if he loved me he wouldn't do this to me and the children. (American)
>
> I just let everything out that I feel. I'm crying and saying everything I have in my heart. (Finn)

American husbands who earlier were constrained during calm discussions of their drinking and limited themselves to countercharges to their wife's accusations, now escalate their defense and exhibit anger when approached about their drinking by an emotion-wrought wife.

American wives describe their husband's reactions to tearful pleading as follows:

> He said, "Well, you go your way and I'll go mine. I'm not an alcoholic." (American)

Finnish men, on the other hand, seem quite touched by a weeping wife and react sympathetically. After a tearful scene they will often promise their spouses not to drink:

> I start to cry, and when I do he consoles me and calms me and says he will do something about his drinking. (Finn)
>
> "Oh yes," he'd say [when I cry], "I'll change. Things will get better. Everything will be okay." (Finn)

This difference in reactions to tears and supplication is probably the result of the more equalitarian stance of men in American marriages as compared to the dominant one in Finland. In American marriages, husbands may feel they are relieved of a portion of the traditional duty to be protective of a spouse's feelings, inasmuch as equals are, by definition, equal in ability to "take it." Not so the Finnish man, apparently, who can easily tell his wife that his drinking is none of her business, but feels responsibility and guilt when she dissolves in tears about it.

However, whether the husband promises to stop excessive drinking as a result of low-key logical persuasion, as with some American husbands, or higher-pitched emotional pleading, as with some Finnish husbands, the promise is honored "more in the breach." In most instances, after a very short stint of sobriety, the drinking is resumed, full force.

If social bonds, especially those in the primary relationship of marriage, are based on shared meanings, reciprocity, and trust (Berger and Kellner 1970; Deutsch 1964), then it is not surprising that a great deal of strain is put on the marriage when the wife experiences the disappointment of a succession of broken promises (Estes 1974:1251):

I felt let down, you know. Somebody, you know, didn't keep their end of the bargain. Now I just don't believe him, and tell him so. (American)

He didn't keep his promises. Well, of course, when he broke his promises, I became deeply depressed. Then I got new hope when he made a new promise, so it was up and down all the time. (Finn)

One Finnish husband made a pledge that took cognizance of probable promise-breaking:

When he talked he said everything will be better when *I* can stand it [his drinking], then it will be easier. He said for *me* not to give up. (Finn)

Further Escalation: Threats to Leave

With talk of failing on all levels, but still believing their husbands can stop drinking, wives of alcoholics turn to threats. Talk of separation or divorce is often used as a weapon to bring about reform.

A problem with threats-as-negotiation is that the indicated sanctions can become progressively more serious and real. The major assumptions of threats-as-negotiation as an approach to behavior change are:

1. the person being threatened must perceive the threat as real;
2. he/she must wish to avoid this punishment or sanction, and thus will agree to the wishes of the threatener;
3. this negates the need to carry out the threat.

The person making the threat must have the means, ability, and psychological readiness to take the action called for, in order not to lose credibility. Likewise, the individual being threatened must care about the possible consequences sufficiently that the value of the desired behavior reform does not seem too high a price to pay. The threatened person also must have the means, ability, and psychological readiness to do what has been requested.

Threatening to terminate a relationship, even temporarily, is not something to be undertaken lightly. Groups and states do not usually secede without war, and when they do, they often must pay a large economic price. Parallel costs are often found at the marital level. A partner will often fight to maintain a relationship, even when he or she apparently has not been enjoying it. Thus, the about-to-be abandoned spouse may launch a tremendous emotional and/or legal campaign to save the marriage.[6]

Initially, American and Finnish wives threaten to leave their husband in order to hasten drinking reformation and ultimately salvage the marriage. These women hope not to have to carry through with the threat. They know they are ill-equipped to handle the emotional upheaval of a divorce, as well as the trauma involved in finding temporary housing and adequate financial support.

American and Finnish wives say:

> At that time, I threatened: "You either stop or I leave." I guess that when I leave him, I hope that it will sort of, you know, make him realize. (American)

> I tried to threaten him with divorce. I remember once when I hid in a big closet and he couldn't find me, and he thought I had left and he felt very badly . . . But, of course, it is hard to *really* leave. (Finn)

Both American and Finnish husbands respond to these threats primarily with general disinterest, although promises such as those made in response to tearful pleas to quit drinking are sometimes made. These drinking husbands appear to know that there is a lack of real seriousness in the threat, or at least they are willing to risk the possibility that their wives are bluffing.

American wives say:

> The threats I used to use on him would roll off his back and he would say, "Well, maybe you're right, maybe we should give it up and quit and get a divorce." You know. (American)

Finnish wives echo this reaction on the part of their husbands:

> I have threatened him many times, "If you don't stop drinking, I'll leave you." He is only smiling. (Finn)

In calling his wife's bluff, the alcoholic husband may be relying, in part, on the economic difficulty she would undoubtedly have trying to manager on her own, especially if small children are involved. Additionally, having experienced earlier threats-as-negotiations that proved hollow, husbands may feel complacent that their wives appear to lack the courage actually to take such a drastic step. Hertzman and Hertzman (1981) point out that an alcoholic is a past master at knowing when family members mean business and will follow through, and when they are bluffing.

Women, themselves, admit to these problems:

> [I threatened] to run out and go away, but I knew that they were threats I couldn't carry out because I had five children and where was I going to go? I think that he knew that my threats couldn't be carried out, and anyway I don't think it means anything to them at all what you do when they are drinking. So I didn't do anything. I didn't do anything at all that time. (American)

I threatened divorce. As he is very much against divorce, that is a good threat—but it only keeps him for drinking a couple of days. (Finn)

American women are in a better position to carry through on a threat of separation or divorce than are their Finnish counterparts, as will be discussed in more detail in a later chapter. Finnish women usually have little discretionary money (even if they work), and the couple's apartment is usually in the husband's name (and many women are unaware of the recent law making it community property). Even when the woman owns the apartment, if the husband refuses to move, it is difficult to get him out. There is no alimony in Finland and child support is hard to collect (The Position of Women in Finnish Society 1984). These difficulties are compounded by (1) a severe shortage of city apartments, (2) a general lack of support from parents (who seldom offer to take their daughter in if she leaves her husband), and (3) the fact that acceptance of welfare is seen as a great disgrace in this quasi-socialist, yet fiercely individualistic country.

Finnish women describe the economic and legal barriers to actually leaving their husbands as follows:

I wouldn't have anything to live on [if I were to divorce my husband]. We could sell the home and split the money. I think Finnish law is that if I leave, I can't claim anything. (Finn)

It is also extremely difficult to get an apartment here in Helsinki. I would have no place to go. (Finn)

I can't force him to leave. The police can't help more because it's his home, too. At least it's that way in Finland. (Finn)

American women usually own the family home jointly with their husband. Even where they do not, these wives have more access to their husband's money than do Finnish wives and more hope of alimony, if not child support. They accept more readily the possibility of going on welfare if need be. (They also seem far more able than Finnish women to convince their husband to move out.) These resources, and willingness actually to use them, mean that American women are in a much stronger position than Finnish women when threatening separation or divorce. Thus, when these wives actually begin to take concrete steps to leave, the threat is often taken seriously by a husband who cuts down on drinking temporarily:

He knows now if he drinks, or really gets drunk, that I really will split. Once, during the last month, I threatened and was ready and said what I was going to do. That was three weeks ago, and he cut all of his classes and stayed home and talked to me the entire day. (American)

And I have laid out my whole plan for him. Before, if I'd have said two years ago, "I'm leaving," he would say, "Ha, you're crazy. How are you going to get along?" And I've said, "I'm leaving tomorrow morning. I've got a part-time job. I can get welfare if I need it. The kids will be provided for. I don't think this is a good situation for them to remain in, or me, or you. I'm leaving." I would say in the last year he has probably consumed one-fourth [the amount] that he had the year previous. (American)

Of course, the woman who can successfully threaten to end a relationship in order to save it (by forcing desirable behavior modification) is also in the best position, both practically and psychologically, actually to give up on reform and rehabilitation as a goal and instead end the relationship once and for all. Thus, a strong push for reform and reconciliation on the one hand, and abandonment of the marriage on the other, are tactically very close to each other.

Focusing on the Supply

At one time or another, desperation drives wives in both cultures to try the most direct approach of all to get their husband to cut down on drinking: they attempt to curtail the supply. They pour out liquor, smash bottles, or hide alcohol. They ask bars or friends not to serve him. This classic strategy is more histrionic than helpful. Supplies of alcohol seem always available to a determined drinker.

Most wives ruefully describe past scenes in which they poured out alcohol—a bit ashamed that they expected so simple an act to accomplish so complex a reform. Finnish wives not only pour out liquor, but they ask various business establishments not to sell replacements. This is no more successful than destruction of the supply:

I have poured out his liquor, which was very silly of me because it does no good whatsoever. The only thing it does—all my efforts made him drink more compulsively. (American)

I tried hiding his bottles and pouring them out. I drank with him so we could finish the bottles faster, but that didn't work and I got sick. (Finn)

The Variety of Indirect Approaches

James and Goldman (1971) and Estes (1974) report that wives of alcoholics often develop an entire repertoire of coping styles; when one fails to produce desired results, another is tried. The findings of this study indicate that this is true for attempts to get their husbands to cease heavy drinking. Wives of alcoholics start with the direct approach, for which the underlying assumption is that the husband can be persuaded by the logic of the wife's argument to stop his heavy drinking; they move on to emotional pleading, nagging, and threats; these efforts dwindle to feeble attempts at cutting off the liquor supply. Most wives admit this last effort is more likely to reduce their own feelings of tension and frustration than to have any lasting effect on their husband's heavy drinking.

Inasmuch as the underlying assumption of all direct attempts at home treatment is that the husband can be persuaded he has more to lose than to gain by continued imbibing, a wife's switch to the indirect approach is, in part, a self-admission that no amount of logic, bribery, or threat can get her husband to give up liquor. The possibility of psychological compulsion to explain his drinking becomes viable and she decides he must somehow be manipulated into cutting down on his alcohol intake without being aware of her efforts to this end.

The Indirect Approach

With this development, the wife's relationship to her drinking spouse changes as she feels a loss of closeness with her husband. She is now aware he will not stop drinking just for her sake, nor does he show much concern at the ritual threat of separation. At the same time, she retains concern for his welfare. Reasoning startlingly like professional therapists, wives explore a range of entirely different approaches. If calm, discussions, tearful sessions, or angry threats, and destruction of supply are not effective, perhaps the manipulation of a husband's environment can be managed in such a way that he has either less desire or less opportunity to drink.[7] The strategies involved in the indirect approach are, almost by definition, those ploys which a concerned therapist would use on someone with little or no motivation to change or with reduced mental and/or physical capacities.

Acting "Normal" or "Natural"

One indirect approach, which, quite interestingly, wives in both cultures have developed and labeled identically as acting normal or natural, is not unlike the so-called therapeutic milieu that enjoyed a great deal of popularity in the treatment of mental illness in the 1960s, *Community as Doctor*. Rapaport (1959) describe this approach quite aptly. Its essence is that professional therapists construct an environment in which the alcoholic lives (usually a hospital ward), so as to make the atmosphere as accepting, loving, and noncritical as possible, without regard for what the patient may have done that brought him or her there. Presumably, in such a setting the individual would experience less stress and have less desire to drink to reduce tensions (or to "act out"—in the case of mental illness).

In the wifely version of the therapeutic milieu, the wife ceases all attempts to persuade her husband to stop his heavy drinking, and instead pretends that the drinking or the drunken behavior is not occurring, even when it is. Often the wife will try this method after deciding the daily hassle of the direct confrontation is useless, as well as hard on her emotions:

> Over a period of years, I've quit nagging at him about his drinking. If we've had supper at night, and at 9 o'clock he combs his hair and goes to the front door and says, "See ya," I don't get all upset and cry, "Where are you going?" I know where he's going. I know he might be home in an hour, he might be home at 2:30, or he might not come home all night. (American)

> I was wearing myself out fighting and crying. I decided to start ignoring the fact that he was drunk. (Finn)

It should be stressed that acting normal or natural is more than just resignation on the part of a wife of an alcoholic. It is a planned behavior intended to elicit the same type of behavior in return. As one American wife put it:

> I acted a lot of ways when he was drunk. Inside [myself], I acted like, "Let's pretend it is not happening." Now I try to act like a normal person (like he thought I was abnormal [otherwise]) *because I thought if I acted normal in some way, that he would act normal,* too. (American) (emphasis mine)

A major setting for these attempts to act natural is the home at the end of the day, when the husband returns quite obviously drunk. The wife then tries to act like she thinks she would act if he were sober:

> [When he came home] I just talked to him like I'm talking to you. I just pretend like nothing is wrong. Sometimes it would work and other times he would keep at me till I got mad. (American)

> When he comes home after a few days with a hangover, I try to act like I believe he's been working. (Finn)

The facade of normal interaction creates strains of its own, however, strains that may be harder on a wife than on professional workers in a hospital ward. Acting natural while inwardly feeling stress and anxiety is much more demanding than those occasions when there is no need to make a conscious effort at normalcy. Playacting at naturalness results in heightened awareness of interaction rather than relaxed behavior in taken-for-granted situations. The person who is successful at acting natural is in a state of constant alert.[8]

> I [act normal] outwardly but not inwardly. It is very difficult. (American)
>
> [Acting normal] was very hard. I used to get all tied up in knots inside. I'd try to read a book because I'm quite an avid reader, but it didn't work out. I guess your thoughts start . . . you know. (American)

One woman went go great lengths to help herself act normal, even fantasizing during embarrassing situations in a manner that comes close to what Hochschild (1979, 1983) refers to as "codifying emotions," or "doing emotion work." However, Hochschild was more concerned with how people shape their emotions to conform with normative expectations, while this wife was molding her feelings to avoid the emotions that might be expected of her in the situation:

> Well, I would actually pretend that he was somebody else's husband. I used to say, "My God! Why doesn't some woman—whoever's husband this is—come and take him away! He is not mine!" You play games like that. I would actually pretend he was someone else's husband and [when] we would be at a dinner party (and because of his position we were usually at the head table) and when his steak would drop, or his face would fall in the salad, I'd just think, "Wow! I'm sure glad I'm not married to that dummy!" I was playing a game. (American)

Talking with an inebriated husband presents special problems to wives who are self-consciously trying to ignore the fragmented or somewhat nonsensical quality of the conversation he makes:

> It's very difficult . . . especially if he's in a mood where he wants to keep telling the same thing over and over again. After a while I get so tired of hearing it, I'm sure he knows it from my voice, and right away, he'll say nobody is interested. My mind is on something else. I catch it wandering. (American)

In an effort to reduce such strain, wives of alcoholics, trying to act normal, use props and activities to aid them. Often they go on a self-conscious and sometimes feverish round of cleaning and cooking activities when their husband comes home drunk, for it is easier to playact at naturalness if one has some concrete role involving behavior that will take up excess nervous energy:

> [I act normal by] being in the garage washing, in the den, or I find something to do—using nervous energy. I am so busy with things that I don't even pass the kitchen to see what he is doing. (American)

the glasses the same. Well, I got to where I couldn't drink that much. (American)

At times . . . I considered drinking as much as he did to show him. I did that one time and that was a disaster—oh, that was really bad! I don't want to—it hurts me more than it hurts him. (American)

I tried to keep up with him, to fight fire with fire. I almost turned into an alcoholic myself. (American)

Other American wives reason that if a husband's drinking can be restricted to the home, he will drink less. To get him to drink at home, they start drinking with him, trying to create a "party" atmosphere in the home that would make it competitive with bars. But, as with the "deplete the supply" or "fighting fire with fire" approaches, these wives find that the "home party" strategy cannot match their husband's stamina and intake:

It was great [drinking with him at home], but then after two or three drinks, I had enough and I was ready to go to bed, but then he was so happy . . . he'd want me to sit with him till three o'clock, and if I refused and say I have to go to work, I don't want to drink more, then, well, he'd go out. So you see, there was no way of stopping him. (American)

No Finnish wife volunteered the fact that she tried drinking with her husband as some sort of indirect method of teaching him social drinking; some, however, admitted to drinking alone to console themselves for the unhappiness and tension they experienced in their marriages. One tried to consume as much as possible to reduce her husband's supply. She succeeded only in making herself ill.

Miscellaneous Indirect Strategies

In their desperation to turn back the tide of their husband's increasingly heavy drinking, wives also try a variety of other strategies— all of them covert in nature:

I tried behavior modification. The biggest behavior mod thing I've done is definitely withhold sex. I will avoid him. (American)

I pushed up dinner from our usual 6:30 time to 6:15 and then 6:00 P.M. I invented reasons why we should start eating earlier, because his pattern was three or four drinks before dinner, then he would not eat dinner. (American)

I tried feeding him continuously because I found that if he ate, he would cease drinking. (American)

[I would do] childish things . . . like washing my clothes, but not his . . . or hide his keys so he could not leave. Just to get back at him and to keep him at home. (American)

The "Hands-Off" Approach

A small minority of American women literally do nothing about their husband's heavy drinking, either overtly or covertly, from the time their concern is first aroused about it. They suffer in silence because they are afraid to confront the existence of the problem openly, or fear making their husband angry:

> [I did] nothing for a long time [after I decided he was an alcoholic]. It was more avoidance on my part. I would take the kids and just go somewhere when he would be drinking. When he did drink, I would be pretty sure that he probably would drink too much. So, as soon as I realized it, I would just get out of there. I didn't talk about it. I covered up for him, just mainly to get away. I didn't know what to do. I just kind of shut it out as far as I was concerned, and we'd see the kids were in bed, and that kind of things. And I just took care of things myself. You try not to think about it, you know. Try not to, because it's no point. There's no point in talking to him about it. He won't talk about it. Well, you shut up, the fact that that's the problem, I guess. It's what you do, and then proceed to do your own thing, whatever that happens to be. Raise your family, whatever, and I since raised the kids myself. (American)
>
> [I did] nothing . . . nothing for a long time . . . it was more avoidance on my part. (American)

Other wives arrive at this position after repeated failures to change their husband's drinking behavior, or after receiving counseling[11] (Albertson 1971; Cook et al. 1983) or help from Al-Anon (Gorman and Rooney 1979). McNamara (1960) has pointed out that many wives are relieved when they give up efforts at the home treatment. Steinglass (1981) suggests that this the establishment of equilibrium in the family, a "stable wet stage."[12]

As will be discussed in Chapter 4, Steinglass (1979a,b, 1981a,b, 1982) sees most of the machinations of the wife of an alcoholic as representing the type of behavior that results when alcohol controls what they believe to be a "family behavior system." Thus they see these attempts on the part of the wife to stop her husband from drinking and to maintain the family through "taking over" as a part of the problem that actually keeps the man drinking. Wives who "let go" (which is also suggested by Al-Anon) are viewed within this framework as not giving up, but stopping the "sick family system," which inevitably encourages drinking.

> I figure after trying everything out, I figure let me leave him alone. It will either kill him or cure him, or something, but let him do it on his own. I cannot fight him. I fight, I get less results, so I figure let me let it be. (American)
>
> I've just become more discouraged; just have given up. (American)

These women also mention that the termination of their personal approaches to curing their husband's alcoholism gives them some relief from the stress and tension of trying and continually failing:

> I can't say that I don't talk to him about it. If he brings it up, I can talk calmly now. I can talk about alcoholism and I can talk about what I think he's doing to us. I don't think I just ignore the problem. I'm calm now when I talk to him, and I'm not so tearful or anything like that. I've finally let go of the problem. I know that, personally, I can't change, he has to change it. There's really nothing I can do to make him stop. (American)

Of course, such detachment may lead to increased mental or even physical separation. Emotional bonds, while composed of many threads, can be weakened when concern about a person is deliberately "turned off," regardless of what he is doing to his health and life. Eventually, withering of other strands of the marital tie may follow. This slackening of care is exemplified below:

> Right now, I'm to the point where, this is what he wants to do, I can't stop him. And I'm not going to live with it, for my sake and my kids' sake. I can't live with him any longer. And I won't. (American)

> I've given up. When he goes out that door, I leave too. Sometimes we end up seeing each other in the same nightclub. We sometimes come home together, but we don't do this too often. I show him I can do it, too. (American)

Some women go full circle and return to the direct approach after having run the gamut of both strategic approaches.

A more frequent development, however, after letting the problem lie fallow for a time, is for the woman to turn to professional help for her husband's alcoholism. She realizes her own inability to do anything to help him, but begins to hope that professional help will hold some answers to the problem. Like the diagnostic and home treatment stages, the search for professional help for her husband, and both his and her experiences with it, is a saga in its own right. It signals a greater acceptance of the illness theory of problem drinking, as well as an end to any hope of keeping the problem within the family (although the likelihood that others are not aware of it by this time is probably minimal).

Summary and Conclusions

The fate of the home treatment is a specific instance of what can happen when a concerned but relatively powerless person offers gratuitous advice and aid. It is often ignored; more often resented.

Safilios-Rothschild (1978), in her discussion of the dimensions of power in the family and its distribution between husbands and wives, suggests that most wives lack "dominance" power. Thus, they cannot force their husbands to make a serious attempt to stop heavy drinking. Nor do they have, these wives discover, sufficient "affective" power—that is, the love of their husbands—to appeal to them on those grounds either. The wielding of "moral" power—a matter in which wives are supposed to excel—turns out to be rather puny in the face of the husbands' desire for alcohol. The wife is not able to persuade her husband that his heavy drinking is wrong for their relationship and for the family as a whole. Threats to leave are not taken seriously.

Indirect approaches—reflecting a movement of the definition of problem drinking from willfulness to compulsion—suffer the same fate. False calmness in the face of drunken comportment fails to stop the drinking. Handling all details of household and living (to give the husband a stress-free environment) or assigning tasks and activities (to keep the husband too busy to drink) has minimal effect also. Equally useless are the manipulation of money and joining him in drinking, the latter having possibly dangerous consequences as well.

With failure to change her husband's drinking pattern as the outcome of every effort, the wife of an alcoholic eventually retreats entirely from attempting to handle the problem within the home.

Greenberg and Saxe (1975) have pointed out that requested help is more likely to produce a sense of obligation to and affection for the donor than volunteered aid; and requested help that is successful is even more appreciated. The wife of an alcoholic finds herself in the opposite position: offering unwanted aid that simply does not work. The stage is set for professionals to take over, if they can be located and if the husband will see one.

Notes

1. As Siegler et al. (1968) describe in detail, the acceptance of a given theoretical "model of alcoholism" logically results in the type of treatment selected.

2. The measurement and comparison of "equalitarianness" of marriages in the United States and Finland is a difficult task because of the subtle mix of this characteristic with male dominance. For instance, American women have fewer career opportunities in the upper-level professions, e.g., dentistry, member of a legislative body, than do Finnish women. Finnish women often keep their maiden names at marriage. However, men in semisocialist Finland, like those in its more socialist neighbor, the Soviet Union, expect a woman to work all day outside the home and then do all the housework without aid. American men, on the other hand, are more likely to pitch in and help their working wives.

3. Among professionals in the field of behavior change, both approaches can be found. To oversimplify: behavior therapists use a direct approach (rewards and punishments) with clients while not believing in totally voluntary change. Rather, they seek to "reprogram" the individual. Psychologists, psychiatrists, and therapist-counselors, depending on theoretical orientation, use both "logical" discussions and efforts to get at and neutralize unconscious motivations of their patients.

Among the lay public, the direct approach to reform, particularly where force issuing from a power relationship is used, is probably the more popular. It is interesting, however, that only the portion of lay attempts at change involving force (e.g., spanking by parents, intercession by police enforcing community norms, sentences to prison) have been studied to any great extent. Little attention has been paid to the details of the interaction between a layperson attempting direct logical persuasion or indirect manipulation as reform mechanisms and the object of his/her attention. Where such interaction has been studied, the would-be change agents are usually professionals in the fields of propaganda and/or mass persuasion techniques (Brown 1963; Zimbardo & Ebbesen 1969; Schudson 1984). Macrolevel societal concerns such as psychological warfare, racial prejudice, motivation to buy, and political propaganda are examined and analyzed.

The Booze Merchants (Jacobson, Atkins, and Hacker 1983) is concerned with the selling of alcoholic beverages by the industry through its advertising agencies. However, publications of Alcoholics Anonymous and the National Council on Alcoholism, which over the years have been directly aimed at turning problem drinkers into abstainers, are seldom tested for their persuasive power. When researchers have investigated attitude and behavior change at the microlevel, the focus is primarily on the effect of the group on the individual. Faules and Alexander (1978:126–37) do attempt some analysis of one-on-one influence. However, they focus on indirect means of persuasion to a great extent, and the discussion is very general.

Such all-time popular self-help publications as *How to Win Friends and Influence People* (Carnegie 1936) and child-rearing books such as *Between Parent and Child* (Ginott 1965), come closer to the everyday, ordinary life techniques by which concerned persons can try to obtain behavior modification in others. Thus, while these wives of alcoholics develop strategies that may ultimately fail, for their sheer variety and the creative thinking represented, they are worth studying.

4. Some social workers believe that complaining wives do drive their husbands to drink, and take as one therapeutic mandate teaching the wife not to be as "hostile" to her husband. (See, for instance, Cheek et al. 1971; McClelland 1972.)

5. Safilios-Rothschild (1969) indicates that women are more likely than men to use emotional means of persuasion because of their subordinate status.

6. Goffman (1952) has written about the problem of "cooling out" losers—starting with ways of getting a "mark" to accept without fuss the fact that he has been "conned" out of his money. Goffman enlarges his analysis to bosses who fire workers, priests and doctors who must tell persons they are dying, and so on. A major point in the essay is that people do not willingly give up a relationship they value.

7. Safilios-Rothschild (1978) calls this latter approach "covert" power and notes that this has been a major source of power for women down through the ages.

8.   The strain of pretending to be or to feel something that is not actually the case has been noted by other investigators. Scott and Lyman (1968), for instance, describe the paranoidlike fears that develop in homosexuals who are trying to pass as heterosexuals.

9.   For a good review of this controversy, see Jacob and Seilhamer (1982).

10.   The movie "Days of Wine and Roses" chronicles a marriage in which the husband is an alcoholic and the wife starts drinking along with him. Eventually, he manages to quit, but by this time, she has become a confirmed alcoholic and apparently cannot stop drinking.

11.   Steinglass (1982:213) has pointed out, however, that family therapists have shown a singular lack of interest in the treatment of family members affected by alcoholism.

12.   Steinglass further suggests that this state of "wet" equilibrium actually encourages the alcoholic to continue drinking.

CHAPTER 4

Seeking Treatment for Alcoholism:
The Polemic between the Potential
Patient, the Concerned Wife,
and the Therapist

Introduction

When the hope of containing and resolving her husband's drinking problem within the home—or at least within the family—fails, the wife of an alcoholic begins to move, slowly and uncertainly, toward acceptance of the idea that alcoholism does not yield to home efforts because it is something beyond her husband's control—an illness or a disease.

The disease concept of alcoholism has a stormy history. Its adherents include the National Council on Alcoholism, AA, and innumerable treatment specialists. More recently, Schuckit's work (1972, 1980, 1985) indicates that some persons may inherit a metabolic tendency toward problem drinking. Viewing alcoholism as an illness also has may detractors who see heavy drinking as the result of a conscious effort. Probably the two most influential have been Fingarette (1988) whose book, *Heavy Drinking: The Myth of Alcoholism as a Disease*, (which may have influenced a negative Supreme Court Decision on the issue [*Los Angeles Times*, (1988)], and Beauchamp (1980) a researcher and policy analyst in the area of public health whose book, *Beyond Alcoholism: Alcohol and Public Health Policy*, calls for a change in focus from treatment to the damage heavy drinkers can do in such areas as industrial and automobile accidents, fires and home accidents, as well as tragedies visited on significant others.[1]

Even a slight belief in the disease concept of alcoholism sets in motion a concerted search for outside aid [in addition to eliciting sympathy for the alcoholic (Golding 1982:128–43)]. Upon location of professional help, a new campaign is launched: to get the man to accept treatment. The wife hopes, of course, that when experts who "really understand" take over, they will succeed in curbing her husband's heavy drinking where she has failed. In this chapter, the various avenues explored by the wife as she looks for help in getting her husband to stop drinking and the unexpected outcomes of treatment (when she is able to get him into it) are discussed.

In trying to accept the disease concept and the need for trained therapists to handle it, the wife is now aided by the media, organizations dealing with alcoholism, and the pronouncements of many persons claiming to understand alcoholism, all of which she had formerly ignored.[2] Logically, giving the label "illness" or "disease" to problem drinking means that the chronic overimbiber can presumably be cast into the now well-known sick role first elucidated by Parsons (1951, 1958) and elaborated, criticized, and modified since.[3] [An alternative conceptualization, used at least 30 years ago by some treatment practitioners, who perhaps wished to avoid having to defend what appears to result from deliberate behavior as a "disease," referred to it as a "dis-ease." That is, the alcoholic was seen as a person ill at ease with him-/herself. More recently, Denzin (1987b:31–32) has used this formulation.]

From their testimony, and from the explanations given it by many professionals, wives' sense of what a disease is comes closer to Parsons's idea of sickness than the idea of dis-ease. However, there are problems with seeing the alcoholic as sick in the Parsonian sense, and the application of this concept to heavy drinking highlights the problems of viewing alcoholism as a disease and the limitations of the sick role concept.

For instance, the sick role starts with the expectation that the patient will acknowledge the presence of an illness and see it as undesirable. Furthermore, the progress of the disease is such that it cannot be coped with through sheer willpower alone. Thus, a person who is sick will show a willingness to seek and accept therapy and cooperate with it. Due to conditions caused by the illness (e.g., fever, pain, weakness), temporary release from ordinary responsibilities by concerned significant others is a right inherent to the sick role. Additionally, the patient him-/herself is seen by others as in no way at fault for becoming ill. Rather it is assumed he/she is the victim of a misfortune (which he/she will attempt to avoid in the future). When the person is cured, he/she is expected to vacate the sick role and return to the responsibilities and privileges of the usual role from which he/she had temporarily departed. It should be obvious from the data presented in earlier chapters that alcoholism, viewed as disease, fits Parsons's initial explication in some ways and not in others. A major departure obviously includes the "patient's" refusal to acknowledge the problem which results from purposeful action. Nevertheless, it is a useful beginning for understanding what the wife goes through when trying to find a treatment that will "cure" her husband of the disease of alcoholism because it mirrors her expectations and highlights her disappointments, as will be seen.

It is obvious that the special case of alcoholism presents a very unusual type of "illness." For instance, Parsons's description appears to begin (and end) with social events shortly after the patient has started treatment (or at least is about to do so). The behavior of concerned significant others is not discussed in any detail. Important areas of related behavior occurring before, during, and following treatment are not covered. These periods were apparently assumed by Parsons to be socially nonproblematic. Yet clearly, they can bring troublesome problems and decisions to the surface, especially in the case of problem drinking.

In addition, alcoholism is seen to be an apparent addiction that has both physical and psychological roots as well as consequences.[4] Further, these aspects can exacerbate each other. Treatment modalities reflect this intertwining of physical and mental problems, with the result that expectations of success may be confounded as well. At the outset, a more comprehensive depiction of a sick role model than Parsons envisages could be subdivided into one part involving the general interaction of an ill person and significant others when disease symptoms are "strictly physical," and the other when psychological elements seem more pertinent. Thus, while alcoholism has sufficient aspects of both physical and mental symptoms to encourage acceptance by wives of the disease concept, they are often unaware of the vacillation between the two.[5]

Realization of these definitional contingencies is crucial to understanding both the problems the wife encounters as she attempts to locate treatment and get his husband into it as well as its ultimate results.

In this chapter, discussion is focused on perceptions and expectations of concerned others as they interact with the alcoholic and therapists, and the way in which these approaches to alcoholism as a disease digresses from the classic sick role that serves as a model for wives' expectations of treatment.

Locating Professional Treatment and Getting the Patient into It

An American wife who decides to seek professional assistance for her husband's drinking problem will find that there is a bewildering jungle of individuals and organizations, some professional, some lay but highly experienced, some willing volunteers, and some highly visible corporate facades providing tax write-offs for their sponsors. Some are government-sponsored, some are commercial enterprises. Furthermore, unlike the fairly close cooperation between various branches of the medical and psychiatric profession, the cooperation between these therapists and institutions for alcoholics is very spotty. Some come into being on an idiosyncratic basis as the result of personal ties across agencies; others not only lack such ties, but are quite hostile to each other's approaches (Wiseman 1979:260–62).

Included among those individuals to whom Americans with a family member having a drinking problem may turn for help are pastors of churches, family counselors, family doctors, psychiatrists, social workers, and representatives of AA—an organization of laypersons that has developed and standardized a unique approach to aid problem drinkers (discussed in greater detail later in this chapter). Concerned loved ones may also start their search with institutions such as the psychiatric or alcoholism wings of general hospitals or their detoxification units, mental hospitals and outpatient clinics accepting alcoholics, as well as commercial sanitariums specializing in alcoholism problems. At this stage in her search, the wife is not yet aware of the many treatment modalities that various professionals, semiprofessionals, and laypersons in the field represent. Later in this chapter, the problem of attempting to understand and evaluate treatment approaches is discussed.

Finnish wives have approximately the same wide array of choices, but their search can be somewhat more focused at the outset because referral networks are better developed in Finland. Government-owned and -operated Social Hospitals exist to deal with intensive inpatient care of approximately two weeks to a month, and numerous A-Clinics are available for outpatient treatment (Osterberg 1977). Both are well publicized. Additionally, AA is well established in Finland. In both countries, the Salvation Army works with alcoholics, although primarily with those who are homeless indigents, and thus families are less likely to get referrals to its facilities.

Wives in both cultures, however, appear to feel that their first concern is not to assess the merit of the content or focus of any given treatment approach, but merely to locate a therapist or organization dealing with drinking problems. Although the concerned loved one of a physically ill person may concentrate on finding the best physician, therapy, or "specialist" for the problem, the wife of an alcoholic usually concentrates on learning where she might turn for any professional help at all. It is only later (usually after some experience with a treatment modality) that she begins to be aware of the existence of a variety of professionals concerned with alcoholics, representing quite disparate approaches.

Complicating the search for aid is the fact that the drinker does not usually accept his need for professional help. Thus, the wife must hunt for the type of aid the husband might accept, and then make the first contact on his behalf. She often continues to act as a go-between, attempting to speak for her spouse's needs to the professionals and then trying to persuade her husband to try her selection.

Emerson and Messinger (1977:127) observe, in their discussion of the social mechanics of trouble, that when persons seek professional help, they often go to "generalists" first. This is primarily because these persons or institutions are accessible. A second reason is because they appear to work with problems of all kinds and thus most people are more comfortable with them when seeking aid for a family member. This is indeed the case with American wives of alcoholics, who often start with a marriage counselor, the family doctor, or a minister before taking their problem to someone who works specifically with alcoholics. That wives seeking help for alcoholism first go to professional family relations "troubleshooters" also indicates the lingering doubt that the heavy drinking is really alcoholism, and further is actually a disease. They still may have some faint hope that their husbands will yield to logical discussion with an authority figure. It is also possible that these women see this expedient as less threatening to a husband who denies he is an alcoholic than more specifically focused treatment, while still offering a platform where she can air fears about his drinking and expect to get some moral support. Unfortunately, however, husbands seldom welcome the idea of any discussion of their drinking with outsiders. They usually deny vigorously they need any help with their marriage— regardless of the woman's urging and protestations of unhappiness. According to their wives, the men's refusal to go is immediate and adamant:

> First, I said, "Let's go to a marriage counselor," because I didn't realize that alcohol was the problem. I thought it was us, and I said, "Let's go to the marriage counselor." And he said, "Hogwash!" (American)

> I told him that he should go see a doctor . . . the doctor that he trusted. I would make the appointment; I would go with him. He said, "No." Then I told him, "Let's go see a minister," and he said, "No." "Let's talk this problem over with someone." He said, "No." He just wouldn't listen to it. (American)

Marriage counselors, whether ministers or professional advisors, are somewhat less frequently a first contact for wives in Finland. Perhaps this is partly because Finland has such a well-developed network of agencies specifically created to deal with alcoholism. Another possible explanation is that the church is less involved in social-welfare activities in Finland and thus is less likely to be a source of family assistance. However, when Finnish wives do try this approach, they suffer the same fate as American spouses:

> I have reserved time at the church's family counseling (I was very nervous myself then). He didn't want to go. He said he is going there only to get lectured. (Finn)

Unfortunately, for couples who do go into church counseling, middle-class ministers and clergymen may not be the best sources of alcoholism treatment referrals (Piedmont 1968). Thus, when ministerial counseling fails to make any appreciable progress with the husband's drinking problem, the wife must look anew for professional aid. It is at this point that many American wives attempt to locate institutions, groups, or individuals specializing in the treatment of problem drinkers. By far the largest group of these women turns to AA and private sanitariums. This may be because both of these sources have made their presence known in the community as dealing almost exclusively with alcoholics.[6] Once wives have contacted an AA group or a hospital, they try to get their husbands interested. Again, the response they most often receive is refusal:

> I have gone to several AA meetings myself—to speak at meetings—so I could try and understand some of the things about my husband. I wish he would go. In fact, I have mentioned it when I can talk about it calmly, but he refused. (American)

> I've tried to push him into [name of sanitarium], but he refuses to go. (American)

For Finnish wives, the major approach to get a drinking husband into professional treatment appears to be suggesting the government-operated A-Clinics, Social Hospitals, or AA. However, the reaction of Finnish men is similar to that of Americans.

The next step, for wives in both cultures, is to launch a campaign, either open or covert, or both, to persuade the husband to give treatment a try. Certainly such efforts by concerned spouses and other relatives are encouraged by professionals in the field (Sisson and Azrin 1986; Golding 1982:185–89; Twerski 1981; McWilliams 1978; Thorne 1983; Dougherty 1985; Logan 1983). However, when wives do try to get alcoholic husbands into treatment, the actions they take differ in both form and content from more conventional, directly persuasive approaches to get an ill person with either physical or mental problems to see a doctor: These women leave educational material about the dangers of continued alcoholic overindulgence lying around in conspicuous places; they ask persons from AA to drop by "casually" for a talk; they leave the telephone number of AA in a handy spot by the phone; they ask the family doctor to talk to the husband and offer to "make an appointment" for him. American wives describe a few of these ploys:

> I went to alcohol and drug abuse class. It gave me information about what happens to the body when you drink—the liver damage and the brain damage and so forth. And I would come home with this information and I would use it as dinner table topics. Ha! Ha! (American)

> I leave [pamphlets] lying around where he'll pick them up, and he'll pick a pamphlet up [and], he says, "What's this crap?" you know, and he'll throw it at me. (American)

> My daughter, she sent him a Christmas card and put the AA telephone number in it. After I found out it was my daughter, I said [to my husband], "Gee, that is somebody that really cares for you. Why don't you call and see who it is?" (American)

For their part, husbands find these less-than-subtle campaigns highly resistible. Most of the time, they continue to deny they are alcoholics. The husband's refusal is often both brief and final.

Some American women go from one treatment agency to another, hoping to find one that will appeal to their husband:

> I went to my minister, and I went to Al-Anon. I called up AA and they sent me forms, but I could not get him to it. My doctor suggested a psychologist; he would not go. He said there was nothing wrong with him. (American)

> I went to the Family Service Association. . . . Then I found Al-Anon and I went there for a year and a half . . . giving him literature and telling him about that. . . . Then I went to pastoral counseling for marriage counseling and dragged him to those things. (American)

Refusal of men to consider treatment for their drinking problem is tantamount, especially for Americans, to closing the door on professional aid. Few individual therapists, AA members, or institutions in the United States will attempt to persuade or coerce a drinker into treatment if he/she is adamant about not needing help. The next possibility would be court commitment proceedings, and these are difficult to handle successfully and are of doubtful value as to therapeutic outcome (Ward 1979). Thus, the American wife is virtually powerless in such cases, and she knows it, or is soon apprised of this fact by the professionals she contacts. The prevailing professional ethos is that treatment for alcoholism in any form should not be forced on those who do not want it:

> I suggested it once or twice but, you know, just like they say, you can't push them; they have got to want to come, so I haven't [pushed AA]. (American)

> Well, you see, I knew that I could not get him any psychiatry help, because that is something the patient has to want themself. (American)

> I tried to commit him, but I can't commit him; they told me it [violates] his constitutional right . . . unless he is violent, or hits me, or threatens the kids. (American)

One woman tried tricking her husband into seeing a doctor, but the ultimate outcome was counterproductive:

> We belong to Kaiser [a closed-panel medical plan]; so I found out that they
> had a doctor for alcoholics; so I called him and talked to him without my
> husband knowing; and I made an appointment for him and he went to this
> doctor. And when he got home he was very, very angry. When he went
> outside, I called the doctor and asked him what he had said to make him
> come home so mad, and the doctor said, "I guess he's mad because I told
> him that he's an alcoholic." Later my husband told me that doctor was
> more crazy than he was. (American)

The anger of the husband is a very real fear for many of these American women. They hesitate to press the issue of treatment by means of
commitment for fear the husband will become angry, drink vindictively,
or turn on them violently:

> I thought of having him arrested, but probably out of fear did not do it.
> (American)
> I'd be afraid when he got out, he might hurt me, hurt the kids. (American)

One fairly new strategy is the "crisis intervention" approach in which
concerned family members (and possibly friends, an employer, or a
family doctor) confront the drinker and inform him/her that a bag has
been packed and a taxi is coming to take him/her to a treatment facility
now (Wholey 1984; Pinkham 1989). The purpose is to allow no time for
excuses, postponements, and so on. No wife in either sample had tried
this bold maneuver.

Sometimes American wives get help from employee assistance programs operated by the organization or company where their husbands
work. Many of these programs are designed to involve and/or aid the
spouse or significant others of the alcoholic as well (see, for instance,
Anderson 1984; Bensinger and Pilkington 1983; Busch 1981; Caldwell
1983; Carone and Krinsky 1982; Johnson 1983). However, wives in the
sample were reluctant to initiate employer intervention for fear of the
effects on their husband's job.[7]

Finnish ethos concerning coercion into treatment is quite different.
The government provides several avenues by which a concerned person
can get a problem drinker into treatment, whether or not he admits he is
an alcoholic. First, the government operates a Social Bureau to which the
wife can report a heavily drinking husband. Husbands are then called in
(or visited in the home if they do not respond) by officials in this bureau
and told to get some treatment at an A-Clinic for their drinking problem.
The Social Bureau has the power to send a husband to a social hospital if
he does not cooperate.[8] On the work front, employers are not allowed to
fire drinking workers summarily. Rather, they must give the worker
earned vacation time immediately, which must be spent in the social

hospital. Alcoholics in Finland have three chances to attain permanent sobriety through this work-furlough program before they are in danger of being fired. Thus, outpatient A-Clinics and inpatient Social Hospitals do accept coerced patients.

As a result of the way these avenues of alcoholism treatment are given social legitimacy by the government, Finnish women are not as hesitant as their American counterparts to force a husband to get help for excessive drinking:

> I though he had to quit before he was ruined. I contacted the Social Bureau and went there. When you go to the Social Bureau they automatically send a card to the husband to come and discuss it. After that [if he fails to respond,] he is ordered in. (Finn)

However, despite government support in forcing treatment on problem drinkers, many Finnish wives are fearful of taking the initiative to get their husband into treatment:

> It is hard to phone secretly to different social offices for him—he gets angry if he hears about it. (Finn)
>
> I am not able to suggest he go to the social hospital—only the social officer could do that. If I said it, he might get violent. (Finn)

Fear of Treatment

Even admission of a possible drinking problem usually does not necessarily mean the husband will immediately go get help. On the contrary, for Americans especially, this is when the various fears about alcoholism treatment surface as well as differences between alcoholism and the commonsense conceptions of illness. While there is some similarity between the alcoholic's fear and fears of treatment harbored by persons with physical ailments or mental illness, there is a unique quality stemming, no doubt in part, from the mystifying nature of alcoholism treatment itself. In resisting entreaties to get some help for their drinking problem, these men offer the following reasons:

The Known Ineffectiveness of Treatment

> [He mentioned] the fact that most of his friends drink and he just doesn't know anybody who has gone through and gotten help successfully. (American)
>
> He had heard from friends that it is no use. When you come out of the social hospital, you just start drinking again. (Finn)

The Fear of Being Labeled

I say, "Get into a hospital. Maybe they can do something for you if you really want to quit." But he says, "No, I'd be disgraced, especially for my job." (American)

I suggested he should go to an alcoholics' institution or hospital, but he didn't want to. He feels it's a shame. (Finn)

The Probable Cost of Treatment

He pointed out that we don't have much money and these hospitals cost a lot and it probably isn't covered with insurance. (American)

This concern is not inconsequential. In a two-part story, a portion of which described the "big bucks in [substance] abuse clinics," Ward (1985) in the *Los Angeles Herald Examiner* quoted charges anywhere from $10,000 for a stay of ten days to a month to $300,000 for several attempts at a "cure" in private hospitals and/or alcoholism wings of general hospitals. These high costs are one reason for the growing popularity of the "social model" of alcoholism treatment, discussed at greater length later in this chapter. Zimmerman (1986) in the *San Diego Union* notes the average cost of this approach to be approximately $600. See also Anonymous (1982, 1984a, 1985) concerning costs and hope for better health insurance coverage for alcoholism treatment.

For Finnish men, as mentioned, time off from work for alcoholism treatment is so institutionalized that there is much less shame. Joining AA is seen as more embarrassing, primarily because it is thought by them to attract a lower-class clientele, or appeal to persons who are not very bright:

He accuses it [AA] of being a religious movement, and he always asks, if I say something, it's that "AA talk." He thinks that the AA has programmed everybody—that they can't think for themselves. (Finn)

Finns, of course, do not have to worry about the cost of treatment, inasmuch as A-Clinics and social hospitals are tax-supported. However, these men often stubbornly insist that treatment is too drastic a step to take for their current drinking behavior and/or their physical condition.

Physical Illness and Treatment Acceptance

When this impasse on seeking professional aid is reached, some wives turn once again to threats of separation or divorce—a strategy undoubtedly used primarily in mental rather than physical illnesses. Some men respond as hoped:

> The only reason I think that he went into treatment was because I was going to leave him. (American)
>
> I got him to go to an A-Clinic when I was arranging a divorce, and he said he would do anything to continue with me. (Finn)

However, the most potent factor in getting a husband into treatment for his drinking problem is the serious physical debilitation that he begins to suffer as a result of his excessive alcoholic intake, inasmuch as the adverse effects of alcoholism are serious and varied:[9]

> He was really sick [when he finally accepted treatment]. He was bleeding and spitting up blood. (American)
>
> He went to a doctor because he thought there was something wrong with his liver or his kidneys. (American)
>
> He was losing weight. He lost about 25 pounds in a month. The doctor explained to him that he gave him some tests and he did have the starting of cirrhosis of the liver. This scared him. This made him decide to stop. (American)
>
> He had broken one tooth and was in very bad shape. . . . He begged the director of the A-Clinic to be able to come [in].
>
> He wanted some kind of short relief from this hangover. They gave him B-vitamins and so on. (Finn)
>
> Finally, his legs suddenly became paralyzed. He collapsed and was unconscious and couldn't stand later when he woke up. That was when he decided to come to the social hospital. (Finn)
>
> He didn't quit [and go into treatment] because of money, or that I'd leave him, but he became so exhausted that he didn't care if he was alive or dead. (Finn)

It is interesting that decisions to go into treatment because of deteriorating health, or loss (or threatened loss) of a job or threatened divorce (or both), have undergone a transformation under the disease label as a result of a certain mystification in the treatment profession called "hitting bottom." Hitting bottom has long been accepted as a significant turning point that occurs when the alcoholic suddenly seems to comprehend the great harm drinking has done to his life, his relationships, and his health, and goes willingly into treatment. However, until he arrives at that stage, according to the theory, he is assumed not to be really ready for therapy.[10] This is certainly an unusual variation of the disease concept, inasmuch as unlike the assumption in most physical ailments—that early treatment is beneficial to the patient—an alcoholic is not assumed to be "ready" for treatment by many therapists until the "disease" has progressed to the point of gravity, that is, he has hit bottom.

Wives indicate an awareness and acceptance of the concept of hitting bottom and its implications:

> He went into treatment by himself because he had hit his bottom in Oregon, and he had come back and decided he was scared. He had been drinking and so on. He didn't tell me the details. (American)
>
> I was told [at Al-Anon] I shouldn't try to speak to him about this—that he had to go to the "bottom" first—so I've left him alone since. (Finn)

When the husband finally does go into treatment for the first time, the wife experiences a flood of relief and hope, just as does a person when a loved, but sick relative is taken to professional treatment. The wife is also pleased to get some respite from the continual struggle she feels committed to wage with her husband for his own good:

> I think, "Gee, someone else is working on him," so I don't have to and so it gives me a little rest. (American)

The Alcoholic Treatment Jungle

These women are not aware, of course, of the continuing turmoil within the field of alcoholism, and the resultant development of what still remain experimental approaches to treatment they locate on their initial search. The etiology of alcoholism continues to elude researchers. Over the years various hypotheses encompassing possible physical, psychological, and social causation have been explored, but without definitive results; nonetheless these frameworks often serve as the heuristic inspiration for the development of a treatment. The result is a bewildering array of therapy techniques, none with what could be termed an impressive record of success (with the possible exception of AA).[11] This high rate of recidivism will be discussed later in this chapter.

Few laypersons are aware of the multitude of treatment approaches when they initially look for treatment. The short discussion that follows can only give a brief sampling.

Keller, an expert in the field and editor emeritus of the *Journal of Studies on Alcohol*, speaking at a gathering of alcoholism researchers (Nelson 1977), noted that the list of treatment approaches being used at that time filled three typewritten pages and "included everything from imprisonment to Alcoholics Anonymous, from psychoanalysis to bio-feedback." Forrest (1978),in his encyclopedic discussion of alcoholism treatment, lists the following broad categories of treatment approaches:

- Individual psychological therapy
- Group therapy
- Behavior modification
- Aversive drugs
- Electric shock therapy
- Applied social learning theory
- Alcoholics Anonymous
- Marital and family therapy

Little has changed since then with the exception of the so-called social model, which continues to gain great popularity in California and other states. This approach reduces the cost of treatment substantially by offering no special medically supervised detoxification, no residential treatment, and no high-priced professional therapists. Rather, it is an outpatient residential program that emphasizes peer counseling and support, as well as numerous alcohol-free situations (both social and recreational) that are intended to show the drinker that it is possible to lead an alcohol-free life and still cope with problems that come up, as well as enjoy oneself from time to time. (Borkman 1984).

All alcoholism treatment modalities may be further subdivided into (1) those treatments with the goal of aiding the drinker to solve his/her personal problems, thus dealing with the presumed basic cause of the drinking; and (2) those that concentrate on treating the symptoms only—in this case, constant excessive drinking. (3) In a class by themselves are AA and the social model, both of which use peer reinforcement to aid sobriety. (4) Another cluster of treatments, aimed at alleviating the debilitating effects of continuous heavy drinking on the body, starts with detoxification and is sometimes extended to amelioration, where possible, of organic damage caused by chronic drinking. Schuckit (1984), for instance, refers to this latter as "acute treatment," as contrasted with rehabilitation that attempts to help the alcoholic reorganize his/her life.

A very brief review of the approaches and purposes of these many therapies is necessary to aid an understanding of reactions of both alcoholics and their wives to them. Unfortunately, these treatment approaches cannot be seen as "choices" in the usual sense of the term, inasmuch as most alcoholics and their spouses are usually unaware of the array of techniques available to them. Additionally, they have no way of knowing which one might be best in their case. Ewing (1980), for instance, discusses the need for a "cafeteria plan" for matching therapy and patients as does Fingarette (1988:114–18), who quotes a study by Sells (1981) indicating that success in a treatment modality is highly dependent on this aspect. Pattison (1982:331–405) also covers the problems connected with this issue, as do Sher and McCrady (1983), who discuss patient and treatment variables.

Individual and group psychological therapies are foremost among treatments that are focused on the "whole person."[12] Briefly, many psychologists, especially of psychoanalytic persuasion, believe that excessive drinking is actually a symptom of some deep-seated personal and/or familial problem; until this can be faced and handled in some way, it is assumed that the drinking or some other maladaptive behavior will continue. Family therapy has the same goal, but sessions include the spouse and possibly other family members considered significant to the drinking (and the hidden problem). Thus, the therapist will try to help the patient locate and confront the problem areas of his/her life. Group therapy has the same purpose, but utilizes group interaction to uncover (presumably) personal problems to be faced. It obviously handles more persons per therapist (often a social worker), thus making it suitable to relatively low-budget treatment programs and/or patients on modest incomes (see, for example, Hart 1970; Moore 1971; Davis 1972).

Behavior modification focuses on stopping the drinking without regard for possible reasons that it occurs. Approaches may include treatments in which the cooperating patient is wired to receive a rather painful electric shock every time he/she reaches for a proffered glass of liquor. Antabuse, a medication that causes violent nausea and vomiting when a person drinks alcohol within 24 hours after taking it, has also been used in an aversive-conditioning manner. All aversive conditioning approaches are intended to cause the drinker mentally to connect the use of alcohol with unpleasant or painful effects, and not with pleasant euphoria and tension reduction. Although the hangover following heavy imbibing indeed does this same thing, it is thought by behavior therapists to be too greatly separated in time from the act of drinking to have the aversive impact necessary. Thus, behavior therapists try to shorten the cause-effect time span with various artificially induced punishing mechanisms such as those just described. [See, for example, Forrest (1978), Davidson (1974), and Miller (1972) for discussions of various approaches to aversion techniques with the goal of behavior modification.]

Over the years, many other therapies have been tried. These include adaptation of the Synanon "game" approach (created originally for drug addicts and featuring a group situation in which a verbal attack on each participant by the rest presumably causes repressed problems to surface; Balgooyen 1974); transcendental meditation (Benson 1974), psychodrama (Blume 1974); family systems therapy based on the theory that the alcoholism of one family member is actually a symptom of disorder in the entire family—discussed at great length later in this chapter; the creation of a therapeutic community (Braun 1972; Fairchild and Wanberg 1974); and hypnosis (Granone 1971) are but a few of the many approaches. Biofeedback has also undergone development as a possible treatment (Green et al. 1974).

AA is a unique approach to treatment (anonymous 1955; Maxwell 1984). Founded by two ex-alcoholics, it depends on a combination of quasi-religious inspiration (Smith 1990; Denzin 1987a,b), group support and identity, plus reinforcement of newly gained sobriety by helping others. A major therapeutic tool is the AA meeting, in which each person offers his/her story of compulsive drinking and its sordid and unhappy consequences. AA ideology includes a special version of the disease concept of alcoholism. The drinker must admit he/she is powerless to stop imbibing (a parallel to the standard sick role); however, he/she must then turn the matter over to a "higher power"—God as the drinker conceives of him (which is not a conventional sick role practice). Furthermore, it is assumed that the "illness" continues to progress through the years even if the alcoholic has ceased drinking. This means that should he/she start again, the disease will be in an advanced state, as though there had never been a period of abstinence. Continued group support in the struggle to maintain sobriety plus responsibilities to aid others to do so are major factors in this approach.

In addition to the many approaches to help people halt their excessive drinking, treatments to handle both the short-term and the long-term physiological effects of heavy alcohol ingestion have also been developed.

Among the most pressing of short-term problems, the physical discomforts of withdrawal can be triggered when a person addicted to alcohol is cut off from the supply. The "DTs" (delirium tremens), in which the drinker may suffer from frightening hallucinations, as well as symptoms that resemble epilepsy, can also be alleviated by medical procedures (Schuckit 1984:67–72).[13] Alcohol poisoning can result from ingesting large amounts within a short period of time and can be fatal. Detoxification centers that deal with these emergencies are available in many large cities. Emergency wards of most city hospitals also take some of the most critical cases (see, for example, Feldman et al. 1974). More recently, however, detoxification has been "demedicalized." The newest approach, part of the social model just discussed, is to view "detox" as something that alcoholics can handle with the aid of coffee, donuts, and understanding companionship. (Schuckit 1984).

Hospitals and sanitariums are also called upon to deal with physical maladies associated with alcoholism. Thus, in addition to one or more of the above therapeutic approaches, vitamin therapy, balanced diet, and tranquilizers are often prescribed. Many sanitariums boast of their beautiful grounds and the opportunities for fresh air and exercise, although the connection between these regimes and alcoholism has never been proved. Many mental hospitals use IT (industrial therapy)—required work on the wards (such as mopping floors), in the kitchens, and on the hospital grounds—as part of the treatment for alcoholism. IT's efficacy in treatment has never been proved either. It does, however, operate to reduce plant overhead (Wiseman 1979:153–54).

Frequently, institutions and therapists offer several different forms of treatment simultaneously, without explaining what each is intended to accomplish or its general success rate (Wiseman 1979:152; Pattison 1982). Thus, the same institution may feature Antabuse, group therapy sessions, AA meetings, plus a regime of vitamins, tranquilizers, good food, rest, and exercise. Equally significant, some of these approaches (especially various versions of group therapy) undergo mystification by their proponents, who give them names like "double whammy," "honesty hour," "family rap meetings," and "insight sessions," intended to make them sound like potent and/or especially created weapons with which to fight alcoholism. Many are based on the theory that the "true self" of the alcoholic must be revealed for progress toward recovery. For instance, according to Denzin (an obvious true believer in AA philosophy and approach):

> If the alcoholic does not penetrate this emotional facade he has placed in front of himself, he will not recover and uncover the deep, underlying reasons that lead him to drink. *The recovery of the self through emotionality is the underlying premise of treatment.* (1987b:37; emphasis in the original)

It should be made clear that the above brief summaries barely do justice to the range and complexity of any one of the treatment programs, and were presented primarily to reveal the array of therapeutic approaches (some with rather cloudy rationale) that confront the wife of an alcoholic and the drinker when seeking help. For more complete discussions of treatment and treatment facilities, see Pattison and Kaufman (1982:821–1076) and Forrest (1978).

Quite often the wife knows so little about these many approaches to alcoholism therapy that she has no idea which one (or ones) her husband is undergoing after she urges him into treatment. Certainly, she is unaware of their generally low rate of success (with the possible exception of AA), a matter to be discussed shortly.

Most concerned wives and their alcoholic husbands are probably unaware, initially at least, that the chances are quite low that any one therapy, or even a combination of them, will stop a drinker's overimbibing. Wiseman (1979:299) noted that the average success rate for any approach is about one-third or less.[14] Edwards (1980a) has suggested that treatment for alcoholism lies somewhere between "guesswork and uncertainty." Valliant (1980) has called treatment an expensive fraud. Recidivism is, in many ways, more the rule than the exception (Slater and Linn, 1982–83).

Treatment Disappointments

Thus, the high hopes wives have that the "disease of alcoholism" will be halted, or "cured," and their spouses returned to them rehabilitated are most often dashed. Entrance into treatment sets the stage for disappointment, more often than not. Husbands sometimes refuse to go back after their first therapy session, or quit treatment after only a few weeks. Even more discouraging to their wives are the men who take a full course of treatment, only to start drinking almost immediately upon its completion.

Quite naturally, wives question their spouse about what "went wrong," and many find that the husband has surprisingly little to say about the failure of the treatment to stop his heavy drinking. Repeatedly, American wives report that their husband offers brief and cryptic explanations:

> He doesn't like it. He says that he doesn't see any sense to it. (American)
>
> He said, "I didn't get a thing out of it." (American)
>
> He never went back [to AA] again. He never told me why. He said, "The only reason I am going is because the judge made me go [to AA]. I see no real value in it. They're not really helping me to stand up there and tell everybody all the bad things I've done while being drunk. I just don't feel anybody's going to learn anything from it." (American)

With the exception of attitudes toward AA, Finnish husbands did not volunteer any reasons at all for terminating treatment. Wives did note, however, the relative lack of success of the outpatient clinics and hospitals.

Those wives who are able to get more detail from their husbands report there is a disjunction between these husbands' expectations of treatment for an illness and what actually occurs during treatment or is accomplished by it. The complaints also indicate the very different nature of treatment for alcoholism as compared to treatment for most physical illnesses.

When drinkers quit their psychiatrists, the reasons they give might, at first glance, be termed nonmedical. At second inspection, however, they reflect what the psychiatric approach to alcoholism may seem like to the inexperienced layperson:

> They [the psychiatrists] said something like he was attached to his mother or something. They just tore him down, but they never built him up. (American)

> He [her husband] told me that the doctor was more crazy than he was. (American)

> The doctor had some problems himself. . . . I think he was just a puppet on a string on the job: that he just pushed pills, and listened to patients talk, and tried with the best of his knowledge to be a psychiatrist—to help, but he just really didn't know how. (American)

Prescription of Antabuse by medical doctors and psychiatrists is also interpreted by their alcoholic patients as ineffective in trying to cure alcoholism. The actual purpose of taking Antabuse pills is to provide the drinker with a strong motivation not to drink, although it has also been used (with strict medical supervision) as a tool in behavior modification, as previously noted. Persons who drink after taking Antabuse experience severe nausea, violent heartbeat, sweating, and trembling. However, when this does occur, the alcoholics do not blame themselves, they blame the medication, according to their wives:

> He tried Antabuse and claimed it made him sick. So he stopped that. (American)

> He also tried Antabuse, but drank with it, and had to go to the hospital. (Finn)

While Denzin (1987b:61–63) has noted that AA offers a "community" to the alcoholic who feels he has lost all social ties, not all persons see it in that light. Husbands who give up on AA complain to their wives about the composition of groups they attended—the type of people they met at AA meetings:

> He has tried AA and after a while they turn out to be a bunch of jerks. (American)

> They [the participants in the group] had been in and out of skid row for years. They were quite old men and my husband is young for his age. (American)

Finnish husbands voiced the same types of complaints:

> So last summer we took part in [an AA] group one month, and after that my husband didn't want to go again because he didn't think the group was the best possible because the people in the group were so different. (Finn)

Related American comments suggested concern about the stigma of being labeled through association with the persons in these groups:

> He said, "Those people are nuts. I'm not that crazy. God, how can you say I'm like that? Don't compare me with those guys. Those guys are no good." (American)

Another closely related complaint by alcoholics in both countries was in inability to relate to or open up to such a group:

> The men there were 60 and 70 years old and had been on booze for 40 to 50 years. He [her husband] just didn't relate to them too much; he didn't want to get up there and tell his big story. (American)
>
> He went to the AA, but according to my opinion he didn't have any "opening up" . . . he hasn't been able to create close relationships. (Finn)

The exact mechanics of the therapy or treatment offered also came in for their share of criticism by wives in both countries:

> I think he thinks that they're [AA members] sitting there listening to other people talking about their escapades. They don't tell you how to stop drinking and things like that. I think that [the idea of AA] is just, if you've made up your mind to stop drinking, you go and socialize with other ex-alcoholics. (American)
>
> I have tried to get him to AA, but he has said they [the other drinkers] are only proud and telling how much they are drinking. . . . I said we could go to another club where there were not these kind of people and he said they were all the same. He said it is nothing to be proud of when you are drinking. (Finn)

When the criticisms alcoholic men have of AA are compared with the usual complaints about doctors and treatment, they seem strangely incongruent. Patients seldom mention the quality or character of a doctor's other patients as a major reason for ceasing medical treatment (although doctors do acquire patients by referrals of trusted friends). The necessity to relate to the doctor's other patients or share one's private life with them is nonexistent, since it has nothing to do with the normal medical treatment of a physical ailment. [Note, however, that Denzin (1987a:184–85) comments on the positive spiritual benefits from AA for persons who relate well to group approaches, benefits that help them maintain sobriety.] Koch's (1973) discussion of the problems of opening oneself to criticism from strangers and other pseudo-intimate features of encounter groups makes clear why their composition is so important to people who join such a gathering for help.

Wives also confuse levels of treatment. Medication for the physical effects of continual heavy drinking—either emergency detoxification centers or longer-term therapy in hospitals—may be mistakenly assumed to be a therapy aimed at stopping the drinking. Additionally, after several disappointments with detoxification and therapy combinations, wives begin to suspect that their husbands use treatment cynically to get in shape for the next drinking bout.

> The doctor talked to him . . . and gave him vitamins . . . and he did quit drinking at that time, for about thirty days. But as soon as he felt great again he went right back at it [drinking] again and he still is. (American)
>
> He hated the institutions. He went to four or five. They dried him out so he could start drinking again. (Finn)

One Finnish wife complained that the clinics actually encourage drinking by helping the alcoholic through the pangs of withdrawal:

> I just want to say when they [alcoholics] are treated in the clinics, they just get back their strength and come back to drink again. I think we should press them hard. The general attitude is too soft. They should be pressed down so that they get ill. (Finn)

This use of the institution to get in shape so as to drink again is not unknown to therapists (Wiseman 1979:135, 312). It may account for an anomaly of alcoholism treatment that has little parallel in the treatment of physical illnesses, whereby patients are dismissed from institutions if they exhibit signs of increased illness—that is, drinking while undergoing treatment. The assumption is that the patient is not sincerely motivated towards helping in his own recovery. Such action is, of course, a disappointment to wives:

> They threw him out the last time because he sneaked off the grounds and drank vodka. (American)
>
> He came home . . . he said a nurse had seen him drinking beer, so he was kicked out. (Finn)

When a patient with physical illness takes a turn for the worse as exemplified by Parsons's sick role, it is more usual that increased efforts and attention are then focused on the patient even though the change was caused by proscribed behavior.

The Triadic Constellation in Alcoholism Therapy

The relationships between members of the alcoholism treatment triad—the alcoholic, the concerned other, and the therapist—undergo quite different changes from those found in either the physical or the mental sick role constellation. The unique shifts that occur are only understandable in terms of the dynamics of the treatment attempts. The failure to understand (and thus the dissatisfaction with available approaches to treatment), the husband's apparent inability to maintain sobriety, and the wife's increasingly severe emotional problems (which may result from her disappointment in and even despair over her husband's continued drinking despite professional efforts) take their toll.

Emerson and Messenger (1977:126–30) point out that when a person concerned about another requests aid through intervention, he/she is usually operating with a theory of how the type of trouble should be handled. These assumptions might not be congenial to the person receiving the request, who may be operating within another framework that offers an alternative way of deciding who or what is to blame and what ameliorative steps to take. In the case of alcoholism, the dynamics of the drinker–concerned-other–therapist triad reflect some factors that seem quite unique to the treatment of alcoholism. The patient and the spouse (and other family members) are often tied together by treatment specialists into some sort of therapeutic package (see Edwards 1982; A. Berger 1981).

The fact that she and her husband are quite frequently treated as a *therapy pair* (Bateman 1971; Anonymous 1984b) can come as a disconcerting surprise to the wife. Two theories of alcoholism causation often used by treatment professionals coalesce (or coexist, depending on the point of view) to bring this about. One sees the wife unconsciously encouraging her husband's heavy drinking because of her own pathological problems of either desiring to suffer or hoping to dominate him (deSaugy 1962; Futterman 1953; Kalashian 1959; Paige et al. 1971; Price 1945; Rae and Drewery 1972; Whalen 1962). The other is more current and is most often referred to as family systems theory. Its major proponents are Steinglass (1982a,b), Steinglass, Weiner, and Mendelson (1971) and Kaufman (1985). A good description of this theory and its proponents is also available in Paolino and McCrady (1977:110–40), Bowen (1974), and Koppisch (1974). Basically, systems theory ignores the idea of the alcoholic as having a disease and looks instead to the "sickness" of the family that may be causing and/or maintaining the drinking (Golding 1982:199–207; Forrest 1978:168–210). Many of the actions taken by wives of alcoholics (described in Chapter 3) as approaches to home treatment (e.g., taking over all responsibilities, acting natural in the presence of his drunkenness, or threatening to leave and failing to make good on the threat) are subsumed within systems theory and used as evidence that the family actually promotes the drinking.

As a result of adherence to either of these theories, wives often find that they are expected to accept or share the blame for contributing to the husband's drinking, instead of receiving praise for their concern about the drinking problem and their attempts at bringing about a cure. Sometimes they are told they need counseling themselves. [There are, of course, numerous variations on treatment of the so-called alcoholic family (see, for instance, Root 1986).] Such a reaction on the part of the therapist almost always dismays them, at least initially:

> He [the husband] comes home and tells me that he went to the chaplain, or something, or somebody there, and they told him I am sick and that I should go see a doctor. (American)

> When I turned to the Social Bureau for his drinking, they contacted him. Then I was asked to come back also, and the man in the Social Bureau said that I was not the kind of person to turn to them. I didn't ask what he meant . . . but I thought maybe my husband told things he believed about my sexual relationships before I met him. But since I am married, I have been faithful to my husband. But he talked. Perhaps, he told the official about this. My husband then said, "There, you got what you deserved." (Finn)

Second, some wives fail to find the idea of going into therapy for their husband's drinking an appealing prospect:

> I said, "Why should I go to your doctor for your drinking problem?" It didn't make sense to me. (American)

> He asked me to go with him to the A-Clinic, as I told you, but . . . I told him it was his problem. (Finn)

Obviously, these partnership approaches to treatment run counter to the idea of the sick role. (Certainly, in Parsons's simplistic conception, responsible others do not need treatment, nor do they need to join the ill person in treatment.) Furthermore, since the rate of recidivism is high, all three members of the alcoholism treatment triad are most often bound together by failure—not success. The ramifications of this negative outcome are several, primarily connected with maneuvering to place the blame.

A major portion of the blame is almost always laid at the feet of the patient if treatment fails to help him. As noted earlier, professionals claim he was not "motivated" enough to participate wholeheartedly in his own treatment. They suggest that possibly he had not hit bottom and thus was not ready for therapy, as discussed earlier in this chapter.

Second, therapists themselves are also targets of blame. As has been discussed, the drinkers tend to see these professionals as offering nothing of real use to overcome their craving for alcohol. Larsen and Rootman (1967) point out that, in the case of physical illness, an important factor in patient satisfaction is whether the doctor's perceived role performance meets expectations. The same is true in the field of alcoholism treatment, especially if some form of psychotherapy is used, where the rate of success is low (Smart 1970:43). When husbands are not cured of their compulsive drinking, wives also express their disappointment by describing the psychiatrist as a person who "doesn't act like a real doctor," indicating again their medical-model perspective on alcoholism treatment. It is also possible this attitude rises out of professionals' antipathy toward alcoholics, which may be sensed by these clients and their spouses (see Sowa and Cutter 1974; Hornstra et al. 1972):

> I have no respect for the psychiatric profession, because I think it's the greatest way to take your money without giving you help of any profession that we have. Did you know, they claim they don't even keep records? If I go to my [regular] doctor, he's got a record from the first day I walk in—"she suffered from bronchitis, nerves from Jim's drinking, or whatever." With Jim (her husband), they said, "What records? We don't keep records!" . . . I said, "Just keep me informed on what you think about my husband and what his chances are." (American)

The Reorganized Treatment Dyad

Eventually, treatment failure can result in a total realignment of patient-therapist ties. A wife who continues to live with a man who is alternately sober when in treatment and drunk shortly after release experiences substantial anxiety. This takes a toll, sooner or later, on her mental health (Howard & Howard 1985; Conway 1981; Cohen-Holmes 1981; Byrne & Holes 1979; Archer 1979). Although at first upset at any suggestion that she needs help, the wife, after many disappointments, turns to the therapist with her own coping problems. Eventually she becomes a more responsible and attentive patient than her husband ever was, and thus far more satisfying to the therapist. In Finland, for instance, the patient rosters of the A-Clinics are filled with spouses (mostly female) who go for help in coping with an alcoholic husband. American wives also turn to professional help when treatment fails:

> I had gotten to where things were going on inside of me emotionally and I could not handle it. I didn't know the reason for it. . . . Going to the doctor did help some, by helping me. (American)
>
> It was a great help to me when I went to the A-Clinic and I could speak to the social worker. And I met the doctor, too. (Finn)

Other women join Al-Anon, where they have an opportunity to meet sympathetic friends and share problems. (This will be discussed in detail in Chapter 7.)

The Career of Alcoholism Viewed as a Disease

When alcoholism is viewed as a disease, with the concomitant implication of the alcoholic as a candidate for the sick role, the conceptual decision creates a far more complicated treatment career than encompassed by the regular medical model focused on physical distress. Treated as an illness, prolonged heavy drinking has trial-and-error, disappointment and revision of expectations components that have, in many cases been glossed over by mystique devised by therapists.

From the wife's point of view, experiences with professional treatment indicate that the disease model fails to offer guidance leading to successful cure. Thus, the concept begins to lose explanatory power in their minds and a majority of wives no longer appear to expect that professional treatment will bring about long-term sobriety.

In both the United States and Finland, these women do not totally give up hope that their husband will someday stop drinking; rather, they speak vaguely of faith in miracles, prayer, or the development of sudden insight on the part of the husband:

> I just feel it [his stopping drinking] will be an act of God. This is what I just pray for so much. (American)
>
> I don't even like to discuss it [whether or not he will ever stop drinking]. That is something you have to have faith in God about. (Finn)
>
> I think he is the type of person who will one day realize that he is destroying himself and a lot with him that is too worthwhile keeping. I would hope that this is what he will think, anyway. (Finn)

A sizable minority of wives lapse into hopelessness after experiencing many treatment failures. They also appear to return to a voluntary theory of alcoholism:

> No, I have no hope [that he will stop drinking]. He just needs it to keep going, and has no intention of quitting. (American)
>
> [He won't quit] because he is not trying, and I don't think anything in this world would make him stop. He has to do it himself. (Finn)

Thus, by the end of several treatment experiences, the wives' attitudes toward their husbands' problem drinking have gone full circle: from first seeing the behavior as voluntary and trying to handle it within the family, to accepting alcoholism as a disease and seeking professional treatment, to once again deciding that the husband drinks because he wants to do so. This is the position that husbands have maintained throughout all of these periods. It is also reinforced by the treatment specialists themselves, who, while calling heavy drinking a disease, will not accept patients who are "not motivated" to quit, thus blaming therapeutic failures on the patient's lack of determination rather than on their treatment paradigm or their administration of it.

Summary and Conclusions

When a wife fails in efforts to persuade her husband to cut down on this drinking, she accepts the idea that alcoholism is a disease that calls for professional treatment. However, her idea of what kind of a disease it is, and how treatment should help it, closely resembles Parsons's simplistic view of the sick role. Experience soon proves otherwise. Alcoholism is a far more complex phenomenon with its combinations of free will and compulsion as well as physiological and psychological aspects.

Getting an alcoholic into treatment and the ultimate results are unique experiences that have some resemblance to physical and mental illness, but many aspects are specific to problem drinking. All phases of the career of al alcoholic sick role—diagnosis by a concerned spouse, home treatment, locating types of treatment available, convincing the patient to accept professional treatment, and the treatment itself—differ in such important ways from general concepts of illness that they cannot be used for guidance by the wife during this trying time.

The wives find it difficult to locate treatment. The men are highly resistant to going to a professional in the alcoholism field, despite a concerted campaign of persuasion, because they do not see their drinking as either uncontrollable or a disease. Husbands usually agree to treatment for alcoholism only when their excessive drinking has made great inroads on their physical health.

Both spouses often fail to understand the goal of a particular therapy. This reflects, to some extent, the chaos present in the field itself. Little is really known about the causes of alcoholism or its cure, and thus there is little standardization; there is, however, a great deal of treatment experimentation. Both wives and husbands have medical-model expectations of the treatment outcome. They assume, initially, that a therapeutic approach will help the man cut down and/or stop drinking entirely. They are most often doomed to disappointment, for there is a high rate of recidivism in all treatments.

The patient–concerned-other–therapist relationship is different from that developing in physical illnesses, and to a lesser extent in the mental illnesses as well, in that failure and mutual blame of one kind or another seem to be endemic where alcoholism is concerned. Repeated failures also change the feelings of both spouses toward treatment. The husband becomes a cynical treatment user, going to a professional only for help in drying out or with serious health problems brought on by alcohol consumption. The wife begins to lose faith in the illness concept of alcoholism and returns to a model in which the husband alone is responsible for his drinking. She often copes with the disappointment of her husband's repeated lack of positive responsiveness to treatment by going into treatment for her own stress. Thus, is many ways, she becomes the true patient—her husband merely an adjunct.

Looking at alcoholism as a disease and tracing its career when treated as such, reveals the flaws both in this view of alcoholism as well as in Parsons's concept of the sick role.

Notes

1.   For further pro and con as to whether alcoholism is a disease see (Gitlow 1982; Makela 1980; Chalfant and Kurtz 1971; Mulford and Miller 1964; Roman and Trice 1968; Edwards 1970, 1980b; and Robinson 1972, 1941). In a study of lay opinion, Ries (1977) found that people do not grant alcoholics full sick role privileges, still seeing them as primarily responsible for their own behavior.

2.   For example, "Hospital Treats Illness" and "Treating Alcoholism as a Disease" were both headlines in a Los Angeles Times story. More recently, alcoholism has been combined with drug use under the rubric of "chemical dependency." See, for instance, Ward "Addiction Industry," Los Angeles Herald Examiner, November 17,1985, cover story, pp. A-1 and A-10. The discussion also refers to alcoholism as a disease.

A history of the medicalization of behavior formerly looked at as bad habits can be seen in Conrad and Schneider's Deviance and Medicalization (1980), in which they speak of disease moving an activity from "badness to sickness."

3.   See, for instance, Freidson (1962), Mechanic (1965) and Britt (1975) for general discussions. Twaddle (1969) and Segall (1976) offer elaborations of the sick role to cover its many variations. "Real-life" enactments of the sick role and its counterroles not only vary by type of physical disease, but also by cultural strictures. The vagaries of mental illness (where etiology is, as yet, unknown and the patient often denies the problem) offer even greater application difficulties.

4.   Those who do not think that alcoholism is properly defined as a physical illness do not necessarily accept it as a mental one either, nor if they believe alcoholism to be a mental illness do they necessarily feel that all problem drinkers are mentally ill (Moore 1972; Sargent 1968; Schuckit 1984).

5.   Bateson (1972:309–39) called attention to some similarities between alcoholism and schizophrenia in his analysis of the AA approach. Denzin (1987a:34) points out that alcoholics have "public symptoms" that are physical, interactional, and mental. (See also Cassell 1976, and Eisenberg 1977.)

6.   AA is listed in all telephone directories, and makes its literature easy to obtain. Commercial hospitals created for the purpose of serving alcoholic (and often drug abuse) clients advertise on television, in newspapers, and with the aid of expensive brochures.

7.   With the new employee assistance programs in large American corporations, company counselors may strongly urge the employee to join AA. Some-

times, however, they also coerce employees (by threatening dismissal) to go to an institution to be dried out and treated for their drinking problem. Smart (1974) compared samples of employees who went in voluntarily and those who were coerced and found that the voluntary patients made the most improvement on an overall rating scale used to assess changes in drinking 12 to 14 months after treatment. However, he also noted that the coerced patients may have benefited from early intervention.

8.   Most of the time, the Social Bureau does not take the rather drastic step of sending the husband to a social hospital upon the initial contact. More often, the alcoholic and his wife receive counseling, and are referred to an outpatient A-Clinic.

9.   Pattison (1982:147–366) and Novick, Hudson, and German (1974) have chronicled some of the long-term health problems that alcoholics often have by the time they enter treatment—or when they go for periodic detoxification. Alcohol can adversely affect the liver, the stomach, the throat, the kidneys, and the brain and central nervous system. Heavy drinking can result in weight gain and later massive loss. These physical problems are part of the rehabilitation complex faced by institutions that treat alcoholics.

10.   Obviously, the concept of hitting bottom also allows the therapist a convenient excuse for treatment failures. They can claim that the patient has not yet hit bottom, and thus cannot respond to treatment. So deeply entrenched in alcoholism treatment ideology is the concept of hitting bottom that some professionals suggest that external pressures be brought to bear on heavy drinkers to help them hit bottom sooner in their drinking careers. In the earlier literature on this subject, Selzer (1958), for instance, suggests manipulating the alcoholic's social world by getting his wife to threaten to leave him, his partner to threaten to quit the business, and so on. Jellinek (1962) also mentions this approach, arguing that expediting the alcoholic to a stage of utter defeat allows earlier application of help. A less manipulative approach is to stop protecting the alcoholic from the consequences of his drinking—an approach urged by Al-Anon and advocates of "tough love" (Twerski 1981; McWilliams 1978). McNamara decried the practice of calling alcoholism an illness. He feared such a label would prevent the drinker from hitting bottom and getting treatment:

> The problem that arises here [as a result of treating the alcoholic as an ill person] is that the alcoholic may be insulated from feeling the consequences of his deviance. He may never "hit bottom," or reach such a low point that he will come to perceive the necessity for controlling his drinking. It is interesting to note that a philosophy and literature on "crisis intervention" has emerged within the last decade among social workers and counselors. [See Brown (1975) for a review of recent theory and research.] In the case of alcoholism, this would mean that such therapists first wait for the crisis to develop, then intervene on a systematic basis to help the client handle it. (1960:463)

Denzin (1987a:123) has suggested that there are really two bottoms: one when the drinker decides to get some help, and a second when he/she decides never to drink again.

11.   Roizen (1977) points out the problems of measuring the outcomes in terms of treatment goals in this field. Much earlier, Braun (1963) discussed treatment outcome differences in Finland.

12.   Jewson (1976) describes the philosophic and lay-professional distinctions between treating a sick man and treating the symptoms of a disease, a difference

that he feels results in fractionating the person and reducing his control over his own treatment.

13.   Tranquilizing drugs are also administered to alcoholics in withdrawal, suffering delusions, tremor, agitation, and sleeplessness. Here, the focus would be on symptoms, rather than the whole person (see Robinson 1972:92).

14.   Because of the very loose or nonexistent formal or informal connections between agencies, institutions, and other types of treatment approaches to alcoholism, actual recidivism is difficult to gauge, inasmuch as alcoholics often move from one institution to another for treatment. Rosenblatt and Mayer (1974) discuss the same problems in connection with the rate of recidivism of mental patients. Sullivan et al. (1981) and Slater and Linn (1982–83) discuss variables that might predict treatment outcome. AA claims a higher rate of abstinence than other approaches, but it is difficult to know how much of this is due to self-selection by the highly motivated. Additionally, AA does not keep records on the people who drop out of its program.

CHAPTER 5

The Malevolent Pendulum: Drunken and Sober Behavior of an Alcoholic as Perceived by His Wife

Introduction

Long-term, excessive intake of alcoholic beverages clearly affects behavior so profoundly that the drinker often seems to others to have literally changed in personality and character. Alcohol consumption can cause people who are normally alert and verbally adept to develop speech that is often illogical, socially inept, disjointed and slurred, and in the later stages even incoherent. The descriptions are legion of individuals who in daily life are described as kind and thoughtful, yet under the influence of alcoholic overindulgence become paranoid, nasty, quarrelsome, and even violent. Characteristically industrious, dependable, hard-working persons may become indolent, careless, sleepy when drunk. Other persons may react to the effects of alcohol ingestion by changing from a normal mode of shyness to periods of charm, wit, and warmth, but they are in the minority.

The preponderance of negative changes may be, in fact, one of the major reasons for the general moral prohibition against overimbibing. In many areas of interaction important to sustaining good relationships with others, the alcoholic behaves in socially unacceptable ways. Importantly, the drinker seldom seems aware of these changes, for alcohol appears to dull self-insight. Rather, concern comes from those persons who must deal with the problem drinker, or—even more serious—must live with him.

Past research on the effects of heavy drinking has emphasized physiological and psychological reactions, featuring "objective" testing of alcoholics or persons under the influence of alcohol. Thus, there is a plethora of data about the effects of alcohol on sensory perception, vision, motor skills, perceptual skills, and thought processes or cognitive abilities. Little or no research has been attempted that might provide some detail on how significant others perceive and cope with the behavioral changes in persons brought about by alternative bouts of heavy drinking and periods of sobering up.

Likewise, there has been little about how an alcoholic who has very recently sobered up acts toward family members. Rather, sobriety in alcoholics or persons who have been drinking is assumed to be a return to "normalcy" (once withdrawal or hangover has passed). Little or no interest is shown in the range of behavior activated by sobriety or abstinence after long bouts of heavy drinking, and, more importantly, what linkages exist between drunken and sober behavior of alcoholics. The purpose of this chapter is to expose that heretofore ignored connection, inasmuch as it offers insights into the mystery of recidivism.

This chapter is concerned with the behaviors by male alcoholics when drunk, and when periodically sober. An important and revealing connection between the two states as they are linked both in time and experience by the drinker and concerned significant others will then be discussed. The marital world of the wife of an alcoholic is delineated by his behavior both drunk and sober. Some of the wife's immediate reactions to her husband's mood changes as they are apparently triggered by either heavy drinking or efforts to remain sober will be discussed. (Chapter 6 will describe the longer-term effects of his drinking on the marriage, while Chapter 7 will be concerned with effects over time on a woman of living with a problem drinker.)

Behavior When Drunk

In *Drunken Comportment* (MacAndrew and Edgerton 1969), a cross-cultural study of behavior of intoxicated persons, the authors show that excessive consumption of liquor does not, as often believed, "dissolve the superego" and disinhibit persons to the point where they will do practically anything. Rather, the behavior of intoxicated persons, while nonnormative and often in sharp contrast with their sober demeanor, is nonetheless almost always in keeping with what a drunken person is permitted or expected to do in the society in which he or she lives. Thus, the range of drunken behavior, rather than being infinite, was found to have definite cultural restrictions.

The drunken behavior of American and Finnish male alcoholics, as perceived by their wives, is similarly restricted to narrow and ultimately predictable paths, considering the vast possibilities. In both cultures, aggression, both verbal and physical, against wives dominates home behavior of the alcoholic while intoxicated. Self-destructive behavior was entirely absent.[1] Furthermore, with the exception of a general surliness of attitude that seems to characterize about half the men when drunk, each man appears to develop only one type of aggressive behavior. For instance, almost half of the sample of American and Finnish wives face anger, quarreling, and sarcasm when their husbands are drunk, but the husbands do not strike their spouses. Another 33 to 40% of the wives in both cultures report that their husbands beat them, slap them, or rough them up in some way.

In terms of other, more infrequent behavior, American husbands appear to be more likely to break up furniture or destroy other property in the home or to accuse their wives of unfaithfulness than are Finnish husbands. Finnish men are more likely to become maudlin and cry when drunk than are American men. A small minority of male alcoholics show increased happiness, charm, and relaxation when initially drunk, but even in these cases, this reaction often diminishes in strength as drinking progresses and is ultimately replaced by belligerence. A few men are, without apparent reason, charming on some occasions when they are drunk, yet angry on others. For still another group of Americans, the physiological effects of liquor gradually reduce either charm or anger through loss of motor and speech control, blackouts, and sleepiness or loss of consciousness. Thus, any activity that takes coordination, memory, or energy is eventually difficult to sustain if sufficient quantities of liquor are ingested.[2]

Although data presented by other researchers suggest that wife abuse of one kind or another is much more likely to occur when the husband is an alcoholic and frequently intoxicated, most researchers find that alcohol is neither a necessary nor sufficient cause of wife beating (Kantor and Straus 1986; Bard and Zacker 1974; Gelles 1974:561–62; Dobash and Dobash 1979; Eberle 1980; Okun 1986; Rosenbaum and O'Leary 1981). For instance, Coleman and Straus (1979) found that, while the frequency of drunkenness is associated with the frequency of physical violence, when the drinking is very heavy, violence declines. To elaborate, their findings indicate that among husbands who are never drunk, the yearly incidents of violence toward the wife is 2.1 per husband; for husbands very often drunk, the rate is 30.8. But the violence rate drops by almost half (to 17.6) for men who are "almost always drunk." Other researchers have indicated that such intrafamily violence is a culturally accepted activity (especially among the working class) even in the absence of heavy drinking (see, for instance, Kantor and Straus 1986; Steinmetz 1977; Strauss 1973, 1976, 1977; Steinmetz and Strauss 1974; Gelles 1974; Strauss and Steinmetz 1973). Gelles (1974:116–17) and Strauss (1977–78), however, suggest that ingestion of alcohol allows a husband to abuse his wife with a clearer conscience and also facilitates the escalation of family fights and thus is an important correlate of wife abuse. Additionally, some researchers have suggested that wives prefer to attribute their battering to their husband's drinking, rather than to an essential cruelty in his character (Kantor and Straus 1986; Dobash and Dobash 1979; Gelles 1974).

In the discussion that follows, the details of how these men, when under the influence of alcohol, behave toward their wives will be presented. A theory to account for the fact that an alcoholic man appears to develop a single style of behavior when drunk and then repeat it over and over will be discussed. Following that, the complex connection between drunken and sober comportment will be shown.

Abusiveness without Physical Violence

General Anger, Quarrelsomeness. For American wives, their husband's verbal aggression takes two major forms: (1) a general belligerence that includes an argumentative demeanor; everything the wife or others say is challenged, answered with anger or argued about, its validity denied, or the veracity of the speaker questioned; and (2) criticism of the way the wife does things (or does not do them), or a general attempt to disparage the wife and others with sarcasm, belittling her efforts, ideas, behavior. These two styles of verbal aggression are seldom found in the same man. Either the man is generally quarrelsome and argumentative, or he is highly critical and tries to show the general inferiority of others around him, especially his wife.

The argumentative husband is described by his wife as follows:

> He is belligerent to anyone that talks to him. If someone comes to the door, his is belligerent; if I talk to him he gets belligerent. He just says, "Damn it, just leave me alone." If someone is at the door he says, "What the hell do you want?" (American)

Criticisms usually center on how badly the wife is performing various aspects of her role. Often, the children are dragged in as audience:

> He would say to the kids, "Your mother didn't do this; your mother won't do this." (American)

> If I'm cooking, he says I'm doing it wrong. If I'm setting up the hose, the hose is set up wrong. If I pull the drapes, the drapes shouldn't be pulled. (American)

> When he came home drunk he usually shouted at me and blamed me for things not done around the house or for things [that happened] way in the past. (Finn)

Accusations of Infidelity. For American wives primarily, a more focused type of verbal belligerence from their husband occurs in the form of suspicion of sexual infidelity. As will be discussed in Chapter 6, a drinking man finds sexual performance difficult. Additionally, his wife may be repulsed by his drunken condition and refuse intercourse. It is not surprising, then, that some of these men develop fears of infidelity. This insecurity manifests itself in almost paranoid suspicion of the most mundane activities (Pfeffer 1958:2b):

> He's like a raging maniac around here. "Where's your mother? Where'd she go to? Who's she going to see?" Just like as if I've got a lover somewhere you know. I can't go to the grocery store and be gone five minutes because [he suspects] I'm out to meet somebody. (American)

> The times I was working, he followed me. He works in another city. He would follow me to the place where I work, take time off of work, to make sure I was not catching a ride with another man, and I was pregnant with my daughter. (American)

> When we were out, he accused me of flirting with someone else, I might just look across the room and he would say, "Who are you looking at?" (American)

A small minority of Finnish wives also complain about sexual accusations and a barrage of "sexual talk" when their husband is drunk.

A few men of both nationalities emulate a version of Merton's self-fulfilling prophesy (1968) and attempt to prove their wife unfaithful by actually trying to force her to be. They bring men home for this purpose:

> He brought home men and wanted me to put on some sort of thin negligee and go out and get a rise out of them. (American)

> He says I am the worst whore he knows. He even brings me men. (Finn)

Abusiveness with Physical Violence

Violence Directed at Wives.   The largest proportion of American wives of alcoholics who experience physical violence from their intoxicated spouses report that their husbands start out acting pleasant, even charming while drunk and gradually become hostile to the point of violence. (Later, aggressiveness might turn to sleepiness.) Women described the slowly developing career of changing moods like this:

> He would go through stages of being funny. He had everyone laughing. . . . Then all of a sudden he would become very quiet. He would not want to talk. Then the third stage, anything anyone said or I said, he took in an offensive way. If he didn't like the shirt someone had on at the other end of the bar, he would go down and tear it off of him. (American)

Other wives have husbands whose physical aggressiveness seems explosive and idiosyncratic. One moment the man will be pleasant; suddenly, he becomes angry and attacks her:

In one incident, I was cooking in the kitchen and he said somebody was on television, and I made a remark back about this particular person being on television . . . and all of a sudden he came up; he thought I was making fun of him. He got a gun, he came into the kitchen, and he said he was going to kill me. I don't know how, but I managed to get away from him. He had me by my slacks, and was dragging me around the house. (American)

Bob got drunk one night, and I was sitting on the couch and his friend was there. I was reading a newspaper and all of a sudden Bob came up and started hitting me, and said, "We did too have a good time in Las Vegas. You won't convince me that we didn't have a good time in Las Vegas." (American)

Wives also mention that their husband will inexplicably switch from words and gestures of love to violence:

Just the other day, he comes in the kitchen and he is loving me and kissing me and hugging me and he goes in and sits down and then grabs me and says, "How come you didn't answer me?" Then he hits me. I didn't hear him say or ask anything. Maybe he did; I didn't hear him. (American)

Sometimes he would say to me when he was drinking, "I love you." He would get very sentimental about how much he loved me and then he would cry. Then he would start calling me long and terrible things, and then he would start to hit me. (American)

Descriptions by Finnish wives of the violence they face from alcoholic husbands is similar:

He gets violent. He has hit me. Today, for instance, I have to go to an ear specialist because he hit me on the side of the head. (Finn)

He has hit me so badly I am nearly crippled. He hit me so hard I was unconscious for a half hour twice. (Finn)

Mistreatment of Children. Even when drunk, most alcoholic men refrain from beating their children. Gil (1973) found that when compiling social workers' checklists of 18 possible circumstances associated with child abuse, only 13% of the cases noted "alcoholic intoxication of the perpetrator." Aarens et al. (1977) surveyed both the domestic and foreign research, and found that on the average less than one-third of American abusive parents had histories of drinking. Foreign studies, however, reported higher associations. The fact that alcoholic men are selective in their beating of family members lends credence to the theory that imbibing of alcohol does not cause aggressive behavior; it only allows it and "excuses" men so they can do something they want to do, but would ordinarily feel constrained not to do. (Only one respondent, for instance, reported that her husband got violent with her mother.)

In this study, those children who are physically attacked by their fathers are not hit or beaten, as the wives are, but brutalized in other ways:

> For instance, one night Janet came in to get something to eat, and the next thing I hear her screaming. He choked her. I took him off her. He came in and attacked her again in her bedroom. . . . So that evening I had to sleep with her because it was really upsetting to her. That's two or three times he'd done that. (American)
>
> We went dune buggy riding . . . he would be drunk before we left, and he would stop the truck as we were going down, because my daughter said something smart, and he threw her out of the truck. (American)

Fathers are more likely, however, to use shouting, sarcasm, and put-downs with their children.

> He talked to my son for three hours while he was really drunk. My son kept saying, "Yes, sir, yes, sir." And he kept yelling at him and said, "Don't 'yes, sir' me." The boy was being respectful and getting yelled at for it. (American)
>
> [He will watch his daughter practicing dancing] and if he's drunk he'll say, "What the hell! You trying to be a ballerina?" (American)

Wives also become upset when children see their father beating the mother or threatening to do so. They worry about the disturbing effect this sort of violence has on a youngster.

> He was shaking me, strangling me. I had the car keys, I didn't want him to drive . . . and my five-year-old got in front of me and started getting hysterical. . . . This time my daughter was five and the other one was, I guess, about eleven. It upset the children. (American)

Destruction of Property. For a small minority of American wives, the fear is not for life or limb, but for furniture, appliances, doors, windows, or anything else that can be broken by human force. Put another way, there exists a group of violence-prone, alcoholic husbands who do not beat their wives, but rather limit their destructive tendencies to material objects (again indicating the limits on drunken comportment). Few husbands both beat their wives and break up furniture. The variety of things these men break while in alcoholic rages, however, is truly amazing:

> We had a beautiful oil painting of a ship and he busted it up. He's broken lots of dishes. One time he ran his fist through the wall. (American)
>
> He threatened to smash the dishwasher. He hates the sound of it. He hit the inside of the washing machine with a hatchet. I have to watch the appliances. (American)

He breaks everything he can get a hold of at home. He has never hurt me
or laid a hand on me or the kids. One time he took all the food and threw it
all over the kitchen walls. (American)

Few Finnish wives mention destruction of property. One, an actress,
described how her husband slashed her entire wardrobe to ribbons.
Others mention that their husbands throw furniture as part of the rage
and violence toward them.

Bizarre Behavior and Scenes.   For some American wives, the violence
they live with goes far beyond what might be termed "routine" flare-ups
and beatings by their husbands. They describe, instead, frightening
scenes of terrible anger, brutality, and loss of control.

A good deal of the activity in such scenes appears to be focused on
dramatic threats and use of weapons. The husband acts like a man well
beyond mere anger—one who could be characterized as a madman.

One wife described several scenes of this sort:

He threatened me with a gun, and a time or two he had his hands around
my neck and acted like he was going to choke me, and he didn't. . . . One
night, in a terrible rage, he picked up my favorite cut-glass ashtray, which
was very big, off of the coffee table, and he aimed it at me, and in the last
second he changed his aim and hit the coffee table with it; the glass flew
out and I got a piece in my eye. When I started to complain about it, he
said it was my way to complain. (American)

He thought he had seen me with another man . . . he came home at seven
in the morning and pulled me out of bed and slapped me three times. He
hit me up against a cement block wall and I got to mild concussion out of
it. . . . One night, because I didn't come and get him when he was drunk,
he started slapping me. I went out of the house, I grabbed his coat . . . I
was stark naked. I had to get away. Before, I had got myself into the
bathroom. I thought I had the door locked, but he came right in. I thought
I was down to my time and I said to myself, "Janet, you better get out of
here." And I did. (American)

He wanted to eat . . . and here it was three in the afternoon. I said, "John,
we are going to eat at 5:30 [when] the kids come in from school." He said,
"I want it now, and I know how to get dinner on that table." He jumped
up and pulled out his pocket knife and put it against my neck . . . and I
said, "John, put your knife away . . . yeah, I'll fix it." So he closed the
knife and put it in his pocket. (American)

On that Sunday afternoon . . . he went and got his gun to kill me. He held
me for about 30 minutes, right in that corner, a German luger at my head,
and my little boy was screaming, and screaming, and the whole neigh-
borhood called the police. (American)

He started screaming and yelling and came upstairs to get me and he
grabbed me and was going to throw me over the bannister. (I was preg-
nant at the time.) He pushed me and I held onto the railing and I fell two

or three steps away, but wasn't hurt, and he got me in the front of the door . . . and then he grabbed me around the neck and began choking me. (American)

For Finnish wives, bizarre behavior appears to reflect the brain damage that occurs after many years of heavy drinking rather than the wild anger described by American wives. This again may indicate the later stage at which Finnish wives become aware of their husband's problems with alcohol:

Sometimes when he comes home drunk late at night and talks a lot of mad things, I start to cry. (Finn)

Once when I was visiting a neighbor he was shouting and he pushed a dustpan through the neighbor's mail box and said I was using it to poison him. (Finn)

Pleasant Behavior

Loving and Charming Behavior. For a minority of women, both American and Finnish, the personality of a drunken husband is actually an improvement over his sober mien. As their mates drink, these American wives report the men become loving, talkative, charming, and exhibit other character improvements:

When he's drunk, he's very sweet and very nice. He shows a personality when he is drunk which he doesn't have when he is sober. When he is sober he is very stiff, very tense. (American)

[When he is drunk] he is all loving. He is happy and he talks. Usually when he is sober, he does not talk, he is very quiet. So we all enjoy it when he is drinking. (American)

Among those few Finnish women whose husband's behavior seems to improve with alcohol intake, descriptions of a loving, agreeable, kind, and considerate man who plays with his children, talks to his wife, and generally emulates the behavior of an exemplary husband are offered. The word "emulate" is important here, however, because the wife knows it is drunken behavior she is witnessing rather than normal activity. Additionally, many wives mention that this behavior occurs only in what they term the "early stages" of drunkenness.

Other Behavior

Becoming Maudlin. The loving but drunken husband can turn maudlin as alcohol ingestion increases. American women do not mention this development, but one-fifth of Finnish wives do:

When he's a little bit drunk, he plays with the children and they are happy.
When he is very drunk he keeps looking at me and asking me not to leave
him. (Finn)

When he gets drunk it isn't long before he is holding on to me and crying
and saying he is afraid he is going to lose me. (Finn)

Lack of Coordination; Slowness to React. American women also mention
that their husband loses physical motor control of their bodies when
drunk. They also notice changes in his face, eyes, and speech when he
has been drinking heavily, as well as his poor balance—as he stumbles
over furniture, knocks things down, and exhibits general unsteadiness:

His face takes on like another person. His features and everything get
ugly. Like putting on a mask. Like day and night. (American)

He gets a "retarded" look on his face; he's red-eyed and droopy.
(American)

Sleepiness. A frequent reaction to heavy drinking for some husbands
is simply to fall asleep. American wives report their husband passes out
regularly—some after incidents of aggressiveness, but more often in
front of television, in a chair immediately following dinner, or in some
cases right at the table during dinner. Their husband's head may actually fall to the table. In such cases, different wives react differently,
depending on how long such behavior has been going on; sometimes
the wife will attempt to move the husband to bed at the end of the
evening; sometimes she will leave him wherever he is sleeping for the
rest of the night. Sometimes she will bring out a blanket and cover him
before she goes to bed.

Blackouts. A few American wives speak of beginning to notice more
frightening symptoms than drowsiness and long periods of sleep. Their
husband starts having blackouts, that is, periods when he does not
remember anything of what he did while drunk. Other men show loss
of memory in selected areas (Finnish wives do not specifically mention
blackouts, but they do notice a decline in memory):

He's told me he doesn't even remember driving the freeways. (American)

He would wake up someplace and not know how he got there. (American)

A frightening aspect of the blackout for the wife is not knowing
whether the husband was actually "out" at the time of the forgotten
behavior, or whether he is "in contact" during the behavior, but has
subsequently blocked the memory of it. Actually, the latter is considered
correct, but many wives are unaware of this.

The Interpersonal Nexus of Styles of Violence While Intoxicated

Frank (1976) in an elaboration of Goffman's (1959) *Presentation of Self,* suggests that violent public scenes result in the development of participants' sense of self. Thus, persons involved in such scenes have not in fact lost control, but are actually managing situations so as to express themselves. In symbolic-interactionist terms, all behavior must occur within the context of a situation (Blumer 1969:85). These alcoholic men appear to be creating situations in which an angry or hurt self can express being upset in strong but still culturally approved ways that are in keeping with the image each man has of himself.

Thus, men who are verbally but not physically aggressive when intoxicated may be creating situations in which they can complain about or disparage other family members, but never physically harm them—this latter restraint aiding them in retaining a positive self-image. On the other hand, some violent men allow themselves to break up furniture when drunk, but not hurt wives, children, or other family members. Most men who when drunk beat their wives do not touch their children or other relatives.

Sudden, unexplained flare-ups of violence and the bizarre behavior of scenes can also be explained within Frank's paradigm. Although these acts seem to be truly senseless behavior in that they are outside an understandable situation, it is possible they are being used by alcoholic men who lack the social ability to create ordinary situations in which they could more logically be abusive. In other words, it may be that these men are taking advantage of the stereotype of senseless brutal behavior brought on by intoxication to vent feelings that they have difficulty organizing for understandable expression.

However, there is another self and another definition of the situation to consider in these episodes of drunken, abusive behavior in the family, inasmuch as all social action is jointly arrived at (Blumer 1969:70–71). Violent behavior in interpersonal relationships poses a threat to the identity of both participants (Hepburn 1973). Certainly the sense of self the wife develops as a result of such maltreatment by her alcoholic husband could well be a degraded one.[3] This appears to be the case for some wives. The constant criticism they receive from their husband takes its toll of their self-esteem, especially if they obtain no feedback to the contrary. Furthermore, the courts and police reinforce the helpless position of the wife by de facto spousal immunity (Straus 1977) despite recent changes in the law.[4] These women say such things as:

> I allowed him to run me down so that I thought I was a lousy wife, a lousy mother, and a lousy housekeeper, and a lousy cook, and I chased men. (American)

The fear of triggering their husband's wrath places these women in a constant state of nervousness and makes them wary of all their interactions with him—certainly a difficult stance over long periods:

> He can act just delightful when he's drunk . . . but as I found out, he can be unpredictable too. He can just turn like *that*. He can become very preoccupied with one thing and be rather cruel and abusive. (American)
>
> His moods shift fast. The littlest thing can set him off. (American)
>
> He is a Jekyll and Hyde when he drinks. (Finn)

Eventually, these women may even see themselves to blame for their husband's brutal behavior, feeling they had somehow precipitated it. This feeling is often reinforced by counselors and therapists:[5]

> He kind of knocked me around a little bit . . . but who knows, I might have egged him on. I was giving him a bad time. (American)
>
> It [being beaten by her husband] doesn't happen very often; mostly when I trigger it off in him. When I am the one that sets it off. (American)
>
> I pushed him too far and he lost his temper. He was supposed to be home in ten minutes and he came home three hours later, drunk. I was really mad, and so I wouldn't talk to him and so he says . . . like he was trying to make me laugh and say little things to me, "I see a smile coming," and little things like that just drive me crazy and I kept pushing him away. I can't stand his breath and so finally he broke my nose. He hit me. See I had to really be careful of what I did. I had to think about every little move before I made it. (American)

Thus, the apparent style limitation and consistency in the violent behavior of the alcoholic husband when drunk may find, in circular manner, a reinforcing attitude on the part of the wife, who through her experiences with her husband during these episodes has developed, for survival purposes, a changed self-image with a behavior style to match his own. Possible factors explaining why these wives continue to live with men who brutalize them are discussed in Chapter 8.

Behavior When Sober

Sober behavior of alcoholics has long been ignored by researchers as an area of investigation. It has been assumed that during those intervals when a heavy drinker is sober, his/her behavior returns to "normal."[6] Actually, this is the experience of the majority of persons who get drunk sporadically, perhaps in the course of a celebration or upon the receipt of bad news. They become intoxicated, perhaps lose control of motor reactions, stop drinking, no doubt suffer self-recrimination and a hangover as well, and then revert to their normal behavior.

This simple model does not fit alcoholics who sober up periodically from drunken episodes. For them, sobriety has many variations. In the first place, they may sober up and/or remain sober voluntarily at home without much outside help, or they may sober up in an institution (either self-committed, or forced) with professional assistance. Obviously, the dynamics of each care are different.[7]

Physiologically, sobriety can result from either a reduction of intake to a point that could be called social drinking or drinking in moderation, or total abstinence from alcohol. The time span for an alcoholic to remain sober may vary anywhere from a couple of hours to several days, weeks, months, or even years.[8] Psychologically, the length of time the alcoholic intends to remain sober appears to be a crucial factor in his behavior during this period, and how it is experienced—by both him and his wife. This is further confounded by the fact that intent and actual behavior of an alcoholic do not necessarily match. Nor do husbands and wives always have the same perspective on the purpose of sobriety during any specific sober time. Further, since recidivism rates are high [somewhere between two out of three or four out of five (Franks 1963; Wiseman 1979:109)], the chances are that, even with the best of intentions, the alcoholic will be drinking heavily again in the near future.[9] The quality of social interaction with others while sober and the ease with which the alcoholic can succumb to temptation are also important variables.

This discussion, consistent with that of other chapters, will be limited to the sober behavior of the alcoholic husband as witnessed by the wife and the social interaction that is a part of it.

When wives of alcoholics describe their husbands' sober behavior and their reactions to it as well, some important characteristics emerge:

1. Just like drunken behavior, the activities of a sober alcoholic are both surprisingly narrow in range and highly self-conscious (rather than broad in range and un-self-consciously normal).
2. There is more than one form of sobriety.
3. Sober behavior is affected by (or reflects awareness of) the drinker's own unpleasant drunken behavior that preceded it, and the wife's reaction to her husband's periods of sobriety.

Three forms of self-induced sobriety (i.e., without the aid of an institution) emerge from the descriptions offered by wives' experience with their husbands:

1. Brief sobriety, resulting from temporary abstinence or a drastic cut in intake. The intent appears to be maintenance of level of acceptable drink and/or behavior for special occasions or people for short periods of time.

2. The withdrawal period that accompanies complete abstinence for a longer period. The intent may be either a temporary or permanent halt in drinking.
3. Long-term abstinence, following withdrawal. Again, the intent may be either temporary or permanent cessation of drinking. (Original sobriety may have been gained either at home or in an institution. However, the expanded time span is usually handled at home.)

Brief Sobriety

Both American and Finnish wives of alcoholics report their husbands have times when they are able to refrain voluntarily from drinking.[10] Some wives said the alcoholic men will not drink in their presence or when in the company of these persons whose goodwill they value. Wives say:

> When we go to Tacoma to see our kids . . . all the time we were there, he did very little drinking. (American)
>
> When we would go back and visit our relatives in the South, he would not drink around my mother at all. (American)
>
> He would try to drink less if he knew older relatives were coming—my parents or grandparents—but not for people our own age. (Finn)
>
> He drank less around his mother. (Finn)

Wives also observe that many of these men were able to withstand the temptation to drink during working hours or related occasions:

> [He doesn't drink] when he has a lot of work . . . [and when] he goes to school. I think that's why he keeps going to night school right after work. (American)
>
> He is still in the military reserve, and he has to take an annual physical, and it seems like I could tell what month it was because he would not drink at all, or minimum one can of beer, every night for three weeks before he took his physical. (American)

Interestingly, American wives say there are also short-lived attempts by their husband to cut down on drinking for its own sake. Lacking the impetus of a special occasion, the alcoholic's focus appears to be a test of (or development of) his own control abilities:

> That's one of the things that puzzles me. The days that he didn't drink, like I say, maybe he'd go three days and then drink every day, and then two days he wouldn't touch it, and it puzzled me how he could just shut it off like that. (American)

When he makes up his mind that he wants to taper down a bit, he does it for no reason at all. (American)

Occasionally he would go out and try to prove to himself that he could [cut down] his alcohol intake. I remember one incident after we were married, he said, "I want to go listen to some music up at the bar; they got a new band up there." He came back in two hours and looked at me with an expression on his face [and said], "I only had one beer. I sat there and listened to them play and only had *one* beer!" It didn't register until several years later. Wow! That was his effort to prove to himself that he could drink socially! (American)

These periods of sobriety are apparently too brief or too public for the wife to react to them, except with relief and pleasure that her husband did not ruin an important occasion. Wives also seem to realize (probably from past experience) that these times of sobriety have little probability of becoming permanent.[11]

Two aspects of this short-term sobriety that occurs (1) for special occasions or (2) to attempt to regain control over consumption—are worth examining. First, the men are self-consciously sober and "on stage," enacting sober behavior (Goffman 1959:17–76) with quite a bit of intensity throughout the crucial period they have selected at the time to maintain sobriety. Second, they do not report suffering any withdrawal, perhaps because they still do take small amounts to drink, or because they know that they will be able to drink again soon.

Withdrawal That Accompanies Longer-Term Sobriety

When alcoholic men do try to stop drinking for a longer period (or permanently), their wives report three prime motivators (not unlike those that get the husband into professional treatment): (1) fear of the serious effects of continuous heavy drinking on health, (2) desire to regain control over drinking,[12] (3) fear that the wife will leave them.

The one time with the ulcer he stopped; I think that really had him scared. (American)

He had high blood pressure and . . . was 15 to 20 pounds overweight. The doctor told him to get that off. He did. He quit drinking completely. He did [it] for about two weeks . . . then he came home and started with the beer. (American)

When I told him I was leaving, he cried . . . and stopped for about a week. (American)

He became so sick and nervous that he stopped for a while, but not for long. (Finn)

Both American and Finnish wives observe that their husbands become nervous and irritate easily during such periods:[13]

He is very jumpy. We have a chime doorbell; we have a chime telephone; and you see him miserably rise off his chair because he is shocked by the noise! People talking, he will start pacing. He is a chain smoker, and he will walk back and forth, back and forth. (American)

He's irritable. You can't ask him anything; he jumps down your throat. (American)

When he has not been drinking, you better watch out, for you're in for a lot of nit-picking and a lot of "Come and see . . . " the yard, the windows, the dresser drawers, everything. Sometimes he would make lists. (American)

Finnish wives say essentially the same thing—that their husbands are very irritable during sobriety.

Some edgy husbands appear to their wives to work with a frenzy while trying to remain sober, perhaps as an attempt to handle nervousness through activity:

[He is] just energy . . . just must be in motion all the time . . . work, work, and more work, mostly around here. (American)

He works a little more in the year, he works more in the house, he goes down and checks the hill, he looks around for things he can do. (Finn)

Just as difficult to be around are the men who become withdrawn and noncommunicative when they try to stop drinking, or the men who are obviously depressed because of it. Such moods may be almost as unpleasant for the wife as is his behavior when drinking:

He comes home and he does not talk to anyone and he doesn't relate to us. (American)

The world's going to come to an end next week, you know. [He has] that type of attitude. (American)

When he was sober between drunks, he didn't talk. He was apathetic, depressed, and didn't feel like doing anything. (Finn)

. . . formerly we went sailing, but once he got nervous and threatened to throw me out of the boat, so I don't go anymore. (Finn)

Despite an apparent awareness of how badly her husband feels during withdrawal from alcohol, a wife will often use this time to complain, either verbally or by her actions. She perceives this as a time when she can safely communicate how he has made her suffer during his drinking and drunken periods. Since she may have endured a husband who spends money that is needed for the household and bills, is irregular in going to work and in doing chores around the house, becomes physically abusive, does not take her or the children to any recreational or social events, seldom eats meals with them, or either becomes very uncommunicative or quarrelsome, it is almost a certainty that the wife has built up a list of complaints. It is not surprising, therefore, that almost from the moment a husband sobers up, a wife takes the opportunity to let off steam—to tell her husband how she feels about the treatment she has received and the things that are going wrong in the family.[14] Wives describe their own behavior during their husband's initial try at abstinence as follows:

> During his sober periods, I was very cold and made sure that he realized just exactly how much he was making me suffer. (American)
>
> I would never hassle him when he was drinking, but when he was sober I would be more likely to try to get something straightened out, or give him a pile of shit about something. Yes, I acted different when he was sober than when he was drinking. (American)
>
> [When he was sober], I'd really give it to him. I couldn't say exactly what I wanted to when he was drinking because I knew I could only push him so far and that was all. {But when he sobered up] the next day, I'd be mad . . . it showed in everything and anything I did. I'd slam doors and cupboard doors, I was so full of hostility and resentment. (American)
>
> I am mean to him [when he is sober]. I hate what he has done to me. I treat him a little bit like a kid. He asks me if I paid the bills and I say, "Why do you want to know? I do it all—pay the bills, care for the kids, and care for you, too." (American)
>
> [When he is sober], I am not ready to forget and forgive like I thought I was . . . I blame him for a lot of things he's done. (Finn)

Sober Comportment during Longer Periods of Voluntary Sobriety

Although it may seem understandable that the withdrawal period is not a return to ordinary sobriety, it might be expected that when this period has been worked through, un-self-conscious normal behavior will return. Such is not the case. Even skid row alcoholics who sober up for long periods after years of heavy drinking have great difficulty in handling and scheduling their sober time. They become nervous or depressed about how they are managing, rather than being self-consciously sober (Wiseman 1973). (Furthermore, inasmuch as these men are no longer in intact marriages, they find they have sobered up without anyone significant to them knowing or caring.)

The still-married husbands in this study have different problems during their long-term sobriety, however. They apparently remain on stage for significant others, playing a special role, impressing persons as to what fine family men they really are, despite past drinking episodes. Most women describe their husband during longer-term sobriety as having a marvelous personality, being generous and loving toward all, and paying special attention to being a good family man. A smaller proportion of wives say that when their husband is sober he becomes nervous, tense, fault-finding, negative, quiet, lethargic, or depressed.[15]

For American wives who report that the longer-term sober behavior of their husband improves dramatically, four clusters of characteristics emerge, each suggesting a person of great charm and consideration. One subcluster of attributes includes such adjectives as charming, gracious, attentive, and talkative. The wives say such things as the following:

> When he's not drinking, he's one of the finest individuals, very warm and sensitive. (American)
>
> He is a beautiful person . . . a perfect-plus gentleman. He is kind, considerate, and lovable. (American)

A second, closely related cluster of descriptions focuses on the unusual amount of generosity and thoughtfulness toward others exhibited by the husband when sober:

> He'll give you the shirt off his back. (American)
>
> [When he's sober] he's a giver . . . he'll just give of himself, you know, without any thought for himself. (American)
>
> He has a good heart . . . he would do anything for anyone. (American)
>
> He bends over backwards to help people. He gets things for people, helps them with odd jobs around the house. He's loaned people money when they asked for it. (American)

In a third cluster of attributes, reported by a substantial minority of wives, husbands are seen as loving or lovable when sober.

A fourth sober-behavior trait cluster could be described as that of the good husband and father. These men, when sober, go out of their way to help around the home, spend time with their children, and do numerous household repairs. One almost gets the picture of an ideal husband, a person who is activated when the effects of heavy alcohol intake and/or withdrawal symptoms wear off:

> He brings me flowers. Helps with the kids and the dishes. He is a good husband. He is a good father. (American)
>
> He is fantastic with the kids . . . he will read to them . . . he spent about three hours the other night making kites for them . . . he takes them places. We do a lot . . . as a family together. (American)
>
> He fixes every damn thing in the house; he cleans the house. (American)

For many Finnish women, the time between drinking bouts represents golden moments in the family—all the more precious because of the contrast with drunken times:

> He was wonderful while he was sober. He came home on time for dinner. Everything was just fine. (Finn)
>
> It's a beautiful day when he's not drinking. (Finn)

The Finnish wife is pleased to see her husband show a renewed interest in the upkeep of the house.

For a minority of wives in both countries, the husband's long-term sobriety results in some somber times in the home. These women describe their spouse going into a shell of shyness, silence, and sometimes sadness:

> He does not talk to us; he does not talk to his children; he does not pay much attention to me . . . just nothing . . . very quiet. (American)
>
> He's very somber and silent and he doesn't want to talk or do anything. He doesn't even read. (Finn)

This longer-term sober comportment is characterized by both drinkers and significant others within a similar and relatively narrow range of behavior. No respondent—either alcoholic or wife—claims that sobriety brought normalcy. There was no report that the drinker acts the way he always had acted before becoming an alcoholic, with a full range of activities and interests. One might hypothesize that the wonderful personality, the joking, and the generous and good family man are all deliberate personality constructions by these husbands as a way of assuaging the guilt they feel at having spent so much time drunk or having acted so badly when they were drinking excessively.

Wives' reaction to longer-term sobriety may also contribute to the husband's heightened sense of awareness of a special state—abstinence—rather than aiding a feeling of returning to normalcy. As wives explain it, they, too, are putting on a performance during their husband's sober time:

> It is very had [when he is sober] because I tried to be the model of a good wife and I guess I was playing a role. (American)
>
> At first, I acted good. I'd been very loving and try to do things right, and try to be a good wife, and try to avoid anything that I would think might make him drink, and I would make all efforts I could to make the house very happy. (American)
>
> I try to let him feel that I am happy about him being sober . . . I try to see if I can help him. I'd say, "Is there anything you would like or need?" (Finn)

At the same time, wives fear, also probably with the justification of past experience, that their husband may resume drinking at any time:[16]

> I'm walking on egg shells [I feel] that any minute he'll go over the edge again. (American)

> When he's sober, I'm very nervous. I can see signs of him giving up. I'm almost relieved when he does. It's like waiting for the other shoe to drop. (American)
>
> I'm holding my breath and I'm saying, "Oh, I'll come home tomorrow, and I'll find him drunk again." (American)

Finnish wives who notice their husband maintain his sobriety beyond the usual time see him develop extreme nervousness. Often this edginess is coupled with a tendency to pick quarrels. This behavior usually increases in intensity until the husband "breaks" under the strain and resumes drinking. Sometimes, by the time her husband starts drinking, a wife will admit to feeling a bit relieved to be past the tension of waiting for it to happen!

Even men who are good-natured when sober apparently give off clues that this state cannot last:

> He's like a human being. He's more gay. Then it's quite okay. We have coffee together and talk—and then, it's too much [for him]. (Finn)

Summary and Conclusion

Two important aspects of the behavior of the alcoholic husband, when alternately drunk and when sober, are (1) the limited clusters of characteristics typical of each state. Neither drunken nor sober behavior apparently encourages a broad range of behavior in alcoholics. (2) The contrasting moods—some extremely unpleasant—to which a wife must accommodate. She must feel sometimes as if she were living with more than one man, and being forced to adjust to each one. A good-natured husband when sober is just as likely to become an angry, even violent man when drunk. A husband who is nervous and quarrelsome when drunk may change to a silent and sad man when he sobers up. Concomitantly, a wife may be careful of his feelings when drunk, but tell him what she things of him the moment he is sober.

As can be seen from the data, intoxication casts its shadow on all stages of sober comportment in the form of bad behavior, withdrawal symptoms, plus guilt and shame for past actions. Likewise, sober comportment, with its heightened awareness by the alcoholic as to how he should be acting, usually is the prelude to another period of drinking.

Eventually, the alcoholic husband becomes discouraged with the maintenance of long-term sober existence. The role of wonderful husband, good family man, and man with an exaggeratedly good personality is obviously a great strain. Other men find they are playing this demanding role opposite a woman who herself is acting the part of a perfect wife. Such role perfection can only increase the strain on both spouses. Still other alcoholic husbands are required to cope with wives who are fearful and suspicious as to how long such nondrinking will last. Thus, in long-term sobriety, as with brief occasions of cutting down, or attempts at abstinence, the various and increasingly burdensome strains of self-conscious interaction with wives and significant others may play an important role in recidivism.

This special part played by the wife in her husband's return to drinking, coupled as it is with her reactions to his behavior while drunk and sober, seems further to refute the theory of an unconscious desire on the part of the wife of an alcoholic to suffer herself or to dominant him touched on earlier (deSaugy 1962; Futterman 1953; Kalashian 1959; Paige et al. 1971; Price 1945; Rae & Drewery 1972; Whalen 1962). In addition to the fairly practical reasons wives give for taking over most aspects of household and daily management for the two of them (described in Chapter 3), the complex interaction between spouses in drunk and sober periods is important to understand, inasmuch as it may lead him to start drinking again. Her behavior is composed out of her reactions to his on-stage personality, her memory of the suffering he has caused her, and her problems with handling a sobered-up husband in a life that she may have restructured in such a way as to manage without him. (See Chapter 7.)

It would seem that alcoholism on the part of the husband plunges the wife into a relationship that can only be understood in the context of his changing behavior. Not only are the husband's actions unpleasant—even dangerous—when drunk, but even in his sober state she knows that the "other man" is lurking, waiting for alcohol to activate much more difficult behavior, behavior that includes frightening irresponsibility and aggressiveness. This very knowledge of difficult times to come coupled with unhappy times in the past may, indeed, have some bearing on how wives act when their husband tries to remain sober, and ultimately on his ability to stay that way.

Notes

1. Only one American respondent claims her husband turned his aggression toward himself. He tried to commit suicide when he was drunk. (He used carbon monoxide.) Another was describing as becoming "self-destructive"; he hurt himself, but this was not seen as done purposely or with intent to kill himself. A few Finnish wives report their husbands were taken to the hospital after a combination of alcohol and drugs had rendered them unconscious, but these instances are rare and were seen as accidental. Thus, while alcoholism has

been described as an unconscious form of slow suicide (Menninger 1938), drinking husbands seem not to be in any hurry to end their existences. See also Snyder, in Clinard (1968:189), who found an absence of meaningful statistics showing any relationship between alcoholism and suicide.

2.   It is interesting to note that only American wives mention blackouts and the reduction in their husbands' physical coordination when drunk. The absence of these symptoms in Finnish responses may be further testimony to a possibility raised in an earlier chapter: that American wives are more likely than the Finnish to see their husbands in both early and late stages of heavy drinking because their husbands drink at home.

3.   Heider (1967:252–65) and Kelman (1973) have speculated that the victims of violence (and others who hear about it) have a tendency to believe that they probably deserved it.

4.   Straus (1976) points out that even though laws that gave husbands the right to discipline wives have been changed, the extralegal spirit of these laws remains. Police are still reluctant to arrest a husband who batters his wife, prosecutors often fail to act, women often drop charges in fear of retaliation by an angry husband, and thus few cases come to trial or result in a guilty plea or conviction. Both Finnish and American women stated their fear of accelerating their husband's anger by either calling the police or preferring charges if they— or a concerned neighbor—try to get official help during a beating crisis.

5.   Nichols (1976) observed that when battered wives go for help to a family agency, the caseworker often suggests the wife's behavior must provoke the husband's wrath; she is thus the one who should reform rather than the husband.

6.   This return to normalcy implies a model that has much in common with Parsons's systems approach (1951), where deviant behavior causes a "disequilibrium" and the removal of this deviance allows the system to return to equilibrium. Mills (1959), on the other hand, argues that human group life is not so simple. Even when the disequilibrium is removed, things can never return to their exact former state.

7.   Rubington (1978), for instance, using a convenience sample that compared the first year of sobriety of halfway house residents with persons who attained initial sobriety in the community, found in general that those drinkers who were living in halfway houses had either fewer problems or problems of less intensity while maintaining sobriety than those remaining in the community.

8.   There appears to be no specific time span of continuous sobriety that insures "recovery" from alcoholism, and alcoholics have been know to "slip off the wagon" after many years of maintaining abstinence. It is difficult to say, therefore, for certain, just when an alcoholic can be termed a cured or even arrested case. Some practitioners in the field of alcoholism rehabilitation, notably AA, believe that once a person becomes an alcoholic, he/she remains one for the rest of his/her life and is always "at risk" in this area. Others in the field suggest that alcoholics can eventually learn to drink normally. To date, the issue remains without resolution, although researchers and therapists are leaning toward believing that alcoholics can never learn to drink moderately. (See also note 12.)

9.   Actual recidivism rates of alcoholism are difficult to know. In the first place, a great deal of alcoholism is hidden (i.e., it is has not yet come to the

attention of significant others or professionals). Second, as discussed in Ch. 4, note 14, it is difficult to keep track of persons who are not successful at maintaining sobriety, inasmuch as alcoholics often go from one treatment institution or agency to another, and these facilities most often have no formal connections with one another and thus no central source of patients' names.

10.   Alcoholism has often been referred to as a compulsion or an addiction. A compulsion is defined in the dictionary as "an irresistible impulse or tendency to perform an irrational act." In the same way, the term "addicted" is defined as "given over to a pursuit, practice, or habit." Certainly, such common language definitions give a picture of an activity that is constant and compulsive, almost like an uncontrollable spasm. Yet if the daily lives of actively drinking alcoholics are examined in detail and over time, there are patterns of short periods of purposeful nonimbibing when the drinker remains sober. Such occurrences should cause investigators to supplement the questions usually asked about alcoholism (e.g., Why do they drink?) with inquiries of an opposing nature: Why don't they continue to drink unabated? Why do they stop—even for a short time? How is this so-called compulsion or addiction overcome—even temporarily?

11.   Although the above discussion seems to indicate that some alcoholics, when motivated, can reach and maintain briefly a state of relative sobriety, continued heavy drinking may ultimately result in the loss of this ability. Continued excessive intake is also believed to account for the increasingly embarrassing behavior of long-term alcoholics. One might hypothesize that a sort of push-pull motivation develops, in which a long-term heavy drinker (who appears to be "addicted" to alcohol and could be referred to as a "compulsive drinker") can temporarily maintain sobriety at will if the situation or relationship means more to him than the pleasure of drinking. One might further posit that persons who continue drinking find fewer and fewer situations that mean more to them than alcohol does. If this is the case, it would follow that in the later stages of alcoholism, no social situation or relationship can exert a claim that is stronger than alcohol.

12.   The jury is still out concerning whether alcoholics can become controlled social drinkers; however, the preponderance of current opinion and evidence is that most cannot, and that their only hope of "recovery" is total abstinence. Beauchamp (1980:78–82) discusses this controversy, which became front-page news when a study by the Rand Corporation, reported at length in Armour, Polich, and Stambull (1978), indicated that longitudinal data proved that alcoholics could return to social drinking. This study was attacked by AA, the National Council on Alcoholism, and the National Institute for Alcohol Abuse and Alcoholism.

13.   Alcoholics, recalling their first year of sobriety for Rubington (1978), describe uncontrollable moods swings as a problem. This phenomenon is probably the "dry drunks" referred to in AA literature as being similar to the behavior an alcoholic exhibits when drinking. Michael Deegan, program coordinator of the Veterans' Administration Medical Center Alcoholism Treatment Program in La Jolla, California, points out that the term is associated with another, "building up to a drunk." This behavior pattern often consists of provoking a fight with a spouse or other close tie, and in this way have an excuse to go out and get drunk.

14.   Family members of alcoholics are warned in Al-Anon meetings and

through such publications as "Living with Sobriety" that they will feel anger toward drinking spouses, parents, or children for all the trouble the drinking has caused. They are urged to let off steam or "take out their garbage" in some acceptable way that does not result in a show of hostility toward the newly sober family member. One suggestion is for them to discuss their feelings with their sponsor and vent their anger in that way.

15.   It is possible that the positive personality characteristics of the sober husband, as perceived by the wife, are an artifact of the wife's hopes for the relationship. No doubt women project their hopes or fears on the man they married in terms of who he "really" is. That is, they undoubtedly want to believe that alcohol is what is causing him to behave badly. Sober, they would prefer to believe, he is a "wonderful man." Such a definition gives wives a reason for staying in the marriage. Indeed, a few mention their husband's wonderful sober personality when they are asked why they do not get a divorce or separation. On the other hand, women who experience their husband as difficult even when sober might well be selectively perceiving negative qualities in a husband they are considering leaving.

16.   One wonders how the wife's anxious expectation of the slide back into excessive drinking and the concomitant apprehension she projects affect her husband's nerves. Wives claim they can predict when their husbands are going to start drinking again from the onset of this nervousness. The result might indeed by a circular one. Superalertness on the part of the wife (to "wait for the other shoe to drop," as one put it) is, in turn, noticed by the man, who then becomes increasingly nervous under such scrutiny. Then, in classic circular fashion described by Gough (1948), Lemert (1967), and Ray (1964), the husband begins acting nervous, escalating his wife's fears, and reflexively increasing his own tension. This period of mutual tenseness and apprehension, which culminates in the man's return to heavy drinking, might even be related in a roundabout way to his violence toward his wife, (which, of course, is conjecture at this point).

CHAPTER 6

The Private Tragedy of Alcoholism: The Failed Marriage Relationship

Introduction

With her hopes that professional aid will put an end to her husband's drinking problem repeatedly dashed, the wife of an alcoholic finds herself married to a man with whom living becomes increasingly difficult. Perhaps the greatest tragedy of alcoholism is this deterioration of the marriage relationship into a state of continuing and, ultimately, permanent mutual alienation.

This chapter will discuss some of the ways the husband's alcoholism curtails, for most wives, any satisfactory marital interaction in four key areas: talk or communications, mealtime, joint recreation and social activities, and sexual intimacy. The increasing failure of the husband to provide satisfaction in these areas leaves the wife almost entirely without a means of role fulfillment as a spouse. Predictably, wives react in anger and sorrow. The drinking husband, also predictably, reacts with hostility to his wife's unhappiness. Ultimately, as will be seen, she withdraws, hurt and alienated, and he is further cut off from the society of nondrinking companions.

The circularity of bad feelings between spouses, which intensifies as time goes on, is not only important in explaining what happens to a majority of marriages of wives of drinking men. Relationships in these four crucial areas of marriage during the husband's drinking appear to be associated in a causal way to the man's ability to stop drinking (as discussed in the epilogue).

It is important at this point to be certain that, in reporting the effect of a drinking husband on a marriage, the interaction problems actually reflect, in general content and/or intensity, the effects of his alcoholism. This is because these areas of conflict are not in any sense unique to marriage with an alcoholic man. The distinction is particularly important inasmuch as wives in the general population are more likely to be unhappy in marriage than their husbands (Schumm et al. 1985; Shafer and Keith 1984; Bernard 1973:25–33). Bernard, in fact, reports that this unhappiness gap increases with the years, and Schumm notes, in a followup study, that it still exists. Additionally, women are more likely to report feelings of loneliness than are men (Borys and Perlman 1985), and Shafer and Keith (1984) note that wives are more likely than husbands to perceive inequity in marital roles that seems unfavorable to them.

Therefore, in order to be more certain that the unique effects of alcoholism on marital interaction and emotional reactions are targeted, a comparative sample of wives in marriages where alcohol is not a problem were questioned about their satisfaction with their husbands in the areas of companionship, mealtimes, sociability, and sexual relations. Data for this purpose were collected from a sample of American wives married to men who are not alcoholics, but who are matched with wives of alcoholics on other important demographic characteristics: income, age, and education. (A more complete description of the sample, its selection, and restrictions can be found in the chapter on methodology.)

Each of the four crucial areas of marriage under study was originally developed as a result of voluntary complaints made by wives of alcoholics concerning the behavior of their drinking husbands. Wives of alcoholics tell how they first felt when they noted the behavior of their husband in each key interaction area, how they reacted to this behavior, and how their husband, in turn, reacted to them. From such data, one can see how marital dissatisfaction builds up to the point where the rift is so great that recapturing original loving feelings in the marriage is extremely difficult.[1] Furthermore, the unique effects of an alcoholic husband on these four important areas of marriage are apparent.

Although each of the four important marriage relationship areas will be discussed separately, it is necessary to note that, in actuality, failures and/or hard feelings emerging in one part of a relationship do not remain isolated and discreet; in actual life, they interpenetrate other areas of marital interaction, a dissatisfaction in each casting a shadow on the others. Thus, if reduction in communication is serious enough, it can affect sexual adjustment as well as joint recreation or meal taking, and so on. Eventually, areas of unhappiness merge or blend to become the general disaffection discussed in offices of family doctors, social workers, psychiatrists, and lawyers.

The Talk Problem in Marriages

It is expected that persons living in the same household, especially in the intimacy of marriage, usually talk and communicate with each other on many aspects of their lives, especially matters of mutual interest and concern. Yet, there are many indications in the research literature that this is not the case. Rather, the absence of communication is an important problem in some marriages.[2]

Approximately two-thirds of the wives of alcoholics complain that their mates will not talk to them. Inasmuch as these women see marital communication as embodying empathy, sympathy, and understanding of their needs and feelings, they feel terribly deprived when their husbands give them the silent treatment. On the other hand, less than one-fifth of the sample in marriages where alcohol is not a problem also feel that their husbands are virtually noncommunicative.

Among a majority of the wives of alcoholics, the absence of talk between themselves and their spouses is a major complaint. In many cases, as will be seen, this situation becomes so bad that eventually neither talks. A negotiated but essentially hostile silence results. Most women blame their husband's drinking, a connection that seems logical in terms of the depressive physiological effects of heavy alcohol ingestion. A more detailed discussion follows.

Effects of Heavy Drinking on Talking and Communication

Alcohol has always been known to affect the quality of social intercourse. Up to a point, small amounts of alcohol are thought to reduce tenseness and put the speaker at greater ease, perhaps even aiding glibness and enjoyment of the interchange. Thus, it is usually provided at parties to "loosen things up." When taken in excessive amounts, however, alcohol can cloud mental capacities; the drinker no longer communicates well. Speech is slurred, reactions are slowed, and energies sometimes appear sapped to the point that even talking is an effort. Persons under the influence of alcohol often say things they may regret or deny when sober. When alcohol is taken in excess over long periods, it can affect the brain cells so that memory is reduced. The ability to communicate is also affected during the sobering-up period, inasmuch as alcoholics experience a great deal of physical discomfort, tenseness, and depression at that time. The tenseness may escalate a tendency to quarrel or to resort to angry retorts; the depression discourages any kind of interpersonal interaction.

The combination of these effects of heavy drinking appears to result in a spouse who avoids conversation unless he can indulge in sarcasm, complaint, or other forms of verbal aggressiveness, as discussed in earlier chapters. Eventually, even this form of communication may become too much of a burden. The wife finds herself living with a person who is no longer companionable. He avoids her company; she tries to find ways to regain his attention. She ultimately reacts to this state of affairs with concern, anger, and finally withdrawal. He further reacts with more coldness and hostility. The process of alienation can be traced through the wives' volunteered descriptions of the talk problem with an alcoholic husband, which follow.

The Drastic Reduction in Talk.   Many women who are married to excessive drinkers claim their husbands will neither talk to them nor listen to what they have to say, regardless of subject. Below are some typical complaints:

> When he is drinking, like I said, at times he is kind of quiet. Sometimes we just sit for hours and don't say a word. (American)
> [He] eats his breakfast and goes to work . . . doesn't say goodbye, go to hell, or anything, and just walks out. (American)
> I told him I had the feeling I could not get contact with him. I said, "When I talk you don't listen. I would like to have more conversation with you." He said that he was always so tired; that he would like to talk but he was too tired. (Finn)

Most wives feel that excessive drinking is the cause of the silent treatment they experience from their husbands. They base this conclusion, at least in part, on the fact that the absence of talk is a noticeable change from the degree of communication they had with their husbands before the drinking had escalated to problem proportions:

> When we first married, we had a very close relationship. We enjoyed doing things together; we communicated. Now, there's no communication in our marriage. (American)
> [Before we were married] when we went together, it was different. He drank, but not so heavily, and was more talkative. Our marriage went well for three years, and then he drank very heavily and became silent and not talkative. (Finn)

A few wives say that their husbands really never were talkers, thus suggesting that the communication problem existed prior to the heavy drinking.

No Talk on Significant Matters.   Gottman (1982) has noted that symmetry in emotional responses during marital communication is essential to satisfaction on the part of spouses. In the case of alcoholics and their wives, the women often claim that certain topics (often referred to by such terms as "deep" ones) are taboo. In such cases, the wives feel that topics that mean a great deal to them do not receive the same emotional weight from their husbands:

We still can't talk about anything in depth about my feelings. I've tried and he just shuts it off. So I don't try. I just keep busy with other things. (American)

Some Finnish wives also complain that while their husbands will talk about mundane, everyday matters, they cannot get a discussion going on important personal issues. Thus, they still feel they are unable to make "real" contact with their spouses:

We never have any "deep talks" because he doesn't talk . . . only when he has a hangover or is drunk. But that kind of talk is not meant. It is not sincere. (Finn)

Strategies to Avoid Talk. It is not easy to avoid conversation with someone who shares the same household. Alcoholic men employ many means. A primary avoidance technique is to absent themselves from their wife's company. Both American and Finnish husbands leave the room (or the house entirely) to avoid discussing an unpleasant or unwanted topic:

When I felt like I needed him because my nephew was killed overseas . . . I couldn't find him the whole time. He would show up for a few minutes . . . then he got nasty about that. "What's everybody feeling so terrible about? At least he doesn't have to be in this rotten world we are in." And he'd go right back to the bar. (American)

Men also will combine two ploys, absenting themselves and paying concerted attention to television:[3]

He stays out in the garage or the garden until dark, and then he comes in and talks to the TV set. (American)

American alcoholic men are more likely than Finns to use the television set as a barrier between themselves and conversations with their wives. Finnish men avoid talk by staying out of range of their wives:

I wanted to talk about it all—to arrange it [a family get-together], but my husband put on his hat and left, and there I sat. (Finn)

Some Finnish men develop this avoidance response to an art, managing to use the home solely as a place to sleep, or creating different living schedules than their wives:

When he would come out of the WC [bathroom], he would go to the bedroom or somewhere I wasn't—he was escaping. Then, he started going to work earlier—before I was awake. (Finn)

In "Holy Deadlock," LeMasters (1971:454–55) discusses how estranged spouses who remain married can manage separate existences under the same roof. Daily schedules chronicled by the wives of Finnish alcoholics sound a great deal like their husbands are moving toward or have accomplished such an arrangement:

> Here is a typical day when he is drinking: He sleeps only a little. He gets up very early in the morning. We have breakfast at 8 A.M. He goes to the office. Sometimes he comes home for lunch, most often not. Sometimes he has had one bottle of beer or two already. He finishes work at 4 P.M. and doesn't come home until 9 or 10 P.M. I have dinner with the children. Then he comes home and goes to bed by way of the kitchen. Sometimes in the winter or weekends he takes the dog out for a walk and comes back at noon drunk and goes to bed. (Finn)

Bernard (1968:110, 140–42) observes that one way people end a conversation is to provide no feedback when a topic is broached, thus letting the subject "fall," and repeatedly leaving the initiative to the other.[4] Such conversation stoppers allow a drinking husband to stay in the same room with his wife and still not talk. Alcoholic husbands often let a topic die rather than make an interested response that would maintain their end of a cooperative conversation effort, or its symmetry, as noted by Gottman (1982). Wives describe the effect:

> When I want to talk . . . he just doesn't even want to listen to it, or he just doesn't want me to get off on a subject, so consequently it just stops there. (American)

> As a general rule, he doesn't ask me anything. He doesn't have an ounce of curiosity. Why even if I said, "Joe Blow was here today," you know, it would be normal to say, "What did he want?" He wouldn't say that. He wouldn't ask me any more. If I didn't say any more that would be the end of it. (American)

The Talking Minority

A minority of women indicate their husband is always willing and able to talk despite his heavy drinking. Some women claim they and their spouse actually talk more since the inception of his heavy drinking.

> When he is drinking, we argue, but when he is sober, we talk. We have some great talks. [Over the years] talks have improved [since he has been drinking heavily]. (American)

> We talk more now that he has begun drinking heavy. (American)

Sometimes the increased talk is seen as an outgrowth of efforts to improve the relationship, which in turn are seen as connected with the drinking either as cause or effect, or both:

> I think we talked more [after he was drinking heavily], because when I faced up to it [the heavy drinking] and we had some really long serious talks about where we are and where we want to be, and why do you think you are drinking and like that. Much more than we could have been in the early part of our marriage. (American)
>
> We discuss his drinking and his stopping very much. We talk about different things. How it is for me when he is drunk. (Finn)

However, even women with talkative drinking husbands report a gradual reduction in conversation as drinking continues over time.

Effects of Absence of Talk

Fear of Loss of Love. The termination of communication, which occurs in the case of most wives of alcoholics, is a very serious symbolic act—be it between individuals, families, or nations. A refusal to talk not only signals the end of sociability and discourse, but it also means that differences cannot be arbitrated—that one party no longer sees anything to gain by messages to or from the other party. Many individuals, groups, and nations use cessation of communications as a public rebuke or punishment for wrongdoing.[5] It can also be seen as a threat of hostilities to come. Thus, it is not surprising that, when their husbands avoid conversations with them, some wives begin to fear that their men have ceased to love them. They ask for reassurance in word or deed, but get none:

> One morning I got up and I just got to ask him and so feeling real brave, I just ask him, "Do you plan on leaving?" And he looked at me and he said, "No, I'm not planning on leaving." Up went the paper in front of his face. He won't look at me, you know. (American)
>
> Perhaps I shouldn't say this, but I felt so cut off when he wouldn't talk to me. I was thinking he didn't love me any more. That was the essence of our battle. (Finn)

Finding the Best Time. Other wives, loath to give up the companionship of their husband, start watching for the most fortuitous times to talk to him, carefully gauging his drinking and sobering-up patterns. For this latter group, time is seen as divided into several periods when communication seems possible: (1) when the husband is freshly sober; (2) when he has worked through a hangover and has been sober a longer period; (3) after the husband has had a few drinks, but is not yet drunk; (4) when the husband seems to be in one of his rare talking moods. A few women said that their husbands were only talkative in bars, so that they would go with them for the opportunity to talk. With the exception of accompanying their husbands to bars, Finnish wives mention the same range of "safe" talking times. Many wives try to talk

to their husbands in the early morning, because this is the time a husband is most likely to be sober and able to understand the discussion
and answer intelligently. As an added plus, he is often contrite for the
past night's drinking and his apologetic mood makes him easier to get
along with:

> You either had to grab or pass, like seven to eight in the morning when he
> was sober, and then sometimes he would be sober between five and
> six . . . sober enough that you would try to get through and might even
> think you got through. But as far as his being rational, those were the best
> times. (American)

> The best time to talk to him would be in the morning, or right at
> lunchtime. And once in awhile, if I could just stick with him so that he
> does not get out at that period, [he could talk] at five or around there.
> (American)

> The best time to talk to him is in the morning when we have coffee
> together. That is when he promises not to drink that day. (Finn)

A few wives try to wait until the husband has gone through a hangover period before they approach him to talk:

> [I talk to him] when he's been sober for 12 hours or longer. It takes a while
> to get it out of his system. When you're sitting down, like if we have a late
> breakfast at times, sometimes that's the time to bring up anything that's
> worth discussing. (American)

> The best time to talk to him is when he has been sober a long time, but
> even then discussing this annoys and irritates him and in a way, speeds up
> the next falling off the wagon. (Finn)

Realizing their own tendency to fight if their husband is drunk or
suffering a hangover, a minority of women not only monitor their husband's moods, watching for the best opportunity to talk to him, but also
keep track of their own feelings in this area:

> [The best time to talk to him is] when he hasn't been drinking, of
> course . . . but I find that I will not talk about it if I cannot remain calm. I
> know I'll do more damage than good. (American)

> The best time is when he's sober or when he's relaxed. The best time is
> when I'm calm. If I'm upset I holler at him. (American)

Inasmuch as sobriety is so often a forerunner of a new period of
nervousness and physical discomfort, some American wives find it best
to say whatever they want to say to their husband during the narrow
band of time that comes after he has had two or three drinks, but before
he gets drunk:

You see, he's up at 12 to one o'clock. Well, from one, there's about three hours in there [when he's not drinking much yet]. (American)

[The best time to talk to him] was usually right after he has had just about two [drinks] and before he gets really gone. I think he has a chance for the alcohol to sort of numb things a little bit and for him to be a little more responsive. (American)

[The best time to talk with him] is when he's had one beer . . . the one-or-two-beer level. When he's had his third drink, it's too late. (American)

Giving Up. Faced with the many difficulties of communication with a drinking man, many wives begin to feel there is really no good time when attempts at communication will succeed. This becomes especially true as drinking progresses and the periods of sobriety become increasingly shorter and blurred by hangovers:

There used to be days like in the morning or in the afternoon, I could talk with him because he was sober. Well, he has so much alcohol in his system [now] he is never really sober. There never really is a time. (American)

When he talked, there was no mind to his talks. (Finn)

We talk, and mostly he talks if he is able to, but he is becoming more and more incoherent. He jumps from one subject to another. (Finn)

Often, the outcome of the wife's attempt to cope with her alcoholic husband's silent and angry moods, as well as her own hurt feelings, is that she gives up and becomes noncommunicative also, as these American wives note:

I don't discuss anything with him. He throws it back at me, you know. So I don't talk to him. (American)

I just quit. I gave up [talking]. (American)

Finnish wives express the same feelings, saying that they "freeze up" as their husband's drinking continues, so it is they who finally terminate communication:

I have lost the wish to try to discuss things with him. I think that our marriage is more like a business relationship than a marriage. I tried to get the "old feeling" back, but now I give up. It's up to him to do something. (Finn)

The end of communication also signals a change in the relationship as a whole, affecting other ares of marital interaction:

No. [We don't talk much.] I am no longer interested in his opinion or anything. (American)

We talk only a little. Like I said, I don't even know how much I love him anymore. (American)

A Finnish wife speaks of the emptiness of a relationship without communication:

Our relationship is dull. He doesn't give me anything. (Finn)

Thus, the circularity of the effect of nontalking can be seen. A hurt or angry partner, shut out from communication and having no outlet for sharing confidences or sounding out ideas, may try to get through at apparently advantageous times, but may eventually become progressively angry and hostile. If talking continues to be a problem, communication by both spouses is eventually frozen, making any return to open discussion increasingly difficult. Such constraints transform talk from a fairly easygoing, unconscious act to one that must be carefully handled. Furthermore, some important areas may never get really discussed at all by both parties and some sore spots or problems may never be arbitrated or clarified. Psychological access of each to the other is closed, for to cease to talk is effectively to withdraw a large part of oneself from the company of the other.

Comparison with Wives in Marriages Where Alcohol Is Not a Problem

When comparing the ramifications of the talk problem faced by wives of alcoholics with complaints on the same subject by American wives in marriages where alcohol is not a problem, some important differences surface. (Quotes from these women are labeled WNA, wife of nonalcoholic.) While some concern is expressed, the talk problem is nowhere nearly as prevalent or serious as it is among wives of alcoholics, as can be seen from the table presented on page 127.

It should be mentioned that of the 83% of these wives not married to alcoholics who were satisfied with communication with their husband, only 11% claimed that conversations between themselves and their husbands were wonderful, totally open, or full of sharing. In fact, when these wives were asked whether or not they could discuss their problems with their husband, slightly less than half (48%) responded yes, and 13% said definitely no. The remaining answers fell somewhere between: the women in marriages where alcohol is not a problem felt they could talk over some issues and not others, and sometimes perceived they had a sympathetic ear in their husband and sometimes not.

Even with these reservations about communication among wives where alcoholism is not a problem, their experience is in sharp contrast to that of wives of alcoholics.

Among the substantial majority of the sample of American women married to a nonalcoholic and claiming to have no major problem with

Table 6.1. Wives' Perceptions of Communications as a Problem in the Marriage

	American wives where alcohol is not a problem (N = 63) %	Wives of Alcoholics	
		American (N = 76) %	Finnish (N = 50) %
Husband noncommunicative; won't talk to wife; won't maintain conversation	17	62	64
Husband talks to wife some or a great deal; communication not a major complaint	83	38	36

Cautionary note: This table is for *general comparison purposes only* of major sample and sub-sample responses. That is, the percentages shown are not based on results to a standardized questionnaire (see Methodology), but rather, on depth interviewing data which allow a great deal of latitude to the respondent in answering fairly open-ended questions. Thus, in addition to the usual variance assumed for in small samples, the approach to gathering the data must be taken into consideration. Nevertheless, the comparisons are useful—especially where there are (a) large differences or (b) where the respondents offer qualitatively different answers to the same question.

communication in their marriage, those who are happiest about this aspect of their relationship describe their ability to discuss things with their husband as follows:

> I talk to him. I have nothing at all that I cannot talk to my husband about—sex, children, anything . . . we ask each other. We are very compatible. (WNA)

> We communicate beautifully no matter what problems we may have, or whatever, we can always sit down and calmly talk things over, and we never really act like children. When we talk, we discuss things. We discuss everything. (WNA)

> He's my closest friend. (WNA)

Some of these women complain about the style of their husband's discussions with them, but seemingly see this as part of his personality, in contrast to wives of alcoholics who ascribe it to his heavy drinking:

> He's unable to communicate. He cannot express what he feels inside. He keeps it all in. (WNA)

> I'd like to find out just what he feels about things. He does not have definite convictions about anything. (WNA)

Several women in marriages where alcohol is not used excessively complain they could not take a problem to their husband because the proposed solution was always too drastic. For instance, if a wife complains about her job, the husband tells her to quit; if she shows concern about the children, he suggests spanking them; if she complains about the behavior of a neighbor, he tells her to call off all relations with the person. What she really wants is a sympathetic, interested audience, rather than an all-encompassing suggestion for a cure.

Wives in this sample also report television is a major barrier to conversation with their husband, who is suspected of using this means to escape having to talk with his wife:

> Well, we have a third party in the house, and it is a little problem—the television (WNA)
>
> I don't know, he would rather watch TV, or work in the garage on a motor, than he would to just sit and talk. (WNA)

Some of these wives also get discouraged and angry. They finally stop trying to talk to their husband, illustrating again how silence by one partner can bring about a total communication shutdown in marriage:

> I talk to my friends and he talks to his. (WNA)
>
> I feel that if I'm having certain emotional inside things going on, that I can relate better to my friend than I can to him. He does not seem to understand me at an emotional level. (WNA)

Although it is true that the latter group complains about the absence of conversation with their husband, this behavior is not nearly as universal as it appears to be among wives of alcoholics, nor does it get progressively more serious as it does where there is continued excessive drinking. However, some wives in both marriages describe the development of a complete companionship standoff and increasing alienation where the husband continues to be noncommunicative, for whatever the reason.

Mealtime and Marriages

Most authorities agree that, taken in moderate quantities, alcohol enhances the taste of food, increases the appetite, and aids digestion. Cocktails are often served prior to meals and wine with dinner because these beverages, taken in conjunction with food, enhance the pleasures of eating. However, heavy and prolonged drinking reverses these sensations. The heavy drinker eventually loses almost all interest in food. If he eats at all, it is at odd times during the day keyed to his drinking rhythm. Many alcoholics in advanced stages stop eating almost entirely.

Thus, despite the high caloric content of various types of liquor, alcoholics have been known to die of malnutrition because of their neglect of a proper diet. With such profound disinterest in food, and having little or no desire to converse with their wives, as already discussed, it is not surprising that alcoholic men avoid mealtimes.

The central place of the meal in the life of family members has been noted by some investigators. Anthropologist Barnouw, for instance, in his discussion of "The Enjoyment of Life," starts his description with the norms and pleasures of family mealtimes:

> The pleasure of eating is surely enhanced or diminished by the nature of the social setting in which it takes place and by cultural traditions about food. In Europe, the United States, China, Japan, and many other regions, there is a tradition of the family meal, where all the family members eat together. When men are away all day at work and the children have lunch at school, this is not always feasible, but the tradition is still maintained, when possible. This custom strengthens the sense of family unity and may be (although it often is not) an occasion for pleasant conversation and relaxed enjoyment. (1971:258)

Shuman and Arnold (1985) pointed out that both parents and children receive socializing experiences at family meals and that the ritual of these meals is a basic source of family social structure. In a classic study of child development, Bossard and Boll describe the social nature of the family meal:

> The two rooms in which the family spends most time as a group are the living and the dining rooms. . . . It is at the dining table, particularly at dinnertime, that the family is apt to be at its greatest ease, both physically and psychologically. . . . The family meal, in short, represents the family in action upon a common interest and a task so absorbing as to let it operate off-guard in other important respects. The family meal, especially the main one of the day, holds the members of the family together for an extended period of time. . . . Mealtime is family council time, particularly today when under the stress of the different interests of its various members the family is not likely to get together at any other time. (1960:232–33)

With the advent of TV dinners, commuting fathers, and working mothers, the ideal of family mealtime councils around the dining room table is, at least partially, a myth. Nevertheless, family meals continue in the media as an aspect of daily life that is taken for granted. Family members who do not get together to eat on some kind of a regular basis may feel some important element is missing from their relationship.[6]

A substantial group of wives of problems drinkers said their husband seldom ate when drunk. Others indicated that even when sober, their husband's appetites or interest in food had been adversely affected by heavy alcohol intake. The general result, in either case, is family meals often not attended by the husband or, if he is present, a mealtime atmosphere that is far from pleasant. For the wife, this dishonoring of the family meal, and of its accompanying sociability, is a major blow.[7] Even with the possible decline in importance of the family meal in Western industrial countries, eating together has suffered nowhere near this eclipse in families where alcohol is not a problem.

For instance, among wives of alcoholics, only one in three said she could count on her husband for dinner and approximately half said his mealtimes with the family are irregular. On weekends, these drinking husbands seem to disappear from mealtimes altogether. In families where alcohol is not a problem, two-thirds of the wives say they usually eat dinner with their husband, and only one in ten claims he cannot be counted on to be present for meals.

Mealtime Problems of Wives of Alcoholics

Avoidance of Family Meals. Men who are heavy drinkers dodge the family meal by some of the same methods they use to avoid talk. They simply do not show up for dinner, or arrive hours late. When this behavior first begins to occur, wives try to maintain a semblance of the family meal and will often hold dinner. Eventually, of course, they give up and eat alone or with the children:

> He'd say he'd be home for dinner . . . he wasn't home by midnight. [I used to] stay awake, trying to be up when he arrived. (American)
>
> Sometimes we don't eat until 10 P.M. I'd like to have my daughter in bed and she sometimes does not get to bed until 12 at night. (American)

Some alcoholic husbands vanish for days (or for the entire weekend) and in this way manage to miss all meals for that period:

> Most of the time he would be gone for meals. The kids hardly ever saw him. (American)

Finnish wives voice the same complaints:

> Breakfast was the only meal he attended when drinking. Other meals he skipped. (Finn)
>
> When he is drinking, we don't have breakfast or dinner together because I don't know when he will be home. He can stay away one night or many nights, or he might leave the house at 4 A.M. and go to a cafe where they serve beer. (Finn)

Husbands often explain their absence at meals with the simple statement that they are not hungry or seem to have permanently lost their appetite:

He used to be a good eater . . . but now he doesn't even get up to have breakfast anymore . . . there's no appetite there. None. (American)

The Absence of Sociability at Family Meals. A part of the reason the husband skips family meals may be to avoid talking to his wife and children:

Sometimes, if you are lucky, you can talk about the weather, or you can mention politics . . . mutual friends we don't have any more. We have got sort of a compatible silence that is comfortable now. (American)

Sometimes I try to talk to him during dinner; sometimes I am too angry. Sometimes he mumbles; sometimes he says nothing and is very quiet. (Finn)

The television set, of course, provides one way to eat together while still eating separately:

[Dinner] changed to where it was just sitting in front of the TV set and on a tray. I didn't mind that . . . I thought it was normal . . . I realize now it was not. (American)

Some American husbands do not bother using television programs as an excuse to avoid interaction, but merely pick up their plate and move to another location apart from their family:

Usually he would stand at the counter and eat his meal. (American)

He used to talk a lot and have dinner with us, and now he won't sit at the table; he just goes to the living room and the kids and me sit [at the table] and eat . . . even when sober, he will not eat dinner with us. (American)

Meal Disruptions. Some men make an obvious effort to be with their family during mealtimes, although the meal may be difficult for all concerned because of the trouble he has eating. However, even though mealtime is not necessarily pleasant and convivial, the fact that husbands do try and the family endures their presence is an indication of mutual caring. This is an important factor in the man's ability to maintain sobriety at a later time, as will be seen in the epilogue.

The last few weeks he has been trying hard and he has been sitting down at mealtime. But if he's drinking, the children would rather he didn't eat, because he is so funny at the table. Sometimes he'll gobble the food down, and it's never been like him to do that, or he'll, he just seems to want to get away, both mentally and physically. (American)

> Sometimes he comes to the table . . . he will try to eat a sandwich and he cannot breathe . . . he strangles if he is drinking. (American)

> We really try to eat together, although it's the same thing—he is sometimes not very skilled at eating because he's shaking. Sometimes when the son sees that the father is in bad shape, he tries to eat ahead of us. (Finn)

Another futile ritual is the family dinner that starts out with a drunken husband and ends with an unconscious one. Some women report this as a regular nightly occurrence:

> Usually about 7:30, he will come to the table and, as soon as he starts to eat, he just passes out right at the table. I just leave him there. Clean up the kitchen and go to bed. That is it. (American)

Other men come home, join the family at dinner, and then manage to break up the sociable aspects of the meal with quarreling:

> If he comes to the table drunk, it's cooked too much, or it has too much salt; everything is wrong. There are nights when I couldn't take that and I would say my piece and the children would usually leave the room in tears. (American)

> We ate meals together and it was terrible. They were terrible because he demanded extremely good manners from the children. He chided the older girl who was fat and the boy who ate with bad manners. (Finn)

Effects of Mealtime Problems; Looking for Reasons; Maintaining Role Vestiges; Developing Eating Irregularities

Many wives consider cooking the most creative task of homemaking, in contrast to keeping house, which is seen as offering no lasting achievement (Berheide 1984). Indeed, research on the everyday lives of London housewives, for example, found that a majority selected cooking and serving meals as representing a pleasant challenge. Many were reported to feel this activity offered the possibility of being raised to an art (Oakley 1974:48–59).[8] How does the wife react to a breakdown in as important a part of the family daily round as the evening meal? Her skills as a cook and homemaker are demeaned, as well as her role as an eating companion to her husband. If the wife had assumed that she and her husband would preside over a dinnertime family hour in which children receive both food and parental attention (especially from a father absent all day at work), this ideal too, is shattered.

The connection between food preparation, its proper reception, and the self-image has been noted.[9]

> If etiquette [of eating] is repeatedly violated, one feels spiritually diminished, because of the significance to the self of such violations of the food value system. (Henry 1965:356)

A sardonic discussion of "The Dinner Hour" in *MS Magazine* highlights the meaning of meal preparation to the self-image of the average married woman:

> The feminine mystique about food lingers on. Whether the fare is bean sprouts and brown rice or *navarin frintanier*, for a woman the table is laid with expectations far beyond taste and nutrition. A meal, especially dinner, is supposed to be a creative act, an expression of love, intelligence, and imagination. The reward? Female fulfillment and our household's adoration. In our collective fantasies, family togetherness rises nightly like a perfect souffle. (Dienstag, 1974:15)

The variety of reactions by wives of alcoholics, including their "solutions" to the meal problem, are quite disparate and complex—testimony to the importance of the ritual of preparing and eating food in their lives.

When the pattern of repeated disregard for meals begins to emerge, the wife first looks for explanations of her husband's lack of appetite that do not reflect on her skills as cook or her desirability as a table companion. For instance, if there is any sign that a husband is eating at times other than designated meal periods, a wife will point out that he is "spoiling his appetite":

> [I told him] "You want to eat at three [in the afternoon] so you can go to sleep. You don't want to eat at normal times." (American)

Finnish wives often express the fear that their cooking does not compare to the free hot lunch served by employers in that country:

> We didn't have breakfast together. He left earlier. Three years ago, he didn't want food at all. I got really angry at this. "Well," I said to him, "I don't have as fine food as you have in your place of work. I think it's terrible you blame me for using so much on food. You don't even eat it." Then I cried. (Finn)

A minority of wives make an early connection between their husband's failure to eat and his heavy drinking, not in terms of alcohol as an appetite killer, but rather awareness that food can kill an alcoholic glow:

> I told him, "I know why you don't want to eat . . . at 5:30 or at normal times, because you would spoil your high, and you want to keep that high." (American)

Regardless of the initial reasons wives offer themselves for their husband's declining interest in mealtimes, many women have such a strong sense of duty, or are so reluctant to give up their roles as cooks and nurturant persons to family members, that they cling to meal preparation with a tenacity that often borders on the fanatic, considering the absence of counterrole affirmation and appreciation.[10] (This sort of behavior has many parallels elsewhere in social life, of course. For instance, the fading movie star who clings desperately to an aura of false glamor, the colonialist in an outpost who dresses for dinner although there is no one there to appreciate it, the doctor or lawyer who goes to his office everyday although his practice has dwindled to almost nothing are all loathe to admit to themselves that a role they have enjoyed in the past is no longer viable.)

Some wives change the household eating schedule to suit their husband's appetite or time of arrival. A modification of this approach is to make the meals on time, and then warm up the husband's portion again when he appears. This latter method is used more often when there are young children in the home, while the former on-demand schedule is used when the couple lives alone:

> I don't fix anything until he walks through the door. I have a pressure cooker, and I can cook real fast, like a whole meal in half an hour. (American)
>
> Our eating habits have changed terribly. I used to get up and have breakfast and a light lunch. Now we eat anytime. Sometimes 11 p.m. (American)
>
> He doesn't care about specific hours of eating. He eats when he's hungry. He wants it "at the moment." (Finn)

Other women continue, day after day, year after year, to cook complete meals, "just in case," even though their alcoholic husband seldom comes home to eat, or ignores the food when he is present at mealtimes. These women who fail to adjust the quantity of their cooking to their husband's current low demand say:

> I've always cooked dinner, lunch, and breakfast for four people whether he ate or not. I cooked dinner for four for 19 whole years, and he may have eaten, I would say, just about a year's worth. (American)
>
> I kept on making meals whether he ate them or not. It was a matter of, I guess, pride with me. (Finn)

When wives fix food on a speculative basis, there is always the possibility of waste. Food thrown out uneaten symbolizes all sorts of failures to her: the meal on which she expended time and effort was not wanted or appreciated; money is being spent on food unnecessarily. The bitterness generated can be noted in the following comment:

> I would say [if I didn't make food I have to throw out,] my food bill would be half of what it is. (American)

The link between self-image of these women and meal preparation is obvious from these statements:

> I cooked nice dinners every night . . . I think I did that as a kind of a proof I was maintaining. (American)

> Interviewer: How has his drinking affected your everyday living? Do you buy fewer groceries because he does not eat as much?
> Respondent: No.
> Interviewer: Do you cook better or worse meals?
> Respondent: I cook better ones.
> Interviewer: Why?
> Respondent: I have to prove something to myself, I guess. I'll make the nicest thing I can. My mom helps me out and she will pay for the food. (American)

As time goes on, however, maintenance of the nonreciprocated role of cook and hostess at meals becomes increasingly difficult. There is no one on whom to test role behavior boundaries or to supply positive feedback concerning dishes prepared. The wife's role has become a mere vestige, interacting with ghost counterrole personnel of the past. It is not surprising then that the behavior of some wives becomes increasingly bizarre. One wife maintained both her pride as a cook and her feelings of anger toward her husband by cooking meals daily, but not always calling (or waking) her husband to tell him that dinner was served!

> I cooked for all four of us. He might be upstairs and I made him come to dinner. Or, if I was mad enough, I would not wake him. I might wake him one time and another time I might not. (American)

Without the incentive of someone to join them at a regularly scheduled meal, some wives of alcoholics begin to eat at odd times. Some gain weight because they consume more food as a compensation for the unhappiness of their marital situation (Charles & Kerr 1986) or merely to use up the leftovers. Others claim they are too upset to eat much of anything and so lose weight. Still others stop cooking, or avoid eating with their husband even when they have a chance. Those who prepare for two and then hate to see the food wasted say:

> He would not eat the meals I fixed for him, and I would end up eating his and mine. (American)

The noneaters claimed to be either too upset to eat or to lack the appetite for food:

[While I waited for him] I was too upset to eat. I mean I couldn't have sat down and eaten a meal. (American)

I was down to 78 pounds. I just couldn't eat. My psychiatrist said I had to start eating, whether my husband came to meals or not. (American)

Finally, I became so upset about his not eating that I broke out in a rash all over my body. My doctor said I had to start eating balanced meals. (American)

Finnish wives also report that they lost their appetites when their husband stopped eating meals with them on a regular basis:

Anyway, some of the time he ate and sometimes he had drunk too much and didn't. I didn't know what to expect. It made me very nervous. I didn't know how much to prepare for. I could hardly eat myself. (Finn)

For other women, the repeated disappointment of fixing food for someone who rarely can be counted on to appear at mealtime takes a different toll. These wives began to dislike cooking; they turn to convenience foods for the children; they stop making balanced meals; some forgo any cooking at all and take their children to eat at fast-food restaurants:

I've gotten so that I don't feel that I want to cook a lot of times. I have gotten so that I hate that time of day. (American)

He rarely eats with the family, so I fix a lot of hot dogs and things that the kids like . . . that are quick to prepare. I used to love to fix the tablecloth and set the table, but I got discouraged because he would never join us, and you know an important part of enjoying [a meal] is having the people that are going to enjoy it. (American)

I used to feel more like cooking. [Now] I just don't feel like fixing food anymore. (Finn)

As the problem continues, men are not the only ones who practice avoidance at meals. Women whose husband joins them at the family meal but then ruins the occasion in some way or another begin to find other locations in which to eat:

I take my plate and eat in the kitchen, or sit where I could read the paper, but I don't want to sit at the table with him. (American)

Of course, he could not keep anything down. A lot of times he could not keep coffee down or I would hear him attempting to and it would come back up again. For my own self-defense . . . I leave and go to a restaurant and have a good breakfast. (American)

Some wives would reschedule their mealtimes so as to ensure that they would eat alone:

> Sometimes I limit myself to two meals, like a late breakfast and then, if I work six to nine, I have something just before I go to work. (American)

Ultimately, as with the absence of conversation, most women resolve the problem of meals by withdrawing all concern over whether their husband eats, or what time he arrives to eat. These wives may make a meal for themselves, and for the children, if there are any. If the wife continues to make meals, she does not bother to heat up food when her husband comes home late. Some even fail to leave their husband some cold leftovers. This unruffled mien is often managed through the aid of Al-Anon:

> After Al-Anon, when he wasn't home, I still went ahead and fed the kids . . . and [it] depends on what kind of mood I was in whether I was going to leave that food on the stove or not. I got tired of having to do dishes at ten o'clock at night . . . [or] having last night's dishes to face in the morning. (American)
>
> I ate earlier with the child. I never fixed him anything. I told him if he had money to drink, he had money to eat. (Finn)

In this way, a major family ritual atrophies to the point where it is ignored by all, and with it, if anthropologists are right, a major linchpin of family unity is gone.

Comparison of Meals in Families Where Alcoholism Is Not a Problem

Comparing the meal problem of wives of alcoholics with family meal complaints from wives living in households where alcohol is not a problem, the difference heavy drinking makes is quite dramatic. Family meals, are, for the most part, still viable in the more "average" households. Where the husbands are not heavy drinkers, the wives are able to get their spouse to dinner on time, to eat normally, and to make civil conversation. There is no indication of the frantic attempt to hold onto the role of cook; it is obviously not in the serious jeopardy felt by wives of drinking men.

As Table 6.2 indicates, there are some major differences between eating patterns of families in which the husband is not an alcoholic and those in which he is. In the former case, almost half of the wives report that the husband is present at family dinners, and only one in ten wives complains that her husband cannot be counted on for meals. Looking at the substance of the wife's concerns in families where alcohol is not a problem, it is obvious that some do have complaints about husbandly mealtime behavior, but their unhappiness is neither profound, nor is it focused on a few serious problems, as is the case of wives of heavily drinking men.

Table 6.2.   Husband's Attendance at Family Meals

General Pattern of Meals Together	American wives where alcohol is not a problem (N = 63)* %	Wives of Alcoholics	
		American (N = 76) %	Finnish (N = 50) %
Two or more meals a day	21	21	22
Dinner (or supper) only	48	17	22
Breakfast only	5	8	8
No meals together most of the time	2	24	16
Irregular schedule; husband cannot be counted on for meals	9	20	30
Husband and wife eat many meals together on weekends	21	—	—
Miscellaneous (sporadic eating habits of family; diet problems, etc.)	5	10	2

* Answers add to more than 100 percent because some of these couples also eat many meals together on weekends.

Cautionary note: This table is for *general comparison purposes only* of major sample and sub-sample responses. That is, the percentages shown are not based on results to a standardized questionnaire (see Methodology), but rather, on depth interviewing data which allow a great deal of latitude to the respondent in answering fairly open-ended questions. Thus, in addition to the usual variance assumed for in small samples, the approach to gathering the data must be taken into consideration. Nevertheless, the comparisons are useful—especially where there are (a) large differences, or (b) where the respondents offer qualitatively different answers to the same question.

One of the most frequent complaints of women married to non-alcoholics is that mealtimes have a harried atmosphere because of the presence of small children at the table:

> Because my kids talk a whole lot, you know, and by the time it comes dinnertime, I've had it with the kids, my husband has had it with the kids, the kids are there yakking and you're going, "Oh, quiet, can't you just shut up?" (WNA)

Others would like a more relaxed atmosphere at family meals, with time for small talk and a bit of gracious living:

> I'd like to be more relaxed, enjoying meals, talk, be a family together . . . say how your day went at work or any problems you have . . . discuss things at the table . . . you know, get our problems out while we're still right there as a bunch, instead of being quiet and not relaxed. (WNA)

Other wives in marriages where alcohol is not a problem mention that they tire of cooking and would like to eat out, or they get tired of their husband watching some sports event on television during mealtime. A substantial number of women who are married to men with no drinking problem said that there were no improvements they would like to see in family mealtime. Their statements are in sharp contrast with the descriptions of mealtimes in homes where the husband is an alcoholic:

> I don't know. Our mealtimes are happy and I really cannot think of a thing that I'd like to change, really. Sometimes, we get in a small argument at dinner time, but not usually. (WNA)

> No [no change]. That is one area where we really seem to enjoy our time the most. (WNA)

The Quality of Joint Recreation in Marriages

In most Western industrial societies, men and women who have more than a passing interest in each other usually deepen and cement their relationship by the joint recreational activity referred to as dating or going together. Recreational compatibility actually plays a crucial and initial role in mate selection, for it is in the context of leisure activities that a couple usually first find themselves to be what they define as "compatible."[11] Later, as Allen and Donnelly (1983) note, family recreation also helps cement feelings of family unity.

In almost all discussions of leisure time activities, however, the need for a partner is taken for granted because a partner is usually a primary structural component. Without a partner, a person often cannot join in the activities or, if he/she can participate, it is done with less personal enjoyment than would have been the case had another person been present to share the fun. Many recreational events (e.g., dancing, bridge, tennis,) are fashioned around partner participation. Other activities such as movies, picnics, and camping are difficult to enjoy without being in the company of at least one familiar, friendly person who heightens the pleasure of the experience by comments, reactions, and joint participation. Anyone who has traveled alone, gone to movies alone, or eaten dinner in a restaurant alone can testify to the increased pleasure a companion can bring to these occasions. Most people take for granted that one advantage of marriage is a dependable companion for social or recreational events.

Wives of alcoholics complain a great deal about the fact that their social life gradually atrophies as their spouse's alcohol problem increases. Eventually, say many of these women, they have little or no outside recreation. Like husband-wife communication and shared meals, the absence of leisure time together is a serious loss.

Although the prime importance of joint recreational activities in the marital dyad fades over time and other, more crucial areas of living gain in importance, the companionship of a husband in whatever recreation is attempted is still close to being a necessity for the wife. A woman can keep house, raise children, work at a job, cook, and maintain many "married activities" alone. However, it is more difficult for her to have fun successfully without a partner, and her married status poses problems in finding a substitute.

The ultimate impact of heavy alcohol ingestion by one partner on the social life of both spouses can be clearly seen when joint recreation is compared with spouses for whom alcohol is not a problem. For instance, while less than 5% of wives of alcoholics in both the United States and Finland say that they have many occasions of joint recreation with their husbands, 80% of women in the control sample claim they and their husbands enjoy numerous joint activities. (The same proportion also have separate activities—in contrast to the 5% of wives of alcoholics who claim any individual recreational activities, indicating how alcoholism cuts into all aspects of social life.)

Effects of Heavy Drinking on Social Activities and Recreation

As pundit-poet Ogden Nash commented on the role of alcohol in oiling the wheels of sociability, "Candy is dandy but Liquor is quicker." Parallel with the apparent positive effects of alcohol ingestion on conversation and enjoyment of food, a little liquor enhances periods of sociability and recreation; a great deal, on the other hand, annihilates both interest and ability. This connection between heavy drinking and reduction in recreational activities is, indeed, one more paradox concerning the effects of alcohol.

Although frowned on during actual sports participation, the "nineteenth hole" in golf and "apres ski" in the snow country are well-known after-sports libation periods. Yet the very ingredient that often seems to ensure a good, relaxed time eventually can destroy participation when taken in increased amounts.

Heavy drinking has a significant effect on social interaction. Being sociable and taking part in recreational events with others means being agreeable and communicative. Heavy drinking makes these behaviors difficult to maintain. A great deal of alcohol ingestion renders the drinker physically unable to handle him-/herself properly, even within the relaxed norms of party behavior. Drunken activity can include rudeness, lascivious conduct, and regurgitation. Even more drinking results in passing out, i.e., losing consciousness entirely. Such behavior, if repeated often enough to gain the drinker a reputation, results in a reduced number of invitations to future recreational events. Gradually, social life becomes quite truncated. Recreation and/or social events become an increasingly problematic area of living for both the alcoholic and his wife. Ultimately, the result is practically no social life at all for either of them.

Such an outcome is linked to the various complaints the wife of an alcoholic has about her marriage. As Kelly (1975) notes an ongoing leisure career is dependent on stability in the roles of participants. The disintegration that is taking place in the marital roles of wives and their alcoholic husbands substantially undermines this base for enjoying leisure together. Furthermore, his public antics while drunk further reduce the possibility for future joint enjoyment.

The Recurrence of Scenes. Inasmuch as a great many leisure time activities involve the company of others or the use of public facilities, one of the first problems the wife of an alcoholic reports is the embarrassment her husband causes when drunk in public or at some social event.[12] For her, early fun is clouded by the almost certain knowledge that social disaster lurks nearby. A heavy-drinking husband gradually becomes drunk; the evening may end with an argument, or some other form of unpleasant behavior. He may fall asleep or pass out. When such scenes become almost inevitable, these women begin to dread social events. They describe the stress of expecting unpleasant and embarrassing occasions during sociability this way:

> We will go over [to her sister's house] to play cards, and he leaves a bottle of booze there and he mixes drinks for himself and we always get in an argument over something. . . . I often wish I had to go to work [then] because [I know] it will be another one of those weekends. (American)

> Sometimes we would go out for a drive . . . [or] to the beach . . . but whenever we went anywhere he always had to stop and get a couple of six-packs or something, so it really wasn't any fun for me because I knew that at the end of the day it would end up in a big fight or something always. (American)

These past performances of alcoholics at social events result in fewer and fewer invitations as hosts begin to protect their gatherings and occasions (Goffman 1963:198). Wives, fearing the worst, begin to skip social engagements that may reveal their husbands as drunks. Eventually, social life with friends becomes a thing of the past (Jackson 1973:56–58):

> Everything evolved from the fact that we could not go out to dinner because he would get drunk. We could not have company because he would get drunk. I could not go anywhere because he would get drunk. I could not go on vacation because when he was taking two weeks off from work, he was drunk at ten o'clock in the morning, and where do you want to go with somebody who is drunk? (American)

We had some friends before he started drinking so much, but now we don't have any because we don't go any place. (Finn)

Earlier . . . we were able to invite guests and go somewhere, but later it wasn't possible, so all social contacts were abandoned. (Finn)

Drinking husbands also tend to prefer the company of less critical others; thus, more and more of their socializing is done away from home, with drinking friends rather than with their wife and family friends. This appears to be especially true in Finland (Haavio-Mannila and Holmila 1986). Spouses take less pleasure in each other's company; the wife, because she fears a drunken scene at the end of the event, and the husband, because he can sense her censure and anxiety. The end result is a dramatic reduction in joint social life.

Effects on Interest in Social and Recreational Events.   Continuous heavy drinking reduces the energy level, leaving the drinker without the motivation necessary for either planning or participating in recreation. Excessive drinking, rather than heightening pleasure in external events, takes the edge off them; as a result, sitting in a chair and doing nothing or going to sleep is more attractive to the heavy drinker than the exertion of social or recreational activities. Those wives who ascribe their husband's lack of interest in leisure activities to a low energy level due to drinking say the following:

We just don't have any recreation anymore because he is too tired or doesn't want to do what I want to do, or something, and we cannot come to an agreement on it. (American)

He will try to do something, but when he is drinking . . . it does not last. By the time he has had two or three cans [of beer], he comes in here and falls asleep (Finn)

Those who talk about the drinker's apparent reduced enjoyment of events say:

He doesn't seem to enjoy the things we do together anymore. He gets bored and irritable in no time. (American)

He's not interested in going anywhere with me. He really feels more comfortable at home. (Finn)

When this point is reached, it extends into the alcoholic's sober periods as well. Many wives point out that even when their husband is sober, he seems to have no energy beyond such activities as going to the grocery store with his wife or working in the yard.

Like the cessation of talk and attendance at meals, the symbolic meanings attached to a husband's behavior in the area of recreation affect the wife's self-image as a person whose company is desirable—either to her husband or to others. First of all, since recreational activities are voluntary (as contrasted, for instance, with employment), a spouse's choice of companionship during free time is an indicator of the company he or she enjoys. It is not surprising, then, that wives interpret their alcoholic husband's reluctance (or inability) to engage in joint recreation as a sign that the relationship is failing. Added to this is the personal stigma a wife feels as a result of her husband's public behavior. When her marriage partner makes a fool or spectacle of himself, it reflects on her, her choice of mate, and her ability to help him control himself. The gradual reduction and ultimate cessation of invitations can also be interpreted as the desertion of her by her friends, as well as their understandable avoidance of her husband and his drunken antics.

When these women talk about the effects of the loss of a social life as a result of their husband's drinking, they speak of their fears that the man has lost interest in their companionship, that the loss of a joint social life affects their whole marital relationship, and that they feel ill at ease with their friends now and so have become doubly reclusive:

> We have done nothing together since we have come to California—about three years ago . . . I just feel that he does not enjoy me as a person. (American)

> Earlier I did have friends and organizations, but now I've lost the wish to spend a healthy life, because even if people are not talking [about the husband's drinking], I am ashamed. (Finn)

Comparison with Recreation in Homes Where Alcohol Is Not a Problem

When alcoholism does not cloud the relationship between spouses, the joint recreation that wives describe is so varied and qualitatively these women sound so much happier about their leisure time activities that the contrast with the complaints of wives of alcoholics is both sharp and poignant. Wives whose husbands are not problem drinkers describe mutual activities with their spouse and family:

> In the summertime we go to the beach, and football games [are at the] head of the list. Well, we like to go out to dinner. We like to go dancing once in awhile. We like to go to dinner, just the two of us, but my husband likes to take out our daughter too, once in a while. Mostly in the summertime, it is just the beach. Nothing too exciting, and some people would think our lives dull, but I don't. (WNA)

> We go camping. We have a camper. And we go and play cards at some friends' houses, or go out to dinner together. (WNA)

We used to go camping, we are in the motel stage now—no more camping. We go swimming or to the show. He is not much for a play, but if I get tickets for a play, he will go. He would probably like to go bowling, but he won't go without me. (WNA)

We go out to dinners and games, football games, or sports, maybe theatre; sometimes we go to the symphony, [and] some of the plays occasionally. (WNA)

Note that the difference in quantity, as well as quality of recreation is marked in Table 6.3.

A substantial number of wives speak proudly of the fact that they and their husband share all of their recreations:

Oh, we don't do anything separately. There were times, that, oh, I'd say earlier in our marriage, the first two or three years, he belonged to a club and that was about the only time that he'd go . . . why if I want to do anything like a sewing class, I do it during the daytime so that it doesn't interfere with our being together. (WNA)

A great many of these husbands and wives have separate recreational activities, but in many cases the wives report this with little or no rancor:

Table 6.3.   Recreation with Husbands as Assessed by Wives of Alcoholics and Wives in Marriages where Alcohol is not a Problem

Nature of Recreational Activities	American wives where alcohol is not a problem (N = 63)* %	Wives of Alcoholics	
		American (N = 76) %	Finnish (N = 50) %
Many or several joint recreation activities	81	4	—
Husband and wife also prefer some separate activities	80	6	—
Only a few joint activities	—	56	62
Little or no activities together	18	34	38

* Answers add to more than 100 percent because of multiple answers.
Cautionary note: This table is for *general comparison purposes only* of major sample and subsample responses. That is, the percentages shown are not based on results to a standardized questionnaire (see Methodology), but rather, on depth interviewing data which allow a great deal of latitude to the respondent in answering fairly open-ended questions. Thus, in addition to the usual variance assumed for in small samples, the approach to gathering the data must be taken into consideration. Nevertheless, the comparisons are useful— especially where there are (a) large differences, or (b) where the respondents offer qualitatively different answers to the same question.

I shop with my girlfriends, or he will go up and have a drink with a buddy or something on the way home from work. He may bowl with a friend. (WNA)

We do most recreation separately. He has his poker and baseball . . . half-day boat rides to fish, and I have Tupperware parties and home parties, and things like that we do separately. (WNA)

An interesting difference, then, between the wives married to alcoholics and those who are not is that in addition to the absence of joint recreation in the marriages of wives of alcoholics, neither spouse does much on his or her own either. On the other hand, where alcohol is not a problem, both spouses do many things together, as well as maintaining separate activities. Some women complain that their husbands have no outside interests or hobbies and are always "underfoot," but the complaint lacks the unhappy quality of those made by wives of alcoholics.

Sexual Problems in Marriages

A significant aspect of the marital dyad is that it includes a sexual relationship. The quality of this area of marriage is, in turn, determined by the way sex partners are sensitive to each other's needs. Sexual satisfaction plays an integral part in a woman's assessment of her marriage, and since the advent of the women's movement, wives have become more outspoken on this issue.[13] Concern about sexual relations figures quite prominently in lists of problem areas of persons unhappily married or those who feel the need of counseling for their marriage.[14]

Wives of alcoholics often voice bitter complaints about the sexual and affective areas of the marriage. Either their husband has become rough and/or undesirable sex partners, or the man has stopped approaching them for intercourse altogether. Either behavior is seen as cause for concern and grief.

There are definitely both qualitative and quantitative differences in sexual relations and sexual problems in marriages where the husband is a heavy drinker compared to those where alcohol is not a problem. The latter group of wives mention dissatisfactions with sex that span a rather wide range. These types of discontent seem much less serious than the more focused list of complaints of wives of alcoholics. Women married to problem drinkers have specific complaints rather than vague feelings of discontent or wishes for more affection, or for more or less intercourse. In fact, the range and seriousness of the assessments of sexual relations in both samples is radically different, making simple com-

Table 6.4a.   Wives in Marriages where Alcohol is not a Problem: Assessment
of Sexual Relations with Husbands

Assessment of sexual relations with husband	Wives who discussed sex in marriage (N = 63) %
Sexual relations good; satisfying, no problems	29
Sexual relations fair; some problems—vague feelings of discontent, need for more information	8
Sexual relations poor; have serious problems (wide variety mentioned)	17
Have had temporary sexual problems	3
Wife wishes for more affection, emotional satisfaction with sex	8
Wife dissatisfied with frequency; either too often or too infrequent	14
No change in sexual relations needed, not specific	3
Miscellaneous changes desired	10
No answer	8

Cautionary note: This table is for *general comparison purposes only* of major sample and sub-sample responses. That is, the percentages shown are not based on results to a standardized questionnaire (see Methodology), but rather, on depth interviewing data which allow a great deal of latitude to the respondent in answering fairly open-ended questions. Thus, in addition to the usual variance assumed for in small samples, the approach to gathering the data must be taken into consideration. Nevertheless, the comparisons are useful—especially where there are (a) large differences, or (b) where the respondents offer qualitatively different answers to the same question.

parison impossible, and calling for two tables, rather than one. (See Tables 6.4a and 6.4b.)

Among the wives of alcoholics, one-third complained that sex with their husband is repugnant to them and one-third complained that their husband either is not interested in sex or could not perform. On the other hand, one-third of wives in marriages where alcohol is not a problem claimed their sex relations were good and the other two-thirds had a variety of complaints that were quite different from the spouses of drinking husbands. They talk, for instance, about dissatisfaction with the frequency of lovemaking, a sense of discontent with sex relations, and the desire for more emotional satisfaction—matters that wives of alcoholics apparently do not see as applicable to them.

Table 6.4b. Wives of Alcoholics: Assessment of Sexual Relations with
Husbands

	American (N = 76) %		Finnish (N = 50) %	
Husband repels wife when drunk; is too disgusting to have intercourse with	12	} 35	10	} 18
Wife feels basic change in relationship; too angry, upset to have intercourse with husband	23		8	
Husband interested but can't perform	6	} 35	2	} 6
Husband not interested in sex	29		4	
No volunteered complaints about sexual relations	30		76**	

** Inasmuch as wives of alcoholics were allowed to bring up areas of marital discontent
voluntarily, it might be that excessive Finnish shyness (claimed by Finns as a national
characteristic) accounts for the low proportion of complaints in the area of sex.

Cautionary note: This table is for *general comparison purposes only* of major sample and sub-
sample responses. That is, the percentages shown are not based on results to a standardized questionnaire (see Methodology), but rather, on depth interviewing data which allow
a great deal of latitude to the respondent in answering fairly open-ended questions. Thus,
in addition to the usual variance assumed for in small samples, the approach to gathering
the data must be taken into consideration. Nevertheless, the comparisons are useful—
especially where there are (a) large differences, or (b) where the respondents offer
qualitatively different answers to the same question.

Sexual Problems of Wives of Sexually Active Alcoholics

Alcoholics as Repugnant Sexual Partners. Like many other activities in
social life, sexual intercourse has its esthetics—varying by cultural
norms, past experiences, and present expectations. Sexual attraction
and/or repugnance is connected to some delicate and some not so delicate erotic feelings. Wives of alcoholics whose husband is still sexually
active[15] claim that many characteristics of a man when drunk make him
a particularly undesirable sex partner:

Well, who wants to make love to a stinking alcoholic? Alcoholics are very
selfish people . . . it is all for him and it is not a partnership kind of thing.
(American)

An alcoholic with sour alcohol on their breath . . . that's pretty foul to be
kissing . . . so I just peck him . . . so actually there our marriage is going
downhill. (American)

Alcohol has not affected his potency and virility. But who wants to have

anything to do with a stinking husband who is half-drunk? I can't go to
bed with anyone unless I have peace of mind. (Finn)

The only time he is interested in sex is when he is repulsive and drunk. He
disgusted me—so I quit having relations with him. (Finn)

Methods of Avoidance.   Wives in both Finland and the United States
who are repulsed by their drinking husband's sexual advances react in
one of the following ways: (1) they refuse intercourse entirely (presumably until he stops his heavy drinking); (2) they refuse intercourse when
he is drunk and cooperate when he is sober; (3) they do not refuse sexual
relations, but rather endure his lovemaking without pleasure.

Wives who refuse intercourse with their alcoholic husband because of
the heavy drinking explain:

> When he is drunk and . . . or . . . coming out of it, before he is all the way
> spaced out, he may become, if he is not being abusive, he may become
> really superaffectionate. Well, that's neat when you're not drunk. But, I
> just pull away from him—won't have anything to do with him. That's
> probably the only situation in which I do that—so it's obvious to him why.
> (American)

Additionally, the hurt feelings and the sense of repugnance some
wives develop during their husband's drinking periods cannot be easily
sloughed off the moment their spouse sobers up:

> Like this morning, he put his arm around me . . . he did not get drunk
> yesterday, he may have been drinking earlier, but I love him. I don't know
> if I love him now or feel sorry for him or what . . . I am very confused
> myself, but he put his arm around me and I didn't push him away. I
> cuddled next to him, *but certainly could not have made love with him.*
> (American) (emphasis mine)

One woman said the bad feeling generated by the drinking has to be
neutralized by "talking it over" before she can have intercourse:

> I won't make out unless we make up . . . unless we have talked and I feel
> good . . . because if he makes overtures, and we haven't [had sex] because
> he has been drunk a couple of days . . . and neither of us has talked about
> it . . . I don't feel good, because to me sex is my expression of my love for
> [him], not just a thing. (American)

Thus, wives describe their sexual problem not as a lack of love, but as
an inability to respond. They just cannot return affectionate gestures,
even if they want to:

> It has become more and more frequent that he does drink and more
> and more frequent that I don't want sex with him. During that year I

was having problems with myself and that [sex] was the last thing on my mind . . . just the last thing. I'm sure this has limited his ability. (American)

For those wives whose husband beats them or abuses them in other ways, the thought of having sexual relations very soon after such treatment is also impossible:

He thinks I should go to bed with him after he abuses me and threatens to kill me, that I should go to bed and have sex with him, and I won't. This is his life as far as he is concerned . . . there is no way I'm going to do it—I can't. I will not have him touch me. (American)

Wives of alcoholics also revert to age-old methods of avoiding intercourse:

I would pretend to be asleep, or tell him to be quiet because the children were sleeping in the next room. (American)

When he came home drunk I'd be in bed and try to give the impression I was deeply in sleep. My heart would jump when I learned how each bang [caused by noise he made in the house] meant how drunk he was. (Finn)

Women also admit they withhold sex vindictively as punishment for their husband's drinking and staying away from home:

Of course, now I feel resentful when he does [want to have sexual relations] because I guess I'm feeling sorry for myself and I want to get back at him still. There is still the feeling that I want to get even and make him pay. (American)

When he was out for two or three days drunk or something, I'd be sitting home thinking, "I'm not going to give him any tonight because he's gonna come and want it and I'm not gonna do it." It was a selfish thing. I'd say, well, he's been out all day today. How do I know who he's been with? That's what would go through my mind. Then I'd think he's probably been with women who got him all aroused and he's gonna come and use me? I'd stay up until I'd hear him in the driveway and then run and get in bed and pretend I was asleep. (American)

As an alternative to an on-the-spot, situational rejection, many wives move out of the bedroom or bed of their husband, thus making it clear that they are not interested in sex at any time.

A few women enjoy sex with their husband when he is sober, although they are repulsed by it when he is drunk. These women manage somehow to have a fairly good sexual relationship, although their preference would be more periods of sobriety and more sex (notwithstanding the fact that their numbers are small, their importance will be seen in a later discussion of alcoholic men who are able to maintain sobriety):

There is less sex in our relationship. I have no interest in sex when he's drunk. But when he's sober, I feel loving towards him. I welcome his advances. (American)

Our sexual relations are all right, but when he was drunk, I avoided him. I didn't want to kiss him. He smelled of wine. He was so awful then, I hated him. But when he was sober, I forgot everything. (Finn)

Some American wives who are sexually turned off by their husband report they cooperate with his advances out of duty, fear, or the practical knowledge that it is easier to get it over with quickly than argue at great length as to why sex is being refused:

I'd say the majority of the time I'd just give in and figure that was the easy way to get around it. Rather than argue now about this or about something else, I'd just go ahead and please him and just get it over with. (American)

Oh, I suffered . . . [it was] just absolutely devastating to me, because I would physically want to cooperate with him, but I would mentally not want to cooperate with him—and God! (American)

He was the kind of person that really had a strong sex drive . . . and when he was drunk he wanted it all of the time. I couldn't stand being close to him. . . but I couldn't fight with him. I was pretty scared of him after all the things that happened, so, I think I'd rather have given in than get beat up. What he wanted, he got. (American)

I realize [if] I want to get a night's sleep I have to tolerate something. Can I tolerate twenty minutes, [or] am I going to fight for six hours and not get any sleep? (American)

Effects of Alcoholism on Sexual Interests and Abilities; Loss of Interest; Development of Impotence

As heavy alcohol ingestion continues year after year, drinking men experience a considerable loss of ability to perform and enjoy the sex act, as well as a reduced interest in it even if they are still functioning (Turner and Dudek 1982; Lemere & Smith 1973). A substantial number of alcoholic men are reported by their wives to have a diminished sex drive and/or interest in intercourse, gauged by the frequency with which they approached their spouses for sex. Wives assume heavy drinking to be the cause of this attrition of sexual performance, although some wives indicate awareness that this loss of interest may also be compounded by age as well:

He does not like sex near as much as I do. Let's put it that way. It's because of his drinking. I know that he does not get it anywhere else. He is just not that interested in it. He usually says he is too tired [for sex]. So then I just drop it. (American)

> When he is home, he is sleeping all the time, and he is not interested in sex. When he is awake he is drinking. (Finn)

> The mistress he once had is out of the picture. He says he is too tired to get a new one. I wish he would. Some activity on his part might benefit me, too. (Finn)

If wives show sexual aggressiveness—not waiting for their husband's initiation—their approaches are often rebuffed:

> He would say [when the wife brought up the matter of sex], "To hell with it . . . forget it," and he would just go to sleep. (American)

Wives say this decreased interest in physical intimacy is of great concern to them, and they often turn to their husband for an explanation, or to others for help:

> I asked him, "What happened? You're not interested in sex anymore." I tell him this when he is sober, on the way to work, when he can't run from it, when he's in the car. I'll mention the fact that he used excuses and says, "I'm tired," or he'll say, "I go to bed earlier than you do. You stay up and watch the news." But if I am in the mood I will just wake him up. Sometimes he cooperates, sometimes he doesn't. Sometimes he'll just say, "Go to sleep. I'm tired." (American)

Finnish wives also mention that they are the ones to question the reduction in the sexual interest by their husband:

> When I told the psychiatrist that we had intercourse only four times a year he said that this happens very often [with alcoholic husbands], but that most women just don't say anything. (Finn)

Some wives suspect their husband's lack of interest in them sexually means that the man is having intercourse with other women:

> I'm sure he had other women, so he was not as interested in me. That made me resentful toward him and . . . cold to him. (American)

A few inquiring wives receive the ultimate blow. Their husband informs them that their lack of sexual attractiveness is the reason for absence of interest in intercourse:

> He used to say I didn't turn him on anymore. (American)

Other women say their husband is affectionate with them, try to make love to them, but cannot manage to get or maintain an erection:

Well, he can't keep an erection, or even with an erection, having any
success during it. (American)
He is warm and loving until we go to the bedroom and then it's all over.
(American)

A few wives experience so many failures with their husband that they
feel certain he is irrevocably impotent as the result of heavy drinking.

It [the sex life] is null and void, period, for the last year and a half. He's
just impotent, that's all . . . between the drinking and diabetes, and everything put together. (American)
Sexually, he is an old man. (Finn)

The absence of sex can last for months, even years. Sometimes wives
mentally mark the time elapsed since their husband last had intercourse
with them:

We just haven't had any sex for two months. . . . I know that alcoholics do
have sex problems. (American)
Sexually, forget it! We went without sex for a long, long time. For about
seven years. (American)

Other wives stop keeping count and speak of the loss of marital sex in
terms that sound final, as though they have little or no hope of ever
reestablishing the relationship. They fear he is impotent.

While one might assume that the onset of impotence in male alcoholics results from a combination of drinking and age, the effect of
interaction between the husband and wife in the intervening years cannot be overlooked as an inhibiting factor in the husband's ability to
perform.

An alcoholic man may still retain sexual interests and abilities. Lemere
and Smith (1973) note that only 8% of 17,000 patients in treatment for
alcoholism complained of impotence. However, as noted, drinking
causes the man to become a less desirable sex partner to his wife—a fact
that she communicates to him either by her obvious reluctance to go to
bed with him or by her outright refusal to do so. This message, coupled
with signs of a decline in the ability to maintain an erection, may have a
circular effect that compounds the sexual problems of both partners. The
downward spiral of their disaffection and defection from each other,
springing from these two factors, seems difficult to ameliorate once it is
in operation. Sex drives appear to be reduced from lack of practice as
well as from the effects of heavy drinking. Wives who had complained
about their husband's lack of sexual appeal while drinking become, in
later years, hurt and puzzled by the drop in their husband's interest in

them. Hurt feelings of both spouses resist healing. Thus, cause and effect may be intertwined and difficult to distinguish.[16]

The following quotes illustrate this circularity:

> Well, [the lack of sex] at first . . . was through my choice. I used all the female tactics you know. "I've got a headache; I've got a backache! Leave me alone I'm tired," I mean the whole bit. I did have headaches, but mostly I think it's because I just didn't want him to touch me. I was just so furious at him. I was so upset inside myself. . . . So, I'd just say, "I'm tired," you know, rather than a fight. But now it seems that he, himself, [would] just as soon leave me alone, just as well as I leave him alone. (American)

> His drinking has affected our sexual relationship. Well, earlier when he came home drunk and wanted to have intercourse with me, I refused. Then last winter, he was not interested at all, even if I wanted to. (Finn)

The actual mechanics of the sexual disaffection between spouses are complex and difficult to isolate. Further, it is quite possible that they change as the processes of the sexual relationship, already complex in the feelings they generate, take on different symbolic meanings as alienation escalates. Wives claim that the husband's drinking causes them to lose feelings of love; they also find themselves unable to be spontaneously affectionate but, rather, are beset by repulsion and resentment caused by the excessive drinking and drunken behavior.[17] Wives of alcoholics find also that other occurrences during the day—disagreements and hurt feelings—spill over into the sexual relationship and change its form. These changes are not mutually exclusive, but cumulative, and it becomes increasingly difficult for the wife to act loving when she does not feel loving. It is difficult for a husband to be repeatedly rejected without lashing back in anger or ceasing to try:

> He stopped drinking and wanted sex, but I couldn't. No. I was still full of resentment and hatred. (American)

> I can wake up the next morning and find him next to me [after one of his drinking binges], and if I don't get out of bed in a hurry, because I'm angry, I know what's going to take place. I decided to let him know [and I said], "Please don't touch me," and out of bed I went. (American)

> We have sex twice a month. He said, "Well, if I had anybody decent to sleep with, it would be different." (American)

> He couldn't reach a climax. He tried and tried and finally acted angry with me and [said] why wasn't I sexy like the neighbor next door. (American)

The same escalation can have another beginning. The husband can avoid sex until the wife loses interest:

So I'm sitting here and will go to bed and even sometimes when he hasn't been drinking and he'll go to bed . . . and hold me in his arms for a minute and kiss me and he'll say, "I've got to sleep; I'm really tired tonight." Or he'll start saying that even before going to bed, "Gee, I'm beat," and I try making a joke of it and say, "Gee, you sound just like a woman." Immediately he flared at me. He didn't like that at all. And I have found that my feelings for him as far as sex are concerned . . . there are times now I cannot respond the way I should. (American)

A man's performance may be affected by the fact that his wife was cool to his advances and even expressed distaste. His performance problems may, in turn, further alienate her from him as a sex partner:

I just wasn't going to bed with the smelly old drunk. . . . They have a hard time reaching climax. They just have a hard time releasing. And an hour and a half is just getting a little ridiculous; and you're just sitting there and getting madder and madder by the minute. (American)

He would try, and then fail, and I would just be upset; so after a few failures, I don't even bother trying. Don't bother me. There have been a few harsh words about it, but I have my ways of avoiding him. (American)

The Unique Aspects of Sexual Problems of Alcoholic Men. It seems obvious that those spouses in marriages where the husband is an alcoholic have sexual problems that bear the unique stamp of that problem. First, the wife is unresponsive to a drunken husband. He, in turn, is hurt by her absence of interest and her obvious avoidance of sex with him, and begins to find her a less than desirable sex partner. Long-term alcohol ingestion takes its toll on his sexual interests and abilities, and his wife is unable to be the kind of sexual partner who might rekindle interest. Where she was once upset by unwanted drunken advances, she now is hurt by his lack of interest and upset by his inability to perform or reach climax. Gradually sexual relations between the two atrophy.

Comparison of Sexual Problems in Marriages
Where Alcohol Is Not a Problem

The variety of reactions to the quality of sexual relations within marriage by women whose husbands are not problem drinkers is in stark contrast to the greatly narrowed range (both in intensity and in type) of complaints offered when wives of alcoholics discuss their sexual problems with their husbands.

Not surprisingly, considering current trends, approximately two-thirds of wives of men who are not alcoholics consider themselves to have some sexual problems in their marriage. Descriptions by wives vary from those portraying sex between themselves and their husband as good but not great to those that say it is quite satisfactory. Some wives complain that sex with their husband is more a physical act for him than an emotional one, and that they would like more affection. Others discuss disappointment with the frequency of intercourse. Either their husband wants sex too often, from their point of view, or not often enough. However, their complaints lack the bitterness and resignation of wives of alcoholics.

Among those wives who consider the sexual relationship with their husband to be good, the following are examples of the many factors that go to make up for satisfaction in this area:

> I think it [the sexual relationship] is perfect. We both enjoy it and don't have this stuff of a headache, just if one or the other really does not feel good, we certainly do not force the other, but we are very compatible in this area, too. (WNA)

> No, that part [sex] is fine. My husband had an operation so we can't have any more children, and so everything is fine. I have no worry at all and everything is fine. (WNA)

Those wives who term their sex lives fair but with some problems do not elaborate, but merely talk in generalities such as the ever-present possibility of improvement, or express the wish for more information on how to accomplish the sex act with more skill.

Among those wives who feel their sex life is poor, the following are good examples of the breadth of the complaints:

> We had a relatively good relationship before our problems. When I was pregnant, I was very, very tired. . . . I would come home from work and I would announce that I was going to bed at 8:30; please don't touch me, you know. If you want to make love to a wet rag, fine. . . . [Then] the doctor told me not to get pregnant for a year, and I didn't want to take the pill and he said foam made him numb. He really didn't like rubbers, but he would use them, because I finally said "No intercourse" unless he would. [Since then,] we have sex fairly frequently but I didn't get anything out of it . . . and I think he was doing it just for release of some sort. (WNA)

> Things could be improved because, as far as sex relations, at present we do not have any. He has high blood pressure and I'm afraid of it [sex]. I want him alive, and as far as our sex relations are concerned, it is very exciting, and it would be too much at this time. (WNA)

The women who complain their husband does not show affection but emphasizes the physical side of sexual intercourse make comments like the following:

> If I say I don't feel good, he just goes ahead, like I'm not even there, like I'm a pillow or something, and I'm not supposed to turn him down, so I don't say anything, and as a result, I'm just about frigid. (WNA)

Complaints about frequency cover the entire continuum from too much to too little:

> He is a very sexual person. He has to have it almost four times a day. I like it, but I don't crave it like he does. . . . I go around this house fighting him. He'd touch me and I'd be out of bed. He'd come in the kitchen and I'd dash in the living room, because I knew that he would touch me and I'd be in bed. He always wants it; I think too much. (WNA)

> I'd like it [sex] a little more often. Because he goes to work and comes home tired sometimes I'm not so tired. You know, I understand when he's tired, so . . . (WNA)

The Erosion of the Marriage Relationship

For many a wife, the loss of a partner to talk, eat, have fun, and sexual intercourse with is so serious as to leave the marriage relationship devastated. Not only does the husband fail to perform his role in these vital areas of the relationship, but his very actions seem to be a symbolic message that he no longer loves her (Argyle 1983; Katz 1976). Copeland, Bugaighis, and Schumm (1984) report that among couples married 30 years or more, feelings of positive regard, empathy, and congruence on significant matters are very important. If this is so, it follows that the marriages of alcoholics and their wives are in trouble, for they have deteriorated to the level of a "quasi-primary relationship" (Wiseman, 1979).[18]

American and Finnish women describe the many facets of their feelings of disappointment in their husbands as follows:

> My feelings towards him have changed and I don't feel that great love for him. I feel more sorry for him, and I don't like this feeling. It is not a good feeling. (American)

> I've got to where I hate him. I don't want him to touch me. I don't want anything to do with him at all. There are times when I dread him coming home. I hate to go home also. (American)

> Our relationship is one in which I sometimes detest him and sometimes pity him, so the right feelings have vanished. (Finn)

> His alcoholism has changed our relationship in some ways . . . . We have become alienated or disconnected from each other so we can't even talk about common experiences, because we don't have any. (Finn)

The loss of a relationship with as important a significant other as a spouse and lover actually results in a loss of certain aspects of the self due to the intense interpersonal role relationship between the two. Wives have noted that the change in their husband and marriage resulted in changed feelings toward the husband, which in turn, has affected the wives as persons:

> He is just very unhappy and so am I. Our marriage has changed. I'm not the woman I used to be because of him. I wasn't always a terrible person. (American)
>
> It's difficult to explain, but we are not so close anymore. We have become strange to each other. (Finn)

In addition to the loss of the relationship, the wives and family of an alcoholic lose an important link to a sense of personal security: viable rules of behavior among family members that can be depended upon. Ford (1983) has pointed out that family rules supply the link between family interaction processes and individual conduct, and that they further help families develop a theory by which they are integrated. The loss of reliance on role [or role equity (Schafer and Keith 1984)] and the withering away of family meal rituals and enjoyment of leisure times together, as well as the absence of times of intimacy based on mutual sexual scripts (Simon & Gagnon 1986), remove the rules of family living and leave a void in their place.

Summary and Conclusions

It is perhaps one of the great ironies of social life that the ingestion of alcohol in large amounts defeats the very behavior it is intended to enhance. People serve alcohol at parties to encourage sociability and conversation, yet continued overindulgence appears to curb these desirable social behaviors. Cocktails often precede food, and wine is served to make the meal more enjoyable and to enhance the taste of the food, yet overimbibing kills the appetite. Alcohol accompanies many recreational events and is thought to aid in their enjoyment, but a drunken man can kill the occasion with untoward behavior. Continued drinking will result in his decreased interest in any recreation whatsoever. Shakespeare noted that alcohol increased sexual desire, but decreased ability to perform. No doubt he was thinking of this as a temporary state. More tragic is the apparently almost permanent effect of long-term heavy alcohol ingestion on both the interest in sex and the potency of men.

Wives of alcoholics are victims of the personal wreckage that alcoholism leaves in its wake. Talking, eating, having fun, and engaging in sexual intercourse are social acts. They can also be used as family "themes" for the construction of family reality (Berg 1985). In the case of families where one member is an alcoholic, these themes become negative in tone. They rule out family unity and make enjoying these activities difficult or impossible. One can read instead of talk, eat alone, go to amusements alone, and masturbate, but the very isolated nature of the acts makes a qualitative difference in their enjoyment. Yet, unless the wife of an alcoholic finds herself other companions, this is her fate. The boundaries of her world are narrowed, constrictions brought on by her husband's heavy drinking. And, as will be seen, it is difficult for either of the spouses to recapture good feelings about the other, a matter that compounds the man's problems in attaining long-term sobriety.

Notes

1. It should be noted that this is quite a different approach to the understanding of marital happiness or unhappiness under normal or special conditions than that which is usually used by sociologists and psychologists. The standard method has been the multi-item scaled questionnaire or index, with its ideal of complete happiness on all items at the top of the scale, covering many specific items of possible marital conflict and/or contentment. The pioneers in this field are Burgess and Cottrell (1939), Burgess and Wallin (1953), Locke (1951), and Terman (1938). Many of these indices of marital happiness or adjustment were developed for the purpose of predicting marriage success or failure in young, engaged couples, and not merely for an assessment of the state of a given marriage. Therefore, the creators were concerned with antecedents and psychological factors preceding the marriage as well as current behavior within it and feelings about it. Scores on these separate items were either added or averaged.

However, this bookkeeping approach to assessing the marital relationship does not really aid the understanding of the developmental or career aspects of the general phenomenon of marital incompatibility. First of all, as mentioned, each type of behavior within the relationship, as well as general feelings each spouse has about the manner in which the other spouse is handling it, is in continual process, with important events resulting in significant turning points (Bolton 1961) in the emotional direction of the relationship. What develops out of this mutual responsiveness is a spiraling effect that is both subtle and complex. Olson et al. (1983) deal with this process by looking at families across the life cycle.

2. Gottman (1982), Murphy and Mendelson (1973), and Scoresby (1977), for instance, found that good communication between marriage partners was essential to adjustment. Conversely, research into the causes of marital problems, or of the problems most mentioned by those persons seeking marital counseling, indicates the absence of talk and communication in the marriage to be a major complaint (DeBurger 1971:235; Levinger 1970:128), thus indicating its importance in the marriage relationship. Cuber and Harroff's analysis of five types of marriage relationships (1966:43–65), for instance, observes that at least two of the less attractive types—the "devitalized" and the "passive-congenial"—offered little in the way of talk between partners because of the absence of mutual interests (and personal interest in each other), in contrast to the marriages termed "vital" or "total," where spouses shared both common experiences and a

joy in each other's company. Bernard (1973:44–46) discusses the familiar problem of the intellectually outgrown housewife, who, through no apparent fault of her own, becomes a less and less interesting companion to her husband as he continues to develop in his career and she is stuck with housewifery and child rearing.

There are also some indications that men may stop talking to their wives more often then the reverse. Rubin (1976) and Komarovsky (1967:148–163) suggest that this is particularly true among lower-class couples, although Rubin (1986) suggests this is also true of married couples in general. Among these blue-collar people, Komarovsky states, the impoverishment of life makes for few topics of conversation: coupled with this is what Komarovsky refers to as the "trained incapacity to share," which seems to afflict men more than women. Among males, their socialization and their psychological make-up militates against open communication. Rubin (1986) and Balswick and Peek (1974:27–34) discuss the socialization of male children to be "inexpressive" as adults, pointing out that this condition may be most noticeable in their relationship with women and must be "unlearned" if they are to have a happy marital relationship with their wives. On the other hand, Bell (1981) notes that men are more likely to talk over personal problems with female friends than with other males.

3. A study of the attitudes of spouses from the general population concerning the effect of watching television on their married life (Grantz 1985) indicates that, on the whole, they feel that TV viewing is a positive force in their marriage, and that they frequently watch together. Likewise, they reported that they did not feel the TV watching disrupted normal activities. Such is not the case with wives of alcoholics, who claim that television has become a successful rival in capturing their husband's attention. Some wives of men who have no drinking problem voice this complaint also.

4. Bienvenu (1970:26) noted mechanisms that result in poor communication in marriage. These include nagging, conversational discourtesies, and uncommunicativeness. Bernard (1968:87–205) discusses both the positive aspects of communication in marriage—in the form of reinforcement or "strokes"—and the types of talk styles that eventually function to discourage conversations. Empathetic feedback or sympathy with the person talking gives the person attempting to communicate a feeling that there exists a certain understanding of the intended contribution and thus results in a rewarding interchange. Another conversation killer, according to Bernard (1968:143), is the ploy of parrying every remark by misinterpretation or overinterpretation, thus evading a response aimed at its true intent. The "put-down" answer is also a conversation killer. A lecturing or debating style on the part of one participant can also kill the joy of conversation for another.

5. One individual may give another the silent treatment, a group may send a member to Coventry (i.e., not speak to him/her under any circumstances), a nation may cut off diplomatic relations and recall its ambassador. All of these acts are seen as sanctions and mean that relations between the two parties are, at the very least, strained.

6. The ritual of a family meal is apparently sufficiently accepted in the United States that sociologists have suggested it be studied *in situ* and in greater detail. Dreyer and Dreyer reported on the dinner ritual of 40 white, middle-class families in their article, "Family Dinner Time as a Unique Behavior Habitat" (1973). Warner's discussion of the significance of family meals resulting from their sheer repetition is worth consideration:

It is significant, in any attempt to appraise the social significance of the family meal, to recall that its role is one of continuing repetition. Many families meet around the table three times a day; most families do so at least once a day. Over a period of years, the simple arithmetic of the situation is enough to emphasize its quantitative effectiveness. (1961:223)

7.   Such a feeling appears to be almost universal. The anthropological literature abounds with both descriptions of food-sharing and analyses of its symbolic meaning. Food-sharing among nonrelated tribesmen is often suggested as creating a familylike bond among them (Warner 1961:335–36) and the end of this cooperation is seen to spell the doom of their cohesion. Johnson and Bond, in their discussion of kinship, friendship, and exchange, make the following point about the symbolic meaning of sharing food:

> Friendship in Muyombe is expressed through the sharing of meals. A man does not eat with his enemies or persons with which he is in serious dispute. Sharing meals regularly implies intimacy, a variety of small favors also are involved which facilitate the conduct of everyday life. (1974:58)

Warner, in his discussion of the ritual meal among the Bantus, saw it as a replica of the family meal:

> The "family" meal provides a perfect set of images for the evocation of the deep feelings involved. Food and drink as facts are in the very center of man's feeling. In the family meal and sharing with brothers, sisters, and parents, the food assumes moral significance. (1961:335–36)

If the family meal is the prototype of a close relationship in action for nonrelated persons, it follows that it must have similar functional attributes for members of real families. Anthropologists and sociologists have usually considered this to be the case.

8.   The etiquette concerned with the art of eating reflects the fact the meal is a production. The person making and serving the food is charged with concocting something tasty and serving it attractively. The challenge gives the task its pleasure, but if the product is not eaten heartily or appreciated, the production can be seen as a failure.

9.   Henry, in *Culture Against Man*, devotes considerable discussion to the relationship between food and self-image. He says: "No matter how miserable, there is scarcely a culture where people have not managed to work out a distinction between foods of high and foods of low status, and where food does not become associated with the self image" (1965:355).

10.   Bochner et al. (1982) and Chadwick, Albrecht, and Kunz (1976) observe that failure to meet expectations in role performance is a major cause of marital unhappiness. Inasmuch as the validation of any role is adequate counterrole performance, the husband's withdrawal from family meals (including his appreciation for them) means that he not only fails to perform his role in that area, but destroys his wife's role as well.

11.   Most of the early marital compatibility prediction or measurement scales include many items about mutual enjoyment of leisure time activities, and low scores here are seen as indicative of incompatibility (see Terman 1938; Locke 1951; Burgess and Wallin 1953; Clark and Wallin 1965).

12.   Early manifestations of an alcoholic's problems in social gatherings can be seen in this letter written by a concerned wife to Letitia Baldrige for her column, "Contemporary Living":

Question: I have not been married very long but, I've already been through two incidents when we were guests in friends' homes and my husband became inebriated, and was really rude and crude. He wasn't mean to me, but he was generally horrible to everyone else.

What should I do about this after it happens? It seems to be an excellent way to lose friends. Should I apologize for my husband right then and there to everyone? Should I write our hostess a letter the next day, or what? (Baldrige 1979:8)

13. See Foote (1954), Lewis and Brissett (1967), and Gordon and Shankweiler (1971). These studies indicate that women are showing more interest in sex and greater expectations of a partner who knows techniques that will give them sexual satisfaction.

14. Krupinski, Marshall, and Yule (1970), Krupinski and Farmer (1973), and DeBurger (1971) are but three studies of couples seeking marriage counseling and/or aid that indicate, by implication, the importance of sexual adjustment to marital happiness.

15. In the early stages of the drinking career of an alcoholic man, interest in sex appears from the data to remain the same as before his problem drinking began—even when he is quite drunk. In fact, some wives indicate their husbands become more amorous as a result of heavy drinking.

16. Komarovsky (1967:164–70) gives us an analogous example of the process of this circularity in action as it operates as a conversation killer. "A Case Study of Progressive Estrangement" discusses the wife of a blue-collar worker who refused to talk to her husband when she was angry with him. He retaliated by withdrawing and watching television most of his waking hours at home. The wife's only access to her spouse then became how she treated their daughter in his presence. If the husband thought she was too harsh with the girl, he became upset, and thus would "notice" his wife's complaints, if only to disagree with them.

17. Of course, there are impersonal role aspects of the sex act that allow a partner to divorce him-/herself from emotional involvement. The wife can, for instance, still interact convincingly by faking interest or orgasms. This sort of bracketing of feeling and action, however, is difficult for persons who would prefer a meaningful relationship and naturally developing feelings of eroticism.

18. The term "quasi-primary relationship" was originally created as a concept to describe the intimate interaction of strangers as they help each other select clothing in secondhand stores, and refers to an absence of emotional closeness, even while the kind of structural and physical proximity that usually indicates such feelings are extant. This is indeed true of wives of alcoholics who testify to a loss of loving feelings toward their husbands while still continuing to live with them.

CHAPTER 7

Ports in a Storm for a "Contagious Disability"

Introduction

If alcoholism can be characterized as a disease, it can also be seen, analogously, as a contagious one—visiting allied troubles and misery on close associates. Alcoholism in a husband not only creates an untenable marriage situation for the wife, but also can create both physical and mental problems for her—often of equal magnitude (Steinglass 1981a). Thus, just as the husband's condition can deteriorate alarmingly as his drinking continues, so can the wife's. Worry about her husband and his changed behavior, compounded by the alienation of relatives and friends, creates an environment that can make sheer survival appear a very difficult task and initiative almost impossible.

This chapter will be concerned with the details of what might be called the social contagion that occurs among an alcoholic husband, his concerned wife, and their relatives and friends. The social-psychological world in which the wife of an alcoholic lives as a result of her husband's drinking behavior and its effect on her will be discussed. Additionally, the kinds of help she can call upon, will be presented. Kin, friends, and Al-Anon—all have limitations, as will be seen.

Wives of alcoholics are particularly prone to stress-associated problems. Earlier chapters have chronicled the many deleterious effects a husband's drinking has upon his wife both mentally and physically. As has been described, early in his drinking career she begins to worry about the amount of intoxicating beverages he is imbibing. It is at this time that her mental problems begin. Her concern is met with such vehement denial of the problem by her husband that in some cases she begins to doubt her own senses and sanity, and her husband often encourages these doubts. When she is rescued from fears of losing her mind by convincing evidence that his drinking has gotten out of control, she goes through an emotional stage in which she tries to help him conquer his alcohol problem with little or no cooperation from him. Eventually, giving up on this home treatment approach, she tries repeatedly to persuade him to get some help or professional treatment. When he does, her hopes soar—only to be dashed when he goes off the wagon, a phenomenon that is repeated with discouraging frequency. Over time, a large proportion of these women are angered and saddened when four important areas of marriage—communication and companionship, meals together, recreation, and sex—are destroyed as a result of the husband's drinking. Added to this is the specter of physical brutality or verbal aggression during drunken episodes.

These ongoing effects of her husbands's drinking are only a part of the drastically reduced quality of existence of the wife of an alcoholic. Many of the wife's waking hours are filled with watching a man she once loved destroy himself physically while he deteriorates mentally and socially.

As the husband's drinking becomes more and more continuous, his memory fades and his mental abilities blur. He becomes irresponsible and undependable so that a wife cannot count on him to handle his share of duties. Financially, the household is often close to ruin, yet he seems incapable of considering this a problem. His deteriorating physical and mental condition exacerbates his wife's own physical and mental problems even more, while at the same time driving away persons who might help her. Eventually, her world—like his own—shrinks and becomes encapsulated by the multitudinous effects of his drinking.

In order to understand the further effects of the husband's drinking as they reflect on his wife, we must first understand how progressive deterioration due to alcohol affects him—and, empathetically, her.

Physical and Mental Effects of Heavy Drinking on the Co-Alcoholic

Coping with Anger and Worry Due to the Husband's Lack of Dependability

When a husband becomes an alcoholic, the understandings that husbands and wives usually develop over the years and come to take for granted—mundane matters such as doing chores around the house, coming home on time, and keeping appointments—become problematic. The normal concern one would expect a man to exercise in the care of children or the use of the car is no longer certain either, and such activities become laden with danger. Thus, in numerous situations where she formerly felt she could predict his behavior, the wife finds she must stop and consider what her husband might do, or what might happen to him.

His increasing irresponsibility around the home means that the wife must assume the entire burden for keeping the household going. These women say:

> You can't depend on him for anything. . . . My husband throws all his responsibilities at me. It seems like it's all up to me. (American)

> He doesn't take care of anything. I have to be responsible for the home. Before, he used to pay the rent and automatically take care of the bills. That has become a task of mine. (Finn)

Alcoholic husbands cannot be trusted to look after small children— even for a short time. Wives know that these men can endanger their youngsters by ignoring what they are doing a good deal of the time:

> I left Billy with his father while I went to visit my mother, and then phoned back to see how things were, and found out Billy was either home alone by himself or Dad was in bed. (American)

> He would be so unconscious . . . if something would happen, he would not help. The children could be out there fighting for an hour, and he wouldn't even know it. (Finn)

Alcoholic husbands may disappear for indefinite periods from time to time. This means that his wife can no longer make plans that include her husband's presence or the certainty of his return if he goes out.

These husbands often fail to appear for a special appointment or date, as well. While being left at home and not knowing when her husband will arrive is inconvenient for a wife, it is even worse to be standing on a corner, or to be ready for a party, and wait and wait in vain. Such experiences are common in the lives of wives of alcoholics:

> I was pregnant and teaching night school and he was supposed to pick me up at 9:45. . . . It was midnight when he picked me up. . . . I never got an apology. (American)

> I'm a nervous wreck . . . like last night at 7:30, I just knew he wasn't coming to pick me up and I waited until 9:00 and he didn't come and I kept calling. He wasn't here and he wasn't at work and I just fell to pieces the last couple hours of my work. (American)

When a drinking husband fails to return home, the wife's level of anger often builds up from the strain as she waits through the night (or even a day or two) for his arrival. Throughout this fearful vigil, wives report a veritable roller coaster of emotions, alternately hating their husband and, at the same time, worrying that he may be in serious trouble and/or hurt:

In the evenings, I would sit and brood about how he left me alone so much, and I was angry and hurt. Then, as time wore on, I would start worrying that he had been in a car accident. (American)

In the evenings, I used to imagine I would kill him, or whatever bad I could do to him. Then, at 2:00 A.M. I would ask God to get him home. Then if God did, I was ready to kill him again. (Finn)

Worry and Frustration Concerning Financial Problems. Although heavy use of alcoholic beverages is not nearly so costly as heavy drug use (primarily because the former is legal while the latter is not), alcohol cannot be described as inexpensive. Thus, it is no surprise that wives report their husband's package liquor and bar purchases take a substantial bite out of the family budget, causing the wife great worry in keeping up with the bills as well as day-to-day expenses. Some husbands will deliberately take money set aside for very important purchases and spend it on alcohol, or will sell household items for this purpose without their wife's knowledge. The worst financial blow, of course, is when the husband loses his job (or moves from job to job with periods of unemployment in between because of his "drinking problem"). American women say this about how the day-to-day financial pressures have built up since their husband began drinking heavily:

Our checking account is always overdrawn. We get these notices from the bank and he tears them up and throws them in the trash. (American)

He let our insurance policies go, because he didn't have the money for the premium. (American)

Finnish wives of heavily drinking men also report themselves to be in constant and desperate need for money, especially for food. Some wives complained bitterly that their husband is eating good meals and drinking in restaurants while they and the children have to make do with very little money. Other wives pointed out that their husband unreasonably expected good meals when he came home, while at the same time giving them very little household money with which to purchase the groceries:

When he gives me money, he keeps the bigger part for himself and still demands much meat. He buys only beer with his money. The other day I said "Give me half the salary and we will see who saves more." (Finn)

He had expensive ways of living when I was terribly poor. The children and I had to get along on what I made. He didn't care what kind of food we had to eat. (Finn)

Wives of alcoholics also find that nothing is safe from their husband if he decides to use it for alcohol:

He took $100 out of our savings just for booze . . . . He will hock anything he can find around here. (American)

He drank all the money he got for a business trip and we had to sell the car to pay for that. He was caught stealing a tape recorder and he drank the money we raised for a fine. (Finn)

When American women tried to discuss the household financial situation with their husband, they rarely made much headway:

I'd say, "This bill has to be paid or that bill has to be paid." I wouldn't come right out and say, "You've blown such-and-such money." I'd say, "What are we gonna do?" He'd say, "Well, don't worry about it. I don't want to sit around here and argue." (American)

Finnish women used other methods:

I often used to plead with him. Finally, he signed a paper allowing me to take money from the bank.[1] (Finn)

I took money from his wallet for the needs of our family. (Finn)

Women who go to work to relieve financial pressures usually find themselves subsidizing, in effect, more alcohol purchases instead:

It got down to the point where I had only one item of underwear to wear and I got sick of that. . . . I started baby-sitting, so I could buy my daughter clothes, and buy me some things and have some cosmetics. Then, he wanted my baby-sitting money. If I didn't give it to him, he would have a temper tantrum. (American)

He would run up bar bills. I went to work and paid off two bar bills. (American)

When he is drinking, he doesn't care about the economic aspects. We are seven persons at home, but he still wants to borrow the household money for drink. When I was working, every week I paid the bills for food and part of the rent and that left him a lot of money to drink on. (Finn)

The biggest economic threat brought on by alcoholism occurs when the husband loses a job because of his drinking. Additionally, the firing may touch off a bout of even heavier drinking. Eventually, the husband may go through a series of hirings and firings culminating in a virtually unemployable status:

Well, you see, he has not worked in two years and it is always his drinking. I don't think he will ever hold down a regular job, and [as] I said, he is a foreman! I mean, I don't think he [can] ever put in a full day's work ever again. His mental span will not go that long. He has brain damage. So where we go from here, I don't know. We have got a nice home. If I could get back in office work, maybe I could get enough. (American)

They were tired of his performance. There was a special meeting of the board and they invited him to appear and they bluntly told him he was out. (Finn)

Some men manage to continue to function and hold a job despite their long-term heavy drinking. Their wives were thus spared financial worry, but continue to experience the heartache of seeing a marital partner and loved one gradually deteriorating and withdrawing from communication:

Well, he would vomit every morning. Now normal people don't vomit every morning. . . . Yet he functioned as a human being and held down a high-paying job, brought his paycheck home, laid it on the table and said, "Just buy my beer out of this. You get the rest." There was never any loss of money. We were paying for our home. I always had food on the table, clothes for my children. I was never without, but the emotional abuse is hard to explain. . . . They [alcoholics] don't know how to love, they withdraw. It's like living with a person that is just existing. They get up; they go to work; they come home; go to bed. Any attempt on my part to get to him is met with, "I go to work. Leave me alone." (American)

Distress at the Gradual Deterioration of the Drinker's Appearance

Heavy drinking often results in a drastic reduction of interest in personal appearance, which manifests itself in changed grooming habits. An alcoholic man may seldom bathe, forget to comb his hair or shave, and see no necessity to wear clean, pressed, or neatly put-together clothing. Wives who were used to being married to a man who was fairly well groomed find these changes very difficult to take.

These women report that the inappropriate dress and general lack of coordination which a drunken man often exhibits is so embarrassing that they often avoid letting non–family members see him. When asked to describe this change in appearance, they said:

When I first met him he was spick-and-span, dressed up like a bandbox— a suit, a tie, always a shoe shine, always a shower . . . he wore clean clothes every day. [Since he started drinking] he got less and less concerned about how he looked and he would go for a couple of days, and not shave and wouldn't bathe. He would go for months and not get a haircut. (American)

He does not wear his teeth half the time. Alcohol pours out of his pores when he sweats. It was too overwhelming, and I would become nauseated. (American)

He does not care what he looks like. His clothes look like he has just been dragged through a sawmill. (Finn)

Concern over Physical Degeneration and Illness

Long-term heavy consumption of alcohol takes a physiological toll. A heavy drinker may exhibit many signs of ill health. He may become bloated, develop a very pale countenance, or a yellow or ruddy complexion. His eyes may look bleary or teary.

Wives become even more concerned by a husband who throws up every time he eats, exhibits excessive drowsiness, vertigo, or general weakness. They see these symptoms as possible forerunners (or indicators) of serious maladies. Eventually, continual heavy drinking does take its toll on various organs—the heart and circulatory system, the kidneys, liver, and ultimately the brain—and wives worry as symptoms increase:

> He has an ulcer. He started bleeding and spitting up blood. (American)
>
> He has a tendency to blood clots and has been told not to drink, but he buys a bottle and sneaks it. He had a terrible time last September with blood clots. . . . We thought . . . he was going to lose a leg or arm or something. (American)
>
> He's had two or three heart attacks. (Finn)
>
> Nowadays he gets sick. He will throw up six or seven hours and fears his heart will stop any minute. (Finn)
>
> When he's tying his shoes he gets very exhausted. He gets an ache in his side when he drinks. (Finn)

Cirrhosis of the liver, a very serious disease, is a classic result of heavy alcohol intake:

> And he [her husband] says, "I know I have to quit. My liver is hanging out . . . clear down to here. I know I'm dying. I can't take it." (American)
>
> He got cirrhosis of the liver and can't move around any more. (Finn)

Malfunction of one organ due to heavy drinking eventually affects other parts of the body adversely, such as the brain or the nervous system. Thus, continued drinking can leave a person in what might best be described as very bad shape. For wives, the development of multiple symptoms and ailments causes continual worry. Often, dramatic, frightening situations in which the man exhibits florid symptoms occur:

> He went into convulsions and we didn't know what to do about it. So I called the police and said, "He is not breathing." The next time he is acting like a crazy person—throwing his arms around. I told him that I would take him to detox but that if he wouldn't go, I wouldn't stay in the house with him. (American)

> He passed out in the family room for two days one time. I can't begin to tell you how unbelievable. I had to call an ambulance. I couldn't sit and watch him die on the floor. (American)
>
> I just can't tell you how bad he was. His eyes would roll under and . . . he was flipping out mentally as well . . . his vital signs stopped at three different occasions . . . not only was alcohol damaging his brain but when your vital signs stop, there is a certain amount of permanent brain damage. (American)

Due to the fact that alcoholics are likely to pass out unexpectedly or hallucinate during withdrawal, there is always the specter of an injury from a fall, a fire from a cigarette that continues to burn after the smoker has lost consciousness, drowning or asphyxiation as the result of passing out while bathing, or choking while vomiting. As a result, some wives feel they must maintain a constant vigil on their husband. Naturally, this hampers their own freedom a great deal.

> He went into convulsions and hit the floor and cracked his head. . . . The hospital wanted to turn him loose, but I said, "You can't turn him loose. He does not know where he is. He will walk out into the street and get hit by a car." But they did discharge him, and I had to watch him every minute. (American)
>
> I was afraid he would fall asleep and not just burn a hole in the blanket [he did that one time] but burn himself. We sort of "baby-sat" him; even the kids would sit with him while he was still awake . . . we would take turns and light a cigarette for him and somebody would watch for the ashtray to keep him from getting burned. Once he burnt himself right through his stomach. I don't think he realized that it happened until he sobered up and it began to hurt. (American)
>
> I can't even take a vacation because I'm afraid he'll fall in the shower. . . . He did fall in the shower one time. . . he got a cut in his head and then he started bleeding profusely. (American)
>
> I was scared and I could not sleep at night because I didn't know when he would get up and fall, or do something to hurt himself, or light a cigarette and we would both be burned in a fire. All of these things really scared me. I guess I lived in fear for a long time. (Finn)

Fear of Evidence of Mental Deterioration

Even more frightening to the wife are the mental problems that accompany long-term drinking and indicate damage to the brain. Loss of memory, hallucinations, depression, and paranoia, which have been discussed in previous chapters, can all result from excessive long-term drinking. Wives voice their concern:

> He seems to be losing his mind. He can't remember things. He suspects people of plotting against him. I am so worried. (American)

I mean that the alcohol has caused some kind of brain damage. He seems to have lost his memory. He can't remember when he came home. (Finn)

Thus, there is what Lavee, McCubbin, and Patterson (1985) refer to as "a pile-up of demands" on the wife of an alcoholic, which greatly increases her stress level.

The Wife's Reaction to a Stressful Life

The exact relationship between stress and physical or mental illness is nebulous (Jacob et al. 1973). However, most researchers and clinicians consider some kind of cause-effect relationship to exist (Beck 1984; Ben-Sira 1984; Heins 1982; Hyman and Woog 1982; Martin 1985; Waring, 1982). The wife of an alcoholic lives in a world of almost constant stress, anger, worry, and fear, which escalate as the years go by. Furthermore, it is an existence in which new problems are continually compounding the older ones—his health, his job, his irresponsibility, his brutality, his deteriorating mind. Not surprisingly, many women turn their fears and hostility inward and develop symptoms of their own, which also have physical and mental components. Others begin to hate their husband or find it increasingly difficult to get along with friends or colleagues. In this way, the alcoholism of their husband has a quality of contagion that is partly responsible for the term, *co-alcoholic*. One woman described how these many fears can come together and affect both physical and mental health:

> When I get up in the morning I say, "Well, is he going to come home today?" And [I] worry about paying the bills. I have people call to collect the money and I have to make up excuses for them. We got into debt further and I just got disgusted. There were times when I thought, "What the hell am I going on for?" I got so I wouldn't eat. (American)

Turning Fear and Hostility Inward

Development of Physical Symptoms. Many women who have lived with an alcoholic for any period of time reported physical health problems of their own that seem notably stress-associated:

> [I] finally started getting up at 5:30 every morning with what you call the dry heaves. That is the only word I know for it. I was just really sick. (American)
> My blood pressure goes sky high [when I fight with him] and I start getting a ringing in my ears. (American)

I was covered with a rash from head to toe. . . . [I was] in the hospital for three weeks. [I was] wrapped in Saran wrap . . . gift-wrapped from nerves. (American)

I get diarrhea . . . due to nerves. (American)

When he is drinking, I don't feel like eating. Since we are married, I lost 15 kilos [about 33 pounds]. (Finn)

My health and my blood system broke down. It was difficult to have energy. Fear struck me. (Finn)

I was exhausted with discussing it [his drinking] and got ill. I noticed that my daughter was suffering. I myself lost 20 kilos [about 45 pounds]. (Finn)

Stress-Related Psychological Problems

Wives of alcoholics develop mental problems as well. Many wives develop a negative self-image. They begin to feel that they are either bad wives and thus guilty of causing their husband's drinking, or they are ashamed of his drinking and feel angry that somehow his stigma rubs off on them in the eyes of others. Such reactions are not unusual, but are found in many spouses of clinically ill persons (Farcas 1980):

If someone keeps calling you nasty things and there's no reason for it, you might get to the place, [where you think] "I must be that, he says so." You lose your backbone, you become nothing when you're living with an alcoholic and you don't have any outside help. You're just like a doormat. It seems like the alcoholic enjoys keeping you that way. (American)

At this point my neurosis was at a high point. It was some kind of point between a terrible fear and a feeling of why did this happen to me? Why was alcohol so powerful? It was fear that this was the destruction of everything—our home, our marriage, our children, ourselves, and nothing could help. Our life has been like this, up-down, up-down, up-down for 11 years. (Finn)

Husbands often compound their wife's feelings of inadequacy, as noted, by pointing out her shortcomings. They may complain about the way the wife keeps house, cooks, or maintains her appearance. Such derogatory remarks eventually take their toll on her self-image:

Alcoholics are so good at playing with your emotions and downgrading you, that pretty soon you begin to believe that you are no good. (American)

He would lash out at me . . . he knew every one of my raw spots, every damn one of them. I could remember him [on] two of the worst ones, over and over again, which was that my father didn't love me and I was a piss-poor mother. If there was anything in life that I felt like I wanted, to do a good job of [it] was being a mother. Another thing in life I had strong feelings about was that I was down deep afraid that my father did not love me. [My husband] would go on and on [about these things] and he would not let me go to sleep . . . until he passed out completely. (American)

I felt as though I had failed at everything that a woman can fail at. My husband was constantly pointing out all my faults. (Finn)

The end result may be that the wife of an alcoholic is thrown into a depression for considerable periods of time. She may develop uncontrollable crying jags:

I'm so depressed most of the time that I can't think. (American)

When I cry about it [his drinking] it's a violent thing. I can't stop and I go on and on. They had to take me to a hospital. (Finn)

I was always sick. I couldn't sleep. I was very nervous. Everyone used to see me as a gay person before marriage, but I'm not gay now. (Finn)

These women report that when their husband comes home drunk they fear for their safety, and when he is sober they are nervous, awaiting the day he will start drinking again. These feelings are sometimes translated into tenseness and artificiality in interaction with their husband.

After he was sober for a while, I became apprehensive. I was wondering when the next one was going to strike. I tried doing everything he wanted me to do. I tried playing every game the way he wanted it played, so that I would not rock the boat so that he would not drink. I'd go with him when he wanted to go somewhere, fix the meals he always wanted—a 360-degree turn on what was really comfortable for me. (American)

In between drinking periods, I am nervous, waiting for the next one—but I try to hide it. I don't want him to know it may come again. (Finn)

The depression and hopelessness that some wives develop apparently lead to a breakdown.

I was aware that I was emotionally extremely upset, I felt like I was ready for a nervous breakdown. . . . It had become difficult for me to concentrate on simple things like preparing meals and having the house in order. (American)

I've been going to a psychiatrist for about seven years. I had a nervous breakdown about four years ago. I was in a hospital for a month. (American)

I got to the point where I put the kids to bed around 5:00 or 5:30 P.M. because in the winter time it was getting dark around that time. I'd sleep until 9:00 or 10:00 the next morning. I'd get up and feed them [the children] and they'd go out to the backyard and play and I'd sleep on the couch. I couldn't stay awake. [Eventually she spent two weeks in a psychiatric hospital.] (American)

I think I wouldn't need these medicines [tranquilizers], I think I wouldn't have to be watched by people all the time in my job—if he would stop drinking. (Finn)

I just returned from the hospital last week. They took me there when I tried to commit suicide. (Finn)

So I sat two nights with a bottle of 50 pills of tranquilizers with me. But I thought there must be some means of going on. I thought I would hurt my child very much if I escape. (Finn)

Some women report that they begin to do very bizarre things:

I can remember sitting in a fetal position on the floor of the bathroom; sitting and rocking with my hands around my knees and moaning and sobbing with the door closed so that no one in the whole wide world would know what I was doing, and trying to figure out what the shit I was going to do. (American)

I remember he loved his boots and I thought somehow . . . if I do something with [them] he won't go drinking, and I would hide them. . . . He had a company truck and I broke the windows. I thought if he didn't have this truck around, he would be home. I spent my nights pacing the floor wondering if he was going to get home safely and praying he would, and praying he wouldn't and I was really insane. (American)

Since he has been drinking, I haven't been able to do anything. I had a breakdown over how he acted. I began to have threatening phone calls. I lost weight. I received strange phone calls. The callers asked for someone who has never lived there, then laughed and said something nasty. Almost immediately my husband came home drunk. I could see he enjoyed my suffering over the phone call. (Finn)

Tranquilizers make life bearable for many of these women and, as has been noted, many Finnish wives see psychiatrists at the A-Clinics long after their husband has dropped out of treatment. However, tranquilizers sap initiative and energy—probably contributing to the general inertia these women experience. As one woman put it:

[The psychiatrist said,] "You go home and relax and take your medication." I said, "I am not going to be on the tranquilizers anymore. I am not going to live in a haze anymore. I've been there and I'm not going to be just floating. I refuse to float. I'm going to face life even if it destroys me. (American)

Turning Fear and Hostility Outward

Some wives mention taking their unhappiness out on their friends, their children, or even their colleagues at work:

I didn't want people to visit. I didn't want to see anyone. I just wanted to be alone. (American)

Your whole life revolves around your husband and his drinking and you'll take it out on the kids. Something will be bugging you and maybe the kids will do some little thing wrong, and you'll give them hell for it. Maybe they've done it a hundred times and you've never said or done nothing [before]. So the kids really get it. They get the worst of it. (American)

I even developed problems at work. I could not get along with my coworkers in the hospital operating room. I had to go from there and work in the recovery room. (American)

I felt my friends were judging me because of my husband's drinking, and I was angry and hurt and stopped seeing them. (Finn)

Not surprisingly, for a substantial proportion of wives, distrust, disappointment, hatred, or a feeling of coldness supplants love. Resentment and feelings of being "fed up" were also reported by wives when they discussed their husband:

I got to where I hated him. I didn't want him to touch me. I didn't want anything to do with him at all. (American)

My feelings toward him have changed, and I don't feel that great love for him; I feel more sorry for him, and I don't like that feeling. (American)

I can hardly remember what it was like [the marriage] when it was good. I can't remember even why I married him. (American)

I feel that because of this I can't trust him in *anything*. He is easy with promises, but often can't remember them. (Finn)

Our relationship is one in which I sometimes detest him and sometimes I pity him, so the right feelings have vanished. (Finn)

Some women indicate their hostility by the way in which they seem to welcome the possibility of their husband's death:

He doesn't have much longer to live now. He strangles two or three times a day, his legs are like fish flopping around. I keep thinking if he dies, I'll have his insurance. He's paid through the years and I'll bury him. If he lives, he'll put me into a mental institution. I've put in 20 years, which is a long time. (American)

I'm sticking it out for the insurance now. How long do you think he has to live? (Finn)

A few women fantasize hurting or killing their husband, although they seem aware of the fact that the difference in physical strength between them would make any real attack a dangerous undertaking:

I used to think of ways to kill him. He's very tall [six foot four], but not very heavy. If he were to come in, I could stand behind the door on a chair with a rolling pin and then hit him; but I was afraid I couldn't hit him hard enough and when he would come to, he would kill me. I'd lay there in bed and think if I used a knife on him, they're gonna know I did it. I didn't want to see blood. I just wanted to hit him real hard and get it over with. I've locked him out, so he couldn't get in and he's broken windows so he could get in and [then] he'd beat the shit out of me. (American)

I hated him so, I wanted to hit him as hard as I could, but I knew he was strong enough and mean enough to make me wish I hadn't tried. (Finn)

The following story told by a wife (the one who described herself earlier as worried about unpaid bills) illustrates rather well how physical, mental, and emotional stress can all converge to produce both external reactions and internal symptoms:

The rent was due. For two months the bills were overdue. I was referred to a psychologist by my doctor. It started by me cancelling an appointment and he called me back and wanted to know why I cancelled the appointment. He asked me if I had anything in the house that would hurt me, and I said no. He asked me, "Right now, what do you want to do?" "Well, when my husband comes home I'm thinking of killing him." I told the truth, because I was. [The psychiatrist warned the husband. It took four men to take the wife to a hospital. For three days she would not speak to the psychiatrist who had arranged for her admission.] When I finally started talking to him, I said, "You think I'm crazy, don't you? That's why you brought me here." And he said to me, "If I thought you were crazy you wouldn't be on this ward with the rest of these people. The woman next to you has pneumonia; the woman across the hall has cancer. No. I would have put you behind bars." I was in there for malnutrition—I was 79 pounds, soaking wet—because I had been drinking coffee all day long. (American)

What Ports in a Storm? The Viability of Various Help Networks

The vagaries of social life almost guarantee that everyone will face serious setbacks, disappointments, problems, and tragedies as years go by. The need we all have for affiliation that gives both support and aid has been discussed by Burchfield, Hamilton, and Banks (1982), Lofland (1985), and Mitchell, Cronkite, and Moos (1983). Other researchers have noted the connection between control of stress and support networks (Ben-Sira 1985; Gerstel et al. 1985; Gottlieb 1985; Mitchell et al. 1983), as well as the strains resulting from lack of family support in times of felt need (Mitchell et al. 1983). Usually the kinship and social relationships that people have developed through the years are very useful during these times when a person is up against a situation so disheartening and overwhelming that he or she cannot cope with it alone. Ideally, most people have at least two networks of social relationships to which they can turn in times of stress: family members and friends.

The reactions of relatives and friends to a loved one beleaguered by an alcoholic husband are instructive, for they allow us to see beyond the generalities of role expectations into the intricacies of involvement and the emotions aroused when the problems of another appear to be of a long-term nature with moral overtones.

Family Help Networks

Many sociologists have studied the presence, absence, or change over time of family help networks. Indeed, the existence of a help network is considered to be a major indicator of family solidarity (Dressler 1985; Speck 1984; Quinn and Keller 1983; McClanahan et al. 1981; Stack 1974; Croog et al. 1972; Bott 1971; Miller, 1965; Sussman et al. 1959, 1962; Young & Willmott 1957). Yet when we look at the case of alcoholism of a family member, we become aware of how situation-specific family help networks are, and how fragile they can become under certain circumstances.

In past research on family helping patterns, little concerning the details of various interpersonal relationships within the family is presented. Rather, members are described in standardized roles fulfilling standardized functions in standardized ways. Loans or gifts of money, aid with baby-sitting, housework, transportation, lending appliances, and other such exchanges are the focus. Details of actual relationships are glossed over and implied as uniformly good, or at least adequate for the assistance needed, or more usually not considered at all. Some note has been taken of this. Gibson (1972) has criticized the absence of more exact operationalization of family contacts and family help. Tietjen (1985) has noted that single mothers in Sweden find that friends are more helpful than family in that particular situation. No one has yet looked at family help patterns as they vary with specific types of family members and types of aid needed.

However, when one scrutinizes family role relationships more closely from the perspective of the wife of an alcoholic, the standard aspects of kin networks fade into the background. We see emerging the types of relatives and the idiosyncratic role relationships familiar to us all: relatives with whom the relationship is so bad or so distant that one would never turn to them for aid; relatives who are known to take sides with one spouse or the other in all disagreements and are thus automatically disqualified on these grounds; relatives who are so inept at giving aid that it is best not to ask them; and relatives who would never recover from the shock of knowing about the problem—to name just a few. Additional complications result from the degree of burden inherent in supplying certain types of aid as well as the length of time it is needed.

Thus, when the wife of an alcoholic seeks help, she must consider if the relationship between herself and any member of her family or that of her husband is good enough to ask for such assistance, and further if that member is the right person to handle such aid.

Types of Aid Needed by Wives of Alcoholics

A major factor in understanding the help relationships of wives of alcoholics and their relatives is that the assistance needed by these women is not trivial (see also Neikirk 1983). Certainly, it goes a great deal beyond picking up a few things at the market or baby-sitting now and then. Wives in both Finland and America talk of wishing that some relative (usually a member of the husband's family) would talk to her husband about quitting drinking or going into treatment. They hope that where their own logic and threats have failed, perhaps his parents or siblings will succeed.

Financial help is also needed. Inasmuch as husbands use money for drinking that should go to pay crucial bills, the wife may need a loan to pay rent or maintain house payments, or to buy food. Wives also speak of money to pay a lawyer, so as to leave their husband, plus assistance in setting themselves up in separate living quarters. Failing that, these women would like a place for themselves and their children to stay when the husband is drunk and frightening or violent. Additionally, they want someone to talk to and to sympathize with them from time to time.

Thus, it can be seen that assistance to these women can put considerable demand on the time and resources of the donor. Additionally, there is little promise of closure on the problem. It can go on interminably despite the best efforts of the family helper. Finally, although there has been a great deal of publicity concerning the view that alcoholism is an illness, family members can feel it really represents a moral or character weakness in a person with whom they would rather not associate, or for whom they would prefer not to sacrifice. On the other hand, some family members, seeing the husband sober from time to time, and feeling affection for him, may doubt a problem exists.

Expectations of Reactions at the Request of Aid

Whenever people consider reactions to something problematic, they play out the possible request and reaction scenario in their minds before deciding how to handle the matter in actuality (Mead 1932:270). This rehearsal allows them to correct possible errors in terms of chances for success, revising modes of approach and/or decisions about whom to ask or whom to avoid. Such future-casting can also reveal details about actual family relationships as they exist in the mind of the subject.

This section will focus on the deliberations by wives of alcoholics when they consider aid from either their family or their husband's family. It will be seen that their appraisal of special types of relatives that would be of help or not when alcoholism is an issue offers a chance to gauge the depth of family commitment beyond the usual errand, baby-sitting, small loans or gifts, and transportation.

General Expectations. Almost half of the wives in both cultures said they had no relatives close enough to them emotionally with whom to discuss their problem and expect help. Some American wives, however, make the general claim that if they were to turn to their family or their husband for help, it would be forthcoming from some member. They say:

> I could call my father and say, "Dad, Roger's gone again drinking. What do you think I ought to do about it? And he would try to talk to him. (American)
>
> My relatives would help. I don't know about his. I've never asked either of them. (American)
>
> Here in this city I have three sisters and two brothers I could go live with. (American)
>
> I'm sure, I know that my folks would [help] if I ever went to them with some kind of problem or want or need . . . so will his mother, even though she is on a very limited budget. (American)

Finnish wives, on the other hand, were more dubious about receiving any aid at all from family members.

As mentioned, in earlier stages of a husband's drinking, American wives are conflicted on whether to let anyone in the family know about the drinking and the problems it is causing. If any geographic distance exists between themselves and relatives, the wife often refrains from ever telling them. Thus, on the whole, these women reveal the problem only when they feel that the family member is going to find out anyway.

> Well, my mother doesn't know. She lives quite a ways from here. (American)
>
> I tried to hide it from just about everybody at first—friends, family, his boss—even the children. (American)
>
> I finally told my brother when he came here to visit me. I never had the guts to tell him before. I told him in the airport while walking to the car. (American)

Some wives feel it is a matter of pride not to let people to know that their marriage is not a happy one.

> I don't want anyone else to know that my life has been such a mess. I want other people to think I handled it well. I have a lot of pride. (American)

Eventually some of the women told relatives in order to have someone to talk to about the problem:

> I finally got so uptight that I had to have someone to talk to. I finally confided in my sisters and brothers. They were all more understanding than I thought they would be. (American)
>
> I told his mother because I didn't want her to blame me if I decided to leave; I wanted to go to his uncle's and needed his telephone in another town. I just wanted to get away for that week because I felt I was going to have a nervous breakdown. (American)
>
> It was an emotional thing, and it was Sunday, and he had not come home yet, and I just called to wish my mother a happy birthday and I think it was Mother's Day, too, and all of a sudden I started to cry—and I told her. (American)

Another small group of American women told everyone—relatives, friends, employer, and children—on the grounds that alcoholism is a disease, should be recognized as such, and thus was nothing to be ashamed of or hide. These women felt that by announcing it openly, they removed the stigma that might be associated with problem drinking, should it be discovered in some other way. However, by making it less a crisis, these women also avoided asking for assistance.

In Finland, quite unlike the United States, wives were, first of all, very reticent about telling in-laws or parents about their husband's drinking problem. They assumed (no doubt erroneously in many cases) that kin would not know unless told.

The strong feeling for privacy, which respondents said was a Finnish cultural trait, appears to account for the reticence Finnish wives have about going to extended family members for aid—even when they would like to share their burden. Husbands are often adamant about contacting others and repeatedly wives say that their husband would not approve of them sharing family problems with relatives outside the immediate family. This is effective in sealing wives' lips on the subject, for a time at least:

> I promised him not to talk about these things to relatives or parents. His parents died without knowing. (Finn)
>
> When his mother visits us, I've tried to act the happy wife. She lives in another city. I think she would worry about this. (Finn)

The reluctance of people to ask kin for help because it means betraying their need for it when they are trying to maintain a trouble-free facade is seldom discussed in the literature on family help networks. Yet it is a real issue and some wives show a shrewd lay awareness of the lasting quality of a stigma, once revealed:

I think I always had hopes that he would straighten out and that it [the heavy drinking] would be something that was in the past. (American)

I thought that if he should stop drinking, then it would not be good for her [the wife's mother] to know that he had [been an alcoholic]. (Finn)

Types of Relatives That Cannot Be Asked for Help

Merely having relatives and even having some kind of a relationship with them does not mean that each and every one is either willing or able to help out when needed for any kind of problem. In fact, as wives consider asking for aid, they automatically eliminate certain relatives that they characterize as either unapproachable or "impossible." Such a cataloguing results in considerable trimming of the list of possible family members eligible to aid them in one way or another with their specific problem.

The Relative who has Already Declined to Help.   Some American and Finnish wives have already experienced rejection from parents, close relatives, and in-laws when they asked for help. Thus, they vow never to ask them again:

Like when we were in Albuquerque, the rent would be due, and I had no relative who would take us in. They told me to go ahead and find a place of my own, because they didn't want any part of it, you know, me with three kids, and they all said they didn't have the room or something. (American)

His folks? No, I won't ask them, but at the same time, they won't offer. When my husband is in the hospital, they won't as much as call and say, "Do you need milk?" They [the children] are the only grandchildren that can carry their last name, but they won't call up and offer. (American)

I don't think [his family] will give any help. They have refused in the past. His mother has never been too interested in him. She's older, about 73, and he is 30. There's such an age difference. (Finn)

In other cases, the wife feels that either she or her husband has already overdrawn the amount of help that they can or should take from a given relative, and thus can expect no more. This is, of course, a major problem with any long-term disability:

My parents have put out so much money for us for food, and even rent, because he is spending so much on drinking, that they will not help me now. (American)

I once borrowed $300 from an aunt to file for divorce from him (I later relented). To this day, I still owe her, so I can't go to her for any other help. (American)

Lack of Emotional Closeness. The more demanding or extensive the assistance requested, the closer the relationship between the supplicant and the possible grantor of aid must be thought to be before the person can be approached. Almost everyone has one or more persons in the family network with whom the relationship can be described as remote, cold, constrained, or even hostile.

I have asked her if maybe she could help him to do something and she is just not the type that—I don't know that she would or could—their personalities are not warm and close—so I don't feel that anything would be gained. [She said] "Well oh . . . it is a shame"—something like that. (American)

I couldn't ask them. . . . His mother is a cold, hard, rejecting woman. . . . She can look at you and it puts me under. . . . She's got a very sharp tongue and there's no way that you can defend yourself with her. (American)

Oh, my brother is a busy man with a grown family. He has a job and he and his wife . . . we are not that close, really, that I could expect help from him. (American)

We were never close to his relatives. We have two cousins here and they visited us once and made it clear they didn't want to see us again. (Finn)

Geographic distance compounds the absence of emotional closeness:

His family—his mother has passed away, and his only sister lives in Indiana and she doesn't realize how much of a problem he has, and I would never tell her because it would just upset her, and she's too far away to help him. (American)

He has a brother stationed in Tokyo. I can't ask him to come and help. (American)

He doesn't have relatives except for a twin brother who lives in Sweden whom he doesn't see for ten years and who drinks as much as he does. (Finn)

The Relative Who Offers Unusable Advice. Some relatives have offered such drastic or implausible advice (from the wife's point of view), that so far as she is concerned, it is just like no help at all. Thus, they do not ask again:

I have not looked for any help other than my family, who made the suggestion that I should throw his ass out. (American)

My mother just died, and it just broke her heart that I would be so unhappy and she would like to see me leave him if he doesn't quit drinking. (American)

My family doesn't see any benefit of living with an alcoholic, so they don't want to help him. (Finn)

The Relative Whose Personality or Condition Rules Out Aid from Them. If people keep contact with their relatives, they have a history of interaction that builds into some kind of idiosyncratic, emotion-laden relationship. Shibutani (1961) calls such relationships "interpersonal roles." The emotional content can be either positive, negative, or mixed, but it must be taken into consideration when asking for what could be extensive assistance. These relationships, with their emotional valences, stand in contrast to the standard familial roles usually used when assessing family help networks and are a significant factor in selecting or rejecting persons from whom to request aid:

His mother is just—just a real funny person. I wouldn't know what she would say. (American)

His mother has never said anything about his drinking except that he's never welcome in their home when he's drinking. . . . I am very uncomfortable with that woman and I don't talk with her really. (American)

If I went to my family, the first thing they would assume . . . say is, "Well, what are you doing wrong?" I can't handle any more blame, so I don't go to my family about it. (American)

My father is a big blabbermouth. He finds out about things, and then he twists them around, and then he takes them and . . . writes letters to everybody and embarrasses me so much that what I'm actually going through at home is not as bad as how he makes me feel. (American)

My brother is very different from me. He's very religious and leads a strained life. My half-sister wouldn't be able to talk to him. If my mother did, he wouldn't listen to her. (Finn)

His mother's religiosity was not severe, but humble. The mother is very humble and she approves of all the faults of her children. (Finn)

Additionally, the vagaries of life ensure that some persons to whom one might ordinarily turn for aid are currently at overload because they have so many problems themselves (financial, health, emotional, etc.) that they cannot possibly undertake another burden—even for a loved one:

My mother is so old that she ought to be in a nursing home. She can't take this and she would be no help. (American)

My dad has cancer and he is dying and it is a matter of time, and he is so happy when he thinks Fred is dry, so I can't tell him. (American)

My dad can't really help me at all, he has made such a mess of his own life so he really can't help me in mine. (American)

They couldn't right now; it would be an imposition. They're both financially stressed for money because of surgery. (American)

My mother is very old—too old to help. He has had little contact with his sister. He has another sister who is mentally ill. (Finn)

I haven't told my mother because her husband drinks a lot. She is ill and I haven't wanted to disappoint her. She thinks my marriage is quite all right. (Finn)

Family Members Who do not Want to get Involved.   Alcoholism is a problem that can last a long time. It has a high rate of recidivism. Financial help for the spouse of an alcoholic can be an almost interminable drain on the budget. Offering unappreciated and largely unwanted advice means taking the side of the wife against the husband. Talking to an alcoholic means being in the company of someone who is often not lucid and who can become violent. Thus, it is not surprising that many relatives, perhaps sensing a long-term problem, make it clear that they do not wish to become involved in a situation where a successful outcome for their efforts seems almost impossible.

My mom came to stay with us when I broke my leg ice skating and she was here a couple of months, so she could see. And I said, "I think John is drinking too much." And she said, "Yeah." Nothing else. She didn't want to get in a conversation about it. She could have said, "Hey, there is a problem," but no, nothing. (American)

I wrote to my husband's father about his drinking and staying out all night. I figured possibly he would be a lot of help and I was really hurt when he didn't answer my letter. As it turned out, he just didn't want to interfere. (American)

I talked to his father about talking to Ken concerning his drinking and he told me that he didn't want to get involved in it. He said he didn't know Ken drank that much and that he had never been able to tell him anything since he was 15. He really didn't want to discuss it with me. (American)

My husband's relatives have told me they don't want to interfere in our marriage and become enemies. (Finn)

I tried to get his mother to help. But she says she can't do anything. She says I should help him. His sister who is a social worker tells me that "Everyone has their own life—you do as you please. I don't want to interfere." (Finn)

My mother says that she had told me the man is no good. Now she doesn't want to hear about it or help me. My father merely said, "God bless you and I hope everything goes well. That is all I can do." (Finn)

Family Members Who do not Believe a Problem Exists.   Many wives report that relatives will take the husband's side against her, and deny he has any drinking problem. This stance is especially true of the husband's family. Often, total disbelief is coupled with hostility toward the wife for suggesting such difficulties with liquor exist. Wives relate:

I have told my sister [about her husband's drinking] and she tells me that I am making a mountain out of a molehill. That he is good with my children, that he provides for us, he works. (American)

His folks don't believe he has a problem. His mother is his drinking buddy. She said, "No dear, he is not an alcoholic. He drinks a lot, but he is not an alcoholic." (American)

When I told his sisters and brothers, they got mad at me and said, "For God's sake, he has a couple of beers and you are calling him the town drunk." Well, they don't have to go to bed with the town drunk. (American)

His relatives thought I was crazy when I talked to them about it. He is a charming person—he can charm everyone. They don't think he's an alcoholic—even today. (Finn)

Once I asked my brother-in-law to talk to him. He said, "Don't worry, he can't be an alcoholic, he still has his job." (Finn)

I have talked to his sisters, but they get angry and say he is not an alcoholic. They say, "Don't talk like that to me," and hang up. (Finn)

Relatives Who Indulge in the Same Behavior for Which the Wife Seeks Assistance. Additionally, some of these relatives appear to the wife to have an alcoholic problem, so they are not the ones to persuade the husband into going into treatment, and they are seldom in position to give the wife financial aid—or any other kind of aid for that matter:

He has two brothers and all three of the men are alcoholics. One of his brothers has been in a hospital for alcoholics in Seattle. (American)

His mother is a heavy drinker. She will not admit that he is an alcoholic. She tried to tell me that he just drinks coke. That kind of put bad things between me and her. His brothers, all except one, are alcoholics. . . . His father and his stepfather are alcoholics. One was institutionalized. (American)

Wives also testify that heavy-drinking relatives will often invite or even encourage the alcoholic man to "have a few with them," or they will serve generous amounts of alcohol when she and her husband are visiting, thus substantially undermining her position that he drinks too much. This effectively robs the wife of any help from that quarter, and at the same time sanctions the husband's drinking as nonproblematic. Wives become very angry when they discuss this:

My brother sometimes went with my husband drinking. Buddy-buddy. (American)

I talked to his father and asked him not to serve alcohol to his son, but he ignored me. (Finn)

His mother gave him money to drink. He couldn't have drunk without her money. (Finn)

Sometimes wives suspect relatives may get a sadistic pleasure out of tempting an alcoholic to drink:

His brother is a psychologist and I have been really angry with him because he has, for some reason, condoned my husband's behavior and he
has come down and enjoyed the wickedness of going out and having the
excitement of having the brother who knows his way around town, who
does drink. . . . I've been bewildered about this and wrote this brother:
"Why do you want Bob to die?" (American)

*The Result of Relatives Trying to Get the Husband to Stop Drinking or Go
into Treatment.* Those relatives who do attempt to talk to the husband
about his drinking do not fare well. Rather they experience anger from
the husband without any positive compensations. Either the husband is
insulted by the family member's general approach (or the brashness of
daring to mention what the drinker considered to be a private matter), or
the relative is offended by the way in which the alcoholic responds to his
talk:

One time his mother came down and she hit him in the face and she never
came down again and she would never try to help me again, either.
(American)

My father tried talking to him when we were living with them, but he
really gets embarrassed by the whole thing. (American)

His grandmother writes him letters which say, "You should stop drinking
and shape up and get right with God." (American)

My husband's older brother talked to him about it and they became enemies. His younger brother once kept him from driving, and they had a
fistfight, and since then no one in the family wants to interfere. (Finn)

Once my sister said to him, "You are not fair. Try to think of the way you
behave." He thought that now his wife's relatives were trying to boss him
around and that he did not like it. (Finn)

At the very least, relatives are usually told to mind their own business: My
husband said [to his father-in-law], "Don't preach to me. When you were
my age, you drank all you could." (Finn)

He told him, "I'll know when I should cut down. I know the time I have to
stop drinking." (Finn)

Attempts to get aid from relatives is short-lived and dwindles in some
cases to a room for the wife when the husband gets violent. Such an
offer indicates both acknowledgment that a problem exists and a helplessness or reluctance to do anything more concrete about it. Wives even
feel they cannot overuse the offer of shelter and some develop a series of
homes for refuge on a rotation basis.

Family Networks and Serious Long-Term Problems

When the problem of a family member is a long-term behavioral one
with moral or character implications, the helping patterns of the kin
network are far more complicated than previous studies would indicate.

The offer of aid cannot be taken for granted, and even when extended, the outcome is by no means certain.

The assessment of family relationships that must be made by the wife of an alcoholic when looking for assistance reveals the fragility of kin help networks. Many relatives are considered, but deemed unsuitable, inept, or lacking in the necessary resources. Additionally, it seems that some persons do not want to become involved in a long-term deviant behavior such as alcoholism, which could be demanding both in terms of time and emotions, as well as creating family conflicts. Those who do try to help by talking with the drinker do so only once, somewhat ineptly apparently, and then suffering the same fate as the wife when she tried the logical persuasion of the "Let's talk this out" or the more emotional "How can you do this to your life?" approaches, they retire to lick their wounds. The result, in any case, is some kind of permanent disengagement or at least long-term alienation.

Friends as a Lost Resource

If relatives are a problematic group for the wife of an alcoholic to approach for help, how about friends? Neighbors and friends are considered by both therapists and researchers to be important support sources in cases of crisis (Willmott 1987; Bishop 1984; Rueveni 1984; Ball 1984; Tietjen 1985). However, when alcoholism is the problem, data indicate that friends have withdrawn from contact quite some time before most wives can contemplate asking them to lend money, open their home to them (and perhaps their children), offer a sympathetic ear about the problem, or to talk to their husband about stopping the drinking. In fact, friends seem to disappear without acknowledging the reason.

Wives describe the loss of friends as a quiet attrition, often without any form of explanation offered:

> Our friends just seemed to slide away. I stopped getting close to people. We don't have any close friends at all. (American)
>
> Our friends won't invite us over and when we invite them over, they decline. One woman said that she didn't want us in her house because of him, which nearly killed me at the time. (American)
>
> Of course, we are social outcasts now. (American)
>
> We don't have very many friends any more. They have just vanished as a result of his drinking, so we seldom go anywhere. (Finn)

Those friends who maintain contact listen to the wife's woes and offer sympathy but indicate no desire to "become involved" in the problem. Wives excuse this, feeling that friends really do not have the power to help in such a serious matter.

Most of these wives do not even consider the possibility of receiving help from friends. What they yearn for is their lost social life—resulting both from the lack of invitations and from their fear of accepting an invitation, or entertaining and having their husband get drunk at their own social gatherings:

> We can't have a social life under this kind of circumstance. If we're invited to go somewhere, he is drunk before we go and he will insult someone. I won't invite my friends here anymore because he just scares them away. (American)

> No one invites us to their house and we never do anything on holidays. It makes me sad to see a bunch of people all together, family and friends, and we don't have any. We are always alone. (American)

> We don't go to parties any more. Either we are not invited, or I am afraid to go to parties where they serve alcohol—that he will overdrink there. (Finn)

It has been noted that male skid row alcoholics lose social margin (the margin for error that people ordinarily allow each other) as a result of drinking, lack of dependability and general life-style (Wiseman 1979: 223–26). To their dismay, wives of alcoholics not on skid row find that they also lose social margin with friends as a result of their association with an alcoholic husband:

> I know that through his drinking and behavior problems that he has alienated people. People don't want to be around those kinds of people. Because I am his wife, I'm a part of that. He has the disease, and I have the stigma. (American)

> I was rejected by friends who felt I never should have been around him. (American)

> When we got married, my husband destroyed my friends. He went at them and shouted and broke the relationships. They blame me for this. (Finn)

Friends, then, are not a reliable resource if the crisis a person faces is alcoholism in a significant other. Long before a wife can work up the courage to ask a friend for help, the friend has quietly ended the friendship. Later, these women make friends with other wives of alcoholics, who do offer a sympathetic ear, but who, because of their own problems, lack such resources as a safe place to stay, financial aid, or help in persuading a husband to go into treatment.

Help from the Church

A few American women go to their ministers or priests for aid. They find that while spiritual comfort is forthcoming, actual help of the type they would like to get is usually beyond the power of these men:

I talked to my minister at the Episcopal Church, and he hasn't really said too much except that, "Well, if he [the husband] takes the Lord as his personal Savior, the Lord will be with him." Garbage! Really and truly that to me is what it is, and I don't want to hear it. (American)

I've talked to the minister of my church. Well, you can only do so much about prayers, you know. Than I just got really more and more involved with God to the point where I couldn't cope with it. (American)

Yes, I talked to the priest. He told me to go to the doctor. He said, "You know your vows, till death do we part." (American)

I talked to Pastor MacDonald. He just told me that I couldn't live like this, that I would have to do something. I would have to do it on my own. Nobody can do it for me. (American)

Where can a distraught wife of an alcoholic turn? Given that many family members cannot or will not help, that she has lost her "couple" friends due to her spouse's drinking, that her new friends are usually also wives of alcoholics with the same scarcity of resources, and the church offers minimal aid, the answer for many wives of alcoholics appears to be Al-Anon.

Al-Anon as an Emotional Shelter

Over three-fourths of American wives of alcoholics in this study say they are getting some kind of counseling in order to cope with the problems created by their husband's alcoholism. Of these, seven out of ten are currently going, or have gone, to Al-Anon. In the Finnish sample, approximately one-third of the wives have had some contact with Al-Anon. (This smaller proportion may be a result of competition from government-operated facilities such as the A-Clinics, whose counselors and psychiatrists also accept spouses of alcoholics as patients.)

What these women find in Al-Anon is an approach for coping with the depression and anxiety they experience in connection with their husband's drinking—a program that offers a way of life for the spouse of an alcoholic, albeit a difficult one to follow. Additionally, they find a congenial support group—which comes to mean a great deal to them:

I was terribly depressed because I could not possible get him to quit drinking. I got so depressed. A week before Christmas I went to Al-Anon and this helped me tremendously. (American)

I hit bottom emotionally, I knew I had to get help. I had so little self-respect. I didn't care if I lived or died, but I knew my kids needed something. (American)

I went to Al-Anon after I had been in counseling for a while. I needed someone to talk to who was in the same boat. (Finn)

> I was very lonely then and one day I saw the AA ad in the paper and phoned there and since then I have taken part in the Al-Anon group. In the group, I listened to the others' stories. I was like a mushroom, taking the nutrition. I felt I had no knowledge of myself. I felt empty. (Finn)

Many of these women attend Al-Anon meetings despite strong objections from their husband, who fears he will be stigmatized when his wife goes to such meetings and openly proclaims she is married to an alcoholic:

> I told him I was going to join the Al-Anon. I said [I was doing this] because I don't have any friends—nobody, just nobody—not even my sister, nor my brother, not even your kids now, because you're drunk and they don't want to come when you're drunk. He thought it was awful [that his wife should go to Al-Anon] because it was a disgrace for him. (American)

> A lot of wives are like me, they don't tell their husbands they're going to Al-Anon. Boy, I went to more Tupperware and Stanley parties—you wouldn't believe! Husbands think that puts the stigma of alcoholism on them. (American)

> He didn't like me going (to Al-Anon). He said it was a "breeding" ground against men. He also said I was going to get even with him, so the whole world would know that I thought he drank too much. (Finn)

Some wives do report that after they have attended Al-Anon meetings for a while, their husband becomes more appreciative of the organization's effect on the woman's behavior:

> He was really glad about it [that she was going to Al-Anon meetings], I was amazed. For a while he seemed to feel that I was being more concerned than critical. (American)

> I think we are a lot closer than we used to be; we have both grown up. . . . It is because, I think, on my part, of the things I have learned in Al-Anon. (Finn)

Al-Anon is an organization that is an offshoot of AA. While intended for spouses of alcoholics of either sex, its membership consists primarily of wives. Very few men attend Al-Anon meetings.

Al-Anon was created in recognition of the fact that alcoholism is not only a problem of the drinker, but a family problem. Al-Anon's program is not unlike that of the parent organization: spouses are given the 12 steps, telling them, among other things, to take one day at a time, to place their fate in a higher power. Additionally, they are assured that they are neither the cause of the husband's or wife's drinking nor can anything they do bring about a cure. Rather, they are to try to see alcoholism as strictly the problem of the drinker and detach themselves from it, channeling their efforts instead into their own self-improvement.

This is not easy. Farcas (1980) has shown that when a loved one acquires a mental or physical illness, or other serious physical and psychological problems, related family members immediately involved are often very guilt-ridden. They ask themselves what they have done wrong; they are angry and filled with anxiety. Spouses of alcoholics are no exception to this wrenching soul searching. Thus, wives of alcoholics testify that they felt a tremendous relief when they were told that their husband's drinking was not the result of something they had done:

> For a while I thought maybe it was my fault. Maybe I nagged in one way or another; maybe I did something like . . . give him four sons when he wanted four daughters. (American)
>
> I learned it was not my fault and I couldn't do anything about it. That was the first two things I learned, and I worked from there. (Finn)

Al-Anon philosophy stays out of the question of divorce, leaving this decision to the spouses. Its major thrust is to try to keep persons married to alcoholics to look on the bright side of life and create a satisfactory existence, while remaining married. Al-Anon has no professional counselors; rather, it offers "twelfth-step work," in which spouses of alcoholics who "get the program" are told to try to help those distraught persons who are newcomers to the group.[2] Thus, the organization provides a network of people who are in the same boat, who can talk to each other about their mutual problems and how to handle them (Al-Anon Family Groups [no date], 1952, 1967, 1979a,b, 1982, 1986).

In discussing the program, however, these women reveal a general inability to describe just exactly what it does for its members. Descriptions of Al-Anon activities are offered in vague terms that seem to assume understanding on the part of the listener, rather than attempting to ensure it. "Getting the program" appears to be somewhat parallel to "getting it" among EST followers (Greene 1976; Fenwick 1973). Most women describe very seriously their difficulty in "doing" or "getting" the program, or one of the "steps":

> We have a step in AA, in Al-Anon, that says to take an inventory. And I sat there and said, "There's nothing wrong with me. I can't take an inventory." Do you know it has taken me four years, and I am only now beginning to see the things that are wrong in my life. (American)
>
> I started trying it [Al-Anon]. It was a very slow process. I was going and it was kind of like in one ear and out the other. I wasn't really getting into it. And I still have a long ways to go. (Finn)

Persons who do claim to get the program talk in two ways about it: either they speak openly of its religious affect on them—their feeling nearer to God or more spiritual—or they talk in terms of its "beauty" and its "way of life":

> [In Al-Anon] they don't give you suggestions so much as they share a certain amount of . . . philosophy . . . rather than "solutions that have worked for them." Making sure that we turn to our higher power each day and let the higher power guide us and not worry about yesterday and not dwell on it . . . not worry about tomorrow. (American)
>
> It helps to believe in God, to follow my higher power to give me my strength to act sane. My normal reaction before [Al-Anon] was anger and hostility. (Finn)

However, regardless of their enthusiasm for the program, the women confess that not only is it difficult to get the program, but it also is difficult to stay on it. Some admit that they have slipped off the program, or that even when working the program, they found that they were not able to utilize it to cope with their husband's alcoholism. Even as they explain their failure, they insist they will continue to try to master the program and improve their abilities to use it in specific incidences in their lives:

> I felt that I had learned so much at Al-Anon, all of a sudden my life was going to be A-1, you know, I had the entire world by the tail now. I was going to use all of the good things that I learned, but I found out that practicing something is not as easy. It took a lot of effort and I was up and down on the program. (American)
>
> I have to prepare myself for what I think is a big downhill slide all of a sudden. I feel that that's coming. So I have to sort of brace myself, and get as much Al-Anon in me, and acquire as much independence as I can from him. . . . What I have to do is read my Al-Anon literature and apply the rules and the principles and the 12 steps and try to get my mind off it [his drinking], and keep myself busy. (American)
>
> Even though I had almost a year at Al-Anon, I had just let everything go out the door—I had forgotten, you know, to let go and let God take care of him . . . that no matter what I do, I will not change it. And I started to worry and I worried. (Finn)

Effect of Al-Anon on Wives.   Wives who attend Al-Anon meetings and who are receptive to the program uniformly change their approach to their husband's drinking to one of noninterference and nonresponsibility, in keeping with the Al-Anon ethos. They begin to devote themselves to improvement of their own lives, while remaining married. The result appears to be a psychological detachment while remaining physically in the same household. This approach is found to a much greater extent among Finnish wives than American wives, perhaps because of the difficulty of getting a divorce there.

It should be mentioned that the detachment of those wives who subscribe to the teachings of Al-Anon is different in character from the detachment of wives who arrive at this state on their own (described in the discussion of the home treatment), what they call "acting natural." These wives, who pretended not to notice their husband's drinking or drunkenness, hoped that they were doing something therapeutic for their mate by the creation of a calm, accepting atmosphere. In their own minds, of course, they were not truly detached.

Wives who, in keeping with suggestions from Al-Anon, cease to try to get their husband to stop drinking, try also to believe that nothing they can do will succeed. Thus, their detachment is more complete and not an act. Additionally, they have an authority to cite Al-Anon, which gives them confidence that they are doing the right thing. These latter wives come closer to those wives who, seeing their husband through several treatments and recidivisms, decide that he is really the only person who can stop his own drinking. Thus, there is a sense of calm among those who feel they know what they are doing when they do nothing. Undoubtedly many of these wives arrive at this juncture as a result of attendance at Al-Anon (Gorman and Rooney 1979).

Upon being told that there is little or no likelihood that they can help their husband stop his excessive drinking, regardless of the approach, wives feel noticeable relief. However, if they are to stop nagging, pleading, and other tactics aimed at making him return to sobriety, it is possible they could be robbed of a focal point in their lives. In actuality, wives active in Al-Anon often speak of being "too busy working on their own self-improvement" or their work of helping other women in the same boat to get caught up any more with attempts to do something about their husband's alcoholism:

It takes a long time for a person to change. For 17 years I was just sure that I was doing the right thing by trying to get him to quit. Now, as a result of Al-Anon, I am concentrating on myself. (American)

[My life] was difficult until I got the tools at Al-Anon to work with—when I learned he was not my responsibility. And when I learned to look to myself and correct my own defects. [Then] I had enough to do keeping my own life straight without looking out for him. (Finn)

Well, during the last six months, when there have been times of heavy drinking, I have liberated myself from it. I have disconnected myself from his drinking. (Finn)

I spend my time helping other women married to alcoholics. I have been in Al-Anon a long time. I am the oldest in the group. (Finn)

Women who do not describe the program as giving them a new alliance with God nevertheless express very strongly the worth of the program for them and their resultant enthusiasm for it.

> It's a way of life for me. (American)
>
> The insights I have learned through Al-Anon, and the Al-Anon program is terribly important to me. I have progressed much slower than many of the other ladies, and I've still got a lot of growing to do. Al-Anon is such a beautiful program. (American)

Some women are so grateful that they have discovered Al-Anon as a guide to the conduct of their lives, that they express thanks for having an alcoholic husband that caused them to turn to it! Some suggest it would be beneficial to the general public, whether plagued with a problem drinker in the family, or not:

> I talk to one [wife of an alcoholic] everyday. I talk to one who is as emotionally upset as I am. . . . I talk at night—people call me. I have constant contact—it's like we hold each other up. It's the most beautiful thing in the world. I wish others could have it. (American)
>
> I think Al-Anon would be good for people who don't have an alcoholic to deal with. It is like you cleansing yourself. (Finn)

Secondary Gains from Al-Anon

There are other attractive aspects to Al-Anon membership besides the release from responsibility for their husbands' drinking. The organization offers an avenue to sociability and a means of feeling socially worthy—both areas of importance to wives of alcoholics inasmuch as, has been discussed, they get little social sustenance or appreciation in their marriages.[3] Additionally, as will be seen in Chapter 8, Al-Anon may act as a catalyst to aid the wife in many facets of building a life of her own.

Sociability. The talk problem between husbands who drink and their wives has been described as one of the companionship areas that becomes seriously eroded as the husband spends more and more time either drinking or drunk, or away from home. Inasmuch as his drinking usually drives both friends and relatives away, a wife finds herself virtually isolated from human companionship just at a time when she would like to discuss her problems with someone. Al-Anon fills this void:

> Al-Anon is my outlet. You don't talk just about the alcoholic. You talk about yourself and the shape you're in, and you sit and they say, "How is he doing, and is he drinking again?" and I go, "Not yet," and they go, "I

hope he makes it." If we had to give up our Saturday nights together, it would tear us up. A part of our lives would be gone. (American)

Since I joined the Al-Anon group, I have lots of friends there. I go every Wednesday, and my time is full. (American)

I have no one with whom I could talk about this. Only at Al-Anon where I have acquaintances. (Finn)

Emotional Support.   Meeting other women who are in the same boat is also a help to these wives. It reduces their feelings of isolation and shame to see that others have the same problem. Additionally, they often hear stories of the husbands of others that make their own marriage seem quite good in comparison. Feelings of self-worthiness increase as well:

I went to Al-Anon for about two years, and . . . I enjoyed being there because I learned it wasn't my own personal cross. I mean there was an awful lot of us, and I wasn't the only human being going through all of this, so that's what it really taught me. (American)

[At Al-Anon] we talked about the things we have in common. How I cope, how they cope, and you hear people tell their whole story. (American)

Before Al-Anon, I didn't talk of this problem. You have to have someone with the same problem. That is why Al-Anon is good. In the group, the people gave me some kind of basis for feeling well—an emotional equilibrium. (Finn)

Like other efforts to make contact with others, twelfth-step work has a circular effect—it helps the woman socially as well as psychologically when she helps others:

So, they ask if I'm able to call a person, and I've had a lot of them. I stay on the phone sometimes for a whole hour. That helps me because I'm telling this girl what she should be doing and thereby reminding myself what I should be doing. It's good when you're helping others. It takes my mind off myself. (American)

Disappointments in Al-Anon.   The Al-Anon program appears to be more successful in building peace of mind in the wife than sobriety in the husband, and for some, this is a disappointment:

From the time I started Al-Anon, I haven't done anything [about her husband's drinking]. But, my husband is still drinking. (American)

You see, I've been in Al-Anon now for almost four and one-half years, and I grasped the program very quickly and I immediately stopped hassling him. So I had hoped, you know, that through this, maybe he would stop, but he didn't. (American)

Others feel the program simply does not work for them.

They teach you that if you have any hope for your own peace of mind, give them [the drinking husbands] back their problems and mind your own business, which sounds real good, but after you've been involved for 17 years with someone and doing it all wrong, the habit is hard to break. (American)

I don't think I'll go to Al-Anon for the very fact that as much as I enjoy being with the ladies and everything, I find myself very depressed, because I realize that there's really no help for us, and the only help there is just like group therapy. And after a while you realize, "My God, how many of us in this world there are; you know we've all got the same problems." (American)

I went to Al-Anon one time and I was very disillusioned. . . . I want to say more than "Gee, isn't that awful." I want to get to the source of the problem, to have them say, "O.K. now, this is what it is, this is the way it is, it's up to you to do something about it." I'm looking for an answer. (American)

I went to only one Al-Anon meeting. I don't feel you can learn there. I feel that it's more of a crutch, more of a hindrance than help. They have lectures, but then they aren't interested in my own alcoholic, they are interested in how I live with it. (Finn)

He saw the change in me, but it didn't help him. They tell us in Al-Anon that we have to change and therefore our husbands will, but for me and him, it does not seem to work. (Finn)

Others find the program calls for too much passivity:

The theme of the [Al-Anon] program is that the wife or the other person should understand the alcoholic, keep hands off, tolerate everything, live one day at a time. But for me, it [her husband's drinking] is more than I can stand. (Finn)

Summary and Conclusions

From the point of view of the effect of the alcoholism of one person on a significant other, it can be said to be contagious. Wives of alcoholics offer a case in point. Not surprisingly, the wife of an alcoholic finds living with him very stressful. Certainly, anyone who goes through a long period of anxiety concerning her husband's heavy drinking before finally deciding he is an alcoholic, who fails to get him to cut down on his intake of alcohol, and who experiences numerous treatment failures would experience stress. This is compounded by the man's many unpleasant and frightening behaviors, including violence toward her, refusal to talk to her, avoidance of meals, embarrassing behavior at recreational events, and either abusiveness during or avoidance of sexual behavior, increased undependability, financial problems, and deterioration in his personal appearance and health.

Wives report developing serious physical and mental symptoms during this time, including high blood pressure, nausea, diarrhea, and significant loss of appetite and weight, as well as symptoms of paranoia, deep depression, hostility toward others, and problematic thought patterns. She feels she needs help. Where can she turn?

Although both the research and therapy literature suggest that people can turn to their network of family, friends, and neighbors for aid in a crisis, when the problem is alcoholism such aid is not necessarily forthcoming. Aid to wives of alcoholics can be long-term and costly. They often need money for rent, food, and other necessities or to hire a lawyer. A place to stay when he is drunk and violent is a major need also, as is a shoulder to cry on. They may request aid in getting him into treatment—obviously not an easy task given his resistance to it.

Wives who consider turning to parents, or siblings on either side of the family, realize that some members are unsuitable to ask for this kind of aid due to past difficulties in the relationship, inability to cope with the problem, absence of resources needed, or a temperament unsuited to handling such a crisis. Many women report that they either decided against asking family members for these reasons, or when did ask, they were either refused or the matter was badly handled.

Friends (and neighbors) cut off their relationship with the husband *and the wife* long before she even contemplates going to them for help. Later, she makes friends with other wives of alcoholics, but they usually lack the resources to do much more than offer sympathy.

The few women who go to a priest or minister of their church get spiritual but not practical aid and advice.

Many of these women eventually drift to Al-Anon, often with the hope that this organization will offer some kind of advice or formula to them that they can use to get their husbands to stop drinking. Although this turns out not to be the case, they do find that Al-Anon is useful for some of the problems they have developed as a result of his alcoholism. They learn how to handle their stress level by focusing their energies on their own lives and relinquishing their concern for his. They get a sense of satisfaction and positive identity by helping other wives in the same boat. They also are presented with a program designed to help them both get through a day and feel better about themselves as well. Finally, they get the sympathy and companionship that they desperately need at this time.

Thus, it can be seen that there is little or no substantial help for wives of alcoholics, aside from the philosophical program of Al-Anon.

Chapter 8 is concerned with how some of these women who remain married to alcoholics build a more acceptable life for themselves, while at the same time others sink further and further into despair. Possible reasons for the development of this dichotomy will be advanced.

Notes

1. As mentioned previously, salaries in Finland are sent directly to the worker's bank, where he or she is the only person allowed to cash checks against it, unless other arrangements are made.

2. This is analogous to the twelfth-step work in AA, which is assigned to persons who have successfully managed to remain dry for a considerable period of time. The work itself refers to acting as a sponsor to someone who has stopped drinking much more recently, and is therefore expected to have problems staying off the bottle. When these new members experience such temptation, they are free to call their sponsor, who is expected to go to them and help them overcome the urge to drink. In Al-Anon, members (usually wives) help other more newly arrived spouses of drinking husbands to maintain detachment from their husband's drinking as well as benefit from other parts of the program.

3. This sort of secondary gain can be noted in other self-help groups as well: Parents without Partners was organized ostensibly to aid divorced and/or widowed persons to raise their children alone, but it is also known as a good way to meet a new partner. AA itself uses sociability as one of its drawing cards.

CHAPTER 8

Managing Their Own Lives:
The Challenge and the Barriers

Introduction

When the wife of an alcoholic has tried and failed to combat her husband's love affair with booze; when she finds herself cut off from most forms of social intercourse, denied sexual fulfillment and marital satisfaction, and at times the object of cruel remarks and brutal beatings during his alcoholic rages; when she finds herself in an increasing state of despair as all professional treatment attempts end in failure, she becomes ever more anxious and fear-ridden. She asks herself, "What is to become of me? What is happening to my life?"

This chapter is concerned with how women handle their lives when they see their marriage relationship atrophy and they have deep fears about the future. To most objective observers, the situation of the wife of an alcoholic can be seen as encapsulating two puzzles: why some women will endure such a bad relationship with a spouse, and how some are able to modify their general living situation to make a better life for themselves within the marriage.

An obvious solution to the anguish of living with an alcoholic would seem to be divorce. This study is concerned with women who do not avail themselves of this way out and who may, in fact, represent a majority of these wives.[1] Rather, they stay with the marriage in what seem to be nearly hopeless circumstances. Their reasons for not obtaining a divorce make sense to them—if not to an objective outsider. An alternative way of viewing this apparent puzzle is to note the social and psychological barriers to any positive action the wife of an alcoholic faces and how meager are the resources upon which she can call to overcome them, as was discussed in Chapter 7. Additionally, her problems proliferate as they cause other difficulties. When such a wife's existence is looked at in this prospective, it becomes obvious that she may not be in any condition to make the plans and take the steps necessary to break away from her husband or to create a satisfactory life of her own, either within or outside the marriage. With this established, the problem becomes not, Why doesn't she do something? but How is she able to do anything at all about her life?

Ultimately, these women who remain married take very divergent paths. Many create a life of reasonably satisfying quality and even some measure of independence for themselves while remaining married to an alcoholic man. Others become immobilized by the deteriorating circumstances of their marriage until they are in an almost constant state of despair. The differences in these outcomes, and the types of women who comprise each group will be discussed in this chapter.

As the data presented indicate, women married to alcoholics are deterred from divorce or permanent separation by a combination of real barriers, both cultural and structural, and assumed ones—psychological fears that reflect their lifetime socialization to dependency and passivity. In some ways, a woman's general position in society can be seen in the options available to her to improve her own life in those cases where she does not marry well. The manner in which many of these wives of alcoholics handle their situation illustrates the societal limits on a woman's autonomy as well as her acceptance of a role that combines dependency and a nurturing approach toward even the most unsatisfactory of husbands.

In her seminal discussion *The Future of Marriage*, Bernard (1973) speaks of women "dwindling into wives," a phenomenon that involves the active reshaping of the personality to conform to the wishes or needs or demands of a husband. The result is the development of the "good-woman" syndrome (Dowling 1981), which appears to weaken women to deal with the outside world while strengthening them for family duties:

> The [good] woman who devotes her entire life to keeping her husband straight and her children "protected" is not a saint, she is a clinger. Rather than experience the terrors of being cut loose, of having to find and secure her own moorings, she will hang on in the face of unbelievable adversity. (Dowling, 1981:154)

Wives of alcoholics epitomize this phenomenon. They react to the possibility of leaving such a man with a paradoxical combination of dependency on their husband, while simultaneously feeling responsible for a man who is often helpless and ill.

These feelings offer further refutation of the psychological theory— that the wife of an alcoholic stays in the marriage because she has an unconscious desire to suffer. From her testimony, it appears that her endurance of such a marriage can be seen in terms of the pushes and pulls she experiences, resulting in a sort of mental balance sheet that may indicate to her that she has more to lose than to gain if she should divorce her drinking husband.

The Bonds of Marriage—The Barriers to Divorce

The bonds of marriage may be constituted of more than mutual love, companionship, and shared experiences, even if they are initially forged on that basis. The barriers to divorce are both economic and cultural— the latter also being apparent in the fears wives of alcoholics have about leaving their drinking husband and the priorities they express.

Certainly, these women do consider leaving their husband. However, as discussed in earlier chapters, they are often only semi-serious, using the threat of divorce as a ploy to get their husband to stop drinking. Most of these women seem too timid to plan actually to end their marriages:

> I would like to divorce him, but I don't have the strength to do it. I could not face him and take his children and say, "I don't want to be married to you anymore." (American)
>
> I've considered leaving him, but not really . . . you see, I've lost my self-confidence. (American)
>
> I haven't thought of anything to do—I can't get myself to leave him. (Finn)
>
> Of course, I'm thinking of divorce. All the time. But I won't do that. (Finn)

An indicator of the unhappiness of these women is their high temporary separation rate, which many of them saw as possibly preceding divorce (Kitson and Langlif 1984). Over half of American wives and four out of ten Finnish wives had been separated from their husbands— some more than once (see Table 8.1).

Table 8.1. Proportion of Wives of Alcoholics who Have Separated from Their Husbands because of His Drinking

	American Wives (N = 76) %	Finnish Wives (N = 50) %
Have been separated	53	40
Have not been separated	39	50
No answer	8	10

Yet for all these signs of wives' dissatisfaction, these separations are not permanent. The reasons these women offer for remaining in an unhappy marriage with a drunken spouse include economic dependence, inability to deal with the mechanics of divorce, a sense of guilt and fear as to the repercussions of this action, and a residual feeling of love toward the husband as well as a sense of responsibility to the children.

Economic Dependence and Fears

Women who have been accustomed to being supported by their husband, and even those who currently work outside the home, say they are afraid to get a divorce because they do not think they could make it on their own without a greatly lowered standard of living:[2]

> I have a nice house . . . he is a good provider . . . and I don't have to worry about bills. (American)
>
> [We] live a little better with him . . . he makes a good income and pays the rent. It's a matter of the security. (Finn)

Their fears are well-grounded and not necessarily a reflection of a dependency syndrome. Both American and Finnish women are at a disadvantage vis-à-vis men on the job market, as well as in the way divorce settlements are made. The average woman's salary in the United States is about 68–75% that of a man's; in Finland, it is 64%.[3] For both groups of women, the realistic prospects are for a reduced standard of living if they have to support themselves—for even when working in the same industry, women are systematically excluded from male-dominated job promotion tracks (and even some nonladder jobs). These are, of course, the channels that eventually lead to higher status and better pay (Haavio-Mannila and Tuominen 1974).

Despite the women's movement, the status of American women in both occupation and income has stagnated or lost ground generally since 1950 (Richards 1986; Congressional Caucus for Women's Issues 1987). In addition to the loss of financial support from their husband (which, in the case of wives of alcoholics could be minimal—given the man's checkered work record and/or perilous employment status), these wives face working at low-paying, repetitive jobs for the most part (Stoll 1982). If they are trying to raise young children, many of them will look for part-time work, which has been termed a "circular trap" for women. Smith (1983), for instance, points out that part-time employment is low paying and has no ladder status, inasmuch as it was designed to use labor efficiently while keeping wages at minimum levels without fringe benefits or job security.

Those women who are not currently employed mention a reluctance to get a job. They voice a fear they could not handle the responsibility, either because of lack of current training and experience, or because of their age and length of time they have been off the job market:

> Right now, I couldn't support myself. What would I do? Making $140 to $250 dollars a week, what could I do? You get in a situation where there's no way out. (American)
>
> What do I think I'm going to do? I don't know. I frankly do not know. He made me quit work over 20 years ago, and I wouldn't know how to begin to go out to look for a job. I was earning good money, but he felt that I was too independent of him and he wanted me right under his thumb. . . . I thought I was doing it all for him. I didn't realize what the outcome would be. (American)
>
> So many times I'd talk to myself, "It's not worth it." I'm at the age now where I wish I had enough confidence in me to go back to work, but I've just kinda gotten beat down and think, "I can't hack it. My nerves are too bad; my eyes are going bad." . . . I've got all these excuses. I just think that I can't do it. (American)
>
> Years ago, I was working at commercial TV; since I quit, I have been without a steady job for years. I have no hopes for a steady job in the future. (Finn)

Ironically, women who have been the sole support of their families (including their drinking husband) for several years, also ask, "But how would I get along?" when queried about leaving their spouses. As Bernard (1973) has said, girls are reared to expect to lean on men. Apparently, in the case of the women quoted, a husband's mere presence gives them a sense of security.

For an American wife, alimony and child support might augment her income, but these alone would not maintain her at her current level of income. Additionally, since the adoption of no-fault divorce legislation, alimony and child support are less frequently awarded and increasingly difficult to collect, even with a positive court decision (Weitzman 1985; U.S. Department of Commerce 1978). Hills (1983) has noted, for instance, that children who grow up in poverty are most likely to be in female-headed households. The result is a growing female underclass in the United States. However, although not a pleasant prospect, an American woman could get financial help from welfare, if needed.

Wives in Finland, on the other hand, receive little in the way of support if they try to seek their independence. Economically, the wife knows that if she leaves her husband, she must go it alone. No alimony is awarded in Finland. Although child support is granted, it is, as in the United States, difficult to collect, especially from a heavily drinking, sporadically employed husband (The Position of Women in Finnish Society 1984:94–95). As one woman put it:

> He'd have to pay 1200 Finnmarks a month for the son, but no alimony. I
> have no profession, so I'd have to do just anything. (Finn)

While Finland's government has created a great deal of social legislation, the acceptance of welfare payments is still considered a disgrace, and few wives in that country countenance this as an acceptable option, given the accompanying stigma. An acute housing shortage in Finland heightens economic problems and increases the difficulty of divorce. As noted earlier, although the Finnish parliament decreed all property acquired during a marriage to be jointly owned by husband and wife (regardless of whose name showed on the deed), many wives seemed unaware of this, and thought that their condominium-type apartment belonged to their husband alone—a misrepresentation he was happy to foster in some cases. Wives in both cultures fear they will have to move out of their current home—along with their children—and will literally have no place to live if they leave their husband. (From testimony discussed in Chapter 7, very few expect to be taken in by family members. Additionally, the experience of many of these women during temporary separations no doubt reinforces a wife's feelings of not being wanted as a long-term guest.) Binney, Harkell, and Nixon (1985) have found that battered women would leave their husband if they had a place to go. This also appears to be the case with wives of alcoholics. Inasmuch as relatives and friends usually do not offer more than a few nights of shelter, they ask themselves, when considering leaving permanently, "Where would I go?" Getting their husbands to move out, getting a temporary settlement, finding an apartment before moving, or finding a relative or friend to move in with for a longer period were seen as extremely difficult to manage:

> I thought about [leaving him]. Where would I go? I can't move in on my
> parents and disrupt another household. (American)
>
> I don't have a place to go to, and in order to move out you have to have
> [that] and money behind you. Where will I go? Motels, hotels are expen-
> sive. [There's] food and medical bills. You can go on welfare . . . but still
> you have to have a place to live. (American)

For Finnish wives, knowledge of a continuing apartment shortage in Helsinki, combined with the fear (whether well-founded or not) that the husband has sole control of the apartment, also helps hold some marriages together. (One woman brought in a letter clipped from a daily Finnish newspaper, in which the wife of an alcoholic predicted that if the apartment shortage were to end, there would be a dramatic increase in the skid row population!) These women say:

> I threatened to leave him last spring. The first thing he said was "The apartment is mine. How do you think you will get along?" (Finn)
>
> If I could get an apartment, I'd leave him in a minute. (Finn)

Even for those Finnish women who owned the apartment before their marriage, the housing problem is not solved. Their husband simply refuses to move out. Under Finnish law, it is quite difficult to force him to leave:

> Even though it's my apartment, he won't move and I couldn't leave the apartment to him because it is mine. Even the lawyer said, "You will have to get the police to get him out." I couldn't sign a paper saying he was moving; he has to sign that himself. (Finn)

There are other reasons, however, not as directly tied to economics, that make wives wary of starting divorce proceedings.

Concern over the Mechanics of Getting Divorced

The steps and money necessary to get a divorce seem to confound wives in both countries. They worry about the cost of an attorney, the evidence they need for a divorce, and the kind of settlement that would be possible. Some wives are so certain that divorce proceedings will not work out to their advantage that they do not even bother see an attorney. Those who do seem to get little in the way of reassurance from lawyers they consult.

Money to pay a lawyer is a major concern. Either wives do not know of the possibility of a contingency fee arrangement, or are unsuccessful in persuading a lawyer to take the case on this basis:

> I have wanted to divorce him, but never have been able to figure out how to manage the money. (American)
>
> I have seen a lawyer three times to start a divorce, but did not have the money to go through with it. I have never been able to figure out how to manage the money, the expense of it, or taking care of the kids if I leave. (Finn)

Alcoholic husbands in the United States sometimes inform their wives that they actually have no grounds for a divorce. Many wives believe them:

> My husband says that I can't divorce him because he has not mistreated me. Physically, he has not hit me. . . . He says that everything that I've

wanted I have gotten. . . . I went to the library and found out that there is
such a thing as mental cruelty. . . . He had me believing for a long time
that I couldn't get a divorce. (American)

I would never walk out on him, I'd have him leave; [this is] because he
said, if I ever walked out on him, he would have papers drawn immediately that I was not to return to the house and that I deserted him—he didn't
desert me. (American)

Finnish wives are not so much threatened by their husbands as by
Finnish divorce law, which seems to favor the man financially—in the
strength of the evidence necessary to obtain a divorce and/or his cooperation with the proceedings:

If I divorce him, I need some kind of evidence he's drinking. (Finn)

I once phoned a lawyer and he said I should have a better motive. You
cannot divorce on grounds of psychic cruelty. To give alcoholism as
grounds for divorce, I have to let our house break down—the bills pile up.
(Finn)

Guilt and Fear as Divorce Inhibitors

Culturally, in both the United States and Finland, marriage is not a
state to be cast aside lightly. The wife of an alcoholic experiences informal social pressures not to desert her husband in his time of need and
not to deprive her children of their natural father. Rather, she is supposed to be trying to help him with his drinking problem at home or get
him into treatment, provide a home upon his return and assist with his
continuing recovery. Divorced women have a lower status in both countries than do married women, but the Finnish divorce is the most culturally stigmatized. (Etaugh and Malstrom, 1981).

Socialized to play a nurturing role in marriage,[4] women in both countries reflect the good-woman syndrome (Dowling 1981; Bernard 1973)
and express feelings of responsibility for their husbands.[4] Wives stay
with a drinking spouse because of a fear that, if they leave, the man's
drinking will rapidly progress to the point where he drifts to skid row. If
this happens, the wives would feel responsible for such deterioration.
They also feel that their presence prevents him from hurting himself
while drunk. Additionally, they reason, if their husband becomes indi-
gent, child support will most certainly not be paid:

If I was not here, that would probably be the surest way to make him go
downhill faster. (American)

Another thing I've been afraid of, if I left, he might hit skid row, and I
wouldn't want to be responsible for that. (American)

But mostly, I don't feel like leaving him alone. *I'm like his guard.* In a way, I'm scared he'll hurt himself. Just the, other day, he hurt his hip. (Finn) (emphasis mine)

There are other reasons why wives are wary of starting divorce proceedings, however, that are less tied to economics and are more a reflection of the way in which their self-doubts and their hesitancy to take risks leave them immobilized.

The Husband's Resistance to Divorce

Alcoholic husbands do not want their wife to leave them. This is true in both Finland and the United States. The question might be asked, Why should men want to stay with a woman who nags them about their drinking? Why stay with a wife they avoid talking to or joining at meals? Why would these men want to keep a wife who is avoiding sex with them, or in whom they have lost sexual interest? Caldwell, Bloom, and Hodges (1984), Bernard (1973), and Pahl and Pahl (1974) have pointed out that husbands prefer the married state and will cling to it when wives wish to dissolve it, often primarily for the services it provides.[5] The threats that men use to intimidate their wife and to impede her instigation of divorce proceedings reveal the fairly practical reasons they have for clinging to the married state:

He said when you get married, it is for life. He said . . . you just stay through sickness and health until death do us part. (American)

When I talk about leaving him or divorcing him, he gets very angry. He wouldn't have a home to leave and come back to after drinking. (Finn)

Other alcoholic men use their reputations for violence, usually established earlier in the marriage, to make their wife fearful of leaving or filing for divorce:

He said, "If you do it [file for a divorce], I swear that I'll kill you before you leave me." (American)

I think I've had a divorce in my mind for some time, but I think that a divorce would not mean I'd get rid of him. I'd have to go to America. Even if he managed to get an apartment for himself, he'd be outside my door all the time. He sometimes says in the evenings, "You'll never leave me," or "We'll never part." (Finn)

One woman, wishing a divorce, but afraid of what her husband would do if she left him, revealed how desperately she views the difficulty of actually getting away from her husband:

I've thought of committing suicide. If it wasn't for my children, I think maybe I would. I'll have to leave this town if I leave him, because that's the type of person he is. (American)

Love as a Habit and a Barrier to Divorce

A substantial proportion of American women still claim to love their heavily drinking husband and do not leave him for this reason. They point out that when you love someone and he gets a disease (in this case, alcoholism), you do not desert him:

I have an awful lot of love for him. I do love him very much. I can't help but love him because I know what he really is. You know he's a beautiful man and that hurts. (American)

Some women say their feelings of love persist partly out of habit, despite the broken promises, verbal abuse, and in some cases the beatings, as the result of years of living together.

It's hard to explain why you do [stay with someone]. I think mostly when you love somebody and you get older, it gets to be a habit of living with someone and being with somebody. (American)

Among Finnish women, love is the least frequently mentioned reason for not divorcing. When these women do mention love, it is obviously intermingled with pity:

First, it must be love that keeps me with him. But, second, we have three children. And then I start to think what would happen to him if he were left alone. Perhaps it is love or pity. He is very nice and kind and he loves me; there's no doubt about it. I feel he needs me and in some way he leans on me. (Finn)

I very seldom think of leaving him. I stay out of pity and some feeling of honor. . . . I would like to meet another man, because he is like an old man—he has lost his energy. . . . He's always tired, sleepy, not feeling well. But I guess being unfaithful to him would be like hurting a child and leaving him would be like leaving a child. (Finn)

Children as an Inhibitor of Divorce

Children act as a barrier to divorce in three ways. First, women hate to break up a family and leave their children without a father, regardless of how inadequate the man is because of drinking. Second, children often beg their mother not to leave their father. Finally, these women fear, as discussed earlier, that they will be unable to support their children (they invariably assume—probably correctly—that they will have to take over this responsibility alone).

Children's pleas "not to leave daddy" are particularly poignant and play a substantial part in the mother's decision to stay with her husband:[6]

> Marsha [the daughter] started crying, and said, "Dad, is it true that you and Mom are getting divorced?" That is really one reason why we went back together. (American)
>
> Earlier they [the children] didn't want to break up the family because they didn't understand how awful things were for me. (Finn)

Some American wives speak of waiting to leave until their children are grown. But they also say they do not expect to be any better prepared several years from now to support themselves, and, as will be seen, they actually find leaving more difficult the longer they wait to attempt it.

In Finland, adult children also exert great pressure on their mother to stay with the drinking father, to "take care of him." Thus, the wife actually loses family support at the very time when it would be possible to leave because the children are finally grown:

> My daughter agrees with my son that there should be no divorce. She thinks I am the strong one and should keep the weak one. I think they are ashamed of divorce. (Finn)

Time, Ambivalence, and the Development of Inertia

Rather than finding that their resolve to leave their alcoholic husband strengthens with time and maturing of children, the wife's sense of dependence seems to increase, and divorce becomes increasingly difficult for the wife to contemplate as the years go by:

> When he was younger, after the war, and when he drank and had other women, I thought it best to divorce him. But he didn't want me to. Now that I am older, I don't think about divorce very much. (American)
>
> In a way, I'm just now in a dead end. I really don't know what to do. I'm mostly at home. I'm no longer thinking of leaving him. (Finn)

Time, then, works against women who are married to alcoholics and want out of the union. First of all, there is the considerable period of doubt when the woman is not certain that alcoholism is the root cause of the problems she and her husband are having. Then, with the diagnosis certain, she usually sees her spouse through several treatment periods that fail to help him stop drinking. At the same time, she sees more and more negative aspects and many obstacles, real or imagined, to divorce. Thus, she finds it easy to yield to her children's pleas for an intact home.

Bernard (1981:502–4) has noted that the duty and love ethos of women becomes increasingly costly to them psychologically. The longer that wives of alcoholics postpone leaving their drinking husbands, the more ambivalent they become about succeeding. The mental balance sheet becomes more and more negative as they attempt to project the effects on their lives of such a move. They know they are getting older. They know they have been off the labor market for a long time, and that the prospects of getting a job (sometimes with outdated skills) and support-ing themselves and their children on what it would pay is truly frightening:

> What do I think I'm going to do? I don't know. I frankly do not know. If I could get separated from him and make sure that he would send at least $1,580 a month, I know that the girls and I would be much better off without him. But I know that if we are separated he will destroy himself completely. So I can't do that. So basically, I really don't know what I'm going to do. I just know what I'd like to do. (American)

The reasons the women themselves give for not leaving their homes and husbands suggest, then, a strong sense of duty combined with growing dependency, and an acute awareness of their precarious eco-nomic position. Additionally, a number of other fears and barriers ap-pear to keep wives in marriages that might not otherwise be expected to hold them. Intrinsic to all of these reasons appears to be an absence of knowledge, a vagueness of thought, an inability to face the problems, and a general failure to think out the necessary steps that would have to be taken to obtain a divorce. The dependent role of the wife appears to have drastically sapped the ability of these women to think about going it alone, as well as to have reduced their psychological readiness to attempt to make the break.

Styles of Living with an Alcoholic Husband:
A Comparison of Approaches

When the wife of an alcoholic decides that divorce is not desirable or feasible, she is faced with continuing life as spouse to a man whose drinking has made her marital existence one of emptiness and some-times fear. She is left with two alternatives: continue to drift along in what Perry (1975) might describe as an emotionally and socially trun-cated existence,[7] or create an independent life of her own, developing her own activities, her own friends, and sources of satisfaction.

The women interviewed who remain married fall into two fairly dis-crete categories. One group (about one-fourth in each culture) is stunned by all that has happened and sinks further and further into inertia, lack of self-confidence, dependence, loneliness, and self-pity. These wives seem unable to leave the house very often to do anything on their own. If they do work outside the home, they do so without interest or enjoyment. A second group of women (approximately three-fourths in both cultures) can be subdivided into those who find satisfaction in life by intensifying their interest in their homes and children (approximately one-third in both cultures) and those who take steps to, in their words, "lead their own lives" while still remaining married (slightly over 40% in each culture). These latter wives obtain jobs that pique their interest and give them both joy and a positive self-image. Some embark on new careers or begin training for one. Others take courses in school and join social clubs. All of them make friends.

Assessment of Possible Factors That Could Make a Difference in Wives' Ultimate Life-Styles

What can account for the difference in life-styles of these wives who elect to stay in their marriages with an alcoholic man? One might at first think in terms of both the usual social factors: resources and barriers to limited but satisfying independence. Age, education, income, employment opportunities, and number and ages of children in the home can all presumably help or hinder a wife to some happiness in life, regardless of her marriage partner.

Yet, when women building an independent life-style are compared with those who are not, few significant differences in the above areas are apparent, with the possible exception of the presence of children—especially teenage children. The presumed problems created by children, however, are not enough to explain such a wide variety in life-style.

From Table 8.2, it can be seen that women building their own lives are, on the average, slightly younger than those women who are not; but an equal proportion of American women over 50 years of age are found in both groups. However, three times as many Finnish women married to alcoholics and building their own lives are between the ages of 21 and 30, than are those of that age group taking no action.

The amount of formal education does seem to make a small difference with Finnish women, although not with Americans. This may be because almost all Finnish women plan to work when their formal education is completed, while many American women 35 or older who went to college at the time did so with the undeclared ultimate goal of marrying and becoming wives and homemakers.

Distribution of annual income within each society appears almost identical for the group of women building their own lives and those taking no action. Contrary to expectations, the apparent effect of having

Table 8.2.   Characteristics of Wives of Alcoholics who are Building Their Own Lives Compared with Wives who Have Taken no Action

	American Wives		Finnish Wives	
	Building Own Lives (N = 34) %	Taking No Action (N = 42) %	Building Own Lives (N = 20) %	Taking No Action (N = 30) %
Age				
Under 21	—	4	—	—
21–30	9	7	35	12
31–40	32	21	25	28
41–50	24	35	25	28
50 and over	35	33	15	26
Refused	—		—	3
Educational level*				
Grade school or less	6	7	25	55
Some high school	15	16	5	27
High school graduate or trade school	39	30	55	44
Some college	25	25	15	12
College graduate or beyond	15	20	20	3
No answer	—	2	5	—
Annual income**				
Low	18	21	65	61
Medium low	34	37	25	15
Medium high	19	14	5	9
High	16	13	5	—
Don't know, no answer	13	15	—	15
Employment status				
Employed outside home	32	52	95	61
Not employed outside home	68	48	5	39
Number of children at home				
None	32	16	30	24
One	25	19	40	40
Two	25	30	15	24
Three or more	9	26	15	12
No answer	9	9	—	—
Ages of children at home	(N = 20)	(N = 32)	(N = 14)	(N = 23)
Young (11 and under)	40	22	65	37
Adolescents (12–20)	40	53	33	56
Children in both age groups	20	25	2	7

* Finnish columns add to more than 100% because of the common practice in that country to stop formal education with elementary schooling and enroll in a vocation or trade school. It should also be mentioned that various "home arts" such as sewing, are taught in these vocational schools as well as more career-oriented subjects.

** See methodology for discussion on salary comparability.

some kind of job outside the home is not a definitive factor in building a more satisfactory life. In the United States, more women not employed outside the home are building lives they describe as satisfactory. Additionally, among the group taking no action to improve their existence, there is little difference between the proportion who are employed and those who are primarily homemakers. Among Finnish wives, however, almost all of those building their own lives are employed outside the home; on the other hand, two-thirds of those taking no action are employed as well.

Wives of alcoholics in both countries building a life of their own are more likely to have no children, or only one child. Wives who are taking no action are likely to have larger families. The differences between the two groups, however, are not conclusive. Perhaps the most important difference is the age of the children rather than the number. Women married to alcoholics who are building satisfactory existences of their own are much more likely to be raising young children than teenagers. This is somewhat surprising, inasmuch as it might be expected that young children would present a greater barrier to building a better existence than adolescents, because of the more constant care that youngsters require. Adolescents, however, while needing less physical care, and offering some sociability, also have the special problems of teenagers.

It is possible that the women are occupied with these maturing children and have less time on their hands to try new approaches to life. Of course, the very presence of youngsters of this age means that the woman is older, has been in the marriage longer, and thus finds it more difficult to force herself to get out and have new experiences. Table 8.3 indicates the proportions of women building lives of their own and those who are not.

If concrete resources and/or barriers to independence of life-style within the marriage do not differ sufficiently to explain why some wives develop a better quality of life and others sink into despair, what might be the cause? An alternative explanation may lie in those ephemeral factors often termed motivation, inner resources, or general attitude. What is the state of mind that enables some wives to bootstrap themselves into a satisfactory life, while others remain mired in discontent? Here, of course, one might expect that Al-Anon and its philosophy of detachment and self-development could play a leading role in aiding wives to develop a better quality of life for themselves. No doubt it does play a part, but given that approximately 4 in 10 women who attend Al-Anon are building a life for themselves (and the remainder of attenders are not), while the same proportions pertain to nonmembers also, mere participation in Al-Anon would seem not to be sufficient explanation.

Table 8.3. Life Style of Wives of Alcoholics who Decide not to Divorce
Their Husbands

	American (N = 76) %	Finn (N = 50) %
Dependent and despondent; almost total inertia	25	28
Intensified interest in home/children	30	32
Building independent life through work, education, and new friends	45	40

Additionally, as mentioned, some women who try Al-Anon are eventually disappointed because working the program does not bring sobriety to her husband. They then quit going to meetings.

Scrutinizing first those wives who seem frozen into an unhappy inertia and seeing what problems they have, it should be possible to see—through subsequent comparison with their mirror image (wives with satisfying life-styles)—what sorts of inner resources and attitudes these women must have to rescue themselves from day-to-day unhappiness. Furthermore, these resources and attitudes—or their absence—may coalesce into an understandable pattern.

Components of Inertia in the Face of Unhappiness

Almost half of all women who cannot seem to develop any satisfactory life-style independent of their husbands literally cannot think of what to do. They answer the question, What have you done to build a more satisfactory life for yourself? tersely:

I don't know what to do. I am still searching. (American)

No. Actually, I wish to God I could think of something. (American)

During many years, I have just lived in a state of fear and haven't known what to do. (Finn)

What could I do? It is so hopeless. As it is now today for me, I don't know what to do. (Finn)

What sort of mental approach do these women have to their problems? What sorts of attitudes or inner resources do they lack?

Muddled Thinking.   To solve any problem, an individual must have the ability to think fairly clearly. Ordinarily, it is necessary that the circumstances involved be assessed and possible alternative courses of action to a given situation be weighed. Some wives of alcoholics claim they cannot seem to get started on such a contemplative project. Their descriptions of their general state of mind on the topic of their future indicate a great deal of muddled thinking:

> I'm not a deep thinker, but at the same time . . . I already know I have to go to school. I already know I have to make a decision as to what I'm going to take. . . . I also have to make a decision as to where I want to live . . . but in the meantime, you feel tied up in knots. You gotta do something, either be more constructive in your thinking I used to say. . . . I'm real sorry for myself. I never went anywhere and so I got in this kind of state where I have to do something. (American)
>
> I haven't done anything for myself. I am so lonely. It is so difficult. I don't know if I could go to work—I haven't tried. I'm afraid of him. (Finn)

Only a few of this group of women are introspective enough to ponder ways of getting out of the apparent trap of marriage to an alcoholic spouse. They seem unable, however, to pull themselves together to do anything about their situation:

> I never really did [try to build a life of my own]. . . . All this time I have just lived from day to day, wondering what was going to happen next. And not really caring. I'd see young kids walking home from school where I lived. I'd wonder what the hell they were so happy about, what is there to live for? That is how I get to feeling. (American)
>
> I'm trying to search in my own self and find out why it was that I settled for as little as I settled for. Sitting home and waiting for him, never going out and making friends, or meeting other people or doing social things . . . this isn't a normal type of reaction. I don't believe most people would have had. I think most women would have done something. (Finn)

One woman spoke of a somewhat frantic effort to "find herself," but she is in a situation of social isolation, so that she has no one to turn to for assistance:

> [I have done] nothing really [to build a life of my own]. I've just been staying here. I go visit my sister. I did go through a period of emptiness until I started going alone to parks; go alone to beaches, go marketing, go for a drive alone, and out there it seemed like I could find myself. I've been trying to find myself all this time. (American)

Inability to Create a Practical Plan of Action. Persons desiring to change any long-term personal situation must think out possible steps to bring about the desired change. The order of these steps is important, as well, since change comes about from building a new situation little by little. Furthermore, a willingness to put forth the effort necessary to move from one step to another is essential. Wives of alcoholics in a state of inertia seem not to have these qualities. American women doing nothing about their lives mention a sort of grocery list of things they would like to do, but this bears little resemblance to any sort of realistic step-by-step plan:

> Ah, I have thought of doing a lot of things. I wanted to go back to school and take another course, and see, and do things for people—I love doing for people. (American)

> I'm not trained for anything. . . . I have thought of moving out and getting a friend to live with and just travel. (American)

There are some woman who try to think more definitively just what they could do. However, they cannot clearly visualize a plan of action because of the obstacles they see and the loss-gain ratio they envisage. Taking risks seems impossible and such an attitude obscures necessary planning:

> Well, I've thought about leaving him. God knows how many times I've thought about that. But there are an awful lot of things that keep me from doing that. Not that I don't want to. I still think that would be the best thing for me, I'm not sure about for him. And then I weigh them and I go back and count everything else, and I'm not sure I'd find myself better off by that other [leaving him]. I wouldn't have to put up with the drinking; it drives me crazy sometimes, but I need his insurance. I need a good many other things that he can give me that I wouldn't have if I left him. You see what I mean. (American)

> It seems like my mother and dad come out to California almost every year. . . . They are with me for about a month, and I look forward to that so much, and I know if I was working, I couldn't do that. . . . Now I should hurry up and get out and get a job, but I don't want to do it because she [my sister] is coming [to visit now]. I want to spend time with her and take her around. (American)

Finnish women seem almost too emotionally exhausted to start to consider making plans at all—even unrealistic or muddled ones. Thus, they talk in very negative terms about making changes in their lives:

> I don't know if it's possible to create a life of my own while we live together. If I were to divorce, it might be quite different. (Finn)

> I hope that this situation—of building my new life—can be done *after* the children are grown. Then I can get their advice. (Finn)

Even getting out of the house briefly seems beyond the capabilities or energies of some of these women:

> I haven't done very much on my own. I have the feeling he wouldn't like it. And then, if I went out, I'd be so tired the next day at work. (Finn)

I could have asked someone to watch the children and then went out, but I didn't feel like it. (Finn)

Lack of a Positive Self-Image and Optimism Concerning New Experiences. Optimism that a conceived plan will succeed and willingness to work hard to accomplish it seem necessary to the creation of a better life. It is hard for a woman to develop such attitudes when she has the negative self-concept that plagues many wives of alcoholics:

I thought maybe about going to work for a while, but I could see other problems coming from that and I didn't do it. I didn't really want to. (American)

If it were not for my age, I would love to work. I have never worked. I don't know what I can do. (American)

Many of these women simply do not see themselves handling any type of work demanding skill, responsibility, and some dedication. Even those women who express an interest in improving their skills and trying to make it on the job market are unsure as to what they want to do. They have been away from work so long that they have no special orientation and seem to flounder about:

When I started my secretary job, I went and took typing before I got the job . . . then I took night school [and] when he [her husband] left in February, I took shorthand, two nights a week. I just dropped both of them, call it lack of interest or I just didn't think I could afford the gas— going that far. Now, if I had a little car. (American)

[I'd like to] become independent, but I'll tell you something, I don't think I can study. I can't remember. I have taken all these courses and I cannot remember. I get them [the courses] and can talk of things later, but to be able to remember enough for exams [for a job], I don't think I can do it. (American)

Absence of Willingness to Go Ahead in the Face of No Support or Even Opposition. Encouragement from significant others is helpful to a person charting the unfamiliar territory of self-development; however, if it is not forthcoming, individuals building independent lives must have the ability to go ahead without it, even ignoring criticism. Women who are doing nothing with their lives and who are married to alcoholics seem unable to develop this sort of single-mindedness, but rather are constantly worried about their husband's attitudes toward their activities. Not surprisingly, they get little encouragement from these men when they approach the possibility of going back to school, getting a job, or trying other activities:[8]

I have thought of getting into different types of activities, just to get out and take my mind off of the problem. Usually [my husband] made excuses about the money, so it seemed like everything I wanted to do took money, so I just never did it. (American)

[I'm] just getting through the next few years. Trying to . . . you see, I'm a peace-at-any-price person. Any type of disharmony upsets me. Any anger, unpleasantness, I can't face it. So, what I do is tolerate it and smile and gunnysack it. (American)

Many Finnish wives claim that it is their husband who prevents them from going out, getting a job, or making new friends:

I'd like to go back to work. I'm much more alert when I work, but my husband thinks I shouldn't. He thinks the state should help with our rent. (Finn)

I don't go anywhere. He wouldn't like it if I did. (Finn)

Sexual jealousy, apparently found more frequently among Finnish men than American, as discussed previously, is cited by these wives as one reason their husbands fear to have them working outside the house:

He suspects me of things. He thinks when I tell him I was somewhere, I am really having a party. He's "very inhibiting"—he even follows me from room to room. (Finn)

He doesn't let me go out alone. He's afraid I'll be meeting some man. (Finn)

Inability to Be Selfish.   Women married to an alcoholic man, who fail to build a satisfactory life for themselves, do not develop any self-centeredness. These women, who neither get a divorce nor seek some improvements in their lives, have been socialized to a nurturing role. They trap themselves because they feel at once needed by a "sick" husband, and guilty because they want a better quality of life. In the end, they give a major portion of their time and effort to fulfilling their husband's needs:

I can't go to work now because I must see to it that he doesn't drive, and [I must] take care of him. (American)

I usually try to get away when he's drunk although sometimes I stay because he can't be trusted alone; he might do anything. (Finn)

It is obvious, from the explanations of these women who have reached a state of unhappy inertia that improvement of life-style takes more than money, time, education, or even access to employment. It takes motivation and the kind of attitude that turns people into optimistic self-starters, either willing to work hard, and able to ignore criticisms and feelings of guilt, or able to find a sense of peace and satisfaction in home, children and mundane activities without the support and company of their husband. Women appearing to have some kind of positive focus in their lives (in differential amounts) are discussed next.

Homemaking as the Focal Point of Life Satisfaction

A fairly sizable portion of women remaining married to an alcoholic (approximately one-third in each culture) create a partial psychic haven by increased emphasis on domesticity and its accompanying skills.

Enjoying the Company of Children and Relatives. Many of these home-oriented women say that as a result of their husband's drinking they have begun to devote more and more time to their children:[9]

> My life is completely devoted to the kids. (American)
>
> Having four children, I just thrive on my children. I keep them active in school [and] encourage them to try out for things at school. Two are cheerleaders; one works. (American)
>
> I try to keep busy, and I like to sew a lot, and my daughter is in Girl Scouts and I get real busy with her activities, and my son's too. (American)

Lacking opportunities to meet nonrelated adults for sociability, the home-oriented woman must also turn to her children or other relatives for her recreation. Of course, most, if not all, of the friendships she and her husband made before his alcoholism became acute are by now defunct:

> We'll go shopping or we'll clean house. We do things just the three of us, my two daughters and myself. We live a life of our own. We'll go to the movies, and we do things without him. (American)
>
> I'm getting involved in everything that my kids are involved in. Wrestling, we went through the wrestling season, and we will start with basketball and football, and even if I don't like hockey I will sit there and we will discuss the players. (American)
>
> I was relieved whenever he went away [to drink]. We had no television, but I would make cocoa for the children and we enjoyed our time together. I read a lot, did handiwork, and invited some of my old friends over. (Finn)

Spending a great deal of time with the children, because of the husband's drinking, is obviously a substitute for the adult activities in which married couples normally engage, as apparent from these quotes:

> At one point I used to have a baby to help me through it [her husband's drinking]. My last baby was very important to me because taking care of her took up all of my time and helped me to forget that he was not home. (American)

I tried to take the kids out for walks and things—just to take them to a park. I didn't have that much in me to have enough patience with them at home. Somehow going to a park and sitting on the green grass and looking at trees and the animals seemed to help make it pleasant for me. . . . I could release my tensions a little better there and seemed I was more at peace with myself that way. (American)

We [she and her children] go on a picnic, we go on a long walk . . . we have a good time, instead of us all staying home being miserable. (Finn)

For adult company and recreation, many wives turn to relatives. While the activities do not sound very exciting, they do get the wife out of the house and give her an opportunity to socialize:

My sister-in-law will call me up and we'll get our hair done. I've got three sisters-in-law and they'll call me up and invite me for lunch. (American)

I would go with my mother window shopping, and have lunch together— anything to get out of the house. (American)

Concentration on Home Arts. Handiwork of all kinds—knitting, crocheting, embroidering, sewing—also appears to help take up the slack in the life of a wife of an alcoholic. Wives describe their skills and activities in this area with some pride.

For other wives, especially the Finnish, housework, unlike child care, is perceived not necessarily as pleasurable, but therapeutic, taking the mind off problems associated with her husband's drinking:

All I do is work here in this house, and . . . when I'm mad, I go work in the yard. (American)

When I was alone, I generally couldn't concentrate on anything. I made food for the children. (Finn)

When he's drinking, I wonder about my life. During the times he is drinking, I wash dishes and clothes, clean the house, anything to keep my mind off it. (Finn)

For one woman, housekeeping became the part of her existence that she could control:

Well, what I have done is become a fanatic in keeping my house clean. I just totally involve myself in my housework. A speck of dirt would just drive me up a wall. . . . If there was just one speck of dirt or the kids would make a mess, oooh, I'd scream and yell at them. . . . The other part of my life, there was nothing I could do. I had no control over it. It was a mess and I couldn't get it straightened out or solved. (American)

Other Approaches to Improve the Quality of Existence within the Home. The extra time that these wives have while their husband drinks is often used to read and watch television:

> I can lose myself in a book . . . or I watch TV. (American)

> My own life? It's a very lonely life; it's very lonely and I don't like it. I seek companionship in my books. I read a lot and that's about it. (Finn)

A surprisingly few American women looked for solace in religion (except as it is represented in Al-Anon). The same was true of Finnish women. One woman did report converting to Christianity when her husband became an alcoholic, but she expressed disillusionment that God did not help her husband to attain sobriety. Others expressed hope for "finding themselves" or "finding strength" through God.

The press for something to do and someone to relate to while doing it can drive a neglected wife to looking for other male companionship. However, only a few wives of alcoholics mentioned this outlet, perhaps because a good proportion are past the age when women have an easy time attracting men:

> I'm talking about keeping busy like with Al-Anon and such, going bowling or whatever. There's times I've been tempted. I figure, "What the heck. I ought to get me a boyfriend on the side." (American)

> Well, I had even thought of maybe developing a relationship, a companion of my own—someone that I could talk to, [a] male, but I could not do it and why I don't understand. (Finn)

Although these women cannot be described as having a totally independent life, they are enjoying their days more than their counterparts who, in a state of inertia, have yet to do anything about their condition. Women who have learned to enjoy whatever home and family have to offer have an outlook that is more optimistic and their thinking is less muddled. They appear to have a more positive self-concept. On the other hand, their activities can, at best, be described as a minimum plan of action. Certainly, they are avoiding any behavior that could bring on criticism, either by their husbands or by others. Even more certainly, they cannot be called selfish about their own development. The contrast between this group and those who are actually creating a life-style of their own, while nominally married, will be seen.

Getting Outside the Home as a Way to Independence

In the discussion that follows, the various paths wives of alcoholics try in seeking a more satisfactory life outside the home will be discussed. How these women formulate plans for their own lives and experience increasing optimism in their execution will be described. Often using some problem as a catalyst, they seem to be able to forge ahead optimistically without the aid of emotional support or the detraction of guilt feelings.

Employment as It Enhances the Quality of Life. One of the problems often facing wives of alcoholics is that of making ends meet financially.[10] The pinch may first be felt as the husband siphons off ever-increasing amounts of money for alcohol. Later, he may lose his job, drift from job to job, or, if a pieceworker, earn on a sporadic basis. Sometime during this downhill slide, the wife decides she must go to work, even if that was not originally her plan after marriage. If already employed, the woman starts concentrating on her job to a greater degree than she did before her husband's drinking threatened their economic status. However, her relationship to her job is strikingly different from that of employed wives who are in a state of despair and inertia. These women increase their concentration on the job, and, as a result find that employment gives many new meanings to their lives. New interest in the job then sparks feelings of independence:[11]

> I like my job. It gives me some money . . . and we needed the income right now; but also I just like the feeling of independence that my own job gives me. (American)

> When he was fired and we had no money, I went back to work. I won't ever quit working now—I enjoy *that*. I really made my life tolerable, in a way, by working. Now I have money of my own so I don't have to ask him. (Finn)

> I decided that I had to start work as soon as I could because of the children and partly because of economical reasons. But it [the decision] was very much because I had to get independent. I wanted to learn to think: that's my life and this is his. (Finn)

But even beyond the possibility of financial independence, employment serves as a means of maintaining mental health, making new friends, and enhancing one's self-image. Some women claim they do not know how they would have survived emotionally without the job. Employment improves these women's outlook on life by providing an alternative setting, where their husband and problems associated with drinking cannot intrude:[12]

> What the job did primarily was to give me a dual self—just like the alcoholic—a Jekyll and Hyde life. It [the job] has given me a normal sane life, and then I can come home to this crazy life! (American)

> When I walked in to where I work, and until I left for the day, I was in another wonderful world. I was doing something constructive and I was away from that alcoholic. (American)

> I am now working on a ship, selling perfume. I got myself such a job because I couldn't wait for a miracle. I had to take care of myself and my children. However, it was a very good solution in another way. I would work outside the home and do not see him drinking. (Finn)

The sense of independence and autonomy that can result from successfully holding a job also helps to create a positive self-image for a wife whose drinking husband has been hard on her ego:

> It [the job] lets me know that I am a person—I'm not a nothing, and I'm needed somewhere. (American)
>
> I'm a teller and I was trained as a teller . . . and I do everything. Now I do safety deposits and work into accounts on Saturdays, and I just have a big time because I go and people give me the strokes that I don't get at home. And they say, "Oh you must love your work you're so good at it." . . . And I think to myself: "I'm a human being. I am a worthwhile person." And I need that right now. (American)

It is not surprising that women who derive all these benefits from employment become determined, even compulsive, workers. Simultaneously she seems to reduce her sense of responsibility toward her husband, as well:

> I always went to work. I never missed any of my work because of it [her husband's drinking]. Even if he was lying there obviously quite sick from one of his drinking bouts, I would go ahead and leave him and I would go to work! (American)
>
> I've gotten myself to the point that I've got two good jobs and I've been doing some typing at home. . . . I've become a compulsive worker. (American)

Commitment to a job, including making it a central part of life, does not come naturally to most women, having been socialized to see their job as a way to supplement the family income (Ferree 1984; Martin and Hanson 1985). A woman's work orientation depends in part on her sex role ideology (Baker and Bootcheck 1985), but traditional sex role attitudes can be changed by experience on the job and educational attainment (Thornton and Camburn 1983). The greater the job scope, its status, and the autonomy and career possibilities available in a job, the more women will make it a central role.

Some of these women become so involved in their work that they also find satisfaction in taking related training and/or pertinent courses, thus improving their job skills and, ultimately, their career chances. Women who develop this kind of identification with their jobs and commitment to work begin to resemble career-oriented men with a self-image that includes moving into more responsible and better-paying positions as a result of additional training or education:

> I went back to school and got a teaching credential and now I have gotten a job that I'll start right after Easter. That I think will probably be my lifetime job. (American)

[I will] go on to college [after finishing high school in June] . . . nursing school . . . I know my mind is set. (American)

Taking Non-Career-Related Courses.   Unlike the blossoming careers women discussed above, a great many of these wives of alcoholics do what they refer to as "taking classes" or "taking courses"—a sort of random enrichment rather than a focused educational vocational program.

Nonetheless, many of these wives testify that such activities help them find themselves, or aid the development of feelings of peace with their position in life. Others feel proud that they are doing something for themselves. Certainly this activity gets them out of the house and into situations where they can meet people—even if some of the courses are not oriented toward career enhancement:

> I am taking educational courses. . . . I took Spanish first, . . . [then] crochet . . . I'm now taking this sewing class in stretch fabrics. (American)
>
> I took German, went to household courses, took up hobby courses, and gymnastics. (Finn)

A small number of women take courses that specifically aid them in handling their own personal feelings about their husband's drinking, their part in the problem, or the meaning of their lives.

Developing a New Social Life.   A happy bonus of working and/or taking courses is the opportunity to meet people. Wives of alcoholics, who are trying to build a life of their own, are open to these chances, and find that these new friends make it easier for them to accept their home situation:

> I've gotten out and I've gotten back into circulation with people and my friends and I'm just really happy now. (American)
>
> In a way, I built a life of my own—[but] not purposely. My job brings me a lot of friends and acquaintances. (Finn)

Finnish wives of alcoholics, more so than American, develop friendships with women in the same boat with whom they can share problems and advice:

> I have a couple of friends who I work with. One has an alcoholic husband, so we exchange views. (Finn)

Joining clubs or organizations offers other possibilities for enjoying life, although not many wives do this and those who do are sometimes actively discouraged by their husband:

Well, a couple of years ago I joined TOPS [a weight-reducing club]. I did that for a while. He put a stop to that because he didn't like that. He didn't mind my going to the meetings weekly, but the annual dinner that we had, he'd make fun of the club. . . . He ended up going to the dinner with me, but sat there through the whole dinner with his arms crossed. I was on the verge of tears, I didn't know what to do. So I didn't go back anymore. (American)

I spent my time being very active in organizations. I *had* to be active. I couldn't stay at home and do nothing. It was a constant conflict—being active in organizations and doing work for them and being depressed by the situation at home. It [his drinking] made you feel like not working, but you had to keep going and do something or you would lose your personality. (Finn)

A few women have pursued their social activities alone—apparently not yet able to look for friends of their own actively. The results are somewhat poignant, although they may reflect a first brave step toward the creation of a life-style:

The past week I went to the Red Coat Inn by myself, just to listen to the band. (American)

Sometimes I just go sight-seeing. I like to get out of the house and see something different. (American)

I've tried to think of a lot of things I really like to do—like dancing and sometimes I go alone or with a girl friend. Sometimes I go alone just to look at cheerful people. I haven't been dancing very many times. Mostly, I find somebody else who is lonely too, and it is a pleasure to talk to this person. (Finn)

The Circularity of Motivation, Attitude, and Self-Image

How can the difference in the life-styles of these two groups be understood? Certainly it is difficult to find clues to explain the way that they handle their lives when one looks at the structural aspects alone, inasmuch as the women who live in despair and those who are actively trying to find a satisfactory quality of life do not vary substantially on important demographic characteristics such as age, income, education, number of children, working outside the home or even membership in Al-Anon. It is also doubtful that personality differences can account for it. Helson, Mitchell, and Hart (1985) have found that women with very different personalities can develop a positive ego and become quite autonomous.

Coser (1986) has said that the socialization of women follows a cultural mandate that they be committed to the gemeinschaft world of home and family. This focus encourages major interest in practical matters of everyday life while at the same time foreclosing thoughts about the abstract and hypothetical. Such thought patterns, Coser feels, means that women are more comfortable coping with problems concerned with the home. In fact, Epstein (1986) has noted that the very language and nonverbal communication that men and women use in their dealings with each other reinforce the world of the home as the ultimate place and perspective for women.

Such a gemeinschaft view of the world results in women who cling to the ideal of having a husband who can offer some measure of security and be a father to the children. Epstein (1984) has maintained that these ideal roles result in the denial of his real behavior and perpetuate maintenance of traditional sex roles in the face of mounting evidence to the contrary.

Additionally, women socialized to a gemeinschaft view of the world believe that self-interest is a proper attitude for men, but not for women (Laws 1979:151–52). Rather than making the most of themselves, their job is to make the most of their husband.

There are clues in the data to explain the women who escape these traditional expectations as well as those who sink into despair. First of all, it would appear that activities and attitudes are cumulative and circular in their effect on the motivation and behavior of these wives, whether the thrust is ultimately toward independence or dependence.

Getting a job or training, or just getting out where other people are, can affect access to social contacts and encourage independence in other areas of life. Thus, women who begin to seek an independent existence find they also experience a changing perspective on themselves and their circumstances as their situation improves. Likewise, staying at home, or going to work without enthusiasm or interest in the job, moves the woman toward ever greater isolation.

The first step is apparently the most difficult. These women, trapped in such disappointing marriages, find they must psych themselves into taking action. Olesen and Whittaker (1968) and Hochschild (1979) discuss the way in which people socialize themselves into expected behavior by "an internal dialogue" or "emotion work," thus convincing themselves both of the rightness of the action and the proper feelings accompanying it. In the same way, it appears that the wives of alcoholics who want to improve the quality of their lives must, in a sense, brainwash themselves into taking chances, working hard, expecting success, or they will never get started or keep going. This self-socialization no doubt aids the woman to handle other aspects of improving her life. She can assess her circumstances, develop a plan, and then, believing in herself and the plan, go ahead with it despite the absence of support. Once started, this momentum continues even in the face of feelings of guilt about unmet responsibilities toward others. Additionally, as her circumstances change, she must be open to opportunities that develop as the very result of her activities.

The fears these women have about being on their own and the way in which they must literally force themselves to take an active rather than a passive part in the structuring of their lives is illustrated by the following detailed description offered by a respondent who developed an independent life while married and eventually called the interviewer to say she had divorced her husband. Despite the fact that she made a final bolder step than the bulk of wives in the sample, her fears and her approach to overcoming them tell a great deal about the circularity of opportunity:

Interviewer: What have you done to build a life of your own?

Respondent: Everything. What I did first was sit on the front steps one night all night long and pictured everything horrible that could happen to me—welfare, loss of my children, poor health without him. I was frightened. I pictured me becoming a slut. I pictured never having another man love me. I pictured everything in the world that could happen to me if I left that man, and not one thing that I could picture, *not one thing* in the world was worse than what I was in; so that is how I made my decision about my divorce.

Then, from then on the stumbles were there, but I got interested in my business. *I wrote myself a prescription about what I could do to start a new life.* I divorced [myself] from all of our old married friends, because I needed new friends. I started going to singles groups, just by saying, "You got to get out and meet other people." I was having a lot of trouble with my two boys at the time with pot, which I thought was horrible. One of them quit school. But what I did to rebuild my life was, actually I felt like, *I gave me a second life.* I learned early in the game that all of the stuff I was saying, "If it was not for James, I would do so and so and so," that when it went right down to it I knew that it was up to me to meet people and do different things I never done before. I never know how to pay a bill, tip anyone, drive at night alone, and *I forced myself to do things that my head knew would be good for me.*

One of the things I did I found really strange is that I had the greatest fear in the world of exposing my body to anyone else in a casual arrangement. Friends of mine were going to a nudist camp, and *I wrote myself a prescription* if I could do that and spend the day there, then there was not any God damn telling what else I could do. I actually did that, and it was true. Once I had done that it opened all forces in other areas. Not just bodily and sex. I don't mean just that. I made better decisions in the office, too. I had an awful time going to bed with a man, and the first time, when I finally did it, he was a doll, and the roof did not fall in and the sky didn't fall. It was just beautiful and I was delighted.

I finally got out of the house that we had lived in for all of that time—sold that. That was a big step. And I got interested in my business and politics and started to travel and explore things I had never done before. There were lots of things I did that my head told me was all right, but

my guts were scared of. Things I did alone. Now, I find that I enjoy living
alone, and enjoy the life I have, and can't think of a thing to improve it.
(American) (emphasis mine)

Obviously, most of the women in the sample couldn't psych themselves up and write prescriptions leading to such a dramatic behavior
and improvement in their lives. However, as the previous description of
wives who remained married but developed independent lives indicated, a substantial proportion are moving in that direction. Wives who
are creating an independent life of their own report feelings of openness
as they decide to change the quality of their lives or are forced to take
measures that have this result. Then, as they gain some success with
contact-making, sociability, developing job proficiency, and other grati-
fying and ego-enhancing activities, they begin to see themselves in a
much more positive way. A few women managed to verbalize the delight they feel in the change that independence from their drinking
husband has made in them:

> I'm working in a different field from what I was; the people I work with are
> real independent—most unmarried women. They give me just a lot of
> ideas about equality. So I'm just a really different person—changing from a
> dependent person into an independent person. (American)

> The things that I did that made me happy with myself, made me proud to
> be Janet. (American)

> My life is changing. I haven't decided how to do it. I try to keep things *open*
> so if he comes it is okay and if he doesn't it is okay. (Finn)

Wives mention with pride arranging social events and recreation of
the type a married woman usually does not do without her spouse:

> [I] go camping with my friends. I've even taken off and gone back East to
> school—that sort of thing; I do my own thing. (American)

> I don't depend entirely upon him to give me . . . let's say, recreation or
> contentment. . . . I really could do without him real easy because I'm
> a . . . I'm quite independent. (American)

> I've been doing things on my own. I've been going into town and dancing
> and doing some things alone. In the beginning of our marriage, I never
> thought I could do these things alone. (Finn)

For many women, a major criterion of independence from her husband is that of learning skills and knowledge that give them the ability to
do things they formerly relied on a man to do for them. That they like
the feeling of self-assurance the development of such abilities gives
them can be noted in the quote that follows:

I have gotten independent, like if my kitchen needs painting, I'll paint it. If something needs fixing, I'll fix it. I can fix my washing machine. I know where to go to fix income tax papers. I know exactly how to call the company and put in for sick leave. . . . I know when you have payments, what to do. I was afraid to get on the freeways to drive. Well, I've gotten on the freeways. I know my way around. . . . I can fix a flat on my car; I can put oil in it. If the car won't work, I know what to check to make sure its not spark plugs. (American)

A few women feel their newly attained independence so keenly they are talking fairly seriously about leaving their husband or maintaining their separate life-style regardless of what he does or does not do (see also Safilios-Rothschild 1970):

Well, I have my job, and like I said, it is good for me and . . . if I walked out on him . . . [I'd] make a life of my own. [It would be] pretty much the same as I am now just by myself. (American)

I'm not to ever become dependent on someone again. . . . I'm not going to just sit at home and clean the house. (American)

Some say they have started making financial preparations for the future possibility of an entirely separate life:

I have a secret bank account that I am adding to every chance I get. (American)

Once the children leave home, more of my weekly wages can go into a savings account, and when that is built up, then I can decide where I want to go and what I want to do; but I will have to build up the money. I don't have any extra money yet. (American)

I will have something to back me up, like if my husband . . . if we were to split up. I would be able to support myself and my baby. I would not have to just kick back on welfare. That is why I went back to school, because I don't ever want to be pushed around. I don't ever want that again. I want to be myself and I want to do whatever I want to do. (American)

If success is cumulative, how do these women who change the quality of their lives get started? One can look at the literature on assertiveness or effectiveness training for women to get further clues to the dynamics of developing autonomy in some of the persons in this sample.[13] This literature contains the types of advice professional counselors offer persons who come for help in improving their lives. Psychologically, such women seeking counseling must deal with problems that are parallel to those of wives of alcoholics. They, too, must overcome the almost paralyzing despair that overtakes them in marriages they have decided are really bad for them.

These women are told that they must rid themselves of self-doubts (Adams 1980; Bloom et al. 1975:212). For persons socialized to defer their own needs to the needs of others while feeling they are dependent upon them, becoming responsible for their lives means a major commitment to giving up dependent status (Bloom et al. 1975:61–64). Such a decision also means the willingness to take risks (Osborn and Harris 1975:173–92).

Although there is absolutely no evidence in the data that any of the women who build an independent life for themselves within their marriages have had any assertiveness or effectiveness training, they embark on a series of steps that are strikingly similar.

First of all, these women pick the areas of their existences that they feel can be changed. Second, they begin to modify their behavior and their outlook on life in such a way that their characteristic thinking about themselves and their family becomes more like that of a man than a traditionally minded woman. This change of orientation seems to have allowed them to cope much better with the exigencies of their existence. Patterson and McCubban (1984), for instance, have found that women with an androgynous gender-role orientation handle stress better than those with a traditional one. Nontraditional sex-role attitudes are seen as associated with less stress for women during marital separation also (Felton et al. 1980).

Third, an important component of the change assertiveness counselors urge is that of attitude toward employment, inasmuch as employment is seen as the route to personal autonomy. By putting more energy into jobs (working longer hours and getting extra training), these wives improve their performances, while, at the same time they gain self-confidence and a better self-image. The more positive the interpersonal aspects of their lives become, the more they experience an improved quality of life (Osborn and Harris 1975:180).

Finally, these wives of alcoholics gradually become aware of the benefits of controlling their own lives. In this way, their general perspective and approach to day-to-day living changes, within the boundaries that they set for themselves of remaining in the marriage (for reasons of financial security or responsibility to a sick husband, or both). However, these women no longer feel dependent and they revel in their newly found sense of autonomy.

On the other hand, turning once more to the wives of alcoholics who are doing nothing for their lives (failing somehow to psych themselves up) the longer these women bear their lives in unhappiness, postponing action, the more likely they will sink further and further into dependency and inertia. They are without goals—a state always more difficult to understand than goal-directed behavior.[14] They are not the only group who reach this state—over the years it is a phenomenon that has been noted by social scientists in all types of people who are isolated for a period of time from the mainstream of life. Riesman et al. (1950) wrote of suburban women "frozen in their cottages," afraid to make new contacts, to have new experiences. Mental patients (Freeman and Simmons 1968), discharged felons (Irwin 1970), nuns who leave the order (Baldwin 1957), alcoholics who sober up permanently (Wiseman 1973), and wives of the British management class (Pahl and Pahl 1971) report on this inability to make plans and "take hold" of things, for a time at least, as the result of prolonged isolation or seclusion. In such a situation, there is a drastic reduction in social catalysts for change. Additionally, however, such dependent feelings have a tendency to feed on themselves. The longer they exist, the more likely the woman is to experience increased feelings of helplessness, seeing herself as alone, and misunderstood (Dowling 1981). Thus, it is to be expected that a good proportion of these women sink into depression and ennui, becoming too enervated and fearful to try to escape or create a more pleasant quality of life for themselves.

Long-term effects of this social deprivation appear to go beyond mere inability to plan the future. There is a close parallel between the mental state of these women and that of persons released from prison and concentration camps, although naturally varying in degree. In a classic paper titled, "Brainwashing, Conditioning and DDD (Debility, Dependency, and Dread)," Farber, Harlow, and West (1961) hypothesize that living under such conditions for extended time spans tends eventually to sap initiative, to increase helplessness, and ultimately to have a strongly adverse effect on the concept of self. The result again seems circular—indirectly reinforcing the doubts such isolates feel about their ability to carry off a plan of future action. The description of the state of mind of prisoners whose existence is filled with debility, dependency, and dread closely parallels the quotes from those wives of alcoholics, who feeling like prisoners in their own homes and in their marriages, have lapsed into a depression that reinforces their inertia. Time is also a factor to consider in the development of inertia in some wives. As the years go by, they literally become less able to take action as employable skills atrophy along with current job experience and references. Middle age is a difficult time for women to make a career comeback under any circumstances.

Earlier I did have friends and have organizations, but now I've lost the wish to spend a healthy life because even if people are not talking [about the husband's drinking], I am ashamed. I do have a couple of friends I go out with sometimes. I have tried to cling to life, but I must say that this thing has influenced me in a way that has depressed me for 20 years, and this cuts down on my possibilities. (American)

I could go to movies, concerts, and so on, but I don't feel like it. In a way, I've had enough of life. (American)

I don't know. I feel that all the fun has passed me by. Somehow I feel scared. (Finn)

I'm desperate. I'd like to get away. I'd like to go separately. And always I am thinking I would like to die. (Finn)

Notes

1.   Because of the general research mandate to study wives of alcoholics, the sample focuses on intact marriages. The exact proportion of women in the general population who divorce alcoholic men is not known, inasmuch as alcoholism is seldom officially recorded as a reason for divorce. There are, however, indications that wives of alcoholics have a low rate of divorce and, in fact, stay in these marriages to a much greater extent than do husbands with a drinking wife. For instance, a newspaper article (*Los Angeles Times* 1984) on this topic, "Wives of Alcoholics Have Lower Divorce Rate Than General Population," jokingly suggested that perhaps one way to keep a marriage intact would be for the husband to become an alcoholic. Viets also reported on this phenomenon in 1969.

2.   In a study of women who remained with a husband who beat them, Gelles (1976) noted that the fewer resources or power a wife had, the more likely she was not to divorce a violent spouse, but to continue to live with him.

3.   This information is drawn from U.S. Department of Labor (1980), Congressional Caucus for Women's Issues (1987), and The Position of Women in Finnish Society (1984).

4.   Feldberg and Kohen (1976) and Bernard (1981), for instance, suggest that women have been socialized to see themselves as the major providers of an emotional life for their husband and the guilt they would feel about robbing him of this benefit, should they leave, often keeps them in an unsatisfying marriage.

5.   Some of the alcoholic men may also realize that in their present state they are unlikely to find another woman who is willing to take care of them and thus, in spite of their antagonism to their current wife, prefer to stay with her. The reluctance of men to allow a wife whose company they do not appear to enjoy to divorce them was discussed in an academic seminar in Finland, and a male professor offered this proposition as an answer: "One cook is as good as another." While this may seem cynical, when Pahl and Pahl (1971) asked managers in Britain to discuss their wife and the state of their marriages, they spoke primarily of their spouse's ability to cook, keep house, take care of the children, and manage on a budget as the criteria for their happiness with their choice of woman.

6.   Ironically, data from this study indicate that older women who stayed with an alcoholic husband "for the good of the children" report that when grown, these children often refuse to help them care for their still-drinking parent. In addition, the children show some inclination to prefer the company of their father (who, when sober may be charming) to that of their mother whom they now see as chronic complainers.

7. Perry (1975) discusses the social position of women in Japan who are either divorced or widowed, and states that they are *socially anomalous*, having little legal or social claim on anyone. Wives of alcoholics, still married but with an almost inoperative husband, are in a parallel position.

8. A study by Hunt and Hunt (1977) indicates that in dual-career families working women in general get much less emotional support from their husbands than husbands receive from their wives. Families are much more supportive, in general, of the husband's career than they are of the wife's.

9. Al-Anon is sometimes credited for pointing out to wives that they can get pleasure from activities with their children without their husband's company. One woman said:

> Well, I have lately, if he's drinking, I've taken them [the children] out a few times and we enjoyed a movie, one Sunday. This is a new thing for me and it's Al-Anon that has helped us. And I've taken them out to eat a couple of times, too. (American)

10. The following interchange, which occurred while an interviewer was at the home of the wife of an alcoholic, indicates how close these families often are to financial disaster. During the interview, the telephone rang. The wife answered it and came back to report:

> I just got a phone call that my husband was fired. His boss wants to see him right now, and he is fired. We will probably go on welfare. We can't live on that. We will probably lose our home. These days, I don't know how he will get another job. Here we go. Now we are going to have to start all over again. (American)

11. For an incisive discussion of the place of work and fulfillment of potential in human needs, see Haworth (1974).

12. One Finnish woman who earned money as a seamstress found through a friend a room that could serve as a sanctuary away from her husband and his drinking:

> But I had become acquainted with a man who took care of the apartment house, and he arranged a room for me where I could work [I started to do sewing], and my husband was not allowed to come to that room when he was drinking. This went on for six or seven years. (Finn)

13. I am indebted to Rae Lesser Blumberg, who suggested I look at this literature for parallels between the advice offered and the steps taken by wives of alcoholics seeking autonomy.

14. Implicitly or explicitly, almost all of the theories and investigations of sociologists and psychologists are focused on assumptions of goal-directed behavior (sometimes called simply "motivation").

Sobriety and the Dynamics of Marital Interaction: The Complex Connection

Introduction

From time to time, some very heavy drinkers go on the wagon and stop drinking for an extended period of time either on their own or with the aid of professional treatment.[1] Often, they announce their intention to stop permanently.

Previous chapters have focused on how wives of alcoholics decide their spouse has become a compulsive drinker, and the ways in which they try to get the man to cut down on his intake or stop drinking altogether. It is a story of ineffectiveness and failure: first, of wives in private attempts, and later, at professional treatment centers. Concomitantly, it is also a study of how the wives react to and cope with the stress brought about by their drinking husband's behavior and his lack of positive response to reasoning, threat, or treatment.

Yet, some alcoholics do recover (or refer to themselves as "recovering" even after years of sobriety), at least to the extent that they stay away from alcohol for long periods of time.[2] Can clues to this successful abstinence be found in the dynamics of marital interaction and relationships? If so, what part might a wife play in her husband's return to sober living?

Wives have certainly been blamed in the past by theorists for their husband's excessive drinking and his failure to stop. As discussed in earlier chapters, however, none of these theories have been proved or disproved.[3] Some research attention has been given to another aspect of alcoholism: whether husband-wife interaction has any effect, positive or negative, on his ability to remain on the wagon once he has made the initial effort to stop drinking (Schroeder 1985; Moos and Billings 1983; Brisett et al. 1980; Finney et al. 1980; Orford et al. 1975). Generally, results of these studies indicate that a good marital adjustment and the ability to stay abstinent are closely associated. However, in these studies, the actual interaction between the alcoholic husband and wife both during the drinking period and after recovery is usually presented in the abstract, not described in detail. No control sample of the marital interaction of still-drinking men and their wives for the same two periods is included for comparison.

What occurs in the interaction between the male alcoholic and his wife during the initial period when he is trying to maintain sobriety—the time span that nearly all authorities agree is crucial to ultimate long-term recovery? Does this relationship improve, stay the same, or worsen once the husband attains the sober state? Does the general marital relationship during the drinking stage prior to the initial abstinence period affect this relationship later, as the husband tries to attain stabilized sobriety? And, in some circular fashion, do these feelings of the husband and wife toward each other in various stages of drinking and abstaining affect the husband's ability to maintain sobriety?

Such questions are predicated on the supposition that drinking periods and stable sobriety are not discrete entities but are part of a continuum in the career of a problem drinker. Thus, the interactions between spouses in one time span may affect interactions in another. Data that can provide information on the effect these connected interactions have on therapy success and/or recidivism deserve attention.

Obviously, as a result of the focus of the major sample—wives of men who currently have a drinking problem—the husbands described in the foregoing chapters have not been able to stop drinking permanently, although some have tried from time to time for brief periods. In order to compare these men with alcoholics who have been able to stay sober for at least a year, a special sample of 25 wives of men who have stopped drinking for a year or more (referred to in the discussion as recovered or recovering alcoholics) was interviewed in depth using the same topic guide as that of the major sample. These women were also volunteers, recruited through an advertisement, as described in the methodology. As with the major sample, this subsample cannot be claimed to be representative (inasmuch as the universe is not known). A broad spectrum of women from all walks of life participated. Furthermore, on important demographic factors like age, education, and income, this subsample closely resembles wives in the major study, including the length of time the husband had been drinking.

In the discussion that follows, the general negative effects that continued excessive consumption of alcohol has on important areas of the marital relationship for women whose husband is still drinking will be very briefly reviewed. These data will then be compared with evaluations of these same areas by wives whose husband can be designated as recovering. The marital relationship of this latter group of wives is covered before the advent of this stable sobriety (that is, during the drinking period), as well as directly afterward, when sobriety has been sustained for at least a year. Possible inferences to be drawn from the apparent differences in husband-wife interactions in these two samples during these two periods and their association with the husband's attainment of long-term sobriety or resumption of drinking are discussed.

Areas of Grief for Wives of Currently Drinking Men

As presented in detail in Chapters 5 and 6, a majority of wives of alcoholics in both Finland and the United States whose husband is still drinking complain that he fails them in crucial areas of the marriage relationship, particularly communications and companionship. These wives also complain about consistently missed meals, as well as ruined social events—the result of their husband's drunken antics and his ultimate loss of interest in joint social activities. A substantial majority of American women comment bitterly about the negative effect of their husband's drinking on their sexual relations. Wives from both cultures describe a still-drinking husband as one who alternates between brutality and excessive kindness, displaying in his drunken moods general anger and quarreling, physical violence, and property destruction, sometimes combined with mistreatment of the children. During this period, not only does his physical and mental health deteriorate, but hers does as well, due to the stress she is experiencing.

Upon sobering up, rather than returning to "normal" un-self-conscious behavior, a majority of men are on stage, enacting the role of the good husband and father in an exaggerated, larger-than-life script of warmth and sensitivity. This generosity and loving demeanor appear to be an elaborate attempt to make up for his heavy drinking days. During this sober period the wife is ambivalent about her husband's good behavior and nervously fearing another fall off the wagon.

In Chapter 5, wives in both cultures describe the bitterness, rage, and tenseness they feel toward their spouse for the suffering they experienced. As a result they are, in turn, cold, sarcastic, and complaining when he becomes sober. Many of these women point out that they have been controlling their anger for some time, suppressing the complaints and problems they want to tell him about, waiting until he is less volatile, and above all "in contact" so he can understand. The result of these expressions of all-too-human feelings and outbursts might be to short-circuit the husband's tenuous sobriety.[4]

Although the wife's anger, her need to punish, her fears that her husband might slip are all understandable, it may also be true that these reactions create a home environment that works against his determination to stop drinking. Certainly, what is conveyed to him by a majority of wives is criticism and blame. This comes at a time when he is physically weak, mentally depressed, and uncertain about his ability to stop drinking permanently.

Additionally, as detailed in Chapter 8, some wives of alcoholics eventually create lives of their own. When this is the case, the "return" of a sober and unusually attentive husband is a mixed blessing.[5] Having become involved with new activities and friends during their husband's drinking period, the wives lack the time or inclination to be receptive to the highly attentive behavior by which the man hopes to assuage his guilt for drinking. These more independent wives say:

> Well, I had forgotten how much time a husband can want. After all, it's been a long time since he could do anything with me. And I just didn't sit home after a while. I went and got my own friends. Now, I don't know what to do. I owe them both. (American)

> He wanted a lot of attention when he sobered up. I was supposed to appreciate him all the time. It was draining, especially since I have other commitments now. (American)

> I have a job I enjoy and in order to be promoted, I put in long hours, plus I am going to school for additional training. Now that he is sober, I am supposed to give all that up, and I just won't. (Finn)

Thus, the special part played by the wife in her alcoholic husband's return to drinking, often posited by psychologists as resulting from an unconscious desire to suffer or dominate him, may be more complex, composed as it is of her memory of the mental and physical suffering he has caused her, her reactions to his on-stage personality, and her problems of fitting an abstinent spouse into a life that she may have restructured in order to manage without him.

Wives of men who have been sober for a year present quite a different picture.

Recovered Alcoholics' Behavior while Drinking and After Maintaining Sobriety

Data from the special sample of wives of successfully abstaining husbands covering the times during their drinking periods as well as after apparent recovery suggest that there are women married to alcoholics who have had a fairly happy marriage relationship, despite the odds against it. A discussion of these wives' attitudes toward their husband, both when he was drinking heavily and after he had remained sober for a year or more, is revealing. It suggests some of the mechanisms in the marital relationship that may aid the husband in attaining sobriety.

The Status of Talk in Marriage during Drinking Days

Among the wives of recovered alcoholics, communication during the period when the husband was drinking appeared to be subtly but qualitatively different than that described by wives of spouses who are continuing to drink. On the whole, there is a less injured tone in the wives' descriptions of communication between themselves and their husbands at an earlier period when his alcohol intake was at a high level.

Unlike their counterparts with still-drinking husbands, few of the wives of recovered alcoholics refer to their communications problem during their spouse's heavy drinking period as dominated by his refusal to talk. None of these wives mentioned long periods of "the silent treatment," or times when the husband was scarcely answering, if he did react at all to conversation attempts by the wife. Few wives gave up all attempts at conversation with their husband, as did wives of currently drinking men. However, some wives describe being forced to wait until their spouse was sober to talk with him. None of these wives describe husbands who use television to avoid social interaction. A sizable number of women in this group said that communication with their spouse was not affected at all by his intake of alcohol. Rather, these couples continued to talk as usual:

> Yes, we did talk. He is a talker, and I feel comfortable listening. We talked on everything and anything. This did not change as he drank more heavily. (American)
>
> In between drinking, we still talked quite a bit—world affairs, our future, and the boy, and since he was disabled, his new goals. (Finn)
>
> We talked about everything, even after he began to drink heavily. (Finn)

Some of these women, married to men who have stopped drinking currently, focus their complaints about communications during their husband's period of overindulgence in alcohol on his abrasiveness. Every attempt to talk seemed to lead to arguments. They recall:

> He was hard to get along with. He complained about everything. (American)
>
> We would just argue about anything at all. (Finn)

Others, like the wives of currently drinking men, complained that during the drinking period their husband would talk only on "surface topics." Some women said they just couldn't seem to "reach" their husband because he kept himself remote, disinterested, and disconnected from either her day-to-day problems or her long-term interests.

Thus, while a wife finds communications is a serious, many-faceted, and escalating problem in those marriages where the husband eventually stopped drinking successfully, spouses never quite sank into the morass of noncommunications reported by wives of currently drinking men. Often, normal discussions were continued, although the husband's tendency to argue and his remoteness did cause concern.

After Sobriety: The Emergence of "Communications"

The descriptions American wives give of conversations with their newly sobered husband verge on the euphoric. Talk between them is described as "marvelous," "growing," and "terrific." The husband has become more "open," "willing to discuss problems," and interested in the "important things in life." Arguments are seen as almost nonexistent and, where there are disagreements, they are described as handled by logical discussions.

It is interesting to note that these wives appear to have developed a new vocabulary to describe talks with spouses. For instance, where they formerly referred to "arguments," they now use the label "disagreements." Many of these women couch their descriptions of talk between themselves and their husband in professional therapy terms. A large number mention "better communications," although their earlier descriptions of the same problem were more usually offered in terms of the absence of "talk" or "conversation":

> At that time we really started to communicate together for the first time, as a family and also just as two people, just he and I. Communicating was what I needed, and now I have it. (Finn)

A favorite phrase these wives use to describe their changed marital interaction is "openness" of communication:

> We can communicate better with each other. The group from the Veteran's Hospital that we got into was really great and helped us to open up our communication. (American)

These wives also speak of being able to "talk things through" with their now-sober husband and are "discussing things" instead of arguing heatedly when disagreements arise. The importance of willing compromise on the part of both spouses is stressed by wives:

> We don't argue, we don't fight, we care. We have time now to communicate. . . . If he wants to do something, we talk about it first. (American)

At this point, it is difficult to say whether the great satisfaction with communications in the marriage is an outburst of general optimism with the relationship, or a revised perception partially reflecting exposure to the vocabulary of professional help. But whichever is the case, wives are happier about accessibility of their husband for conversations.

Mealtime Behavior during Drinking Days

Wives of men who have been sober for a year or more have memories concerning mealtime problems similar to those of their counterparts with husbands still excessively imbibing. However, there is not quite as much bitterness and despair (at least retrospectively) as found in the descriptions of the spouses of currently drinking men.

A major reason for this more sanguine attitude appears to be that these husbands who have since managed sobriety successfully made it a rule to be present at a minimum of one meal a day with their wives and/or families—even during their heavy drinking period. Often, these men would not eat during this meal, and sometimes they would be nasty and quarrelsome. But this important link to family and connubial solidarity was routinely maintained, although in truncated form.

A large proportion of wives of recovered alcoholics gave descriptions concerning mealtime attendance and its general ambience during the time their husband was drinking heavily:

> He would always show up for a least one meal, and try to get through dinner without falling in his plate, and try to do things so we would not argue in front of the kids. He was good about that [when he was drinking], he always came home. (American)
>
> We always had breakfast, and if he felt like it, quite often dinner. (Finn)

Similar to wives in the major sample, some spouses of men who have stopped drinking also say they continued to make meals during the period when their husband was not very interested in eating. In fact, they claim to have actually made better meals during his heavy drinking days than usual. Their reasoning for this seemingly extraordinary action was substantially different from that of wives of currently drinking men.

This group of women, whose husband eventually attained sobriety, hoped to tempt their husband's alcohol-jaded appetites. (There were also a few wives who sounded like counterparts of spouses whose husband still drinks. They cooked for him daily to show they were "maintaining," and then bitterly threw the food away when he did not eat.)

What is missing from these descriptions, in comparison to those offered by wives whose husband is still drinking, is significant. Unlike those latter women, no one in this group of wives of recovered drinkers reported waiting until a husband comes home at 10:00 or 11:00 P.M. to eat dinner. Likewise, no wives reported that they were routed out of bed in the very early morning to fix a snack for a husband who had just found his appetite. Only one wife reported that her husband would not eat at the table with the rest of the family, while this was fairly common among wives whose husband was still drinking. Furthermore, these women apparently did not spend mealtimes with a husband who would be fighting the compulsion to vomit (not always successfully), or who would literally pass out at the table during the meal (sometimes with his face falling in his plate), although one woman spoke about the ever-present possibility of this occurring.

Additionally, these women whose husbands eventually sobered up appeared not to resort to the aberrant eating patterns of wives of currently drinking alcoholics. They continued to eat with their children, they continued to make meals for themselves (they did not resort entirely to convenience foods), and they neither ate too much (to keep from wasting food prepared for their husband) nor too little (thus suffering malnutrition themselves).

All in all, a striking characteristic about meals during the time this group's husbands were drinking is that both husband and wife managed in some way or other. Men tried to sit through meals for the sake of the family, even when not hungry. Wives grieved about wasting prepared food and the erratic meal attendance of a husband, but did not react in the more extreme ways found among the group of women whose husband is still drinking. Although the talk at the table might turn into quarreling, at least there was some conversation, and apparently both spouses attempted to retain the feeling of togetherness essential to a family meal.

Family Meals after Maintenance of Sobriety

When a husband remains sober for a year or more, the improvement in mealtime behavior is dramatic. Those women who complained that meals (especially dinner) with their husband were beginning to dwindle, despite his efforts to maintain the contact, happily report that many aspects of the family dinner are improving. Sometimes the wife reports that she and her husband find the joy of togetherness so pleasurable (after the crisis of alcoholism) that they attempt to have all meals together or at least some contact for all meals:

> [We have] breakfast and dinner together. Weekends, it is three meals together. (American)
>
> Breakfast we eat together . . . and we sit and talk while we are eating. . . . Supper we eat together. Everything we do, we do it together now. (Finn)

Others, whose husbands had not stopped appearing at meals, say that this time has become more pleasant because the husband's mood and appetite have improved to such a great extent.

The Quality of Joint Recreation during Drinking Days

The recreational patterns of drinking spouses who later control their alcoholic intake is strikingly different from the embarrassing behavior and withdrawal from interest in social events described by wives whose husband is currently excessively imbibing. Rather, these women married to a now abstinent man are more likely to describe their husband when drinking as a partying man with whom they went from bar to bar, and with whom, both drunk and sober, they maintained some kind of social partnership.

Most of these women reported they joined their husband's recreation on a regular basis. Although his social activities usually involved drinking, nevertheless there is a certain richness to the patterns of fun together that the wives describe, which is noticeably absent from the group of continuing drinkers and their wives described earlier:

> As long as it involved drinking, we could do anything. As long as we would go to the beach, and he could take the booze, then we would go. And the same thing with drive-in movies, car races, bowling, anything, any place, as long as it had booze, too. (American)
>
> [We went] out dancing, to dinner, bars, drinking, and home to bed. Boating with drinks, too. (Finn)

Many husbands and wives in this group were involved in joint recreational activities before the husband's drinking got out of hand and continued with them:

> We joined a little theater group where we were living. . . . he was electrician and sound man and prop man. And we really had a real good time. And that continued to be a good thing in our lives. (American)

I would take him to the psychology workshop, and I would read poems to him, and sit and read. I would sing to him, too. I played the piano . . . I was involved in a religious group and we sang. He would come to the concerts that we could go to when he was sober. (American)

Other wives, especially Finnish, speak of confining recreation to visits with friends and family or to games of cards, but more importantly, these social activities remain joint and, on the whole, enjoyable for the wife despite the drinking.

Joint Recreation after Recovery

Descriptions of what husbands and wives do together after the man attains sobriety indicate that these are couples who find enhanced enjoyment in each other's company. The wife is often ecstatic about her husband's companionship and their good times together:

I feel like a teenager, and I cannot stand to be away from him. We have fun together, and we never had good times like this. We fly to Mexico for several days, and come home and drive up the coast, and shoot and it is just great. Everyday is a wonderful day. (American)

Like I say, we enjoy doing things together now, and we enjoy everything we do together. We even shop together now and pick out clothing for each other. (American)

We have a ball, you know, invite friends to come over, and he will be there and that will be just a delight, and to be invited to go somewhere and not worry about his not coming home . . . and to be able to make plans. (American)

Finnish wives' descriptions are somewhat lower key:

We are back to where we can talk about anything and everything and really enjoy it, and watch TV and go out to dinner, too. It is so nice, really nice. (Finn)

Sexual Interaction during Drinking Days

Sexual relations of recovered alcoholics and their wives, even before the men attained sobriety, are substantially more positive in quality. Few wives express dismay, because they did not enjoy intercourse with a rough, drinking husband or say that their sex life was almost nonexistent during this time. Rather, a substantial number of women in the subsample claim that the sexual side of their marriage remained quite satisfactory throughout their husband's alcoholism period:

There were no problems in the sexual relationship because of his drinking. (American)

> Sexually it stayed the same either way for us . . . good [i.e., whether the husband drank or not]. (Finn)

One wife mentioned that she later discovered her husband had sex regularly with her when he was sober in order to make up for the periods when he was drunk. This behavior does indicate some thoughtfulness on his part, and some aspects of playing the good husband after a drinking bout, as previously discussed:

> Right up until the last year it [the sexual relationship] was fairly regular, but when he was drunk he could not do anything, nothing. Afterwards, I found out that sex [during sober periods] was sort of an apology. (American)

Wives married to this group of apparently recovered alcoholics (much more than spouses of the currently drinking men) mention being interested in sex themselves. This, combined with a husband who also maintained sexual interest, even while drinking excessively, resulted in ongoing sexual interaction. Fewer women were repelled by their husband's advances while he was drinking, and even these claim they were often accommodating. Furthermore, during times when their sexual relationship attenuated to the point that the problem could not be ignored, some wives report that they tried to be understanding, or blamed themselves partially for the failure.

Almost totally missing from this group of women, in contrast to wives of currently drinking men, are those women who punished their husband for drinking by withholding sex, those women who claim they made all the advances, and those women who maneuvered themselves out of opportunities for sexual intercourse, or openly refused or grudgingly cooperated to get it over. Some wives of recovered alcoholics mention impotence as an ongoing problem, but say that they and their husband were trying to cope with it during the drinking phase. It seems apparent from a comparison of wives' retrospective accounts of sexual relations with a drinking husband that these couples tried in one way or another to maintain a sexual relationship. Nowhere in the testimony of these women does one see the spiral of resentment resulting from unsatisfactory sex relations that is apparent in the group of wives whose husband is still drinking. On the contrary, wives of men who later recovered do not state that they have lost love for their husband during his drinking period. They do not claim to feel cold sexually. They appear to be less condemning and more encouraging to a semi- or totally impotent husband than are women with a spouse who is still drinking excessively.

Sex after Stabilized Sobriety

After the heavy drinking of the husband ceases, wives who had sex with their spouse during his drinking period continue to have it. The wife does maintain, however, that sex has improved as a result of her husband's sobriety. On the other hand, those couples in this group who had stopped having sex relations for one reason or another during the husband's excessive drinking were still having problems with sex after the husband's sobriety stabilized.

For women who had sexual relations with their husband while he was drinking, sexual activity after his sobriety occurred less frequently, but was reported as more pleasurable. Wives testify that the husband has become a considerate lover:

> It [the sex relationship] is great and is not an every night thing. When he goes to make love to me, there is always foreplay, and afterwards he will ask me if I am satisfied, [or] is there anything he can do to help me, and we hug afterwards and he will kiss me, and now I know it is not [like] an immediate trip to the bathroom. (American)

Many women, both Finnish and American, merely give short descriptions of their sex lives since their husband's sobriety such as "wonderful," "fine," "like it should be," "very good, no problem now," "no change, still good," and "sex has always been one of the strong points of our relationship."

For those wives whose husband remains impotent from drinking, there is a note of sympathetic understanding (as well as regret) when they discuss the apparent permanent loss of their sex life:

> We have a very nice marriage, and despite the fact that we don't have sex in our marriage, ours is a very loving marriage, and a very giving marriage. (American)
>
> Our sex life is nonexistent. He is impotent. It is the price of all that drinking. A doctor is trying to help, and I am trying to be patient. (Finn)

The Absence of Brutality Alternating with Exaggerated Caring

None of the wives of men who had attained stable sobriety spoke of a husband who became aggressive and brutal during drinking periods. Likewise, they either did not notice or defined quite positively the husband's enhanced good behavior during alternating times of brief sobriety. Certainly, they seemed to enjoy these times of sobriety and, rather than nervously fearing this effort would end at any moment, did what they could to see that it continued.

Attaining Sobriety in a Supportive Environment

Perhaps pivotal to the husband's ability to stay dry is the way in which his wife greets the advent of the man's long-term sobriety. Unlike most wives of men still drinking excessively, who take the opportunity of cessation to unload their grievances on a now-conscious man, a majority of wives of men who were able to cease drinking for a year claim their primary reaction was one of happiness when he tried to quit initially. Furthermore, they indicated their pleasure to their husband in many supportive ways, some of which seem, intentionally or not, to simulate behavior modification strategies:

> I would try to be extra loving and sweet and hope that he would think if he stayed sober, [that] this is the nice woman he would have. (American)
>
> I would try to make everything good and right while he was sober so that everyone got along, and so that maybe he would think about this and stay sober. (American)
>
> I showed him my happiness when he didn't drink. (Finn)

Other women claimed they did not change their general behavior at all when their husband was sober.

> Oh, [I act] just the way I always do. Very loving, we have a very loving relationship and I adore him. (American)

The Noncomplaining Minority of Wives of Men Still Drinking

Looking once again at the major sample of wives of men still drinking, there are, of course, a minority of these women who do not complain about their marriage. That is, a minority of these women married to a currently drinking alcoholic do not describe a communication problem with their husband; they claim their man can be counted on to appear at meals, that he does take part with them in some enjoyable social occasions, and that their sexual relations are satisfactory even now.

This noncomplaining minority seems to match, in terms of attitude and experiences, the cohort sample of wives of men who have been sober for a year or more. From the data presented, one could hypothesize that the husbands of these women may be the recovered alcoholics of the future, on the following grounds: (1) that the way some husbands act toward their wife while drinking and the very natural reaction of the wife to this conduct become important influences on the wife's behavior. (2) In turn, the wife's reactions to the man's behavior results in encouraging or discouraging long-term sobriety in the man if he, too, is interested in attaining it.

Summary and Conclusions

If the above general differences in relationships between spouses in marriages where the husband is an active alcoholic and those where the man has stopped drinking for a year are not an artifact of selective memory and/or sampling, then the data presented here provide a clue to an important ingredient of successful sobriety. The findings seem especially significant because they are consistent across two cultures. The husband's successful recovery appears to turn on his behavior while drinking, which must not be so cruel and/or thoughtless as to alienate his wife from the marriage totally. The wife, in turn, must attempt to understand her husband's drinking problem and view it with compassion. Throughout this time of trial for the marriage, and after the husband attains a stable condition of sobriety, a thread of concern and love must continue to be manifest. It is possible that the building of the road back must be started during the drinking period, or it can deteriorate to a point of no return, which bad relationships seem to reinforce and intensify.

Obviously, the complicated dynamics between marital relationships and the effects of heavy drinking by a spouse have yet to be completely unraveled. These data indicate that where the couple had a good relationship during the drinking years, sobriety is easier for the husband to maintain. However, it is also possible that despite the apparent similarity of the length of heavy-drinking careers, husbands who manage sobriety for a year are not as deeply enmeshed in compulsive overimbibing as those husbands who have destroyed the four basic areas of interaction between spouses.

It does seem clear, however, that in those cases where the man attains stable sobriety, the husband and wife had remained psychologically a dyad throughout his drinking career and beyond. These wives, in talking about the trials and tribulations of being married to an alcoholic and seeing him through a year or more of sobriety, say the following:

> He used to send me flowers, and now I mail him cards [that say], "Hey, I love you. You're all right. Congratulations, Baby, you made it for another day." And I even bought him flowers. (American)

> *Interviewer:* Do you get along better now [that he has stopped drinking]?
> *Respondent:* Oh, yes we do. We get along really great.

Interviewer: Is he a better companion to you now?
Respondent: No. He always was, drinking or not. (Finn)

The marital relationship in this group, then, was never destroyed during the period when the husband was an alcoholic. These wives say:

We love each other very much. And I think once in a while I would get through to him. He would admit that he loved me very deeply. I think that's the one strong, strong thing that kept us together. (American)

I was not ready to live without him. I didn't want to give up. I knew that one day he would stop [drinking], too. (Finn)

Notes

1. The phenomenon of spontaneous remission is not well understood. Neither is the rather low record of successful recovery (approximately 30%) from various treatment therapies.

2. "Recovery" from alcoholism is a slippery term, as has been discussed in earlier chapters. Inasmuch as an alcoholic can slip back into heavy drinking after years of abstinence, it is difficult to know when any alcoholic has actually recovered. That is why some prefer the term "recovering." One year of sobriety, however, is considered a significant indicator of possible recovery.

3. In fact, the exact mechanisms by which a wife, whether pathological or just unhappy, is supposed to be able to keep a husband continually imbibing (even if he wants to stop) have never been detailed. Only in fiction or the theatre is there revealed the precise psychological "button" that will result in the wife sending her husband on an alcoholic binge despite his desperate desire to remain sober [see *The Country Girl* (Odets 1951), and *Come Back, Little Sheba* (Inge 1950)].

4. Family members of alcoholics are warned in Al-Anon meetings and publications that they will feel anger toward drinking spouses, parents, or children for all the trouble their drinking has caused. They are urged to let off steam or "take out their garbage" in some acceptable way that does not result in a show of hostility toward the newly sober family member. One suggestion is for them to call their sponsor and vent their anger in that way.

5. See also "An Alternative Role for the Wife of an Alcoholic in Finland" (Wiseman 1975), which presents in detail how some of these women refill the time usually taken by a husband with careers, courses, and social activities with others.

Methodology

The goal of this study is to explore the life of wives of alcoholics from their point of view in order better to understand how problem drinking affects the nondrinking woman and how this, in turn, affects a husband's problem drinking. Issues investigated include the criteria these women develop for diagnosing their husband as being an alcoholic, the strategies of "home therapy" and its success, as well as attempts to get the husband into professional treatment and his reactions to it. Information on the effects over time of living and coping with an alcoholic and the resources available (or unavailable) to the wife through kin networks, and friends were also sought.

This research was not initially planned as a cross-cultural comparative study; originally, it started as an investigation funded by the Finnish Foundation for Alcohol Studies. However, after data were gathered in Finland, it was thought that comparison with the situation of wives in the United States would add power to the analysis. In some instances it has, but one of the major findings is that, despite cultural differences, the effect of the alcoholism of the husband on the wife has been very similar in both countries—as though the strength of the phenomena of an alcoholic spouse wiped out any cultural differences. The American study was funded by a grant from the National Institute for Alcohol Abuse and Alcoholism, PHS AAQ-1456. As each part of the study progressed, two subsamples were added in order to ensure validity of the results. These will be discussed in turn.

Sample Selection

The Major Sample

Fifty wives of currently drinking alcoholics living in Finnish cities and 76 in a city in the United States were interviewed in depth and also answered a five-page structured questionnaire that focused on pertinent background data.[1] The Finnish subjects were interviewed with the aid of a simultaneous translator. All interviews in Finland were conducted by the principal investigator. American interviews were conducted by trained, mature, women interviewers, and the principal investigator.

Locating wives of alcoholics willing to be interviewed on the details of their interactions with their husband is fraught with problems. They are an unknown universe. Although the problem could have been solved by turning to some of the organizations to which wives of problem drinkers belong, such as Al-Anon, it was thought that using this source alone would bias the data, since Al-Anon offers a distinct philosophy of life to wives of problem drinkers. Thus, members of Al-Anon were interviewed only as they surfaced through the more general contact method described below.

In order to encourage the widest possible range of respondents, it was decided that primary attempts to contact wives of alcoholics for interviews would be through the use of the following advertisement in the personals section of the classified advertisements of newspapers in the sample cities:

> Wives: Does your husband have a drinking problem? How have you handled it? An (American[2]) professor wants to talk to you. Call [telephone number]. All discussions kept confidential.

While the entire sample of American wives was recruited through the advertisements, a total of 38 Finnish women respondents were ultimately obtained through this channel. (Ten others answered the ad, but failed to keep their appointments.[3]) As a result, the remainder of the Finnish sample was recruited through the aid of persons who manage the Finnish outpatient clinics and inpatient hospitals for alcoholics. These officials contacted wives of current and recent patients and invited them to participate in the study.

Although, as mentioned, the actual universe of alcoholics in either country is not known and therefore cannot be compared with the sample, important demographic characteristics of the two samples indicate that a broad range of women participated in the study. Tables 9.1 to 9.5 show, respectively, the distribution by age of the wives and their husbands, length of time married, yearly income, educational attainment, and length of time the husband has had a drinking problem.

It should be emphasized that the sample procured for this study by the means described above is actually composed of wives who label their husbands alcoholics. It is recognized that there may be some cases

Table 9.1. Age Distribution of American and Finnish
Wives of Alcoholics and their Husbands[a]

Age	American (N = 76)		Finnish (N = 50)	
	Wives %	Husbands %	Wives %	Husbands %
20 or under	1	1	—	—
21–30	20	8	18	12
31–40	22	26	30	24
41–50	30	32	28	34
51–60	22	27	18	24
Over 60	5	6	6	6

[a] Age of husbands was supplied by wives.

in which the men are not really alcoholics and that their protestations that they are not should be given more weight than their wives' pronouncements that they are. This dilemma will have to remain unresolved. There is no way to "certify" the men as alcoholics (as is amply discussed in Chapter 2). Inasmuch as wives often came secretly for the interview, the husbands could not be contacted. Other indicators were equally difficult to check. Some husbands often did all or most of their drinking away from home—especially in Finland—so that the amount of intake is seldom seen. However, all the husbands reported on had been in some sort of treatment for their alcohol problem at least twice. Additionally, the consistencies in the behavior of the husbands, and the

Table 9.2. Distribution of Length of
Time Married of American
and Finnish Wives of
Alcoholics

Years married	American (N = 76) %	Finnish (N = 50) %
Less than 1	7	—
1–3	12	16
4–6	10	16
7–10	12	8
11–20	28	36
Over 20	31	24

Table 9.3. Distribution of Yearly Family
             Income of American and Finnish
             Wives of Alcoholics[a]

Income level	American (N = 72) [b] (before taxes)	Finnish (N = 44) [b] (after taxes)
Low	7%	11%
Medium low	13	12
Medium	35	46
Medium high	15	19
High	15	10
Don't know	15	2

[a] This table is an attempt to indicate rough comparability of income between American and Finnish
households. Finns always refer to their salaries in
monthly terms after taxes; Americans in yearly terms
before taxes. Finns receive substantially more medical
and social benefits than Americans. Thus all that can
be said about this table is that it offers the general
spread in the standards of living of respondents, and
indicates that not all respondents have close to the
same standard of living.
[b] Refusals were excluded from the base.

wives' reaction to it that occur across the samples, lend credence to the
belief that a uniform population is being studied. Furthermore, the men
apparently present their wives with sufficient problematic behavior and
exhibit enough overt drinking or drunkenness to justify the label.

Supplementary Samples

As the research progressed, the need for various subsamples to answer questions posed by findings in the original sample became apparent from time to time. Each of these will be discussed in turn.

Wives in Marriages Where Alcohol Is Not a Problem.   Later in the study, a
sample of 63 American wives in marriages where alcohol is not a problem was interviewed. These wives were selected by a quota sample with
the controls of age, income, and educational levels reflecting the general
composition of the American wives of alcoholics in the major sample as
presented in Tables 9.1 through 9.5. The purpose of this auxiliary sample
was to serve as a base of comparative data for the marital relationship
and interaction between spouses as described by wives of alcoholics.
Inasmuch as all marriages have problems (some very serious, as indi-

Table 9.4. Distribution of Educational Attainment of American and Finnish Alcoholic Husbands and Their Wives[a]

	American		Finns	
	Husbands [b] (N = 72) [c]	Wives (N = 72) [c]	Husbands [b] (N = 49) [c]	Wives (N = 48) [c]
Year in school completed	%	%	%	%
Elementary school	7	—	37	20
Some high school	16	22	4	24
Vocational school [d]	3	12	35	32
High school and vocational	—	—	4	10
High school graduate	36	32	—	2
Some college	24	22	6	4
College graduate	6	8	14	8
Postgraduate	8	4	—	—

[a] Because of drinking problems, current occupational status of men may not be as indicative of their general position in the class structure (or of their possible status had they not become alcoholics) as educational attainment which was probably reached before drinking became a problem. Educational attainment of both drinker and his wife is therefore presented here to give additional indication of the scope of the sample.

[b] Husband's educational level provided by wife.

[c] No answers were excluded from the base.

[d] In Finland, vocational school is often an alternative to high school; thus the great disparity between these two samples in the proportion of high school graduates.

Table 9.5. Distribution of Length of Time American and Finnish Husbands Have Had a Drinking Problem as Perceived by Their Wives[a]

	American (N = 76)	Finnish (N = 50)
Years husband has had drinking problem	%	%
Less than 1	1	2
1–5	9	12
6–10	21	20
11–15	13	16
16–20	26	8
21–30	11	20
31 or more	15	4
Not certain, drank before marriage, etc.	4	18

[a] The length of time the husband has had a drinking problem (as perceived by his wife) also indicates that the volunteer sample contains a broad range of persons.

cated by the high divorce rate in the United States), it was thought that only by examining data gathered from wives in marriages where alcohol is not a problem, could one see whether the impact of alcoholism per se on the marital relationship is greater, or in some ways unique, as compared to the typical problems in marriages generated by numerous other short-term or long-term conditions not associated with problem drinking. Put another way, it seemed possible that the phenomena of reduced contact and companionship in marriages where one spouse is an alcoholic could be common to all or many middle-aged marriages and thus not necessarily derived from the drinking and its attendant behavior. Data from this sample are presented in Chapter 6.

Wives of "Recovered" or "Recovering" Alcoholics. Another subsample was collected among wives of men who had been free of an alcoholic problem for a year or more. These women were also volunteers, contacted by variations on the following newspaper advertisement:

> Wives, did your husband have an alcohol problem? Has he maintained sobriety for a year or more? We would like to talk to you.

The purpose of collecting data from this sample was to see if comparisons made between the interaction of spouses in marriages where the husband is an active alcoholic and those in marriages where he has managed to stop drinking for a year yield some clues to the dynamics of abstinence and/or recidivism. Additionally, I hoped that there might be some pertinent information in the early career of wife-husband interaction (when the husband was just beginning to drink to excess and the wife was becoming concerned and using various strategies to get him to stop) that would be useful in understanding the ongoing relationship of men who were finally able to stop drinking as compared with that of men who are still drinking to excess.

Twenty-five American wives and 22 Finnish wives answered the advertisement and were interviewed in depth; however, one Finnish woman refused to answer many of the questions on the background data sheet and as a result the tables reflect this with a base of 21. The distributions of characteristics of this sample is shown in Tables 9.6 through 9.10.

In all samples, respondents were restricted to Caucasians, primarily because the first portion of the investigation was conducted in Finland, which has very few nonwhites. Since only Caucasians were available to interview there, it was thought that the comparability of the data would be jeopardized if other races were included in the American sample.

Table 9.6. Age Distribution of American and Finnish Wives of Recovered Alcoholics and Their Husbands[a]

Age	American (N = 25)		Finnish (N = 21)	
	Wives %	Husbands [b] %	Wives %	Husbands [b] %
20 or under	—	—	29	10
21–30	12	4	19	38
31–40	32	24	28	28
41–50	24	24	10	10
51–60	24	28	14	14
Over 60	8	12	—	—
Recently deceased	—	8		

[a] Although actual recovery from alcoholism is problematic, the term is used here to refer to alcoholics who have stopped drinking for a year or more.
[b] Husband's age furnished by wife.

Table 9.7. Distribution of Length of Time Married of American and Finnish Wives of Recovered[a] Alcoholics

Years married	American (N = 25) %	Finnish (N = 21) %
Less than 1	—	—
1–3	4	10
4–6	12	5
7–10	8	33
11–20	32	19
Over 20	40	29
Living together	4	—
No answer	—	4

[a] Although actual recovery from alcoholism is problematic, the term is used here to refer to alcoholics who have stopped drinking for one year.

Table 9.8. Distribution of Yearly Income [a]
of American and Finnish Wives
of Recovered Alcoholics [b]

Income level	American (N = 25) % (before taxes)	Finnish (N = 21) % (after taxes)
Low	—	14
Medium low	24	24
Medium	40	34
Medium high	16	11
High	16	10
Don't know	4	7

[a] This table is an attempt to indicate rough comparability of income between American and Finnish households. Finns always refer to their salaries in monthly terms after taxes; Americans in yearly terms before taxes. Finns receive substantially more medical and social benefits than Americans. Thus all that can be said about this table is that it offers the general spread in the standards of living of respondents, and indicates that not all respondents have close to the same standard of living.

[b] Although actual recovery from alcoholism is problematic, the term is used here to refer to alcoholics who have stopped drinking for a year or more.

Data Collection

Primary means of data collection was a detailed, in-depth interview lasting one and one-half to two and one-half hours. Inasmuch as little is known about the diagnosis, treatment, and coping procedures as well as ultimate life adjustment of wives of alcoholics, it was thought that a highly structured questionnaire would be premature and might well rule out serendipitous findings. A preliminary topic guide was created and served as a means of ensuring that all respondents covered all subjects pertinent to the study. This topic guide was revised several times during the gathering of Finnish data, and again during interviewing of American wives. Respondents were allowed to move from subject to subject in any order they wished, as well as to offer discussion of topics not on the guide; however, interviewers were instructed to ask eventually for discussion on subjects not covered spontaneously by the respondent. (Topic guide follows this chapter.)

Table 9.9. Distribution of Educational Attainment of American and Finnish Wives of Recovered Alcoholics [a]

| | American (N = 25) | | Finnish (N = 21) | |
| | Husbands [b] | Wives | Husbands [b] | Wives |
Year in school completed	%	%	%	%
Elementary school	4	—	19	33
Some high school	4	20	19	5
Vocational school [c]	—	—	28	19
High school and vocational	—	—	—	—
High school graduate	36	32	10	19
Some college	28	24	19	19
College graduate	8	12	5	5
Postgraduate	12	12	—	—
No answer	8	—	—	—

[a] Although actual recovery from alcoholism is problematic, the term is used here to refer to alcoholics who have stopped drinking for a year or more.
[b] Educational level of husband supplied by wife.
[c] In Finland, vocational school is often an alternative to high school; thus the great disparity between these two samples in the proportion of high school graduates.

Table 9.10. Distribution of Length of Time American and Finnish Recovered [a] Alcoholic Husbands had a Drinking Problem as Perceived by Their Wives

| | American (N = 25) | Finnish (N = 22) |
Years husband has had a drinking problem	%	%
Less than 1	—	—
1–5	8	13
6–10	4	23
11–15	20	27
16–20	24	5
21–30	12	9
31 or more	24	9
Not certain, drank before marriage, etc.	8	14

[a] Although actual recovery from alcoholism is problematic, the term is used here to refer to alcoholics who have stopped drinking for a year or more.

Procedures for interviewing take into consideration National Institute of Mental Health protocols for the protection of human subjects. Volunteers were first given a short explanation of the purposes of the study and told that they were free to talk as much or as little (or not at all) on each topic as it was raised. They were also told that they could terminate the interview at any time. Respondents were assured of the confidentiality of their answers. Their anonymity was protected by a numbering system that kept their identity separate from their interview data. A statement describing the project was then given respondents to read (after the verbal description). No one was interviewed unless he or she signed the statement, declaring (1) an understanding of the purpose of the research; (2) awareness of safeguards for confidentiality; and (3) willingness to be interviewed. In the United States respondents were paid $10 for their time while being interviewed.

Getting comparative information from wives in marriages where alcohol is not a problem presented some difficulties, inasmuch as the interview guide lacked the focus (on alcoholism and its attendant problems) that the interview of the wives of alcoholics had. The approach here was to take all the marital problem areas mentioned by wives of alcoholics and ask questions about them that were as open and nondirective as possible.

Problems of Validity, Reliability, and Analysis

In the usual survey research approach, validity refers to whether the data collected represent that which they purport to represent. In this study, the validity problem is not to ensure that the data represent the phenomenon from an objective point of view, but rather that the social world of the actor be represented as she herself sees it. Thus, the question of validity reshaped to suit the purposes of the study is as follows:

1. Do the social actors in question build the concepts and constructs of their daily social reality out of the same data that the investigator has and with the same general forms emerging?
2. How valid are the conclusions the investigator draws from the constructs being used to depict the special social world of the group of actors selected for study?

The investigative talents required to establish validity in each case are somewhat different. In the first case, the researcher must be sensitive enough to apprehend the important ingredients of the constructs of another's world. The second is more the sociological enterprise: the investigator must be able to generalize from the constructs and causal inferences to other instances of the same phenomenon in sociologically technical terms. This allows the world under study to be compared and contrasted (in part or as a whole) with other worlds and other findings. Needless to say, the validity of this more analytic procedure is much more difficult to ensure or demonstrate with any certainty.

For the first type of validity testing—that of building constructs purporting to have close resemblance to those of the social order—two procedures have been used. First, wives of alcoholics in both cultures had the opportunity to attend colloquia based on analyzed material and were invited to comment on and suggest changes where they felt that the materials did not reflect what really happened in their lives.

A further important validity check has been previously mentioned. Thirty American men and 15 Finnish men in treatment for alcoholism were interviewed. This meant that the husband was currently as close to being a "certified" alcoholic as is possible to get. The husbands' perception of their behavior and their actions, as well as how each man perceived those of his wife, were then compared with the larger samples of the wives' in-depth interviews (as well as with answers given by their wives). In general, the data from each source are very similar.

Reliability refers to the consistency of the data obtained. Would the same results be obtained in successive gatherings of data using the same instrument? The concern here is that should another investigator choose to replicate the study using the same approach, his or her findings (in terms of the raw data especially) would not deviate sharply. The reliability problem in this study is, then, as follows:

Does the data offered by respondents in the form of attitudes, descriptions, and recall of behavior constitute commonly accepted phenomena in the world of the wife of an alcoholic, or are the data not representative because:

1. the persons interviewed or observed are not truly representative of the social actors in this behavior system,
2. the person interviewed lies to the investigator or is a chronic complainer and a malcontent.

The first is difficult to know because we do not know the true universe of alcoholics and their wives. However, as demonstrated by the tables presented earlier, we do know that a broad spectrum of wives is represented in the sample. The second concern is more easily checked. Disregarding the unlikely possibility of a great conspiracy that extends to all respondents, information that comes up repeatedly from many respondents has been assumed worth using and analyzing.

An important aspect of validity and reliability is also a vital part of the analysis. The manner in which the data seem to hold together to form a sort of model of what life is like for the wife of an alcoholic simultaneously provide both insight on substantive findings and a check on their authenticity.

It is hoped that this study, which has tried to strike a methodological balance between openness to serendipitous finding and sufficient care about problems of sampling, data collection, coding, and analysis, will provide new insights into the drama of the struggle with alcoholism, which starts on the home front long before it involves professional aid or official sanctions, and continues well after such intercession takes place. Such interactive behavior is an important link in understanding alcoholism as a phenomenon that develops and continues in a very personal social milieu.

Glaser and Strauss (1966) indicate the importance of integrating methods of data collection with theory and suggest that analysis, testing of hypotheses, and data collection should go on simultaneously. In that way, theory can be revised to fit the empirical facts as they are discovered and further types of facts can be searched as theory points the way to unanswered questions. Ultimately, by alternating between analysis and data collection, theory will be revised and data collection will be modified and elaborated as the theory is eventually "grounded" in the empirical world. Thus, any approach to data gathering must, of necessity, undertake to be consistent with the analytic framework of the study, even though they are conceptually independent.

The theoretical guide for the conduct of this research will be the theories of George Herbert Mead (1932), W. I. Thomas (1928), and Herbert Blumer (1969). All share an emphasis on the importance of the actor's subjective assessment of his/her situation to understand his/her actions. Blumer calls attention to the importance of investigating actual interaction between individuals as interpreted by each and acted on by each to understand that the motivation to act is a changing, growing process.

Guided by such a framework, the histories or careers of these wives have been traced through retrospective data in terms of how they view their world. Data gathering was amended as new insights emerged. This means that questions were added to the topic guide from time to time. Through both induction and deduction, large portions of their world as they see it is pieced together, followed by investigative attempts to get details about these portions as well as locate the links among them. The final analytic goal is a reconstruction of the wives' points of view as it emerges through interaction with an alcoholic husband.

Notes

1.   The protocol for protection of human subjects under which the NIAAA sponsored the study, called for keeping the name of the cities where the interviews were conducted anonymous.

2.   This designation was, quite naturally, used only in Finland.

3.   Finns claim that shyness is a national characteristic, and this may account for reluctance on the part of some women to be interviewed. Alternatively, fear of physical abuse from an angry husband or shame concerning his condition may also have played a part.

Interview Topic Guide

(Note: When doing depth interviewing, the topic guide is elaborated and/or amended as more is learned about the subjects in the sample. Therefore, this topic guide is not the one with which the interviewers started out. Data from subsequent interviews is reviewed from time to time in order to expand or change the topic guide if necessary.)

Labeling

- When did you first suspect your husband was an alcoholic?
- What led to your first suspicion that your husband had a drinking problem?
- What other events made it seem even more likely?
- What was the final event that decided it for you?

Reactions by Wife: Counterreactions by Husband

- When you first decided he was an alcoholic, what did you do about it?
- How did he react to that?
- When you first decided he was an alcoholic, what did you know about alcoholism?
- What else have you done in an attempt to stop him from drinking so much? What else?
- What was his reaction?
- Have you changed your tactics through the years? Why?
- What do you think has worked best? Not well at all? Why?
- What are some things you have considered doing about his drinking but so far have not done? Why not?

Actions by Husband

- How does your husband act when drunk?
- How does he act when sober?

- Has this changed over the years?
- Has his drinking pattern changed over the years?
- How does he act when he tries to stop drinking for a period?
- Are there any occasions when he does not drink as much as usual?

Reactions by Wife

- How do you act when he is drunk?
- How do you act when he is sober?
- How do you act in front of the children when he is drunk? Sober?
- Do you ever pretend not to notice he is drunk and act natural? How do you do this? Is it difficult? (This question was added after the topic was raised spontaneously.)
- How do the children act when he is drunk? Sober?
- Does his appearance change?

Family Effects

- Describe a typical weekday at your home when your husband has been drinking.
- Describe a typical weekend at your home when your husband has not been drinking.
- How do weekends differ when your husband is drunk or sober?
- How has drinking affected your everyday living? For instance, do you buy less groceries because he doesn't eat as much? Do you move things he might fall over out of the way? Do you cook better or worse meals? Do you keep sharp knives out of his reach? etc. What things do you have to think about with an alcoholic in the house?
- What things do you think a husband and wife should do together?
- What things do you and your husband do together these days?
- What things did you and your husband used to do together before he started drinking so heavily?
- In what other ways has your relationship changed?
- In what other ways has your relationship stayed the same?
- Do you and your husband have meals together? Which ones?
- Has this changed since he began drinking very heavily?
- Do you and your husband talk much? Has this changed since he began drinking so heavily?
- Aside from getting your husband to stop drinking, what other things do you persuade him to do? How do you do it? How successful are you?
- Does he often promise he will stop drinking? How do you feel

when he breaks this promise? Has your reaction to broken promises changed over the years?

- How has your relationship with your husband changed over the
years?

Significant Others

- Whom have you told about this problem? Why?
- Whom did you try to keep from finding out about your husband's
drinking? Why? (Cover children, wife's family, husband's family,
friends.)
- Who does know about the problem? (How did they find out?)
- Have you enlisted the help of others (listed above)? What was their
reaction?
- If you asked relatives to help you get him into treatment, take you
in their home, give you financial help, would they?
- Have any relatives or friends been lost or alienated because of his
drinking (or for other reasons connected with it)?

Making Life Tolerable

- What have you done to build a life of your own?
- What have you thought of doing?
- What have you done to make life tolerable?
- Has anyone helped you with this: family, friends, children?

Attitudes toward Clinics, etc.

- Have you ever thought of trying to get your husband into Alcoholic
Anonymous? Some outpatient clinic or alcoholism program? A
hospital or sanatorium that treats alcoholism?
- Why, or why not?

Current Attitudes

- Do you think your husband will ever stop drinking? Why or why
not?
- Have you ever thought of divorcing or leaving him? Why or why
not?
- Is your husband against a divorce? Why?
- How do your children feel about a divorce? Why?
- What do you know about alcoholism that you didn't know when
you first discovered your husband was an alcoholic?

Advice to Others

- How to help husband quit drinking so much: What worked best for you? What worked least? Is there a better time to talk to him?
- What to do about your own life?
- What to do about relatives and children?
- If a young woman came to you and said, "I think my husband is an alcoholic. What shall I do?" What would you tell her? What else?

References

(No author). 1955. *Alcoholics Anonymous*. New York: Alcoholics Anonymous Publishing, Inc.

(no author). 1978. "Finland Highest in Deaths from Binges." *Los Angeles Times* July 9, 1978. p. 1–17.

(no author). 1982. "A Woman in Finland." The Council for Equality Between Men and Women. (mimeo)

Aarens, Marc, Tracy Cameron, Judy Roizen, Ron Roizen, Robin Room, Dan Schneberk, and Deborah Wingard. 1977. "Alcohol, Casualties and Crime." Report No. C-18, University of California, Social Research Group, Berkeley.

Adams, Linda. 1980. *Effectiveness Training for Women: E. T. W.* New York: Wyden.

Alasuutari, Pertti. [no date]. "The Male Suburban Pub-Goer and the Meaning Structure of Drinking." (mimeo)

Al-Anon Family Groups. n.d. "A Guide for the Family of the Alcoholic." Pamphlet. New York: Al-Anon Family Group Headquarters.

———. 1952. "Lois' Story: Al-Anon from the Beginning." Pamphlet. New York: Al-Anon Family Group Headquarters.

———. 1967. "This is Al-Anon." Pamphlet. New York: Al-Anon Family Group Headquarters.

———. 1979a. "Homeward Bound." Pamphlet. New York: Al-Anon Family Group Headquarters.

———. 1979b. *Living with Sobriety*. New York: Al-Anon Family Group Headquarters.

———. 1982. "Alcoholism is a Family Disease." Pamphlet. New York: Al-Anon Family Group Headquarters.

Albertson, Robert. 1971. "Identifying Alcoholism as a Problem." Pp. 33–46 in *Casework with Wives of Alcoholics*, edited by P. C. Cohen and M. S. Krause. New York: Family Service Association of America.

Aldous, Joan. 1981. "From Dual-Earner to Dual-Career Families and Back Again." *Journal of Family Issues* 2:115–25.

Ahlström-Laakso, Salme. 1973. "European Drinking Habits: A Review of Research and Some Suggestions for Conceptual Integration of Findings." Paper delivered at Conference on Anthropology and Alcohol Studies. Chicago.

———. 1971. "Arrests for Drunkenness—Two Capital Cities Compared." *Scandinavian Studies in Criminology* 3:89–105.

Allen, L. R. and M. A. Donnelly. 1985. "An Analysis of the Social Unit of Participation and the Perceived Psychological Outcomes Associated with Most Enjoyable Recreation Activities." *Leisure Sciences* 7:421–41.

Anderson, S. E. 1984. "The Outpatient Alternative." *EAP Digest* 4:18–21,23.

Anonymous. 1982. "Health Insurance Should Pay for Alcoholism Treatment in Order to Reduce Costs of Treating Related Illnesses, According to the National Institute on Alcohol Abuse and Alcoholism." *Medical World* 36:38.

———. 1984a. "ALCARE: When There Is No Insurance." *Alcoholism: The National Magazine* 5:27,72.

———. 1984b. "Family Members Focus of Kemper EAP (Employee Assistance Program)." *Alcohol and Health Research World* 8:52–53.

———. 1985. "Study: Alcoholism Treatment Costs." *ADAMHA News* 11:1,7.

Archer, N. Sidney. 1979. "Perceptions and Attitudes of Family Members (Codependents): Pre- and Post-treatment." *Labor-Management Alcoholism: Clinic and Journal* 9:75–80.

Argyle, M. 1983. "Why Do Marriages Break Down?" *New Society* 64:259–60.

Armour, David J., J. Michael Polich, and Harriet B. Stambull. 1978. *Alcoholism and Treatment*. New York: Wiley.

Asch, S. E. 1946. "Forming Impressions of Personality." *Journal of Abnormal Social Psychology* 41:258–90.

Baker, Therese I. and Judith A. Bootcheck. 1985. "The Relationship of Marital Status and Career Preparation to Changing Work Orientations of Young Women: A Longitudinal Study." *Research in Sociology of Education and Socialization* 5:327–49.

Baldrige, Letitia. 1979. "Contemporary Living." *Los Angeles Times* January 4, p. 8.

Baldwin, Monica. 1957. *I Leap over the Wall*. New York: Signet.

Balgooyen, Theodore J. 1974. "Comparison of the Effect of Synanon 'Game' Verbal Attack Therapy and Standard Group Therapy Practice on Hospitalized Chronic Alcoholics." *Journal of Community Psychology* 2:54–58.

Ball, R. E. 1984. "Family and Friends: A Supportive Network for Low-Income American Black Families." *Journal of Comparative Family Studies* 14:51–65.

Balswick, Jack O., and Charles W. Peek. 1974. "The Inexpressive Male: A Tragedy of American Society." Pp. 27–34 in *Process in Relationship*, edited by Edward A. Powers, Mary W. Lees, Frank A. Fear, and J. P. Golinvauz. St. Paul: West Publishing Company.

Bard, Morton and Joseph Zacker. 1974. "Assaultiveness and Alcohol Use in Family Disputes: Police Perceptions." *Criminology* 12:281–92.

Barnouw, Victor. 1971. *An Introduction to Anthropology. Volume Two: Ethnology.* Homewood, IL: Dorsey Press.

Bateman, Mildred E. 1971. "Engaging the Alcoholic Man and His Wife in Casework Treatment." Pp. 60–77 in *Casework with Wives of Alcoholics*, edited by P. C. Cohen and M. S. Krause. New York: Family Service Association of America.

Bateson, Gregory. 1972. *Steps to an Ecology of the Mind.* San Francisco: Chandler.

Beauchamp, Dan E. 1980. *Beyond Alcoholism: Alcohol and Public Health Policy.* Philadelphia: Temple University Press.

Beck, Jane. 1984. "Problems Encountered by the Single Working Mother." *Ergonomics* 27:577–84.

Belknap, Ivan. 1956. *Human Problems in a State Mental Hospital.* New York: McGraw-Hill.

Bell, Robert R. 1981. *Worlds of Friendship.* Beverly Hills, CA: Sage.

Bensinger, A. and C. F. Pilkinton. 1983. "An Alternative Method in the Treatment of Alcoholism: The United Technologies Corporation Day Treatment Program." *Journal of Occupational Medicine* 25:300–303.

Ben-Sira, Zeev. 1984. "Chronic Illness, Stress, and Coping." *Social Science and Medicine* 18:725–36.

———. 1985. "Potency: A Stress-Buffering Link in the Coping-Stress-Distress Relationship." *Social Science and Medicine* 21:397–406.

Benson, Herbert. 1974. "Decreased Alcohol Intake Associated with the Practice of Meditation: A Retrospective Investigation." Pp. 174–77 in *Annals of the New York Academy of Sciences* 233, edited by F. A. Seixas, R. Cadoret, and S. Eggleston.

Berg, Dale H. 1983. "Reality Construction at the Family/Society Interface: The Internalization of Family Themes and Values." *Adolescence* 20:609–18.

Berger, A. 1981. "Family Involvement and Alcoholics' Completion of a Multiphase Treatment Program." *Journal of Studies on Alcohol* 42:517–21.

Berger, Bennett M. 1981. *The Survival of a Counterculture: Ideological Work and Everyday Life among Rural Communards.* Berkeley: University of California Press.

Berger, Peter and Hansfried Kellner. 1970. "Marriage and the Construction of Reality." Pp. 50–71 in *Recent Sociology No. 2,* edited by Hans Peter Zeitzel. New York: Macmillan.

Berheide, C. W. 1984. "Women's Work in the Home: Seems Like Old Times." *Marriage and Family Review* 7:37–55.

Bernard, Jessie. 1968. *The Sex Games.* Englewood Cliffs, NJ: Prentice-Hall.

———. 1973. *The Future of Marriage.* New York: Bantam.

———. 1981. *The Female World.* New York: Free Press.

Bienvenu, Millard J. 1970. "Measurement of Marital Communication." *The Family Coordinator* 19:26–31.

Binney, V. G. Harkell and J. Nixon. 1985. "Refugees and Housing for Battered Women." Pp. 166–78 in *Private Violence and Public Policy: The Needs of Battered Women and the Response of the Public Service,* edited by J. Pahl. Boston: Routledge and Kegan Paul.

Bishop, S. M. 1984. "Perspectives on Individual-Family-Social Network Relationships." *International Journal of Family Therapy* 6:124–35.

Bloom, Lynn Z., Karen Coburn, and Joan Pearlman. 1975. *The New Assertive Woman.* New York: Delacorte.

Blume, Sheila B. 1974. "Psychodrama and Alcoholism." Pp. 123–27 in *Annals of the New York Academy of Sciences* 233, edited by F. A. Seixas, R. Cadoret, and S. Eggleston.

Blumer, Herbert. 1969. *Symbolic Interactionism: Perspective and Method*. Englewood Cliffs, NJ: Prentice-Hall.

Bochner, Arthur P., Dorothy L. Krueger, and Terrence I. Chmielewski. 1982. "Interpersonal Perceptions and Marital Adjustment." *Journal of Communications* 32:135–47.

Bolton, Charles D. 1961. "Mate Selection as the Development of a Relationship." *Marriage and Family Living* 23:234–40.

Borkman, Thomasina. 1984. "The Social Model Approach to the Treatment of Alcoholism." Report to the State of California. (mimeo).

Borys, S. and D. Perlman. 1985. "Gender Differences in Loneliness." *Personality and Social Psychology Bulletin* 11:63–74.

Bossard, James H. S. and Eleanor Stoker Boll. 1960. *The Sociology of Child Development*. New York: Harper.

Bott, Elizabeth. 1971. *Family and Social Network*. New York: Free Press.

Bowen, M. 1974. "Family Systems Approach to Alcoholism." *Addictions* 21:28–39.

Braun, J. J. 1972. "The Administration of the Therapeutic Community: The Dream and Reality." In *Proceedings of the 30th International Congress of Alcoholism and Drug Dependence*. Amsterdam: International Council on Alcohol Addictions.

Brisett, D., et al. 1980. "Drinkers and Nondrinkers at Three and a Half Years after Treatment: Attitudes and Growth." *Journal of Studies on Alcohol* 41:945–52.

Britt, David W. 1975. "Social Class and the Sick Role: Examining the Issue of Mutual Influence." *Journal of Health and Social Behavior* 16:178–82.

Brown, Arthur H. 1975. "A Use of Social Exchange Theory in Family Crisis Intervention." *Journal of Marriage and Family Counseling* 1:259–67.

Brown, J. A. C. 1963. *Techniques of Persuasion: From Propaganda to Brainwashing*. Baltimore: Penguin.

Bruun, Kettil. 1963. "Outcome of Different Types of Treatment of Alcoholics." *Quarterly Journal of Studies on Alcohol* 24:280–88.

Burchfield, Susan R., Kathy Hamilton, and Karsi L. Banks. 1982. "Affiliative Needs, Interpersonal Stress and Symptomatology." *Journal of Human Stress* 8:5–9.

Burgess, Ernst W. and Leonard S. Cottrell. 1939. *Predicting Success or Failure in Marriage*. New York: Prentice-Hall.

Burgess, Ernest W. and Paul Wallin. 1953. *Engagement and Marriage*. New York: Lippincott.

Busch, Edwin J. 1981. "Developing an Employee Assistance Program." *Personnel Journal* 60:708–11.

Byrne, Margaret M. and James H. Holes. 1979. "Co-Alcoholic Syndrome." *The Labor-Management Alcoholism Journal* 9:68–74.

Caldwell, Bernice. 1983. "Assistance Programs Stress Individual Needs." *Employee Benefit Plan Review* 38:76,78.

Caldwell, R. A., B. L. Bloom, and W. F. Hodges. 1984. "Sex Differences in Separation and Divorce: A Longitudinal Perspective." Pp. 103–20 in *Social* and *Psychological Problems of Women; Prevention and Crisis Intervention*, edited by Annette U. Rickel, Meg Gerrard, and Ira Iscoe. Washington, DC: Hemisphere.

Carnegie, Dale. 1936. *How to Win Friends and Influence People*. New York: Simon and Schuster.

Carone, Pasquale A. and Leonard W. Krinsky. 1982. "A Program Geared Specifically to Industry by the Private Psychiatric Hospital." *Psychiatric Hospital* 13:84–87.

Cassell, Eric J. 1976. "Disease as an 'It': Concepts of Disease Revealed by Patients' Presentation of Symptoms." *Social Science and Medicine* 10:143–46.

Chadwick, Bruce A., Stan L. Albrecht, and Phillip R. Kunz. 1976. "Marital and Family Role Satisfaction." *Journal of Marriage and the Family* 28:431–40.

Chafetz, Morris E. 1983. *The Alcoholic Patient: Diagnosis and Management*. Oradell, NJ: Medical Economics Books.

Chalfant, H. Paul and Richard A. Kurtz. 1971. "Alcoholics and the Sick Role: Assessments by Social Workers." *Journal of Health and Social Behavior* 12:66–71.

Charles, Nickie and Marion Kerr. 1986. "Food for Feminist Thought." *Sociological Review* 34:537–72.

Cheek, Frances E., Cyril M. Franks, Joan Laucius, and Vasanti Burtle. 1971. "Behavior-Modification Training for Wives of Alcoholics." *Quarterly Journal of Studies on Alcohol* 32:456–61.

Clark, Alexander and Paul Wallin. 1965. "Women's Sexual Responsiveness and the Duration and Quality of Their Marriages." *American Journal of Sociology* 71:187–96.

Clausen, John A. and Marian Radke Yarrow. 1955. "Paths to the Mental Hospital." *Journal of Social Issues* 11:3–64.

Clayton, Richard R. 1975. *The Family, Marriage and Social Change*. Lexington, MA: Heath.

Clinard, Marshall (ed.). 1968. *Anomie and Deviant Behavior*. New York: The Free Press of Glencoe.

Cohen-Holmes, S. 1981. "Patients in Their Own Right, Families of Alcoholics Deserve Equal Attention in Treatment." *Focus on Alcohol and Drug Issues* 4:5–26.

Coleman, Diane H. and Murray A. Straus. 1979. "Alcohol Abuse and Family Violence." Paper read at annual meetings of American Sociological Society, Boston.

———. 1973. *Report of the Committee on the Position of Women in Finnish Society*. Helsinki: Government Printing Centre.

Congressional Caucus for Women's Issues. 1987. *The American Woman 1987–88: A Report in Depth*. Washington, DC: Women's Research and Education Institute.

Conrad, Peter and Joseph W. Schneider. 1980. *Deviance and Medicalization: From Badness to Sickness*. St. Louis: Mosby

Conway, J. 1981. "Significant Others Need Help Too: Alcoholism Treatment Just as Important to Rest of Family." *Focus on Alcohol and Drug Issues* 4:17–19.

Cook, F., C. Fewell, and J. Riolo. 1983. *Social Work Treatment of Alcohol Problems.* New Brunswick, NJ: Rutgers Center of Alcohol Studies.

Copeland, J. M., M. A. Bugaighis, and W. R. Schumm. 1984. "Relationship Characteristics of Couples Married Thirty Years or More: A Four-Sample Replication." *Lifestyles* 7:107–14.

Coser, Rose Laub. 1986. "Cognitive Structure and the Use of Social Space." *Sociological Forum* 1:1–26.

Criteria Committee, National Council on Alcoholism. 1972. "Criteria for the Diagnosis of Alcoholism." *American Journal of Psychiatry* 129:127–35.

Croog, Sydney H., Alberta Lipson, and Sol Levine. 1972. "Help Patterns in Severe Illness: The Roles of Kin Network, No-family Resources and Institutions." *Journal of Marriage and the Family* 34:32–41.

Cuber, John G., with Peggy B. Harroff. 1966. *The Significant Americans.* New York: Appleton-Century.

Davidson, William S., II. 1974. "Studies of Adversive Conditioning for Alcoholics: A Critical Review of Theory and Research Methodology." *Psychological Bulletin* 81:571–81.

Davis, Melvin. 1972. "A Self-confrontation Technique in Alcoholism Treatment." *Quarterly Journal of Studies on Alcohol* 33:191–92.

DeBurger, James E. 1971. "Marital Problems, Help-Seeking, and Emotional Orientation as Revealed in Help-Request Letters." Pp. 413–28 in *People as Partners,* edited by Jacqueline P. Wiseman. San Francisco: Canfield.

Denzin, Norman. 1987a. *The Alcoholic Self.* Beverly Hills, CA: Sage.

———. 1987b. *The Recovering Alcoholic.* Beverly Hills, CA: Sage.

deSaugy, D. 1962. "L'Alcoolique et sa Femme; Etude Psychosociale et Statistique sur les Condition de leur Development Individual et de leur Vie en Commun." *Hygiene Mental* 51:81–128, 145–201.

Deutsch, Morton. 1964. "Cooperation and Trust, Some Theoretical Notes." In *Interpersonal Dynamics,* edited by Schein, Berlew, and Steele. Homewood, IL: Dorsey Press.

Dienstag, Eleanor. 1974. "The Dinner Hour." *Ms. Magazine* 3(September):15–17.

Dion, K., E. Berscheid, and E. Walster. 1972. "What Is Beautiful Is Good." *Journal of Personality and Social Psychology* 24:285–90.

Dobash, R. Emerson and Russell Dobash. 1979. *Violence Against Wives:A Case Against Patriarchy.* New York: Free Press.

Dougherty, Ed. 1985. "Intervention Counseling." Pp. 45–48 in *Alcoholism and the Family,* edited by Sharon Wegscheider-Cruse and Richard W. Esterly. Wernersville, PA: The Caron Institute.

Dowling, Colette. 1981. *The Cinderella Complex: Women's Hidden Fear of Independence.* New York: Summit.

Dressler, William W. 1985. "Extended Family Relationships, Social Support, and Mental Health in a Southern Black Community." *Journal of Health and Social Behavior* 26:39–48.

Dreyer, Cecily A. and Albert S. Dreyer. 1973. "Family Dinner Time as a Unique Behavior Habitat." *Family Process* 12:291–321.

Ebbeson, Ebbe B. 1980. "Cognitive Processes in Understanding Ongoing Behavior." Pp. 179–225 in *Person Memory: The Cognitive Basis of Social Perception*, edited by Reid Hastie, et al. Hillsdale, NJ: Lawrence Erlbaum Associates.

Eberle, Patricia A. 1980. "Alcohol Abusers and Non-Users: A Discriminant Analysis of Differences between Two Sub-Groups of Batterers." Paper presented at the annual meeting of the Society for the Study for Social Problems, Toronto.

Edwards, D. W. 1982. "Spouse Participation in the Treatment of Alcoholism: Completion of Treatment and Recidivism." Pp. 41–48 in *Social Groupwork and Alcoholism*, edited by Marjorie Altman and Ruth Crocker. New York: Haworth.

Edwards, Griffith. 1970. "The Status of Alcoholism as a Disease." Pp. 140–61 in *Modern Trends in Drug Dependence and Alcoholism*, edited by R. V. Phillipson. New York: Appleton-Century-Crofts.

———. 1980a. Alcoholism Treatment: Between Guesswork and Certainty." In *Alcoholism Treatment in Transition*, edited by Griffith Edwards and Marcus Grant. Baltimore: University Park Press.

———. 1980b. "What Alcoholism Isn't Borrowing." Pp. 37–42 in *Alcoholism Treatment in Transition*, edited by Griffith Edwards and Marcus Grant. Baltimore: University Park Press.

Eisenberg, Leon. 1977. "Disease and Illness: Distinctions between Professional and Popular Ideas of Sickness." *Culture, Medicine and Psychiatry* 1:9–23.

Emerson, Robert M. and Sheldon L. Messinger. 1977. "the Micro-politics of Trouble." *Social Problems* 25:121–34.

Epstein, Cynthia Fuchs. 1984. "Ideal Images and Real Roles:The Perpetuation of Gender Inequalities." *Dissent* 31:441–47.

———. 1986. "Symbolic Segregation: Similarities and Differences in the Language and Non-Verbal Communication of Women and Men." *Sociological Forum* 1:27–49.

Estes, Nada J. 1974. "Counseling the Wife of an Alcoholic Spouse." *American Journal of Nursing* 74:1251–55.

Etaugh, Claire and Joann Malstrom. 1981. "The Effect of Marital Status on Person Perception." *Journal of Marriage and the Family* 43:801–05.

Ewing, John A. 1980. "Matching Therapy and Patients: The Cafeteria Plans." Pp. 399–405 in *Alcoholism Treatment in Transition*, edited by Griffith Edwards and Marcus Grant. Baltimore: University Park Press.

Fairchild, Donald M. and Kenneth W. Wanberg. 1972. "Therapeutic Community (Residential Treatment Center) as a Treatment Modality for Chronic Alcoholics." P. 3–7 in *Selected Papers from the Twenty-Third Annual Meeting of Alcohol and Drug Problems Association of North America*. Washington, D.C.: ADPA.

Farber, I. E., Harry Harlow, and Loius Jolyon West. 1961. "Brainwashing, Conditioning, and DDD (Debility, Dependency and Dread)" Pp. 106–16 in *Studies in Behavior Pathology*, edited by Theodore R. Sarbin. New York: Holt, Rinehart and Winston.

Farcas, Susan W. 1980. "Impact of Chronic Illness on the Patient's Spouse." *Health and Social Work* 5:39–46.

Faules, Don F. and Dennis C. Alexander. 1978. *Communication and Social Behavior:*

A Symbolic Interaction Perspective. Addison-Wesley Publishing Co., Reading, Massachusetts.

Feldberg, Roslyn and Janet Kohen, 1976. "Family Life in an Anti-Family Setting: A Critique of Marriage and Divorce." *The Family Coordinator* 25:151–59.

Feldman, Daniel J., E. Mansell Pattison, Linda C. Sobell, Theresa Graham, and Mark B. Sobell. 1974. "Outpatient Alcohol Detoxification: Initial Findings on 564 Patients." *American Journal of Psychiatry* 132: 407–12.

Felton, B. J., et al. 1980. "The Coping Function fo Sex-Role Attitudes during Marital Disruption." *Journal of Health and Social Behavior* 21:240–48.

Fenwick, Sheridan. 1973. *Getting It: The Psychology of est.* Philadelphia: J. Lippincott Company.

Ferree, M. M. 1984. "The View from Below: Women's Employment and Gender Equality in Working Class Families." *Marriage and Family Review* 7:57–75.

Festinger, Leon. 1964. *Conflict, Decision and Dissonance.* Stanford: Stanford University Press.

———. 1954. *A Theory of Cognitive Dissonance.* Stanford: Stanford University Press.

Fingarette, Herbert. 1988. *Heavy Drinking: The Myth of Alcoholism as a Disease.* Berkeley: University of California Press.

Finney, John W., Rudolf H. Moos, and C. R. Mewborn. 1980. "Post-treatment Experiences and Treatment Outcome of Alcoholic Patients Six Months after Hospitalization." *Journal of Consulting and Clinical Psychology* 48:17–29.

Foote, Nelson. 1954. "Sex as Play." *Social Problems* 1:159–63.

Ford, F. R. 1983. "Rules:The Invisible Family." *Family Process* 22:135–45.

Forrest, Gary G. 1978. *The Diagnosis and Treatment of Alcoholism.* Springfield, IL: Charles C. Thomas.

Frank, Arthur W., III. 1976. "Making Scenes in Public: Symbolic and Social Order." *Theory and Society* 3:395–416.

Franks, C. M. 1963. "Behavior Therapy, the Principles of Conditioning and the Treatment of the Alcoholic." *Quarterly Journal of Studies on Alcohol* 24:511–29.

Freeman, Howard E. and Ozzie G. Simmons. 1968. "Mental Patients in the Community: Family Settings and Performance Levels." Pp. 427–37 in *The Mental Patient: Studies in the Sociology of Deviance,* edited by Stephen Spitzer and Norman K. Denzin. New York: McGraw-Hill.

Freidson, Eliot. 1962. "The Sociology of Medicine." *Current Sociology* x/xi:3.

Futterman, S. 1953. "Personality Trends in Wives of Alcoholics." *Journal of Psychiatric Social Work* 23:37–41.

Gelles, Richard. 1974. *The Violent Home.* Beverly Hills, CA: Sage.

———. 1976. "Abused Wives: Why Do They Stay?" *Journal of Marriage and the Family* 38:659–68.

Gerstel, Naomi, Catherine Kohler Riessman, and Sarah Rosenfeld. 1985. "Explaining the Symptomatology of Separated and Divorced Women and Men: The Role of Material Resources and Social Networks." *Social Forces* 64:84–101.

Gibson, Geoffrey. 1972. "Kin Family Network: Overheralded Structure in Past Conceptualizations of Family Functioning. *Journal of Marriage and the Family* 34:13–23.

Gil, David G. 1973. *Violence Against Children*. Cambridge: Harvard University Press.

Ginott, Haim. 1965. *Between Parent and Child*. New York: Macmillan.

Gitlow, S. E. 1980. "Alcoholism: A Practical Treatment Guide." Pp. 129–43 in *Alcoholism: A Modern Perspective*, edited by P. Golding. Lancaster, England: MTP Press.

Glaser, Barney and Strauss, Anselm. 1967. *The Discovery of Grounded Theory*. New York: Aldine.

Goffman, Erving. 1952. "Cooling the Mark Out: Some Aspects of Adaptation to Failure." *Psychiatry* 15:451–63.

———. 1955. "On Face-work: An Analysis of Ritual Elements in Social Interaction." *Psychiatry* 18:213–31.

———. 1959. *The Presentation of Self in Everyday Life*. Garden City, NY: Doubleday Anchor Books.

———. 1963. *Behavior in Public Places*. New York: Free Press.

———. 1968. "Insanity of Place." *Psychiatry* 32:357–88.

Golding, A. P. 1982. *Alcoholism: A Modern Perspective*. Ridgewood, NJ: George A. Bogden.

Gollin, Eugene S. 1958. "Organizational Characteristics of Social Judgment: A Developmental Investigation." *Journal of Personality* 26:139–54.

Gordon, Michael and Penelope J. Shankweiler. 1971. "Different Equals Less: Female Sexuality in Recent Marriage Manuals." *Journal of Marriage and Family* 33:459–66.

Gorman, Joan M. and James F. Rooney. 1979. "The Influence of Al-Anon on the Coping Behavior of Wives of Alcoholics." *Journal of Studies on Alcohol* 40:1030–38.

Gottheil, Edward, A. Thomas McLellan, and Charles C. Thomas. 1981. *Matching Patient Needs and Treatment Methods in Alcoholism and Drug Abuse*. Springfield, Ill.

Gottlieb, Benjamin H. 1985. "Social Networks and Social Support: An Overview of Research, Practice, and Policy Implications." *Health Education Quarterly* 12:5–12.

Gottman, J. M. 1982. "Emotional Responsiveness in Marital Conversation." *Journal of Communication* 32:108–20.

Gough, Harrison. 1948. "A Sociological Theory of Psychopathy." *American Journal of Sociology* 49:359–66.

Granone, Franco. 1971. "Hypnotism in the Treatment of Chronic Alcoholism." *Journal of the American Institute of Hypnosis* 12:32–40.

Grantz, W. 1985. "Exploring the Role of Television in Married Life." *Journal of Broadcasting and Electronic Media* 29:65–78.

Green, Elmer E., Alyce M. Green, and Dale E. Walters. 1974. "Biofeedback Training for Anxiety Tension Reduction." Pp. 157–61 in *Annals of the New York Academy of Sciences* 223, edited by F. A. Seixas, R. Cadoret, and S. Eggleston.

Greenberg, Martin S. and Leonard Saxe. 1975. "Importance of Locus of Help Initiation and Type of Outcome as Determinants of Reaction to Another's Help Attempt." *Social Behavior and Personality* 3:101–10.

Greene, William. 1976. *est: Four Days to Make Your Life Work*. New York: Pocket Books.

Gross, A. E. and C. Crofton. 1977. "What Is Good Is Beautiful." *Sociometry* 40:85–90.

Haas, Linda. 1986. "Wives Orientation Toward Breadwinning: Sweden and the United States." *Journal of Family Issues* 7:331–58.

Haavio-Mannila, Elina and Eeva-Liisa Tuominen. 1974. "The Situation of Women in the Work World in Finland." *Sociologie et Societes* 6:93–103.

——— and Kyllikki Kari. 1980. "Changes in the Life Patterns of Families in the Nordic Countries." *Yearbook of Population Research in Finland*. 23:7–34.

——— and Riitta Jallinoja. 1980. *Changes in the Life Patterns of Families in Finland*. Helsinki: University of Helsinki, Department of Sociology. (mimeo)

———. 1983. "Economic and Family Roles of Men and Women in Northern Europe." Pp. 243–60 in *The Changing Position of Women in Family and Society: A Cross National Comparison*. Edited by Eugen Lupri. Leiden: E. J. Brill.

———, Riitta Jallinoja, and Harriet Strandell. 1983. *Changes in the Life Patterns of Families in Europe*. Helsinki: University of Helsinki, Department of Sociology. (mimeo)

——— and Marja Holmila. 1986. "Drinking Companionship and the Restriction of Drinking as Expressions of Family Relations." *Sociologia* 12:117–26.

Hariton, Theodore. 1970. *Interview: The Executive's Guide to Selecting Personnel*. New York: Hastings House, Publishers.

Harnett, John and Donna Elder. 1973. "The Princess and the Nice Frog: Study in Person Perception." *Perceptual and Motor Skills* 37:863–66.

Hart, H. L. A. 1965. "The Ascription of Responsibility and Rights." Pp. 151–74 in *Logic and Language*, edited by Anthony Flew. Garden City, NY: Doubleday.

Hart, William T. 1970. "The Treatment of Alcoholism in a Comprehensive Mental Health Center." *American Journal of Psychiatry* 126:1275–79.

Haworth, John. 1974. "Human Needs, Work and Leisure." *Society and Leisure* 6:5–24.

Heider, Fritz. 1967. *The Psychology of Interpersonal Relations*. New York: Wiley.

Heilman, M. E. and L. E. Saruwatari. 1979. "When Beauty Is Beastly; the Effects of Appearance and Sex on Evaluations of Job Applicants for Managerial and Non-managerial Jobs." *Organizational Behavior and Human Performance* 23:360–72.

Heins, T. 1982. "Marital Interaction and Depressed Women." *Australian Journal of Family Therapy* 3:155–58.

Heller, Joseph. 1962. *Catch-22*. New York: Dell.

Helson, Ravenna, Valory Mitchell, and Barbara Hart. 1985. "Lives of Women Who Became Autonomous." *Journal of Personality* 53:257–85.

Henry, Jules. 1965. *Culture Against Man*. New York: Vintage.

Hepburn, John R. 1973. "Violent Behavior in Interpersonal Relationships." *Sociological Quarterly* 14:419–29.

Hertzman, Marc and R. Z. Hertzman. 1981. "Marital Conflicts Caused by Alcoholism." *Medical Aspects of Human Sexuality* 15:69–83.

Hills, M. S. 1983. "Female Household Headship and the Poverty of Children." Pp. 324–76 in *Five Thousand American Families: Patterns of Economic Progress*,

Vol. 10, edited by G. J. Duncan and J. N. Morgan. Ann Arbor: University of Michigan Institute for Social Research.

Hochschild, Arlie R. 1979. "Emotion Work, Feeling Rules and Social Structure." *American Journal of Sociology* 85:551–75.

———. 1983. *The Managed Heart*. Berkeley and Los Angeles: University of California Press.

Holmila, Marja. 1985. "The Guardian Angel or a Drinking Companion." Paper presented at the Cultural Studies Conference on Drinking and Drinking Problems. Helsinki, Finland.

Hornstra, Robin K., Bernard Lubin, Ruth V. Lewis, and Beverly S. Willis. 1972. "Worlds Apart: Patients and Professionals." *Archives of General Psychiatry* 27:553–57.

Howard, Donald and Nancy Howard. 1985. "Treatment of the Significant Other." Pp. 137–62 in *Practical Approaches to Alcoholism Psychotherapy*, edited by S. Zimberg, J. Wallace, and Sheila B. Blume. New York: Plenum.

Hunt, Janet G., and Larry L. Hunt. 1977. "Dilemmas and Contradictions of Status: The Case of the Dual-Career Family." *Social Problems* 24:407–16.

Hyman, Ruth B. and Pierre Woog. 1982. "Stressful Life Events and Illness Onset: A Review of Crucial Variables." *Research in Nursing and Health* 5:155–63.

Imada, A. S. and M. D. Hakel. 1977. "Influence of Nonverbal Communication and Rater Proximity on Impressions and Decisions in Simulated Employment Interviews." *Journal of Applied Psychology* 62:295–300.

Inge, William. 1950. *Come Back, Little Sheba*. New York: Random House.

Irwin, John. 1970. *The Felon*. Englewood Cliffs, NJ: Prentice-Hall.

Jackson, Joan K. 1954. "The Adjustment of the Family to the Crisis of Alcoholism." *Quarterly Journal of Studies on Alcoholism* 15:562–86.

———. 1973. "The Adjustment of the Family to the Crisis of Alcoholism." Pp. 52–67 in *Deviance: The Interactionist Perspective*, edited by Earl Rubington and Martin S. Weinberg. New York: Macmillan.

Jacob, Theodore, and Ruth Ann Seilhammer. 1982. "The Impact on Spouses and How They Cope." Pp. 114–26 in *Alcohol and the Family*, edited by Jim Orford and Judith Harwin. London and Canberra: Croom Helm.

Jacob, Theodore, Alison Favorini, Susan S. Meisel, and Carol M. Anderson. 1973. "The Alcoholic's Spouse, Children and Family Interactions: Substantive and Methodological Findings." *Journal of Studies on Alcohol* 39:1231–47.

Jacobson, Michael, Robert Atkins, and George Hacker. 1983. *The Booze Merchants*. Washington, DC: CSPI Books.

James, Jane E. and Morton Goldman. 1971. "Behavior Trends of Wives of Alcoholics." *Quarterly Journal of Studies on Alcoholism* 32:3773–81.

Jellinek, E. M. 1962. "Phases of Alcohol Addiction." Pp. 356–68 in *Society, Culture and Drinking Patterns*, edited by David J. Pittman and Charles R. Snyder. New York: Wiley.

Jewson, N. D. 1976. "The Disappearance of the Sick-man from Medical Cosmology, 1870–1977." *Sociology* 2:225–44.

Johnson, Allen and George C. Bond. 1974. "Kinship, Friendship, and Exchange in Two Communities: A Comparative Analysis of Norms and Behavior." *Journal of Anthropological Research* 30:55–68.

Johnson, E. L. 1983. "Alcoholism: The Workplace." Pp. 65–78 in *Alcoholism: New Perspectives*, edited by H. K. Cleminshaw and E. B. Truitt. Akron, OH: University of Akron Press.

Kalashian, Marion M. 1959. "Working with the Wives of Alcoholics in an Outpatient Clinic Setting." *Journal of Marriage and the Family* 21:130–33.

Kantor, Glenda Kaufman and Murray A. Straus. 1986. "The Drunken Bum Theory of Wife Beating." Paper presented at the National Alcoholism Conference on Alcohol and the Family, San Francisco.

Karlen, Herman. 1965. "Alcoholism in Conflicted Marriages." *American Journal of Orthopsychiatry* 32:326–27.

Katz, Judith Milstein. 1976. "How Do You Love Me? Let Me Count the Ways. (The Phenomenology of Being Loved.)" *Sociological Inquiry* 46:17–22.

Kaufman, Edward. 1985. "Family Systems and Family Therapy of Substance Abuse: An Overview of Two Decades of Research and Clinical Experience." *International Journal of the Addictions* 20:897–916.

Kauppinen-Toropainen, Kaisa, Elina Haavio-Mannila, and Irja Kandolin. 1984. "Women at Work in Finland." Pp. 183–208 in *Women and Work*. Edited by M. J. Davidson and C. I. Cooper. New York: John Wiley & Sons Ltd.

Keenan, A. 1976. "Effects of the Nonverbal Behavior of Interviewers on the Candidates' Performance." *Journal of Occupational Psychology* 49:171–76.

———. 1977. "Some Relationships between Interviewers' Personal Feelings about Candidates and Their General Evaluation of Them." *Journal of Occupational Psychology* 50:275–83.

Keller, Mark. 1958. "Alcoholism: Nature and Extent of the Problem." *Understanding Alcoholism: Annals of the American Academy of Political and Social Science* 315:1–11.

———. 1972. "On the Loss-of-Control Phenomenon in Alcoholism." *British Journal of Addictions* 67:151–66.

Kelly, John R. 1975. "Life Styles and Leisure Choices." *The Family Coordinator*, 24:185–90.

Kelman, Herbert C. 1973. "Violence without Moral Restraint: Reflections on the Dehumanization of Victims and Victimizers." *Journal of Social Issues* 29:25–61.

Kitson, G. C., and J. K. Langlif. 1984. "Couples Who File for Divorce but Change Their Minds." *Journal of Ortho-Psychiatry* 34:469.

Kiviranta, Pekka. 1969. *Alcoholism Syndrome in Finland*. The Finnish Foundation for Alcohol Studies, (monograph series 27).

Koch, Sigmund. 1973. "The Image of Man in Encounter Groups." *American Scholar* 42:636–52.

Komarovsky, Mirra. 1967. *Blue-Collar Marriage*. New York: Vintage.

Koppisch, Arthur. 1974. "Alcoholism and the Family." *Journal of Perth Amboy General Hospital* 3:18–23.

Krupinski, Jerry and Robyn Farmer. 1973. "A Study of Aspects of Marital Life and Roles in Marriage Guidance Clients and Non-client Marriages." *Journal of Comparative Family Studies* 4:295–308.

Krupinski, Jerry, E. Marshall, and V. Yule. 1970. "Patterns of Marital Problems in Marriage Guidance Clients." *Journal of Marriage and the Family* 32:138–43.

Kuehn, L. L. 1974. "Looking Down a Gun Barrel: Person Perception and Violent Crime." *Perceptual and Motor Skills* 39:1159–64.

Larsen, Donald E. and Irving Rootman. 1967. "Physician Role Performance and Patient Satisfaction." *Social Science and Medicine* 10:29–32.

Lavee, Yoav, Hamilton I. McCubbin, and Joan M. Patterson. 1985. "The Double ABCX Model of Family Stress and Adaptation: An Empirical Test by Analysis of Structural Equations with Latent Variables." *Journal of Marriage and the Family* 47:811–25.

Laws, Judith Long. 1979. *The Second X: Sex Role and Social Role.* New York: Elsevier.

LeMasters, E. E. 1971. "Holy Deadlock." Pp. 454–55 in *People as Partners.* Edited by Jacqueline P. Wiseman. San Francisco: Canfield Press.

Lemere, F., and J. W. Smith. 1973. "Alcohol Induced Impotence." *American Journal of Psychiatry* 130:212–13.

Lemert, Edwin M. 1967. "Paranoia and the Dynamics of Exclusion." Pp. 197–211 in *Human Deviance, Social Problems, and Social Control.* Englewood Cliffs, NJ: Prentice-Hall.

Levinger, George. 1970. "Marital Cohesiveness and Dissolution." Pp. 126–32 in *Families in Crises.* Edited by Paul H. Glasser and Lois N. Glasser. New York: Harper and Row.

Lewis, Lionel S., and Dennis Brissett. 1967. "Sex as Work: A Study of Avocational Counseling." *Social Problems* 15:8–18.

Lewis, Margaret L. 1954. "The Initial Contact with Wives of Alcoholics." *Social Casework* 35:8–14.

Li, Jason T. and Robert A. Caldwell. 1987. "Magnitude and Directional Effects of Marital Sex-Role Incongruence on Marital Adjustment." *Journal of Family Issues* 8:97–110.

Locke, Harvey J. 1951. *Predicting Adjustment in Marriage: A Comparison of a Divorced and a Happily Married Couple.* New York: Henry Holt and Company.

Logan, David G. 1983. "Getting Alcoholics to Treatment by Social Network Intervention." *Hospital and Community Psychiatry* 34:360–61.

Lofland, Lyn. 1985. "The Social Shaping of Emotion: The Case of Grief." *Symbolic Interaction* 8:171–90.

London, M. and J. R. Poplawski. 1976. "Effects of Information on Stereotype Development in Performance Appraisal and Interview Contexts." *Journal of Applied Psychology* 64:199–205.

Los Angeles Times. 1978. "Hospital Treats Illness," and "Treating Alcoholism as a Disease." April 3, Section 8, pp. 1, 22–24, 26.

———. 1984. "Wives of Alcoholics Have Lower Divorce Rate Than General Population," October 19, p. C-1.

MacAndrew, Craig and Robert B. Edgerton. 1969. *Drunken Comportment.* Chicago: Aldine.

Mäkelä, Klaus. 1971. "Concentration of Alcohol Consumption." *Scandinavian Studies in Criminology* 3:77–88.

———. 1980. "What Can Medicine Properly Take On?" Pp. 225–33 in *Alcoholism Treatment in Transition,* edited by Griffith Edwards and Marcus Grant. Baltimore: University Park Press.

Martin, Del. 1976. *Battered Wives.* San Francisco: Glide.

Martin, J. K. and S. L. Hanson. 1985. "Sex, Family Wage-Earning Status, and Satisfaction with Work." *Work and Occupations* 12:91–109.

Martin, John B. 1985. "The Stress-alexithymia Hypothesis: Theoretical and Empirical Considerations." *Psychotherapy and Psychosomatics* 43:169–76.

Maxwell, Milton A. 1984. *The AA Experience.* New York: McGraw-Hill.

MacLanahan, Sara S., Nancy V. Wedemeyer, and Tina Adelberg. 1981. "Network Structure, Social Support, and Psychological Well-Being in the Single-Parent Family." *Journal of Marriage and the Family* 43:601–12.

McClelland, David C. 1972. *The Drinking Man.* New York: Free Press.

McNamara, John H. 1960. "The Disease Conception of Alcoholism: Its Therapeutic Value for the Alcoholic and His Wife." *Social Casework* 41:460–65.

McWilliams, James J. 1978. "Tough Love: A Method of Coping with the Alcoholic and Motivating Her/Him to Accept Treatment." Pamphlet, Kansas City National Council on Alcoholism.

Mead, George Herbert. 1932. *Mind, Self, and Society.* Chicago: University of Chicago Press.

Mechanic, David. 1965. "Perception of Parental Responses to Illness: A Research Note." *Journal of Health and Human Behavior* 6:253–57.

Menninger, Karl A. 1938. *Man Against Himself.* New York: Harcourt Brace.

Merton, Robert K. 1968. *Social Theory and Social Structure.* New York: Free Press.

Miller, Peter M. 1972. "The Use of Behavioral Contracting in the Treatment of Alcoholism: A Case Report." *Behavioral Therapy* 3:593–96.

Miller, S. M. 1965. "The American Lower Class: A Typological Approach." Pp. 27–29 in *New Perspectives on Poverty,* edited by Arthur B. Shostak and William Gomberg. Englewood Cliffs, NJ: Prentice-Hall.

Mills, Theodore. 1959. "Equilibrium and the Process of Deviance and Control." *American Sociological Review* 24:671–79.

Mitchell, Roger E., Cronkite, Ruth C., and Moos, Rudolf H. 1983. "Stress, Coping, and Depression among Married Couples." *Journal of Abnormal Psychology* 92:433–48.

Money, Jess. 1985. "Alcoholism Is the Result of a Conscious Decision." *Los Angeles Times,* Editorial pages, September 21.

Moore, R. A. 1971. "Alcoholism Treatment in Private Psychiatric Hospitals: A National Survey." *Quarterly Journal of Studies on Alcohol* 32:1083–85.

———. 1972. "The Diagnosis of Alcoholism in a Psychiatric Hospital: A Trial of the Michigan Alcoholism Screening Test (MAST)." *American Journal of Psychiatry* 128:1565–69.

Moos, Rudolf H., and Andrew G. Billings. 1983. "Psychosocial Processes of Recovery among Alcoholics and Implications of Clinicians and Program Evaluators." *Addictive Behaviors* 8:205–18.

Mulford, Harold A. and Donald E. Miller. 1964. "Measuring Public Acceptance of the Alcoholic as a Sick Person." *Quarterly Journal of Studies on Alcohol* 25:319–23.

Murphy, Donald C. and Lloyd A. Mendelson. 1973. "Communication and Adjustment in Marriage." *Family Process* 12:317–26.

National Institute on Alcohol Abuse and Alcoholism. 1971. *Alcohol: Some Questions and Answers.* Washington, DC: U.S. Government Printing Office.

————. 1972. *Alcohol and Alcoholism: Problems, Programs and Progress*, Publication No. (HSM) 72-9127. Washington, DC: DHEW.

Nätkin, Ritva. 1984. "The Suburban Pub—Women's Viewpoint." Helsinki, Finland: The Finnish Foundation for Alcohol Studies. (mimeo)

Neikirk, J. O. 1983. "Grief, Loss—Constant in Alcoholic Families." *Focus on Family and Chemical Dependence* 6:13–14.

Nelson, Harry. 1977. "No 'Best Cure' for Alcoholism, Experts Agree." *Los Angeles Times*, June 13.

Nichols, Beverly B. 1976. "The Abused Wife Problem." *Social Casework* 1:27–32.

Niemi, I., S. Kiiski, and M. Liikkanen. 1981. *Use of Time in Finland*. Studies 65, Helsinki: Central Statistical Office of Finland.

Niitamo, Olavi E., and Jorma Hyppola. 1985. *Women and Men at Work*. Tutkimuksia Undersokningar Studies Nro. 116. Helsinki, Finland: Central Statistical Office of Finland.

Novick, Lloyd, Henry Hudson, and Elaine German. 1974. "In-hospital Detoxification and Rehabilitation of Alcoholics in an Inner City Area." *American Journal of Public Health* 64:1089–94.

Oakley, Ann. 1974. *The Sociology of Housework*. New York: Pantheon.

Odets, Clifford, 1951. *The Country Girl*. New York: Viking.

Okun, Lewis. 1986. *Women Abuse: Facts Replacing Myths*. Albany: State University of New York Press.

Oleson, Virginia and Elvi Whittaker. 1968. *The Silent Dialogue*. San Francisco: Jossey Bass.

Olson, D. H. et al. 1983. *Families: What Makes Them Work*. Beverly Hills: Sage.

Orford, J., S. Guthrie, P. Nicholls, E. Oppenheimer, S. Egert, and C. Hensman. 1975. "Self-Reported Coping Behavior of Wives of Alcoholics and Its Association with Drinking Outcome." *Journal of Studies on Alcohol* 36:1254–67.

Osborn, Susan M. and Gloria G. Harris. 1975. *Assertive Training for Women*. Springfield, IL: Charles C. Thomas.

Österberg, Ingalill. 1977. "Alcohol and the Finns." *Finland* 58(January):56–68.

Ostrom, Thomas M., John M. Lingle, John B. Pryor, and Nehemia Geva. 1980. "Cognitive Organization of Person Impressions." Pp. 55–88 in *Person Memory: The Cognitive Basis of Social Perception*, edited by Reid Hastie, et al. Hillsdale, NJ: Lawrence Erlbaum Associates.

Pahl, J. M. and R. E. Pahl. 1971. *Managers and Their Wives: A Study of Career and Family Relationships in the Middle Class*. London: Allen Lane, Penguin.

Paige, P. E., W. La Pointe, and A. Krueger. 1971. "The Marital Dyad as a Diagnostic Treatment Variable in Alcohol Addiction." *Psychology Savannah* 8:64–73.

Paolino, Thomas J. and Barbara S. McCrady. 1977. *The Alcoholic Marriage: Alternative Perspectives*. New York: Grune & Stratton.

Parsons, Talcott. 1951. *The Social System*. Glencoe, IL: Free Press.

————. 1958. "Definitions of Health and Illness in the Light of American Values and the Social Structure." Pp. 165–87 in *Patients, Physicians and Illness*, edited by E. Gartley Jaco. Glencoe, IL: Free Press.

Patterson, J. M. and H. I. McCubbin. 1984. "Gender Roles and Coping." *Journal of Marriage and the Family* 46:95–104.

Pattison, E. Mansell. 1982. *Selection of Treatment for Alcoholics*. New Brunswick, NJ: Rutgers University Press.

Pattison, E. Mansell and Edward Kaufman, eds. 1982. *Encyclopedia Handbook of Alcoholism*. New York: Gardner.

Peltoniemi, Teuvo. 1984a. "Alcohol and Family Violence." Paper presented at Second National Conference for Family Violence Researchers, Durham, N.H.

———. 1984b. "Strategies for Coping with Family Violence among the Finnish and the Swedish Population." Paper presented at the Fifth International Congress on Child Abuse and Neglect, Montreal, Quebec, Canada.

Perry, Linda L. 1975. "Being Socially Anomalous: Wives and Mothers without Husbands." *Journal of Asian and African Studies* 10:32–41.

Pewers, Barbara Holland and Paul F. Secord. 1973. "Developmental Changes in Attribution of Descriptive Concepts to Persons." *Journal of Personality and Social Psychology* 27:120–28.

Pfeffer, Arnold Z. 1958. *Alcoholism*. New York: Grune & Stratton.

Piedmont, Eugene B. 1968. "Referrals and Reciprocity: Psychiatrists, General Practitioners and Clergymen." *Journal of Health and Social Behavior* 9:29–41.

Pinkham, Mary Ellen. 1989. *How to Stop the One You Love from Drinking: I Know Because Intervention Worked for Me*. New York: Berkley.

Pokorny, A. D., B. A. Miller, and H. B. Kaplan. 1972. "A Brief MAST: A Shortened Version of the Michigan Alcoholism Screening Test." *American Journal of Psychiatry* 129:342–45.

Polich, J. Michael, David J. Armour, and Harriet B. Stambull. 1980. "Patterns of Alcoholism over Four Years." *Journal of Studies on Alcohol* 31:35–62.

Poloma, Margaret M., Brian F. Pendleton, and T. Neal Garland. 1981. "Reconsidering the Dual-Career Marriage: A Longitudinal Approach." *Journal of Family Issues* 2:205–24.

Powers, J. S. and A. Spickard. 1984. "Michigan Alcoholism Screening Test to Diagnose Early Alcoholism in General Practice." *Southern Medical Journal* 77:853–56.

Price, G. M. 1945. "A Study of the Wives of Twenty Alcoholics." *Quarterly Journal of Studies of Alcohol* 5:620–27.

Quinn, William H. and James F. Keller. 1983. "Older Generations of the Family: Relational Dimensions and Quality." *American Journal of Family Therapy* 11:23–34.

Rae, J. B. and J. Drewery. 1972. "Interpersonal Patterns in Alcoholic Marriages." *British Journal of Psychiatry* 120:615–21.

Rapaport, Robert N. 1959. *Community as Doctor: New Perspectives on a Therapeutic Community*. London: Tavistock.

Ray, Marsh. 1964. "The Cycle of Abstinence and Relapse Among Heroin Addicts." Pp. 163–67 in *The Other Side*, edited by Howard S. Becker. New York: Free Press.

Reiss, Ira L. 1976. *Family Systems in America*. 2nd ed. Hinsdale, IL: Dryden.

Richards, Robert K. 1986. "The Declining Status of Women . . . Revisited." *Sociological Focus* 19:315–32.

Ries, Janet K. 1977. "Public Acceptance of the Disease Concept of Alcoholism." *Journal of Health and Social Behavior* 18:338–44.

Riesman, David, Reuel Denney, and Nathan Glazer. 1950. *The Lonely Crowd: A Study of the Changing American Character.* New Haven, CT: Yale University Press.

Robinson, David. 1941. *From Drinking to Alcoholism: A Sociological Commentary.* London: Wiley.

———. 1972. "The Alcohologist's Addiction." *Quarterly Journal of Studies on Alcohol* 33:1028–42.

———. 1973. "Alcoholism as a Social Fact: Notes on the Sociologist's Viewpoint in Relation to a Proposed Study of Referral Behavior." *British Journal of Addictions* 68:91–97.

Roizen, Ron. 1977. "Alcoholism Treatment's Goals and Outcome Measures: Conceptual, Pragmatic, and Structural Sources of Controversy in the Outcome Debate." Social Research Group Working Paper No. P61, University of California, Berkeley.

Roman, Paul M. and H. M. Trice. 1968. "The Sick Role, Labeling Theory, and the Deviant Drinker." *International Journal of Social Psychiatry* 14:245–51.

Root, Laure E. 1986. "Treatment of the Alcoholic Family." *Journal of Psychoactive Drugs* 18:51–56.

Rose, Arnold M. 1958. "Cultural Factors in Mental Health Attitudes." *Midwest Sociologist* 20:65–71.

Rosenbaum, Alan and K. Daniel O'Leary. 1981. "Marital Violence: Characteristics of Abusive Couples." *Journal of Consulting and Clinical Psychology* 49:63–71.

Rosenblatt, Aaron and John E. Mayer. 1974. "Recidivism of Mental Patients." *American Journal of Orthopsychiatry* 44:687–706.

Rubin, Lillian. 1976. *Worlds of Pain.* New York: Basic Books.

———. 1986. *Intimate Strangers.* New York: Harper & Row.

Rubington, Earl. 1978. "The Natural History of Sober Careers." Unpublished paper.

Rueveni, U. 1984. "Family Network in the 1980's: A Postscript." *International Journal of Family Therapy* 6:55–57.

Safilios-Rothschild, Constantina. 1969. "Patterns of Familial Power and Influence." *Sociological Focus* 22:7–19.

———. 1970. "The Influence of the Wife's Degree of Work Commitment upon Some Aspects of Family Organization and Dynamics." *Journal of Marriage and the Family* 32:681–91.

———. 1978. "The Dimensions of Power Distribution in the Family." Pp. 135–49 in *Marriage Problems and Their Treatment,* edited by Jacob Christ and Henry Grunebaum. Boston: Little, Brown.

Sargent, Margaret H. 1968. "The Conception of Alcoholism as a Mental Illness: Comment on the Article by R. A. Moore and a Sociological Alternative." *Quarterly Journal of Studies on Alcohol* 29:974–78 (Part B).

Sariola, Sakari. No date. "Prohibition in Finland 1919 to 1932: Its Background and Its Consequences." Helsinki, Finland: The Foundation for Study of the Alcohol Question. (mimeo)

Scanzoni, John. 1980. "Contemporary Marriage Types." *Journal of Family Issues* 1:125–40.

Schafer, R. B. and P. M. Keith. 1984. "Equity in Marital Roles Across the Family

Life Cycle." Pp. 375–83 in *Family Studies Review Yearbook*, Vol. 2, edited by D. H. Olson and B. C. Miller. Beverly Hills, CA: Sage.

Schneider, David J., Albert H. Hastorf, and Phoebe C. Ellsworth. 1979. *Person Perception*. Reading, MA: Addison-Wesley.

Schroeder, Emily. 1985. "Reorganization of the Family after Aftercare." Pp. 53–62 in *Alcoholism and the Family: A Book of Readings*, edited by Emily Schroeder and Richard W. Easterly. Warnersville, PA.: The Caron Institute.

Schuckit, Marc A., Donald A. Goodwin, and George Winokur. 1972. "A Study of Alcoholism in Half Siblings." *American Journal of Psychiatry* 128:123–27.

———. 1980. "Self-Rating of Alcohol Intoxication by Young Men With and Without Family Histories of Alcoholism." *Journal of Studies on Alcohol* 41:242–49.

———. 1984. *Drug and Alcohol Abuse: A Clinical Guide to Diagnosis and Treatment.* New York: Plenum.

———. 1985. "Genetics of and the Risk for Alcoholism." *Journal of the American Medical Association* 254:2614–17.

Schudson, Michael. 1984. *Advertising: The Uneasy Persuasion*. New York: Basic Books.

Schumm, Walter R., Anthony P. Jurich, Stephen R. Bollman, and Margaret A. Bugaighis. 1985. "His and Her Marriage Revisited." *Journal of Family Issues* 6:221–27.

Scoresby, A. Lynn. 1977. *The Marriage Dialogue*. Reading, MA: Addison-Wesley.

Scott, Marvin and Stanford Lyman. 1968. "Paranoia, Homosexuality and Game Theory." *Journal of Health and Social Behavior* 9:179–87.

Segall, Alexander. 1976. "Sociocultural Variation in Sick Role Behavioral Expectations." *Social Science and Medicine* 10:47–51.

Sells, S. B. 1981. "Matching Clients to Treatments: Problems, Preliminary Results, and Remaining Tasks." Pp. 33–50 in *Matching Patient Needs and Treatment Methods in Alcoholism and Drug Abuse*, edited by Edward Gottheil, A. Thomas McLellan, and Keith A. Druley. Springfield, Ill.: Charles C. Thomas.

Selzer, M. 1958. "On Involuntary Hospitalization for Alcoholics." *Quarterly Journal of Studies on Alcohol* 19:660–67.

Shaver, Kelly G. 1975. *An Introduction to Attribution Processes*. Cambridge, MA: Winthrop.

Sher, Kenneth J. and B. S. McCrady. 1983. "Alcoholism Treatment Approaches: Patient Variables; Treatment Variables." Pp. 309–73 in *Medical and Social Aspects of Alcohol Abuse*, edited by Boris Tabakoff, Patricia B. Sutker, and Carrie L. Randall. New York: Plenum.

Shibutani, Tomatsu. 1961. "Sentiments and Interpersonal Roles." Pp. 323–66 in *Society and Personality*. Englewood Cliffs, NJ: Prentice-Hall.

Shuman, A., R. Browning, and L. E. Arnold. 1985. "Nutrition, Nurture and Changing Family Rituals." Pp. 95–113 in *Parents, Children, and Change*, edited by L. E. Arnold. Lexington, MA: D. C. Heath.

Siegler, Miriam, Humphry Osmond, and Stephens Newell. 1968. "Models of Alcoholism." *Quarterly Journal of Studies on Alcoholism* 29:571–90.

Sigelman, C. K., S. F. Elias, and P. Danker-Brown. 1980. "Interview Behaviors of

Mentally Retarded Adults as Predictors of Employability." *Journal of Applied Psychology* 65:67–73.

Silva, Shelley, et al. 1985. "Alcoholism: Is It a Disease?" *Los Angeles Times*, Letters to the editor, September 29.

Simon, William and John H. Gagnon. 1986. "Sexual Scripts: Permanence and Change." *Archives of Sexual Behavior* 15:97–100.

Sisson, R. W. and N. M. Azrin. 1986. "Family-member Involvement to Initiate and Promote Treatment of Problem Drinkers." *Journal of Behavior Therapy and Experimental Psychiatry* 17:15–21.

Skard, Torild and Elina Haavio-Mannila. 1984. "Equality Between the Sexes—Myth or Reality in Norden?" *Daedalus* 113:141–67.

Slater, Elisa J. and Margaret W. Linn. 1982–83. "Predictors of Re-hospitalization in a Male Alcoholic Population." *American Journal of Drug and Alcohol Abuse* 9:211–20.

Smart, Reginald G. 1970. "The Evaluation of Alcoholism Treatment Programs." *Addictions* 17:41–47.

———. 1974. "Employed Alcoholics Treated Voluntarily and under Constructive Coercion: A Follow-Up Study." *Quarterly Journal of Studies on Alcohol* 35:196–209.

Smith, Annette. 1991. *Alcoholics Anonymous: A Social World Perspective.* Unpublished doctoral dissertation. University of California, San Diego.

Smith, Vicki. 1983. "The Circular Trap: Women and Part-Time Work." *Berkeley Journal of Sociology* 28:1–17.

Snyder, Charles R. 1968. "Inebriety, Alcoholism, and Anomie." Pp. 189–212 in *Anomie and Deviant Behavior*, Marshall Clinard, editor. New York: The Free Press of Glencoe.

Sowa, Patricia A. and Henry S. Cutter. 1974. "Attitudes of Hospital Staff Toward Alcoholics and Drug Addicts." *Quarterly Journal of Studies on Alcohol* 35:210–14.

Speck, R. V. 1984. "Family Network in the 1980's: A Postscript." *International Journal of Family Therapy* 6:136.

Stack, Carol. 1974. *All Our Kin: Strategies for Survival in a Black Community.* New York: Harper & Row.

Statistical Abstract of the United States. 1990. Table 204, p. 125. Washington, DC: United States Bureau of the Census.

Steinglass, Peter. 1979. "Longitudinal Study of Interaction Behavior in Alcoholic Families." *Alcoholism: Clinical and Experimental Research* 3:196–204.

———. 1981a. "The Impact of Alcoholism on the Family: Relationship between Degree of Alcoholism and Psychiatric Symptomatology." *Journal of Studies on Alcohol* 42:288–303.

———. 1981b. "The Alcoholic Family at Home: Patterns of Interaction in Dry, Wet and Transitional Stages of Alcoholism." *Archives of General Psychiatry* 38:578–84.

———. 1982a. "The Roles of Alcohol in Family Systems." Pp. 127–50 in *Alcohol and the Family*, edited by Jim Orford and Judith Harwin. London and Canberra: Croom Helm.

———. 1982b. "Experimenting with Family Treatment Approaches to Alcoholism, 1950–1975." Pp. 194–211 in *Selection of Treatment for Alcoholics*, edited by E. Mansell Pattison. New Brunswick, NJ: Rutgers Center of Alcohol Studies.

Steinglass, Peter, S. Weiner, and J. H. A. Mendelson. 1971. "A Systems Approach to Alcoholics. A Model and Its Clinical Application." *Archives of General Psychiatry* 24:402–408.

Steinmetz, Suzanne K. 1977. *The Cycle of Violence: Assertive, Aggressive and Abusive Family Interaction*. New York: Praeger.

Steinmetz, Suzanne K., and Murray A. Straus, eds. 1974. *Violence in the Family*. New York: Dodd Mead.

Stoll, Clarice Szatz. 1982. "Room at the Bottom." *Working Papers for a New Society* 1:28–41.

Straus, Murray A. 1973. "A General Systems Theory Approach to a Theory of Violence between Family Members." *Social Science Information* 12:105–25.

———. 1976. "Sexual Inequality, Cultural Norms, and Wife-beating." Pp. 543–59 in *Victims and Society*, edited by Emilio C. Viano. Washington, DC: Visage.

———. 1977. "Societal Morphogenesis and Intrafamily Violence in Cross-cultural Perspective." *Annals of the New York Academy of Sciences* 285:719–30.

———. 1977–78. "Wife Beating: How Common and Why?" *Victimology* 2:443–58.

Straus, Murray A. and Suzanne K. Steinmetz. 1973. "The Family as the Cradle of Violence." *Society* 10:50–58.

Sulkunen, Pekka, Pertti Alasuutari, Merja Kinnunen, and Ritva Natkin. 1984. "The Suburban Pub—The Contradiction of Being Man and Woman." Paper presented at the Study for the Conference on Public Drinking, Banff, Alberta, Canada.

Sullivan, A. C. et al. 1981. "Variables Related to Outcome of Treatment for Inpatient Alcoholics." *Alcohol Health and Research World* 6:58–60.

Sussman, Marvin B. and Lee Burchinal. 1959. "The Isolated Nuclear Family: Fact or Fiction?" *Social Problems* 6:333–40.

———. 1962. "Kin Family Network: Unheralded Structure in Our Current Conceptualizations. *Marriage and Family Living* 24:231–40.

Suuronen, Kerttu. 1973. "Traditional Festive Drinking in Finland According to Responses to an Ethnological Questionnaire A18/73." Helsinki, Finland: Reports from the Social Research Institute of Alcohol Studies, The State Alcohol Monopoly.

Swenson, Wendell M. and Robert M. Morse. 1975. "The Use of a Self-Administered Alcoholism Screening Test (SAAST) in a Medical Center." *Mayo Clinic Proceedings* 50:204–208.

Terman, Lewis M. 1938. *Psychological Factors in Marital Happiness*. New York: McGraw-Hill.

The Position of Women in Finnish Society. 1984. Helsinki: Government Printing Centre.

Thomas, W. I. 1928. *The Unadjusted Girl*. Boston: Little Brown.

Thomas, W. I. and Florian Znaniecke. 1918–1920. *The Polish Peasant in Europe and America*. New York: Dover.

Thorne, Daniel R. 1983. "Techniques for Use in Intervention." *Journal of Alcohol and Drug Education* 28:46–50.

Thornton, A., D. F. Alwin, and D. Camburn. 1983. "Causes and Consequences of Sex Role Attitudes and Attitude Change." *American Sociological Review* 48:211–27.

Tietjen, Anne Marie. 1985. "The Social Networks and Social Support of Married and Single Mothers in Sweden." *Journal of Marriage and the Family* 47:489–96.

Trice, Harrison M. 1966. *Alcoholism in America.* New York: McGraw-Hill.

Tuller, W. L., T. W. Mullins, and S. A. Caldwall. 1979. "Effects of Interview Length and Applicant Quality on Interview Decision Time." *Journal of Applied Psychology* 64:669–74.

Turner, D. S. and Dudek, F. A. 1982. "An Analysis of Alcoholism and Its Effects on Sexual Functioning." *Sexuality and Disability* 5:143–57.

Twaddle, Andrew C. 1969. "Health Decisions and Sick Role Variations: An Exploration." *Journal of Health and Social Behavior* 10:105–15.

Twerski, Abraham J. 1981. *Caution: "Kindness" Can Be Dangerous to the Alcoholic.* Englewood Cliffs, NJ: Prentice-Hall.

U.S. Department of Commerce. 1978. "Child Support and Alimony," Current Population Reports Special Studies, Series P-23, No. 112, U.S. Bureau of the Census, Washington, DC.

U.S. Department of Health, Education and Welfare. 1974. *Task Force for Second Special Report to the U.S. Congress on Alcohol and Health.* Washington, DC.

U.S. Department of Labor. 1980. *Handbook of Labor Statistics,* Bulletin 2070:118. Washington, DC.

Valliant, George E. 1980. "The Doctor's Dilemma." Pp. 13–23 in *Alcoholism Treatment in Transition,* edited by Griffith Edwards and Marcus Grant. Baltimore: University Park Press.

Vatz, Richard E. and Lee S. Weinberg. 1985. "The Indulgence Epidemic." *Los Angeles Times,* Editorial pages, Aug. 11.

Viets, Jack. 1969. "Alcohol and Marriage—A Surprising Report." *San Francisco Chronicle.* January 31, p. 48.

Ward, David A. 1979. "The Use of Legal Coercion in the Treatment of Alcoholism: A Methodological Review." *Journal of Drug Issues* 22:387–98.

Ward, Leslie. 1985. "The Addiction Industry." *Los Angeles Herald Examiner.* November 17 and 18, A-1, A-10.

Waring, E. M. 1982. "Marriage and Non-Psychotic Emotional Illness." *The International Journal of Social Psychiatry* 28:111–18.

Warner, W. Lloyd. 1961. *The Family of God: A Symbolic Study of Christian Life in America.* New Haven, CT: Yale University Press.

Weitzman, Lenore J. 1985. *The Divorce Revolution: the Unexpected Social and Economic Consequences for Women and Children in America.* New York: Free Press.

Whalen, H. C. 1962. *Delinquency and Child Neglect.* London: George Allen and Unwin.

Wilde, William. 1968. "Decision-making in a Psychiatric Screening Agency." *Journal of Health and Social Behavior* 9:215–21.

Willmott, Peter. 1987. *Friendship Networks and Social Support.* London: Policy Studies Institute.

Wholey, Dennis (ed.). 1984. *The Courage to Change: Hope and Help for Alcoholics and Their Families. Personal Conversations with Dennis Wholey.* Boston: Houghton Mifflin.

Wiseman, Jacqueline P. 1973. "Sober Time: The Neglected Variable in the Recidivism of Alcoholic Persons." Pp. 165–84 in *Psychological and Social Factors in Drinking and Treatment and Treatment Evaluation.* Proceedings of the Second Annual Alcoholism Conference of NIAAA. Washington, DC: U.S. Government Printing Office.

———. 1975. "An Alternative Role for the Wife of an Alcoholic in Finland." *Journal of Marriage and the Family* 37:172–79.

———. 1979. *Stations of the Lost: The Treatment of Skid Row Alcoholics.* Chicago: University of Chicago Press.

———. 1987. "The Development of Generic Concepts in Qualitative Research through Cumulative Application." *Qualitative Sociology* 10:318–38.

Yarrow, Marian Radke, Charlotte Green Schwartz, Harriet S. Murphy, and Leila Calhoun Deasy. 1978. "The Psychological Meaning of Mental Illness in the Family." Pp. 35–45 in *Deviance: The Interactionist Perspective,* edited by Earl Rubington and Martin S. Weinberg. New York: Macmillan.

Yearbook of Nordic Statistics. 1989–90. Table 165, p. 255. Copenhagen: Nordic Council of Ministries and the Nordic Statistical Secretariat.

Young, Michael and Peter Willmott. 1957. *Family and Kinship in East London.* Baltimore: Penguin.

Zimbardo, Philip and Ebbe B. Ebbesen. 1969. *Influencing Attitudes and Changing Behavior.* Reading, MA: Addison-Wesley.

Zimmerman, Robert. 1986. "High, Low Cost Roads to Sobriety." Editorial in *San Diego Union,* February 23.

Index